The French Revolution
A History
Vol. III

by

Thomas Carlyle

The French Revolution
A History
Vol. III

by Thomas Carlyle

ISBN: 978-93-60462-48-2

Published by

DOUBLE 9 BOOKS

2/13-B, Ansari Road
Daryaganj, New Delhi – 110002
info@double9books.com
www.double9books.com
Tel. 011-40042856

ABOUT THE AUTHOR

Thomas Carlyle was a British writer, historian, and philosopher who was born on December 4, 1795, and died on February 5, 1881. He was from the Scottish Lowlands. He was one of the most important writers of the Victorian age and had a big impact on art, literature, and philosophy in the 1800s. Born in Ecclefechan, Dumfriesshire, Scotland, Carlyle went to the University of Edinburgh and invented the Carlyle circle while there. When the arts course was over, he worked as a schoolmaster and studied to become a minister in the Burgher Church. He gave up on these and other things before he decided to write for the Edinburgh Encyclopaedia and work as a translator. Early on, he was successful by introducing little-known German literature to English readers through translations, his 1825 book Life of Friedrich Schiller, and review essays he wrote for a number of magazines. His first big book was called Sartor Resartus and came out between 1833 and 1834. After moving to London, his book The French Revolution (1837) made him famous, which led to the collection and reissue of his writings as Miscellanies.

CONTENTS

BOOK 3.II.
REGICIDE

BOOK 3.III.
THE GIRONDINS

VOLUME III
THE GUILLOTINE

Alle Freiheits-Apostel, sie waren mir immer zuwider;
Willkür suchte doch nur Jeder am Ende für sich.
Willst du Viele befrein, so wag' es Vielen zu dienen.
Wie gefährlich das sey, willst du es wissen? Versuch's!

GOETHE.

BOOK 3.I.
SEPTEMBER

Chapter 3.1.I.
The Improvised Commune

Ye have roused her, then, ye Emigrants and Despots of the world; France is roused; long have ye been lecturing and tutoring this poor Nation, like cruel uncalled-for pedagogues, shaking over her your ferulas of fire and steel: it is long that ye have pricked and fillipped and affrighted her, there as she sat helpless in her dead cerements of a Constitution, you gathering in on her from all lands, with your armaments and plots, your invadings and truculent bullyings;—and lo now, ye have pricked her to the quick, and she is up, and her blood is up. The dead cerements are rent into cobwebs, and she fronts you in that terrible strength of Nature, which no man has measured, which goes down to Madness and Tophet: see now how ye will deal with her!

This month of September, 1792, which has become one of the memorable months of History, presents itself under two most diverse aspects; all of black on the one side, all of bright on the other. Whatsoever is cruel in the panic frenzy of Twenty-five million men, whatsoever is great in the simultaneous death-defiance of Twenty-five million men, stand here in abrupt contrast, near by one another. As indeed is usual when a man, how much more when a Nation of men, is hurled suddenly beyond the limits. For Nature, as green as she looks, rests everywhere on dread foundations, were we farther down; and Pan, to whose music the Nymphs dance, has a cry in him that can drive all men distracted.

Very frightful it is when a Nation, rending asunder its Constitutions and Regulations which were grown dead cerements for it, becomes *trans*cendental; and must now seek its wild way through the New, Chaotic,—where Force is not yet distinguished into Bidden and Forbidden, but Crime and Virtue welter unseparated,—in that domain of what is called the Passions; of what we call the Miracles and the Portents! It is thus that, for some three years to come, we are to contemplate France, in this final Third Volume of our History. Sansculottism reigning in all its grandeur and in all its hideousness: the Gospel (God's Message) of Man's Rights, Man's *mights* or strengths, once more preached irrefragably abroad; along with this, and still louder for the time, and fearfullest Devil's-Message of Man's weaknesses and sins;—and all on such a scale, and under such aspect: cloudy "death-birth of a world;" huge smoke-cloud, streaked with rays as of heaven on one side; girt on the other as with hell-fire! History tells us many things: but for the last thousand years and more, what thing has she told us of a sort like this? Which therefore let us two, O Reader, dwell on willingly, for a little; and from its endless significance endeavour to extract what may, in present circumstances, be adapted for us.

It is unfortunate, though very natural, that the history of this Period has so generally been written in hysterics. Exaggeration abounds, execration, wailing; and, on the whole, darkness. But thus too, when foul old Rome had to be swept from the Earth, and those Northmen, and other horrid sons of Nature, came in, "swallowing formulas" as the French now do, foul old Rome screamed execratively her loudest; so that, the true shape of many things is lost for us. Attila's Huns had arms of such length that they could lift a stone without stooping. Into the body of the poor Tatars execrative Roman History intercalated an alphabetic letter; and so they continue Ta-r-tars, of fell Tartarean nature, to this day. Here, in like manner, search as we will in these multi-form innumerable French Records, darkness too frequently covers, or sheer distraction bewilders. One finds it difficult to imagine that the Sun shone in this September month, as he does in others. Nevertheless it is an indisputable fact that the Sun did shine; and there was weather and work,—nay, as to that, very bad weather for harvest work! An unlucky Editor may do his utmost; and after all, require allowances.

He had been a wise Frenchman, who, looking, close at hand, on this waste aspect of a France all stirring and whirling, in ways new, untried, had been able to discern where the cardinal movement lay; which tendency it was that had the rule and primary direction of it then! But at forty-four years' distance, it is different. To all men now, two cardinal movements or grand tendencies, in the September whirl, have become discernible enough: that stormful effluence towards the Frontiers; that frantic crowding towards Townhouses and Council-halls in the interior. Wild France dashes, in desperate death-defiance, towards the Frontiers, to defend itself from foreign Despots; crowds towards Townhalls and Election Committee-rooms, to defend itself from domestic Aristocrats. Let the Reader conceive well these two cardinal movements; and what side-currents and endless vortexes might depend on these. He shall judge too, whether, in such sudden wreckage of all old Authorities, such a pair of cardinal movements, half-frantic in themselves, could be of soft nature? As in dry Sahara, when the winds waken, and lift and winnow the immensity of sand! The air itself (Travellers say) is a dim sand-air; and dim looming through it, the wonderfullest uncertain colonnades of Sand-Pillars rush whirling from this side and from that, like so many mad Spinning-Dervishes, of a hundred feet in stature; and dance their huge Desert-waltz there! —

Nevertheless in all human movements, were they but a day old, there is order, or the beginning of order. Consider two things in this Sahara-waltz of the French Twenty-five millions; or rather one thing, and one hope of a thing: the *Commune* (Municipality) of Paris, which is already here; the National Convention, which shall in few weeks be here. The Insurrectionary Commune, which improvising itself on the eve of the Tenth of August, worked this ever-memorable Deliverance by explosion, must needs rule over it, — till the Convention meet. This Commune, which they may well call a spontaneous or "improvised" Commune, is, for the present, sovereign of France. The Legislative, deriving its authority from the Old, how can *it* now have authority when the Old is exploded by insurrection? As a floating piece of wreck, certain things, persons and interests may still cleave to it: volunteer defenders, riflemen or pikemen in green uniform, or red nightcap (of *bonnet rouge*), defile before it daily, just on the wing towards Brunswick; with the brandishing of arms; always with some touch of Leonidas-eloquence, often with a fire of daring that threatens to outherod Herod, — the Galleries, "especially the Ladies, never done with applauding."[512] Addresses of this or the like sort can be received and answered, in the hearing of all France: the Salle de Manége is still useful as a place of proclamation. For which use, indeed, it now chiefly serves. Vergniaud delivers spirit-stirring orations; but always with a prophetic sense only, looking towards the coming

Convention. 'Let our memory perish,' cries Vergniaud, 'but let France be free!'—whereupon they all start to their feet, shouting responsive: 'Yes, yes, *périsse notre mémoire, pourvu que la France soit libre!*'[513] Disfrocked Chabot abjures Heaven that at least we may 'have done with Kings;' and fast as powder under spark, we all blaze up once more, and with waved hats shout and swear: 'Yes, *nous le jurons; plus de roi!*'[514] All which, as a method of proclamation, is very convenient.

For the rest, that our busy Brissots, rigorous Rolands, men who once had authority and now have less and less; men who love law, and will have even an Explosion explode itself, as far as possible, according to rule, do find this state of matters most unofficial unsatisfactory,—is not to be denied. Complaints are made; attempts are made: but without effect. The attempts even recoil; and must be desisted from, for fear of worse: the sceptre is departed from this Legislative once and always. A poor Legislative, so hard was fate, had let itself be hand-gyved, nailed to the rock like an Andromeda, and could only wail there to the Earth and Heavens; miraculously a winged Perseus (or Improvised Commune) has dawned out of the void Blue, and cut her loose: but whether now is it she, with her softness and musical speech, or is it he, with his hardness and sharp falchion and aegis, that shall have casting vote? Melodious *agreement* of vote; this were the rule! But if otherwise, and votes diverge, then surely Andromeda's part is to weep,—if possible, tears of gratitude alone.

Be content, O France, with this Improvised Commune, such as it is! It has the implements, and has the hands: the time is not long. On Sunday the twenty-sixth of August, our Primary Assemblies shall meet, begin electing of Electors; on Sunday the second of September (may the day prove lucky!) the Electors shall begin electing Deputies; and so an all-healing National Convention will come together. No *marc d'argent*, or distinction of Active and Passive, now insults the French Patriot: but there is universal suffrage, unlimited liberty to choose. Old-constituents, Present-Legislators, all France is eligible. Nay, it may be said, the flower of all the Universe (*de l'Univers*) is eligible; for in these very days we, by act of Assembly, "naturalise" the chief Foreign Friends of humanity: Priestley, burnt out for us in Birmingham; Klopstock, a genius of all countries; Jeremy Bentham, useful Jurisconsult; distinguished Paine, the rebellious Needleman;—some of whom may be chosen. As is most fit; for a Convention of this kind. In a word, Seven Hundred and Forty-five unshackled sovereigns, admired of the universe, shall replace this hapless impotency of a Legislative,—out of which, it is likely, the best members, and the Mountain in mass, may be re-elected. Roland is getting ready the *Salles des Cent Suisses*, as preliminary rendezvous for them; in that void Palace of the Tuileries, now void and National, and not a Palace, but a Caravansera.

As for the Spontaneous Commune, one may say that there never was on Earth a stranger Town-Council. Administration, not of a great City, but of a great Kingdom in a state of revolt and frenzy, this is the task that has fallen to it. Enrolling, provisioning, judging; devising, deciding, doing, endeavouring to do: one wonders the human brain did not give way under all this, and reel. But happily human brains have such a talent of taking up simply what they can carry, and ignoring all the rest; leaving all the rest, as if it were not there! Whereby somewhat is verily shifted for; and much shifts for itself. This Improvised Commune walks along, nothing doubting; promptly making front, without fear or flurry, at what moment soever, to the wants of the moment. Were the world on fire, one improvised tricolor Municipal has but one life to lose. They are the elixir and chosen-men of Sansculottic Patriotism; promoted to the forlorn-hope; unspeakable victory or a high gallows, this is their meed. They sit there, in the Townhall, these astonishing tricolor Municipals; in Council General; in Committee of Watchfulness (*de Surveillance*, which will even become *de Salut Public*, of Public Salvation), or what other Committees and Sub-committees are needful;—managing infinite Correspondence; passing infinite Decrees: one hears of a Decree being "the ninety-eighth of the day." Ready! is the word. They carry loaded pistols in their pocket; also some improvised luncheon by way of meal. Or indeed, by and by, *traiteurs* contract for the supply of repasts, to be eaten on the spot,—too lavishly, as it was afterwards grumbled. Thus they: girt in their tricolor sashes; Municipal note-paper in the one hand, fire-arms in other. They have their Agents out all over France; speaking in townhouses, market-places, highways and byways; agitating, urging to arm; all hearts tingling to hear. Great is the fire of Anti-Aristocrat eloquence: nay some, as Bibliopolic Momoro, seem to hint afar off at something which smells of Agrarian Law, and a surgery of the overswoln dropsical strong-box itself;—whereat indeed the bold Bookseller runs risk of being hanged, and Ex-Constituent Buzot has to smuggle him off.[515]

Governing Persons, were they never so insignificant intrinsically, have for most part plenty of Memoir-writers; and the curious, in after-times, can learn minutely their goings out and comings in: which, as men always love to know their fellow-men in singular situations, is a comfort, of its kind. Not so, with these Governing Persons, now in the Townhall! And yet what most original fellow-man, of the Governing sort, high-chancellor, king, kaiser, secretary of the home or the foreign department, ever shewed such a phasis as Clerk Tallien, Procureur Manuel, future Procureur Chaumette, here in this Sand-waltz of the Twenty-five millions, now do? O brother mortals,—thou Advocate Panis, friend of Danton, kinsman of Santerre; Engraver Sergent, since called *Agate* Sergent; thou Huguenin, with the tocsin in thy heart! But, as Horace says, they wanted the sacred memoir-writer (*sacro vate*); and we know them not. Men bragged of August and its doings, publishing them in high places; but of this September none now or afterwards would brag. The September world remains dark, fuliginous, as Lapland witch-midnight;— from which, indeed, very strange shapes will evolve themselves.

Understand this, however: that incorruptible Robespierre is not wanting, now when the brunt of battle is past; in a stealthy way the seagreen man sits there, his feline eyes excellent in the twilight. Also understand this other, a single fact worth many: that Marat is not only there, but has a seat of honour assigned him, a *tribune particulière*. How changed for Marat; lifted from his dark cellar into this luminous "peculiar tribune!" All dogs have their day; even rabid dogs. Sorrowful, incurable Philoctetes Marat; without whom Troy cannot be taken! Hither, as a main element of the Governing Power, has Marat been raised. Royalist types, for we have "suppressed" innumerable Durosoys, Royous, and even clapt them in prison,—Royalist types replace the worn types often snatched from a People's-Friend in old ill days. In our "peculiar tribune" we write and redact: Placards, of due monitory terror; *Amis-du-Peuple* (now under the name of *Journal de la République*); and sit obeyed of men. "Marat," says one, "is the conscience of the Hôtel-de-Ville." *Keeper*, as some call it, of the Sovereign's Conscience;— which surely, in such hands, will not lie hid in a napkin!

Two great movements, as we said, agitate this distracted National mind: a rushing against domestic Traitors, a rushing against foreign Despots. Mad movements both, restrainable by no known rule; strongest passions of human nature driving them on: love, hatred; vengeful sorrow, braggart Nationality also vengeful,—and pale Panic over all! Twelve Hundred slain Patriots, do they not, from their dark catacombs there, in Death's dumb-shew, plead (O ye Legislators) for vengeance? Such was the destructive rage of these Aristocrats on the ever-memorable Tenth. Nay, apart from vengeance, and with an eye to Public Salvation only, are there not still, in this Paris (in round numbers) "thirty thousand Aristocrats," of the most malignant humour; driven now to their last trump-card?—Be patient, ye Patriots: our New High Court, "Tribunal of the Seventeenth," sits; each Section has sent Four Jurymen; and Danton, extinguishing improper judges, improper practices wheresoever found, is "the same man you have known at the Cordeliers." With such a Minister of Justice shall not Justice be done?—Let it be swift then, answers universal Patriotism; swift and sure!—

One would hope, this Tribunal of the Seventeenth is swifter than most. Already on the 21st, while our Court is but four days old, Collenot d'Angremont, "the Royal enlister" (crimp, *embaucheur*) dies by torch-light. For, lo, the great *Guillotine*, wondrous to behold, now stands there; the

Doctor's *Idea* has become Oak and Iron; the huge cyclopean axe "falls in its grooves like the ram of the Pile-engine," swiftly snuffing out the light of men?" *"Mais vous, Gualches,* what have you invented?" *This?*—Poor old Laporte, Intendant of the Civil List, follows next; quietly, the mild old man. Then Durosoy, Royalist Placarder, "cashier of all the Anti-Revolutionists of the interior:" he went rejoicing; said that a Royalist like him ought to die, of all days on this day, the 25th or Saint Louis's Day. All these have been tried, cast,—the Galleries shouting approval; and handed over to the Realised Idea, within a week. Besides those whom we have acquitted, the Galleries murmuring, and have dismissed; or even have personally guarded back to Prison, as the Galleries took to howling, and even to menacing and elbowing.[516] Languid this Tribunal is not.

Nor does the other movement slacken; the rushing against foreign Despots. Strong forces shall meet in death-grip; drilled Europe against mad undrilled France; and singular conclusions will be tried.—Conceive therefore, in some faint degree, the tumult that whirls in this France, in this Paris! Placards from Section, from Commune, from Legislative, from the individual Patriot, flame monitory on all walls. Flags of Danger to Fatherland wave at the Hôtel-de-Ville; on the Pont Neuf—over the prostrate Statues of Kings. There is universal enlisting, urging to enlist; there is tearful-boastful leave-taking; irregular marching on the Great North-Eastern Road. Marseillese sing their wild *To Arms,* in chorus; which now all men, all women and children have learnt, and sing chorally, in Theatres, Boulevards, Streets; and the heart burns in every bosom: *Aux Armes! Marchons!*—Or think how your Aristocrats are skulking into covert; how Bertrand-Moleville lies hidden in some garret "in Aubry-le-boucher Street, with a poor surgeon who had known me;" Dame de Staël has secreted her Narbonne, not knowing what in the world to make of him. The Barriers are sometimes open, oftenest shut; no passports to be had; Townhall Emissaries, with the eyes and claws of falcons, flitting watchful on all points of your horizon! In two words: Tribunal of the Seventeenth, busy under howling Galleries; Prussian Brunswick, "over a space of forty miles," with his war-tumbrils, and sleeping thunders, and Briarean "sixty-six thousand"[517] right-hands,—coming, coming!

O Heavens, in these latter days of August, he is come! Durosoy was not yet guillotined when news had come that the Prussians were harrying and ravaging about Metz; in some four days more, one hears that Longwi, our first strong-place on the borders, is fallen "in fifteen hours." Quick, therefore, O ye improvised Municipals; quick, and ever quicker!—The improvised Municipals make front to this also. Enrolment urges itself; and clothing, and arming. Our very officers have now "wool epaulettes;" for it is the reign of Equality, and also of Necessity. Neither do men now *monsieur* and *sir* one another; *citoyen* (citizen) were suitabler; we even say *thou,* as "the free peoples of Antiquity did:" so have Journals and the Improvised Commune suggested; which shall be well.

Infinitely better, meantime, could we suggest, where arms are to be found. For the present, our *Citoyens* chant chorally *To arms;* and have no arms! Arms are searched for; passionately; there is joy over any musket. Moreover, entrenchments shall be made round Paris: on the slopes of Montmartre men dig and shovel; though even the simple suspect this to be desperate. They dig; Tricolour sashes speak encouragement and *well-speed-ye.* Nay finally "twelve Members of the Legislative go daily," not to encourage only, but to bear a hand, and delve: it was decreed with acclamation. Arms shall either be provided; or else the ingenuity of man crack itself, and become fatuity. Lean Beaumarchais, thinking to serve the Fatherland, and do a stroke of trade, in the old way, has commissioned sixty thousand stand of good arms out of Holland: would to Heaven, for Fatherland's sake and his, they were come! Meanwhile railings are torn up; hammered into pikes: chains themselves shall be welded together, into pikes. The very coffins of the dead are raised; for melting into balls. All Church-bells must down into the furnace to make cannon; all Church-plate into the mint to make money. Also behold the fair swan-bevies of *Citoyennes* that have alighted in Churches, and sit there with swan-neck,—sewing tents and regimentals! Nor are Patriotic Gifts wanting, from those that have aught left; nor stingily given: the fair Villaumes, mother and daughter, Milliners in the Rue St.-Martin, give "a silver thimble, and a coin of fifteen *sous* (sevenpence halfpenny)," with other similar effects; and offer, at least the mother does, to mount guard. Men who have not even a thimble, give a thimbleful,—were it but of invention. One Citoyen has wrought out the scheme of a wooden cannon; which France shall exclusively profit by, in the first instance. It is to be made of *staves,* by the coopers;—of almost boundless calibre, but uncertain as to strength! Thus they: hammering, scheming, stitching, founding, with all their heart and with all their soul. Two bells only are to remain in each Parish,—for tocsin and other purposes.

But mark also, precisely while the Prussian batteries were playing their briskest at Longwi in the North-East, and our dastardly Lavergne saw nothing for it but surrender,—south-westward, in remote, patriarchal La Vendée, that sour ferment about Nonjuring Priests, after long working, is ripe, and explodes: at the wrong moment for us! And so we have "eight thousand Peasants at Châtillon-sur-Sèvre," who will not be ballotted for soldiers; will not have their Curates molested. To whom Bonchamps, Laroche-jaquelins, and Seigneurs enough, of a Royalist turn, will join themselves; with Stofflets and Charettes; with Heroes and Chouan Smugglers; and the loyal warmth of a simple people, blown into flame and fury by theological and seignorial bellows! So that there shall be fighting from behind ditches, death-volleys bursting out of thickets and ravines of rivers; huts burning, feet of the pitiful women hurrying to refuge with their children on their back; seedfields fallow, whitened with human bones;—"eighty thousand, of all ages, ranks, sexes, flying at once across the Loire," with wail borne far on the winds: and, in brief, for years coming, such a suite of scenes as glorious war has not offered in these late ages, not since our Albigenses and Crusadings were over,—save indeed some chance Palatinate, or so, we might have to "burn," by way of exception. The "eight thousand at Chatillon" will be got dispelled for the moment; the fire scattered, not extinguished. To the dints and bruises of outward battle there is to be added henceforth a deadlier internal gangrene.

This rising in La Vendée reports itself at Paris on Wednesday the 29th of August;—just as we had got our Electors elected; and, in spite of Brunswick's and Longwi's teeth, were hoping still to have a National Convention, if it pleased Heaven. But indeed, otherwise, this Wednesday is to be regarded as one of the notablest Paris had yet seen: gloomy tidings come successively, like Job's messengers; are met by gloomy answers. Of Sardinia rising to invade the South-East, and Spain threatening the South, we do not speak. But are not the Prussians masters of Longwi (treacherously yielded, one would say); and preparing to besiege Verdun? Clairfait and his Austrians are encompassing Thionville; darkening the North. Not Metz-land now, but the Clermontais is getting harried; flying hulans and huzzars have been seen on the Chalons Road, almost as far as Sainte-Menehould. Heart, ye Patriots, if ye lose heart, ye lose all!

It is not without a dramatic emotion that one reads in the Parliamentary Debates of this Wednesday evening "past seven o'clock," the scene with the military fugitives from Longwi. Wayworn, dusty, disheartened, these poor men enter the Legislative, about sunset or after; give the most pathetic detail of the frightful pass they were in:—Prussians billowing round by the myriad, volcanically spouting fire for fifteen hours: we, scattered sparse on the ramparts, hardly a cannoneer to two guns; our dastard Commandant Lavergne no where shewing face; the priming would not catch; there was no powder in the bombs,—what could we do? 'Mourir! Die!' answer prompt voices;[518] and the dusty fugitives must shrink elsewhither for comfort.—

Yes, *Mourir*, that is now the word. Be Longwi a proverb and a hissing among French strong-places: let it (says the Legislative) be obliterated rather, from the shamed face of the Earth;—and so there has gone forth Decree, that Longwi shall, were the Prussians once out of it, "be rased," and exist only as ploughed ground.

Nor are the Jacobins milder; as how could they, the flower of Patriotism? Poor Dame Lavergne, wife of the poor Commandant, took her parasol one evening, and escorted by her Father came over to the Hall of the mighty Mother; and "reads a memoir tending to justify the Commandant of Longwi." *Lafarge, President,* makes answer: 'Citoyenne, the Nation will judge Lavergne; the Jacobins are bound to tell him the truth. He would have ended his course there (*termine sa carrière*), if he had loved the honour of his country.'[519]

Chapter 3.1.II.
Danton

But better than rasing of Longwi, or rebuking poor dusty soldiers or soldiers' wives, Danton had come over, last night, and demanded a Decree to *search* for arms, since they were not yielded voluntarily. Let "Domiciliary visits," with rigour of authority, be made to this end. To search for arms; for horses,—Aristocratism rolls in its carriage, while Patriotism cannot trail its cannon. To search generally for munitions of war, "in the houses of persons suspect,"—and even, if it seem proper, to seize and imprison the suspect persons themselves! In the Prisons, their plots will be harmless; in the Prisons, they will be as hostages for us, and not without use. This Decree the energetic Minister of Justice demanded, last night, and got; and this same night it is to be executed; it is being executed, at the moment when these dusty soldiers get saluted with *Mourir*. Two thousand stand of arms, as they count, are foraged in this way; and some four hundred head of new Prisoners; and, on the whole, such a terror and damp is struck through the Aristocrat heart, as all but Patriotism, and even Patriotism were it out of this agony, might pity. Yes, Messieurs! if Brunswick blast Paris to ashes, he probably will blast the Prisons of Paris too: pale Terror, if we have got it, we will also give it, and the depth of horrors that lie in it; the same leaky bottom, in these wild waters, bears us all.

One can judge what stir there was now among the "thirty thousand Royalists:" how the Plotters, or the accused of Plotting, shrank each closer into his lurking-place,—like Bertrand Moleville, looking eager towards Longwi, hoping the weather would keep fair. Or how they dressed themselves in valet's clothes, like Narbonne, and "got to England as Dr. Bollman's famulus:" how Dame de Staël bestirred herself, pleading with Manuel as a Sister in Literature, pleading even with Clerk Tallien; a pray to nameless chagrins![520] Royalist Peltier, the Pamphleteer, gives a touching Narrative (not deficient in height of colouring) of the terrors of that night. From five in the afternoon, a great City is struck suddenly silent; except for the beating of drums, for the tramp of marching feet; and ever and anon the dread thunder of the knocker at some door, a Tricolor Commissioner with his blue Guards (*black*-guards!) arriving. All Streets are vacant, says Peltier; beset by Guards at each end: all Citizens are ordered to be within doors. On the River float sentinal barges, lest we escape by water: the Barriers hermetically closed. Frightful! The sun shines; serenely westering, in smokeless mackerel-sky: Paris is as if sleeping, as if dead:—Paris is holding its breath, to see what stroke will fall on it. Poor Peltier! *Acts of Apostles*, and all jocundity of Leading-Articles, are gone out, and it is become bitter earnest instead; polished satire changed now into coarse pike-points (hammered out of railing); all logic reduced to this one primitive thesis, An eye for an eye, a tooth for a tooth!—Peltier, dolefully aware of it, ducks low; escapes unscathed to England; to urge there the inky war anew; to have Trial by Jury, in due season, and deliverance by young Whig eloquence, world-celebrated for a day.

Of "thirty thousand," naturally, great multitudes were left unmolested: but, as we said, some four hundred, designated as "persons suspect," were seized; and an unspeakable terror fell on all. Wo to him who is guilty of Plotting, of Anticivism, Royalism, Feuillantism; who, guilty or not guilty, has an enemy in his Section to call him guilty! Poor old M. de Cazotte is seized, his young loved Daughter with him, refusing to quit him. Why, O Cazotte, wouldst thou quit romancing, and *Diable Amoureux*, for such reality as this? Poor old M. de Sombreuil, he of the *Invalides*, is seized: a man seen askance, by Patriotism ever since the Bastille days: whom also a fond Daughter will not quit. With young tears hardly suppressed, and old wavering weakness rousing itself once more—O my brothers, O my sisters!

The famed and named go; the nameless, if they have an accuser. Necklace Lamotte's Husband is in these Prisons (*she* long since squelched on the London Pavements); but gets delivered. Gross de Morande, of the *Courier de l'Europe*, hobbles distractedly to and fro there: but they let him hobble out; on right nimble crutches;—his hour not being yet come. Advocate Maton de la Varenne, very weak in health, is snatched off from mother and kin; Tricolor Rossignol (journeyman goldsmith and scoundrel lately, a risen man now) remembers an old Pleading of Maton's! Jourgniac de Saint-Méard goes; the brisk frank soldier: he was in the Mutiny of Nancy, in that "effervescent Regiment du Roi,"—on the wrong side. Saddest of all: Abbé Sicard goes; a Priest who could not take the Oath, but who could teach the Deaf and Dumb: in his Section one man, he says, had a grudge at him; one man, at the fit hour, launches an arrest against him; which hits. In the Arsenal quarter, there are dumb hearts making wail, with signs, with wild gestures; he their miraculous healer and speech-bringer is rapt away.

What with the arrestments on this night of the Twenty-ninth, what with those that have gone on more or less, day and night, ever since the Tenth, one may fancy what the Prisons now were. Crowding and Confusion; jostle, hurry, vehemence and terror! Of the poor Queen's Friends, who had followed her to the Temple and been committed elsewhither to Prison, some, as Governess de Tourzelle, are to be let go: one, the poor Princess de Lamballe, is not let go; but waits in the strong-rooms of La Force there, what will betide further.

Among so many hundreds whom the launched arrest hits, who are rolled off to Townhall or Section-hall, to preliminary Houses of detention, and hurled in thither, as into cattle-pens, we must mention one other: Caron de Beaumarchais, Author of *Figaro;* vanquisher of Maupeou Parlements and Goezman helldogs; once numbered among the demigods; and now—? We left him in his culminant state; what dreadful decline is this, when we again catch a glimpse of him! "At midnight" (it was but the 12th of August yet), "the servant, in his shirt," with wide-staring eyes, enters your room:—Monsieur, rise; all the people are come to seek you; they are knocking, like to break in the door! "And they were in fact knocking in a terrible manner (*d'une façon terrible*). I fling on my coat, forgetting even the waistcoat, nothing on my feet but slippers; and say to him"—And *he,* alas, answers mere negatory incoherences, panic interjections. And through the shutters and crevices, in front or rearward, the dull street-lamps disclose only streetfuls of haggard countenances; clamorous, bristling with pikes: and you rush distracted for an outlet, finding none;—and have to take refuge in the crockery-press, down stairs; and stand there, palpitating in that imperfect costume, lights dancing past your key-hole, tramp of feet overhead, and the tumult of Satan, "for four hours and more!" And old ladies, of the quarter, started up (as we hear next morning); rang for their *bonnes* and cordial-drops, with shrill interjections: and old gentlemen, in their shirts, "leapt garden-walls;" flying, while none pursued; one of whom unfortunately broke his leg.[521] Those sixty thousand stand of Dutch arms (which never arrive), and the bold stroke of trade, have turned out so ill!—

Beaumarchais escaped for this time; but not for the next time, ten days after. On the evening of the Twenty-ninth he is still in that chaos of the Prisons, in saddest, wrestling condition; unable to get justice, even to get audience; "Panis scratching his head" when you speak to him, and making off. Nevertheless let the lover of Figaro know that Procureur Manuel, a Brother in Literature, found him, and delivered him once more. But how the lean demigod, now shorn of his splendour, had to lurk in barns, to roam over harrowed fields, panting for life; and to wait under eavesdrops, and sit in darkness "on the Boulevard amid paving-stones and boulders," longing for one word of any Minister, or Minister's Clerk, about those accursed Dutch muskets, and getting none,—with heart fuming in spleen, and terror, and suppressed canine-madness: alas, how the swift sharp hound, once fit to be Diana's, breaks his old teeth now, gnawing mere whinstones; and must "fly to England;" and, returning from England, must creep into the corner, and lie quiet, toothless (moneyless),—all this let the lover of Figaro fancy, and weep for. We here, without weeping, not without sadness, wave the withered tough fellow-mortal our farewell. His Figaro has returned to the French stage; nay is, at this day, sometimes named the best piece there. And indeed, so long as Man's Life can ground itself only on artificiality and aridity; each new Revolt and Change of Dynasty turning up only a new stratum of *dry-rubbish*, and no *soil* yet coming to view,—may it not be good to protest against such a Life, in many ways, and even in the Figaro way?

Chapter 3.1.III.
Dumouriez

Such are the last days of August, 1792; days gloomy, disastrous, and of evil omen. What will become of this poor France? Dumouriez rode from the Camp of Maulde, eastward to Sedan, on Tuesday last, the 28th of the month; reviewed that so-called Army left forlorn there by Lafayette: the forlorn soldiers gloomed on him; were heard growling on him, 'This is one of them, *ce b—e là*, that made War be declared.'[522] Unpromising Army! Recruits flow in, filtering through Dépôt after Dépôt; but recruits merely: in want of all; happy if they have so much as arms. And Longwi has fallen basely; and Brunswick, and the Prussian King, with his sixty thousand, will beleaguer Verdun; and Clairfait and Austrians press deeper in, over the Northern marches: "a hundred and fifty thousand" as fear counts, "eighty thousand" as the returns shew, do hem us in; Cimmerian Europe behind them. There is Castries-and-Broglie chivalry; Royalist foot "in red facing and nankeen trousers;" breathing death and the gallows.

And lo, finally! at Verdun on Sunday the 2d of September 1792, Brunswick is here. With his King and sixty thousand, glittering over the heights, from beyond the winding Meuse River, he looks down on us, on our "high citadel" and all our confectionery-ovens (for we are celebrated for confectionery) has sent courteous summons, in order to spare the effusion of blood!—Resist him to the death? Every day of retardation precious? How, O General Beaurepaire (asks the amazed Municipality) shall we resist him? We, the Verdun Municipals, see no resistance possible. Has he not sixty thousand, and artillery without end? Retardation, Patriotism is good; but so likewise is peaceable baking of pastry, and sleeping in whole skin.— Hapless Beaurepaire stretches out his hands, and pleads passionately, in the name of country, honour, of Heaven and of Earth: to no purpose. The Municipals have, by law, the power of ordering it;—with an Army officered by Royalism or Crypto-Royalism, such a Law seemed needful: and they order it, as pacific Pastrycooks, not as heroic Patriots would,—To surrender! Beaurepaire strides home, with long steps: his valet, entering the room, sees him "writing eagerly," and withdraws. His valet hears then, in a few minutes, the report of a pistol: Beaurepaire is lying dead; his eager writing had been a brief suicidal farewell. In this manner died Beaurepaire, wept of France; buried in the Pantheon, with honourable pension to his Widow, and for Epitaph these words, *He chose Death rather than yield to Despots.* The Prussians, descending from the heights, are peaceable masters of Verdun.

And so Brunswick advances, from stage to stage: who shall now stay him,—covering forty miles of country? Foragers fly far; the villages of the North-East are harried; your Hessian forager has only "three sous a day:" the very Emigrants, it is said, will take silver-plate,—by way of revenge. Clermont, Sainte-Menehould, Varennes especially, ye Towns of the *Night of Spurs;* tremble ye! Procureur Sausse and the Magistracy of Varennes have fled; brave Boniface Le Blanc of the *Bras d'Or* is to the woods: Mrs. Le Blanc, a young woman fair to look upon, with her young infant, has to live in greenwood, like a beautiful Bessy Bell of Song, her bower thatched with rushes;—catching premature rheumatism.[523] Clermont may ring the tocsin now, and illuminate itself! Clermont lies at the foot of its *Cow* (or *Vache,* so they name that Mountain), a prey to the Hessian spoiler: its fair women, fairer than most, are robbed: not of life, or what is dearer, yet of all that is cheaper and portable; for Necessity, on three half-pence a-day, has no law. At Saint-Menehould, the enemy has been expected more than once,— our Nationals all turning out in arms; but was not yet seen. Post-master Drouet, he is not in the woods, but minding his Election; and will sit in the Convention, notable King-taker, and bold Old-Dragoon as he is.

Thus on the North-East all roams and runs; and on a set day, the *date* of which is irrecoverable by History, Brunswick "has engaged to dine in Paris,"—the Powers willing. And at Paris, in the centre, it is as we saw; and in La Vendée, South-West, it is as we saw; and Sardinia is in the South-East, and Spain is in the South, and Clairfait with Austria and sieged Thionville is in the North;—and all France leaps distracted, like the winnowed Sahara waltzing in sand-colonnades! More desperate posture no country ever stood in. A country, one would say, which the Majesty of Prussia (if it so pleased him) might partition, and clip in pieces, like a Poland; flinging the remainder to poor Brother Louis,—with directions to keep it quiet, or else *we* will keep it for him!

Or perhaps the Upper Powers, minded that a new Chapter in Universal History shall begin here and not further on, may have ordered it all otherwise? In that case, Brunswick will not dine in Paris on the set day; nor, indeed, one knows not when!—Verily, amid this wreckage, where poor France seems grinding itself down to dust and bottomless ruin, who knows what miraculous salient-point of Deliverance and New-life may have already come into existence there; and be already working there, though as yet human eye discern it not! On the night of that same twenty-eighth of August, the unpromising Review-day in Sedan, Dumouriez assembles a Council of War at his lodgings there. He spreads out the map of this forlorn war-district: Prussians here, Austrians there; triumphant both, with broad highway, and little hinderance, all the way to Paris; we, scattered helpless, here and here: what to advise? The Generals, strangers to Dumouriez, look blank enough; know not well what to advise,—if it be not retreating, and retreating till our recruits accumulate; till perhaps the chapter of chances turn up some leaf for us; or Paris, at all events, be sacked at the latest day possible. The Many-counselled, who "has not closed an eye for three nights," listens with little speech to these long cheerless speeches; merely watching the speaker that he may know him; then wishes them all good-night;—but beckons a certain young Thouvenot, the fire of whose looks had pleased him, to wait a moment. Thouvenot waits: *Voilà*, says Polymetis, pointing to the map! That is the Forest of Argonne, that long stripe of rocky Mountain and wild Wood; forty miles long; with but five, or say even three practicable Passes through it: this, for they have forgotten it, might one not still seize, though Clairfait sits so nigh? Once seized;—the Champagne called the Hungry (or worse, Champagne *Pouilleuse*) on their side of it; the fat Three Bishoprics, and willing France, on ours; and the Equinox-rains not far;—this Argonne "might be the Thermopylae of France!"[524]

O brisk Dumouriez Polymetis with thy teeming head, may the gods grant it!—Polymetis, at any rate, folds his map together, and flings himself on bed; resolved to try, on the morrow morning. With astucity, with swiftness, with audacity! One had need to be a lion-fox, and have luck on one's side.

Chapter 3.1.IV.
September in Paris

At Paris, by lying Rumour which proved prophetic and veridical, the fall of Verdun was known some hours *before* it happened. It is Sunday the second of September; handiwork hinders not the speculations of the mind. Verdun gone (though some still deny it); the Prussians in full march, with gallows-ropes, with fire and faggot! Thirty thousand Aristocrats within our own walls; and but the merest quarter-tithe of them yet put in Prison! Nay there goes a word that even these will revolt. Sieur Jean Julien, wagoner of Vaugirard,[525] being set in the Pillory last Friday, took all at once to crying, That he would be well revenged ere long; that the King's Friends in Prison would burst out; force the Temple, set the King on horseback; and, joined by the unimprisoned, ride roughshod over us all. This the unfortunate wagoner of Vaugirard did bawl, at the top of his lungs: when snatched off to the Townhall, he persisted in it, still bawling; yesternight, when they guillotined him, he died with the froth of it on his lips.[526] For a man's mind, padlocked to the Pillory, may go mad; and all men's minds may go mad; and "believe him," as the frenetic will do, "*because* it is impossible."

So that apparently the knot of the crisis, and last agony of France is come? Make front to this, thou Improvised Commune, strong Danton, whatsoever man is strong! Readers can judge whether the Flag of Country in Danger flapped soothing or distractively on the souls of men, that day.

But the Improvised Commune, but strong Danton is not wanting, each after his kind. Huge Placards are getting plastered to the walls; at two o'clock the stormbell shall be sounded, the alarm-cannon fired; all Paris shall rush to the Champ-de-Mars, and have itself enrolled. Unarmed, truly, and undrilled; but desperate, in the strength of frenzy. Haste, ye men; ye very women, offer to mount guard and shoulder the brown musket: weak clucking-hens, in a state of desperation, will fly at the muzzle of the mastiff, and even conquer him,—by vehemence of character! Terror itself, when once grown transcendental, becomes a kind of courage; as frost sufficiently intense, according to Poet Milton, will *burn.*—Danton, the other night, in the Legislative Committee of General Defence, when the other Ministers and Legislators had all opined, said, It would not do to quit Paris, and fly to Saumur; that they must abide by Paris; and take such attitude as would put their enemies in fear,—*faire peur;* a word of his which has been often repeated, and reprinted—in italics.[527]

At two of the clock, Beaurepaire, as we saw, has shot himself at Verdun; and over Europe, mortals are going in for afternoon sermon. But at Paris, all steeples are clangouring not for sermon; the alarm-gun booming from minute to minute; Champ-de-Mars and Fatherland's Altar boiling with desperate terror-courage: what a *miserere* going up to Heaven from this once Capital of the Most Christian King! The Legislative sits in alternate awe and effervescence; Vergniaud proposing that Twelve shall go and dig personally on Montmartre; which is decreed by acclaim.

But better than digging personally with acclaim, see Danton enter;—the black brows clouded, the colossus-figure tramping heavy; grim energy looking from all features of the rugged man! Strong is that grim Son of France, and Son of Earth; a Reality and not a Formula he too; and surely now if ever, being hurled *low* enough, it is on the Earth and on Realities that he rests. 'Legislators!' so speaks the stentor-voice, as the Newspapers yet preserve it for us, 'it is not the alarm-cannon that you hear: it is the *pas-de-charge* against our enemies. To conquer them, to hurl them back, what do we require? *Il nous faut de l'audace, et encore de l'audace, et toujours de l'audace,* To dare, and again to dare, and without end to dare!'[528] —Right so, thou brawny Titan; there is nothing left for thee but that. Old men, who heard it, will still tell you how the reverberating voice made all hearts swell, in that moment; and braced them to the sticking-place; and thrilled abroad over France, like electric virtue, as a word spoken in season.

But the Commune, enrolling in the Champ-de-Mars? But the Committee of Watchfulness, become now Committee of Public Salvation; whose conscience is Marat? The Commune enrolling enrolls many; provides Tents for them in that Mars'-Field, that they may march with dawn on the morrow: praise to this part of the Commune! To Marat and the Committee of Watchfulness not praise;—not even blame, such as could be meted out in these insufficient dialects of ours; expressive silence rather! Lone Marat, the man forbid, meditating long in his Cellars of refuge, on his Stylites Pillar, could see salvation in one thing only: in the fall of "two hundred and sixty thousand Aristocrat heads." With so many score of Naples Bravoes, each a dirk in his right-hand, a muff on his left, he would traverse France, and do it. But the world laughed, mocking the severe-benevolence of a People's-Friend; and his idea could not become an action, but only a fixed-idea. Lo, now, however, he has come down from his Stylites Pillar, to a *Tribune particulière;* here now, without the dirks, without the muffs at least, were it not grown possible,—now in the knot of the crisis, when salvation or destruction hangs in the hour!

The Ice-Tower of Avignon was noised of sufficiently, and lives in all memories; but the authors were not punished: nay we saw Jourdan Coupetete, borne on men's shoulders, like a copper Portent, "traversing the cities of the South."—What phantasms, squalid-horrid, shaking their dirk and muff, may dance through the brain of a Marat, in this dizzy pealing of tocsin-miserere, and universal frenzy, seek not to guess, O Reader! Nor what the cruel Billaud "in his short brown coat was thinking;" nor Sergent, not yet *Agate*-Sergent; nor Panis the confident of Danton;—nor, in a word, how gloomy Orcus does breed in her gloomy womb, and fashion her monsters, and prodigies of Events, which thou seest her visibly bear! Terror is on these streets of Paris; terror and rage, tears and frenzy: tocsin-miserere pealing through the air; fierce desperation rushing to battle; mothers, with streaming eyes and wild hearts, sending forth their sons to die. "Carriage-horses are seized by the bridle," that they may draw cannon; "the traces cut, the carriages left standing." In such tocsin-miserere, and murky bewilderment of Frenzy, are not Murder, Ate, and all Furies near at hand? On slight hint, who knows on how slight, may not Murder come; and, with *her* snaky-sparkling hand, illuminate this murk!

How it was and went, what part might be premeditated, what was improvised and accidental, man will never know, till the great Day of Judgment make it known. But with a Marat for keeper of the Sovereign's Conscience—And we know what the *ultima ratio* of Sovereigns, when they are driven to it, is! In this Paris there are as many wicked men, say a hundred or more, as exist in all the Earth: to be hired, and set on; to set on, of their own accord, unhired.—And yet we will remark that premeditation itself is not performance, is not surety of performance; that it is perhaps, at most, surety of *letting* whosoever wills perform. From the purpose of crime to the act of crime there is an abyss; wonderful to think of. The finger lies on the pistol; but the man is not yet a murderer: nay, his whole nature staggering at such consummation, is there not a confused pause rather,—one last instant of possibility for him? Not yet a murderer; it is at the mercy of light trifles whether the most fixed idea may not yet become unfixed. One slight twitch of a muscle, the death flash bursts; and he is it, and will for Eternity be it;—and Earth has become a penal Tartarus for him; his horizon girdled now not with golden hope, but with red flames of remorse; voices from the depths of Nature sounding, Wo, wo on him!

Of such stuff are we all made; on such powder-mines of bottomless guilt and criminality, "if God restrained not; as is well said,—does the purest of us walk. There are depths in man that go the length of lowest Hell, as there are heights that reach highest Heaven;—for are not both Heaven and Hell made out of him, made by him, everlasting Miracle and Mystery as he is?— But looking on this Champ-de-Mars, with its tent-buildings, and frantic enrolments; on this murky-simmering Paris, with its crammed Prisons (supposed about to burst), with its tocsin-miserere, its mothers' tears, and soldiers' farewell shoutings,—the pious soul might have prayed, that day, that God's grace would restrain, and greatly restrain; lest on slight hest or hint, Madness, Horror and Murder rose, and this Sabbath-day of September became a Day black in the Annals of Men.—

The tocsin is pealing its loudest, the clocks inaudibly striking *Three*, when poor Abbé Sicard, with some thirty other Nonjurant Priests, in six carriages, fare along the streets, from their preliminary House of Detention at the Townhall, westward towards the Prison of the Abbaye. Carriages enough stand deserted on the streets; these six move on,—through angry multitudes, cursing as they move. Accursed Aristocrat Tartuffes, this is the pass ye have brought us to! And now ye will break the Prisons, and set Capet Veto on horseback to ride over us? Out upon you, Priests of Beelzebub and Moloch; of Tartuffery, Mammon, and the Prussian Gallows,—which ye name Mother-Church and God! Such reproaches have the poor Nonjurants to endure, and worse; spoken in on them by frantic Patriots, who mount even on the carriage-steps; the very Guards hardly refraining. Pull up your carriage-blinds!—No! answers Patriotism, clapping its horny paw on the carriage blind, and crushing it down again. Patience in oppression has limits: we are close on the Abbaye, it has lasted long: a poor Nonjurant, of quicker temper, smites the horny paw with his cane; nay, finding solacement in it, smites the unkempt head, sharply and again more sharply, twice over,—seen clearly of us and of the world. It is the last that we see clearly. Alas, next moment, the carriages are locked and blocked in endless raging tumults; in yells deaf to the cry for mercy, which answer the cry for mercy with sabre-thrusts through the heart.[529] The thirty Priests are torn out, are massacred about the Prison-Gate, one after one,—only the poor Abbé Sicard, whom one Moton a watchmaker, knowing him, heroically tried to save, and secrete in the Prison, escapes to tell;—and it is Night and Orcus, and Murder's snaky-sparkling head *has* risen in the murk!—

From Sunday afternoon (exclusive of intervals, and pauses not final) till Thursday evening, there follow consecutively a Hundred Hours. Which hundred hours are to be reckoned with the hours of the Bartholomew Butchery, of the Armagnac Massacres, Sicilian Vespers, or whatsoever is savagest in the annals of this world. Horrible the hour when man's soul, in its paroxysm, spurns asunder the barriers and rules; and shews what dens and depths are in it! For Night and Orcus, as we say, as was long prophesied, have burst forth, here in this Paris, from their subterranean imprisonment: hideous, dim, confused; which it is painful to look on; and yet which cannot, and indeed which should not, be forgotten.

The Reader, who looks earnestly through this dim Phantasmagory of the Pit, will discern few fixed certain objects; and yet still a few. He will observe, in this Abbaye Prison, the sudden massacre of the Priests being once over, a strange Court of Justice, or call it Court of Revenge and Wild-Justice, swiftly fashion itself, and take seat round a table, with the Prison-Registers spread before it;—Stanislas Maillard, Bastille-hero, famed Leader of the Menads, presiding. O Stanislas, one hoped to meet thee elsewhere than here; thou shifty Riding-Usher, with an inkling of Law! This work also thou hadst to do; and then—to depart for ever from our eyes. At *La Force*, at the *Châtelet*, the *Conciergerie*, the like Court forms itself, with the like accompaniments: the thing that one man does other men can do. There are some Seven Prisons in Paris, full of Aristocrats with conspiracies;—nay not even *Bicêtre* and *Salpêtrière* shall escape, with their Forgers of Assignats: and there are seventy times seven hundred Patriot hearts in a state of frenzy. Scoundrel hearts also there are; as perfect, say, as the Earth holds,—if such are needed. To whom, in this mood, law is as no-law; and killing, by what name soever called, is but work to be done.

So sit these sudden Courts of Wild-Justice, with the Prison-Registers before them; unwonted wild tumult howling all round: the Prisoners in dread expectancy within. Swift: a name is called; bolts jingle, a Prisoner is there. A few questions are put; swiftly this sudden Jury decides: Royalist Plotter or not? Clearly not; in that case, Let the Prisoner be enlarged With *Vive la Nation*. Probably yea; then still, Let the Prisoner be enlarged, but without *Vive la Nation;* or else it may run, Let the prisoner be conducted to La Force. At La Force again their formula is, Let the Prisoner be conducted to the Abbaye.—'To La Force then!' Volunteer bailiffs seize the doomed man; he is at the outer gate; "enlarged," or "conducted," —not into La Force, but into a howling sea; forth, under an arch of wild sabres, axes and pikes; and sinks, hewn asunder. And another sinks, and another; and there forms itself a piled heap of corpses, and the kennels begin to run red. Fancy the yells of these men, their faces of sweat and blood; the crueller shrieks of these women, for there are women too; and a fellow-mortal hurled naked into it all! Jourgniac de Saint Méard has seen battle, has seen an effervescent Regiment du Roi in mutiny; but the bravest heart may quail at this. The Swiss Prisoners, remnants of the Tenth of August, "clasped each other spasmodically," and hung back; grey veterans crying: 'Mercy Messieurs; ah, mercy!' But there was no mercy. Suddenly, however, one of these men steps forward. He had a blue frock coat; he seemed to be about thirty, his stature was above common, his look noble and martial. 'I go first,' said he, 'since it must be so: adieu!' Then dashing his hat sharply behind him: 'Which way?' cried he to the Brigands: 'Shew it me, then.' They open the folding gate; he is announced to the multitude. He stands a moment motionless; then plunges forth among the pikes, and dies of a thousand wounds."[530]

Man after man is cut down; the sabres need sharpening, the killers refresh themselves from wine jugs. Onward and onward goes the butchery; the loud yells wearying down into bass growls. A sombre-faced, shifting multitude looks on; in dull approval, or dull disapproval; in dull recognition that it is Necessity. "An *Anglais* in drab greatcoat" was seen, or seemed to be seen, serving liquor from his own dram-bottle;—for what purpose, "if not set on by Pitt," Satan and himself know best! Witty Dr. Moore grew sick on approaching, and turned into another street.[531] —Quick enough goes this Jury-Court; and rigorous. The brave are not spared, nor the beautiful, nor the weak. Old M. de Montmorin, the Minister's Brother, was acquitted by the Tribunal of the Seventeenth; and conducted back, elbowed by howling galleries; but is not acquitted here. Princess de Lamballe has lain down on bed: 'Madame, you are to be removed to the Abbaye.' 'I do not wish to remove; I am well enough here.' There is a need-be for removing. She will arrange her dress a little, then; rude voices answer, 'You have not far to go.' She too is led to the hell-gate; a manifest Queen's-Friend. She shivers back, at the sight of bloody sabres; but there is no return: Onwards! That fair hindhead is cleft with the axe; the neck is severed. That fair body is cut in fragments; with indignities, and obscene horrors of moustachio *grands-lèvres*, which human nature would fain find incredible,—which shall be read in the original language only. She was beautiful, she was good, she had known no happiness. Young hearts, generation after generation, will think with themselves: O worthy of worship, thou king-descended, god-descended and poor sister-woman! why was not I there; and some Sword Balmung, or Thor's Hammer in my hand? Her head is fixed on a pike; paraded under the windows of the Temple; that a still more hated, a Marie-Antoinette, may see. One Municipal, in the Temple with the Royal Prisoners at the moment, said, 'Look out.' Another eagerly whispered, 'Do not look.' The circuit of the Temple is guarded, in these hours, by a long stretched tricolor riband: terror enters, and the clangour of infinite tumult: hitherto not regicide, though that too may come.

But it is more edifying to note what thrillings of affection, what fragments of wild virtues turn up, in this shaking asunder of man's existence, for of these too there is a proportion. Note old Marquis Cazotte: he is doomed to die; but his young Daughter clasps him in her arms, with an inspiration of eloquence, with a love which is stronger than very death; the heart of the killers themselves is touched by it; the old man is spared. Yet he was guilty, if plotting for his King is guilt: in ten days more, a Court of Law condemned him, and he had to die elsewhere; bequeathing his Daughter a lock of his old grey hair. Or note old M. de Sombreuil, who also had a Daughter:—My Father is not an Aristocrat; O good gentlemen, I will swear it, and testify it, and in all ways prove it; we are not; we hate Aristocrats! 'Wilt thou drink Aristocrats' blood?' The man lifts blood (if universal Rumour can be credited);[532] the poor maiden does drink. 'This Sombreuil is innocent then!' Yes indeed,—and now note, most of all, how the bloody pikes, at this news, do rattle to the ground; and the tiger-yells become bursts of jubilee over a brother saved; and the old man and his daughter are clasped to bloody bosoms, with hot tears, and borne home in triumph of *Vive la Nation*, the killers refusing even money! Does it seem strange, this temper of theirs? It seems very certain, well proved by Royalist testimony in other instances;[533] and very significant.

Chapter 3.1.V.
A Trilogy

As all Delineation, in these ages, were it never so Epic, "speaking itself and not singing itself," must either found on Belief and provable Fact, or have no foundation at all (nor except as floating cobweb any existence at all),—the Reader will perhaps prefer to take a glance with the very eyes of eye-witnesses; and see, in that way, for himself, how it was. Brave Jourgniac, innocent Abbé Sicard, judicious Advocate Maton, these, greatly compressing themselves, shall speak, each an instant. Jourgniac's *Agony of Thirty-eight Hours* went through "above a hundred editions," though intrinsically a poor work. Some portion of it may here go through above the hundred-and-first, for want of a better.

"*Towards seven o'clock*" (Sunday night, at the Abbaye; for Jourgniac goes by dates): "We saw two men enter, their hands bloody and armed with sabres; a turnkey, with a torch, lighted them; he pointed to the bed of the unfortunate Swiss, Reding. Reding spoke with a dying voice. One of them paused; but the other cried *Allons donc;* lifted the unfortunate man; carried him out on his back to the street. He was massacred there.

"We all looked at one another in silence, we clasped each other's hands. Motionless, with fixed eyes, we gazed on the pavement of our prison; on which lay the moonlight, checkered with the triple stancheons of our windows.

"*Three in the morning:* They were breaking-in one of the prison-doors. We at first thought they were coming to kill us in our room; but heard, by voices on the staircase, that it was a room where some Prisoners had barricaded themselves. They were all butchered there, as we shortly gathered.

"*Ten o'clock:* The Abbé Lenfant and the Abbé de Chapt-Rastignac appeared in the pulpit of the Chapel, which was our prison; they had entered by a door from the stairs. They said to us that our end was at hand; that we must compose ourselves, and receive their last blessing. An electric movement, not to be defined, threw us all on our knees, and we received it.

These two whitehaired old men, blessing us from their place above; death hovering over our heads, on all hands environing us; the moment is never to be forgotten. Half an hour after, they were both massacred, and we heard their cries."[534] —Thus Jourgniac in his *Agony* in the Abbaye.

But now let the good Maton speak, what he, over in La Force, in the same hours, is suffering and witnessing. This *Résurrection* by him is greatly the best, the least theatrical of these Pamphlets; and stands testing by documents:

"Towards seven o'clock," on Sunday night, "prisoners were called frequently, and they did not reappear. Each of us reasoned in his own way, on this singularity: but our ideas became calm, as we persuaded ourselves that the Memorial I had drawn up for the National Assembly was producing effect.

"At one in the morning, the grate which led to our quarter opened anew. Four men in uniform, each with a drawn sabre and blazing torch, came up to our corridor, preceded by a turnkey; and entered an apartment close to ours, to investigate a box there, which we heard them break up. This done, they stept into the gallery, and questioned the man Cuissa, to know where Lamotte (Necklace's Widower) was. Lamotte, they said, had some months ago, under pretext of a treasure he knew of, swindled a sum of three-hundred livres from one of them, inviting him to dinner for that purpose. The wretched Cuissa, now in their hands, who indeed lost his life this night, answered trembling, That he remembered the fact well, but could not tell what was become of Lamotte. Determined to find Lamotte and confront him with Cuissa, they rummaged, along with this latter, through various other apartments; but without effect, for we heard them say: 'Come search among the corpses then: for, *nom de Dieu!* we must find where he is.'

"At this time, I heard Louis Bardy, the Abbé Bardy's name called: he was brought out; and directly massacred, as I learnt. He had been accused, along with his concubine, five or six years before, of having murdered and cut in pieces his own Brother, Auditor of the *Chambre des Comptes* of Montpelier; but had by his subtlety, his dexterity, nay his eloquence, outwitted the judges, and escaped.

"One may fancy what terror these words, 'Come search among the corpses then,' had thrown me into. I saw nothing for it now but resigning myself to die. I wrote my last-will; concluding it by a petition and adjuration, that the paper should be sent to its address. Scarcely had I quitted the pen, when there came two other men in uniform; one of them, whose arm and sleeve up to the very shoulder, as well as the sabre, were covered with blood, said, He was as weary as a hodman that had been beating plaster.

"Baudin de la Chenaye was called; sixty years of virtues could not save him. They said, '*À l'Abbaye:*' he passed the fatal outer-gate; gave a cry of terror, at sight of the heaped corpses; covered his eyes with his hands, and died of innumerable wounds. At every new opening of the grate, I thought I should hear my own name called, and see Rossignol enter.

"I flung off my nightgown and cap; I put on a coarse unwashed shirt, a worn frock without waistcoat, an old round hat; these things I had sent for, some days ago, in the fear of what might happen.

"The rooms of this corridor had been all emptied but ours. We were four together; whom they seemed to have forgotten: we addressed our prayers in common to the Eternal to be delivered from this peril.

"Baptiste the turnkey came up by himself, to see us. I took him by the hands; I conjured him to save us; promised him a hundred louis, if he would conduct me home. A noise coming from the grates made him hastily withdraw.

"It was the noise of some dozen or fifteen men, armed to the teeth; as we, lying flat to escape being seen, could see from our windows: 'Up stairs!' said they: 'Let not one remain.' I took out my penknife; I considered where I should strike myself,"—but reflected "that the blade was too short," and also "on religion."

Finally, however, between seven and eight o'clock in the morning, enter four men with bludgeons and sabres!—"to one of whom Gerard my comrade whispered, earnestly, apart. During their colloquy I searched every where for shoes, that I might lay off the Advocate pumps (*pantoufles de Palais*) I had on," but could find none.—"Constant, called le Sauvage, Gerard, and a third whose name escapes me, they let clear off: as for me, four sabres were crossed over my breast, and they led me down. I was brought to their bar; to the Personage with the scarf, who sat as judge there. He was a lame man, of tall lank stature. He recognised me on the streets, and spoke to me seven months after. I have been assured that he was son of a retired attorney, and named Chepy. Crossing the Court called *Des Nourrices*, I saw Manuel haranguing in tricolor scarf." The trial, as we see, ends in acquittal and *resurrection*.[535]

Poor Sicard, from the *violon* of the Abbaye, shall say but a few words; true-looking, though tremulous. Towards three in the morning, the killers bethink them of this little *violon*; and knock from the court. "I tapped gently, trembling lest the murderers might hear, on the opposite door, where the Section Committee was sitting: they answered gruffly that they had no key. There were three of us in this *violon*; my companions thought they perceived a kind of loft overhead. But it was very high; only one of us could reach it, by mounting on the shoulders of both the others. One of them said to me, that my life was usefuller than theirs: I resisted, they insisted: no denial! I fling myself on the neck of these two deliverers; never was scene more touching. I mount on the shoulders of the first, then on those of the second, finally on the loft; and address to my two comrades the expression of a soul overwhelmed with natural emotions.[536]

The two generous companions, we rejoice to find, did not perish. But it is time that Jourgniac de Saint-Méard should speak his last words, and end this singular trilogy. The night had become day; and the day has again become night. Jourgniac, worn down with uttermost agitation, has fallen asleep, and had a cheering dream: he has also contrived to make acquaintance with one of the volunteer bailiffs, and spoken in native Provençal with him. On Tuesday, about one in the morning, his *Agony* is reaching its crisis.

"By the glare of two torches, I now descried the terrible tribunal, where lay my life or my death. The President, in grey coats, with a sabre at his side, stood leaning with his hands against a table, on which were papers, an inkstand, tobacco-pipes and bottles. Some ten persons were around, seated or standing; two of whom had jackets and aprons: others were sleeping stretched on benches. Two men, in bloody shirts, guarded the door of the place; an old turnkey had his hand on the lock. In front of the President, three men held a Prisoner, who might be about sixty" (or seventy: he was old Marshal Maillé, of the Tuileries and August Tenth). "They stationed me in a corner; my guards crossed their sabres on my breast. I looked on all sides for my Provençal: two National Guards, one of them drunk, presented some appeal from the Section of Croix Rouge in favour of the Prisoner; the Man in Grey answered: 'They are useless, these appeals for traitors.' Then the Prisoner exclaimed: 'It is frightful; your judgment is a murder.' The President answered; 'My hands are washed of it; take M. Maillé away.' They drove him into the street; where, through the opening of the door, I saw him massacred.

"The President sat down to write; registering, I suppose, the name of this one whom they had finished; then I heard him say: 'Another, *À un autre!*'

"Behold me then haled before this swift and bloody judgment-bar, where the best protection was to have no protection, and all resources of ingenuity became null if they were not founded on truth. Two of my guards held me each by a hand, the third by the collar of my coat. 'Your name, your profession?' said the President. 'The smallest lie ruins you,' added one of the judges,—'My name is Jourgniac Saint-Méard; I have served, as an officer, twenty years: and I appear at your tribunal with the assurance of an innocent man, who therefore will not lie.'—'We shall see that,' said the President: 'Do you know why you are arrested?'—'Yes, Monsieur le President; I am accused of editing the Journal *De la Cour et de la Ville*. But I hope to prove the falsity'"—

But no; Jourgniac's proof of the falsity, and defence generally, though of excellent result as a defence, is not interesting to read. It is long-winded; there is a loose theatricality in the reporting of it, which does not amount to unveracity, yet which tends that way. We shall suppose him successful, beyond hope, in proving and disproving; and skip largely,—to the catastrophe, almost at two steps.

"'But after all,' said one of the Judges, 'there is no smoke without kindling; tell us why they accuse you of that.'—'I was about to do so'"— Jourgniac does so; with more and more success.

"'Nay,' continued I, 'they accuse me even of recruiting for the Emigrants!' At these words there arose a general murmur. 'O Messieurs, Messieurs,' I exclaimed, raising my voice, 'it is my turn to speak; I beg M. le President to have the kindness to maintain it for me; I never needed it more.'—'True enough, true enough,' said almost all the judges with a laugh: 'Silence!'

"While they were examining the testimonials I had produced, a new Prisoner was brought in, and placed before the President. 'It was one Priest more,' they said, 'whom they had ferreted out of the Chapelle.' After very few questions: '*À la Force!*' He flung his breviary on the table: was hurled forth, and massacred. I reappeared before the tribunal.

"'You tell us always,' cried one of the judges, with a tone of impatience, 'that you are not this, that you are not that: what are you then?'—'I was an open Royalist.'—There arose a general murmur; which was miraculously appeased by another of the men, who had seemed to take an interest in me: 'We are not here to judge opinions,' said he, 'but to judge the results of them.' Could Rousseau and Voltaire both in one, pleading for me, have said better?—'Yes, Messieurs,' cried I, 'always till the Tenth of August, I was an open Royalist. Ever since the Tenth of August that cause has been finished. I am a Frenchman, true to my country. I was always a man of honour.'

"'My soldiers never distrusted me. Nay, two days before that business of Nanci, when their suspicion of their officers was at its height, they chose me for commander, to lead them to Lunéville, to get back the prisoners of the Regiment Mestre-de-Camp, and seize General Malseigne.'" Which fact there is, most luckily, an individual present who by a certain token can confirm.

"The President, this cross-questioning being over, took off his hat and said: 'I see nothing to suspect in this man; I am for granting him his liberty. Is that your vote?' To which all the judges answered: '*Oui, oui;* it is just!'"

And there arose vivats within doors and without; "escort of three," amid shoutings and embracings: thus Jourgniac escaped from jury-trial and the jaws of death.[537] Maton and Sicard did, either by trial, and no bill found, lank President Chepy finding "absolutely nothing;" or else by evasion, and new favour of Moton the brave watchmaker, likewise escape; and were embraced, and wept over; weeping in return, as they well might.

Thus they three, in wondrous trilogy, or triple soliloquy; uttering simultaneously, through the dread night-watches, their Night-thoughts,— grown audible to us! They Three are become audible: but the other "Thousand and Eighty-nine, of whom Two Hundred and Two were Priests," who also had Night-thoughts, remain inaudible; choked for ever in black Death. Heard only of President Chepy and the Man in Grey!—

Chapter 3.1.VI.
The Circular

But the Constituted Authorities, all this while? The Legislative Assembly; the Six Ministers; the Townhall; Santerre with the National Guard?—It is very curious to think what a City is. Theatres, to the number of some twenty-three, were open every night during these prodigies: while right-arms here grew weary with slaying, right-arms there are twiddledeeing on melodious catgut; at the very instant when Abbé Sicard was clambering up his second pair of shoulders, three-men high, five hundred thousand human individuals were lying horizontal, as if nothing were amiss.

As for the poor Legislative, the sceptre had departed from it. The Legislative did send Deputation to the Prisons, to the Street-Courts; and poor M. Dusaulx did harangue there; but produced no conviction whatsoever: nay, at last, as he continued haranguing, the Street-Court interposed, not without threats; and he had to cease, and withdraw. This is the same poor worthy old M. Dusaulx who told, or indeed almost sang (though with cracked voice), the *Taking of the Bastille*,—to our satisfaction long since. He was wont to announce himself, on such and on all occasions, as *the Translator of Juvenal*. 'Good Citizens, you see before you a man who loves his country, who is the Translator of Juvenal,' said he once.—'Juvenal?' interrupts Sansculottism: 'who the devil is Juvenal? One of your *sacrés Aristocrates*? To the *Lanterne!*' From an orator of this kind, conviction was not to be expected. The Legislative had much ado to save one of its own Members, or Ex-Members, Deputy Journeau, who chanced to be lying in arrest for mere Parliamentary delinquencies, in these Prisons. As for poor old Dusaulx and Company, they returned to the Salle de Manége, saying, 'It was dark; and they could not see well what was going on.'[538]

Roland writes indignant messages, in the name of Order, Humanity, and the Law; but there is no Force at his disposal. Santerre's National Force seems lazy to rise; though he made requisitions, he says,—which always dispersed again. Nay did not we, with Advocate Maton's eyes, see 'men in uniform,' too, with their 'sleeves bloody to the shoulder?' Pétion goes in tricolor scarf; speaks 'the austere language of the law:' the killers give up, while he is there; when his back is turned, recommence. Manuel too in scarf we, with Maton's eyes, transiently saw haranguing, in the Court called of Nurses, *Cour des Nourrices*. On the other hand, cruel Billaud, likewise in scarf, "with that small puce coat and black wig we are used to on him,"[539] audibly delivers, "standing among corpses," at the Abbaye, a short but ever-memorable harangue, reported in various phraseology, but always to this purpose: 'Brave Citizens, you are extirpating the Enemies of Liberty; you are at your duty. A grateful Commune, and Country, would wish to recompense you adequately; but cannot, for you know its want of funds. Whoever shall have worked (*travaillé*) in a Prison shall receive a draft of one louis, payable by our cashier. Continue your work.'[540] —The Constituted Authorities are of yesterday; all pulling different ways: there is properly not Constituted Authority, but every man is his own King; and all are kinglets, belligerent, allied, or armed-neutral, without king over them.

"O everlasting infamy," exclaims Montgaillard, "that Paris stood looking on in stupor for four days, and did not interfere!" Very desirable indeed that Paris had interfered; yet not unnatural that it stood even so, looking on in stupor. Paris is in death-panic, the enemy and gibbets at its door: whosoever in Paris has the heart to front death finds it more pressing to do it fighting the Prussians, than fighting the killers of Aristocrats. Indignant abhorrence, as in Roland, may be here; gloomy sanction, premeditation or not, as in Marat and Committee of Salvation, may be there; dull disapproval, dull approval, and acquiescence in Necessity and Destiny, is the general temper. The Sons of Darkness, "two hundred or so," risen from their lurking-places, have scope to do their work. Urged on by fever-frenzy of Patriotism, and the madness of Terror;—urged on by lucre, and the gold louis of wages? Nay, not lucre: for the gold watches, rings, money of the Massacred, are punctually brought to the Townhall, by Killers sans-indispensables, who higgle afterwards for their twenty shillings of wages; and Sergent sticking an uncommonly fine agate on his finger ("fully meaning to account for it"), becomes *Agate*-Sergent. But the temper, as we say, is dull acquiescence. Not till the Patriotic or Frenetic part of the work is finished for want of material; and Sons of Darkness, bent clearly on lucre alone, begin wrenching watches and purses, brooches from ladies' necks "to equip volunteers," in daylight, on the streets,—does the temper from dull grow vehement; does the Constable raise his truncheon, and striking heartily (like a cattle-driver in earnest) beat the "course of things" back into its old regulated drove-roads. The *Garde-Meuble* itself was surreptitiously plundered, on the 17th of the Month, to Roland's new horror; who anew bestirs himself, and is, as Sieyes says, "the veto of scoundrels," Roland *veto des coquins*.[541] —

This is the September Massacre, otherwise called "Severe Justice of the People." These are the Septemberers (*Septembriseurs*); a name of some note and lucency,—but lucency of the Nether-fire sort; very different from that of our Bastille Heroes, who shone, disputable by no Friend of Freedom, as in heavenly light-radiance: to such phasis of the business have we advanced since then! The numbers massacred are, in Historical *fantasy*, "between two and three thousand;" or indeed they are "upwards of six thousand," for Peltier (in vision) saw them massacring the very patients of the Bicêtre Madhouse "with grape-shot;" nay finally they are "twelve thousand" and odd hundreds,—not more than that.[542] In Arithmetical ciphers, and Lists drawn up by accurate Advocate Maton, the number, including two hundred and two priests, three "persons unknown," and "one thief killed at the Bernardins," is, as above hinted, a Thousand and Eighty-nine,—no less than that.

A thousand and eighty-nine lie dead, "two hundred and sixty heaped carcasses on the Pont au Change" itself;—among which, Robespierre pleading afterwards will "nearly weep" to reflect that there was said to be one slain innocent.[543] One; not two, O thou seagreen Incorruptible? If so, Themis Sansculotte must be lucky; for she was brief!—In the dim Registers of the Townhall, which are preserved to this day, men read, with a certain sickness of heart, items and entries not usual in Town Books: "To workers employed in preserving the salubrity óf the air in the Prisons, and persons "who presided over these dangerous operations," so much,—in various items, nearly seven hundred pounds sterling. To carters employed to "the Burying-grounds of Clamart, Montrouge, and Vaugirard," at so much a journey, per cart; this also is an entry. Then so many francs and odd sous "for the necessary quantity of quick-lime!"[544] Carts go along the streets; full of stript human corpses, thrown pellmell; limbs sticking up:—seest thou that cold Hand sticking up, through the heaped embrace of brother corpses, in its yellow paleness, in its cold rigour; the palm opened towards Heaven, as if in dumb prayer, in expostulation *de profundis*, Take pity on the Sons of Men!—Mercier saw it, as he walked down "the Rue Saint-Jacques from Montrouge, on the morrow of the Massacres:" but not a Hand; it was a Foot,—which he reckons still more significant, one understands not well why. Or was it as the Foot of one *spurning* Heaven? Rushing, like a wild diver, in disgust and despair, towards the depths of Annihilation? Even there shall His hand find thee, and His right-hand hold thee,—surely for right not for wrong, for good not evil! "I saw that Foot," says Mercier; "I shall know it again at the great Day of Judgment, when the Eternal, throned on his thunders, shall judge both Kings and Septemberers."[545]

That a shriek of inarticulate horror rose over this thing, not only from French Aristocrats and Moderates, but from all Europe, and has prolonged itself to the present day, was most natural and right. The thing lay done, irrevocable; a thing to be counted besides some other things, which lie very black in our Earth's Annals, yet which will not erase therefrom. For man, as was remarked, has transcendentalisms in him; standing, as he does, poor creature, every way "in the confluence of Infinitudes;" a mystery to himself and others: in the centre of two Eternities, of three Immensities,—in the intersection of primeval Light with the everlasting dark! Thus have there been, especially by vehement tempers reduced to a state of desperation, very miserable things done. Sicilian Vespers, and "eight thousand slaughtered in two hours," are a known thing. Kings themselves, not in desperation, but only in difficulty, have sat hatching, for year and day (nay De Thou says, for seven years), their Bartholomew Business; and then, at the right moment, also on an Autumn Sunday, this very Bell (they say it is the identical metal) of St. Germain l'Auxerrois was set a-pealing—with effect. [546] Nay the same black boulder-stones of these Paris Prisons have seen Prison-massacres before now; men massacring countrymen, Burgundies massacring Armagnacs, whom they had suddenly imprisoned, till as now there are piled heaps of carcasses, and the streets ran red;—the Mayor Pétion of the time speaking the austere language of the law, and answered by the Killers, in old French (it is some four hundred years old): '*Maugré bieu, Sire*,—Sir, God's malison on your justice, your pity, your right reason. Cursed be of God whoso shall have pity on these false traitorous Armagnacs, English; dogs they are; they have destroyed us, wasted this realm of France, and sold it to the English.'[547] And so they slay, and fling aside the slain, to the extent of "fifteen hundred and eighteen, among whom are found four Bishops of false and damnable counsel, and two Presidents of Parlement." For though it is not Satan's world this that we live in, Satan always has his place in it (underground properly); and from time to time bursts up. Well may mankind shriek, inarticulately anathematising as they can. There are actions of such emphasis that no shrieking can be too emphatic for them. Shriek ye; acted have they.

Shriek who might in this France, in this Paris Legislative or Paris Townhall, there are Ten Men who do not shriek. A Circular goes out from the Committee of *Salut Public*, dated 3rd of September 1792; directed to all Townhalls: a State-paper too remarkable to be overlooked. "A part of the ferocious conspirators detained in the Prisons," it says, "have been put to death by the People; and it," the Circular, "cannot doubt but the whole Nation, driven to the edge of ruin by such endless series of treasons, will make haste to adopt *this* means of public salvation; and all Frenchmen will cry as the men of Paris: We go to fight the enemy, but we will not leave robbers behind us, to butcher our wives and children." To which are legibly appended these signatures: Panis, Sergent; Marat, Friend of the People;[548] with Seven others;—carried down thereby, in a strange way, to the late remembrance of Antiquarians. We remark, however, that their Circular rather recoiled on themselves. The Townhalls made no use of it; even the distracted Sansculottes made little; they only howled and bellowed, but did not bite. At Rheims "about eight persons" were killed; and two afterwards were hanged for doing it. At Lyons, and a few other places, some attempt was made; but with hardly any effect, being quickly put down.

Less fortunate were the Prisoners of Orléans; was the good Duke de la Rochefoucault. He journeying, by quick stages, with his Mother and Wife, towards the Waters of Forges, or some quieter country, was arrested at Gisors; conducted along the streets, amid effervescing multitudes, and killed dead "by the stroke of a paving-stone hurled through the coach-window." Killed as a once Liberal now Aristocrat; Protector of Priests, Suspender of virtuous Pétions, and his unfortunate Hot-grown-cold, detestable to Patriotism. He dies lamented of Europe; his blood spattering the cheeks of his old Mother, ninety-three years old.

As for the Orléans Prisoners, they are State Criminals: Royalist Ministers, Delessarts, Montmorins; who have been accumulating on the High Court of Orléans, ever since that Tribunal was set up. Whom now it seems good that we should get transferred to our new Paris Court of the Seventeenth; which proceeds far quicker. Accordingly hot Fournier from Martinique, Fournier l'Americain, is off, missioned by Constituted Authority; with stanch National Guards, with Lazouski the Pole; sparingly provided with road-money. These, through bad quarters, through difficulties, perils, for Authorities cross each other in this time,—do triumphantly bring off the Fifty or Fifty-three Orléans Prisoners, towards Paris; where a swifter Court of the Seventeenth will do justice on them.[549] But lo, at Paris, in the interim, a still swifter and swiftest Court of the *Second*, and of *September*, has instituted itself: enter not Paris, or that will judge you!—What shall hot Fournier do? It was his duty, as volunteer Constable, had he been a perfect character, to guard those men's lives never so Aristocratic, at the expense of his own valuable life never so Sansculottic, till some Constituted Court had disposed of them. But he was an imperfect character and Constable; perhaps one of the more imperfect.

Hot Fournier, ordered to turn thither by one Authority, to turn thither by another Authority, is in a perplexing multiplicity of orders; but finally he strikes off for Versailles. His Prisoners fare in tumbrils, or open carts, himself and Guards riding and marching around: and at the last village, the worthy Mayor of Versailles comes to meet him, anxious that the arrival and locking up were well over. It is Sunday, the ninth day of the month. Lo, on entering the Avenue of Versailles, what multitudes, stirring, swarming in the September sun, under the dull-green September foliage; the Four-rowed Avenue all humming and swarming, as if the Town had emptied itself! Our tumbrils roll heavily through the living sea; the Guards and Fournier making way with ever more difficulty; the Mayor speaking and gesturing his persuasivest; amid the inarticulate growling hum, which growls ever the deeper even by hearing itself growl, not without sharp yelpings here and there:—Would to God we were out of this strait place, and wind and separation had cooled the heat, which seems about igniting here!

And yet if the wide Avenue is too strait, what will the Street *de Surintendance* be, at leaving of the same? At the corner of Surintendance Street, the compressed yelpings became a continuous yell: savage figures spring on the tumbril-shafts; first spray of an endless coming tide! The Mayor pleads, pushes, half-desperate; is pushed, carried off in men's arms: the savage tide has entrance, has mastery. Amid horrid noise, and tumult as of fierce wolves, the Prisoners sink massacred,—all but some eleven, who escaped into houses, and found mercy. The Prisons, and what other Prisoners they held, were with difficulty saved. The stript clothes are burnt in bonfire; the corpses lie heaped in the ditch on the morrow morning.[550] All France, except it be the Ten Men of the Circular and their people, moans and rages, inarticulately shrieking; all Europe rings.

But neither did Danton shriek; though, as Minister of Justice, it was more his part to do so. Brawny Danton is in the breach, as of stormed Cities and Nations; amid the Sweep of Tenth-of-August cannon, the rustle of Prussian gallows-ropes, the smiting of September sabres; destruction all round him, and the rushing-down of worlds: Minister of Justice is his name; but Titan of the Forlorn Hope, and *Enfant Perdu* of the Revolution, is his quality,—and the man acts according to that. 'We must put our enemies in fear!' Deep fear, is it not, as of its own accord, falling on our enemies? The Titan of the Forlorn Hope, he is not the man that would swiftest of all prevent its so falling. Forward, thou lost Titan of an *Enfant Perdu;* thou must dare, and again dare, and without end dare; there is nothing left for thee but that! '*Que mon nom soit flétri,* Let my name be blighted:' what am I? The Cause alone is great; and shall live, and not perish.—So, on the whole, here too is a swallower of Formulas; of still wider gulp than Mirabeau: this Danton, Mirabeau of the Sansculottes. In the September days, this Minister was not heard of as co-operating with strict Roland; his business might lie elsewhere,—with Brunswick and the Hôtel-de-Ville. When applied to by an official person, about the Orleans Prisoners, and the risks they ran, he answered gloomily, twice over, 'Are not these men guilty?' —When pressed, he "answered in a terrible voice," and turned his back.[551] Two Thousand slain in the Prisons; horrible if you will: but Brunswick is within a day's journey of us; and there are Five-and twenty Millions yet, to slay or to save. Some men have tasks,—frightfuller than ours! It seems strange, but is not strange, that this Minister of Moloch-Justice, when any suppliant for a friend's life got access to him, was found to have human compassion; and yielded and granted "always;" "neither did one personal enemy of Danton perish in these days."[552]

To shriek, we say, when certain things are acted, is proper and unavoidable. Nevertheless, articulate speech, not shrieking, is the faculty of man: when speech is not yet possible, let there be, with the shortest delay, at least—silence. Silence, accordingly, in this forty-fourth year of the business, and eighteen hundred and thirty-sixth of an "Era called Christian as *lucus à non*," is the thing we recommend and practise. Nay, instead of shrieking more, it were perhaps edifying to remark, on the other side, what a singular thing Customs (in Latin, *Mores*) are; and how fitly the Virtue, *Vir-tus*, Manhood or Worth, that is in a man, is called his *Morality*, or *Customariness*. Fell Slaughter, one the most authentic products of the Pit you would say, once give it Customs, becomes War, with Laws of War; and is Customary and Moral enough; and red individuals carry the tools of it girt round their haunches, not without an air of pride,—which do thou nowise blame. While, see! so long as it is but dressed in hodden or russet; and Revolution, less frequent than War, has not yet got its Laws of Revolution, but the hodden or russet individuals are Uncustomary—O shrieking beloved brother blockheads of Mankind, let us close those wide mouths of ours; let us cease shrieking, and begin considering!

Chapter 3.1.VII.
September in Argonne

Plain, at any rate, is one thing: that the *fear*, whatever of fear those Aristocrat enemies might need, has been brought about. The matter is getting serious then! Sansculottism too has become a Fact, and seems minded to assert itself as such? This huge mooncalf of Sansculottism, staggering about, as young calves do, is not mockable only, and soft like another calf; but terrible too, if you prick it; and, through its hideous nostrils, blows fire!— Aristocrats, with pale panic in their hearts, fly towards covert; and a light rises to them over several things; or rather a confused transition towards light, whereby for the moment darkness is only darker than ever. But, What will become of this France? Here is a question! France is dancing its desert-waltz, as Sahara does when the winds waken; in whirlblasts twenty-five millions in number; waltzing towards Townhalls, Aristocrat Prisons, and Election Committee-rooms; towards Brunswick and the Frontiers;— towards a New Chapter of Universal History; if indeed it be not the *Finis*, and winding-up of that!

In Election Committee-rooms there is now no dubiety; but the work goes bravely along. The Convention is getting chosen,—really in a decisive spirit; in the Townhall we already date *First year of the Republic*. Some Two hundred of our best Legislators may be re-elected, the Mountain bodily: Robespierre, with Mayor Pétion, Buzot, Curate Grégoire, Rabaut, some three score Old-Constituents; though we once had only "thirty voices." All these; and along with them, friends long known to Revolutionary fame: Camille Desmoulins, though he stutters in speech; Manuel, Tallien and Company; Journalists Gorsas, Carra, Mercier, Louvet of *Faublas;* Clootz Speaker of Mankind; Collot d'Herbois, tearing a passion to rags; Fabre d'Eglantine, speculative Pamphleteer; Legendre the solid Butcher; nay Marat, though rural France can hardly believe it, or even believe that there *is* a Marat except in print. Of Minister Danton, who will lay down his Ministry for a Membership, we need not speak. Paris is fervent; nor is the Country wanting to itself. Barbaroux, Rebecqui, and fervid Patriots are coming from Marseilles. Seven hundred and forty-five men (or indeed forty-nine, for Avignon now sends Four) are gathering: so many are to meet; not so many are to part!

Attorney Carrier from Aurillac, Ex-Priest Lebon from Arras, these shall both gain a *name*. Mountainous Auvergne re-elects her Romme: hardy tiller of the soil, once Mathematical Professor; who, unconscious, carries in petto a remarkable *New Calendar*, with Messidors, Pluvioses, and such like;—and having given it well forth, shall depart by the death they call Roman. Sieyes old-Constituent comes; to make new Constitutions as many as wanted: for the rest, peering out of his clear cautious eyes, he will cower low in many an emergency, and find silence safest. Young Saint-Just is coming, deputed by Aisne in the North; more like a Student than a Senator: not four-and-twenty yet; who has written Books; a youth of slight stature, with mild mellow voice, enthusiast olive-complexion, and long dark hair. Féraud, from the far valley D'Aure in the folds of the Pyrenees, is coming; an ardent Republican; doomed to fame, at least in death.

All manner of Patriot men are coming: Teachers, Husbandmen, Priests and Ex-Priests, Traders, Doctors; above all, Talkers, or the Attorney-species. Man-midwives, as Levasseur of the Sarthe, are not wanting. Nor Artists: gross David, with the swoln cheek, has long painted, with genius in a state of convulsion; and will now legislate. The swoln cheek, choking his words in the birth, totally disqualifies him as orator; but his pencil, his head, his gross hot heart, with genius in a state of convulsion, will be there. A man bodily and mentally swoln-cheeked, disproportionate; flabby-large, instead of great; weak withal as in a state of convulsion, not strong in a state of composure: so let him play his part. Nor are naturalised Benefactors of the Species forgotten: Priestley, elected by the Orne Department, but declining: Paine the rebellious Needleman, by the Pas de Calais, who accepts.

Few Nobles come, and yet not none. Paul François Barras, "noble as the Barrases, old as the rocks of Provence;" he is one. The reckless, shipwrecked man: flung ashore on the coast of the Maldives long ago, while sailing and soldiering as Indian Fighter; flung ashore since then, as hungry Parisian Pleasure-hunter and Half-pay, on many a Circe Island, with temporary enchantment, temporary conversion into beasthood and hoghood;— the remote Var Department has now sent him hither. A man of heat and haste; defective in utterance; defective indeed in any thing to utter; yet not without a certain rapidity of glance, a certain swift transient courage; who, in these times, Fortune favouring, may go far. He is tall, handsome to the eye, "only the complexion a little yellow;" but "with a robe of purple with a scarlet cloak and plume of tricolor, on occasions of solemnity," the man will look well.[553] Lepelletier Saint-Fargeau, Old-Constituent, is a kind of noble, and of enormous wealth; he too has come hither:—to have the Pain of Death *abolished?* Hapless Ex-Parlementeer! Nay, among our Sixty Old-Constituents, see Philippe d'Orléans a Prince of the Blood! Not now

D'Orléans: for, Feudalism being swept from the world, he demands of his worthy friends the Electors of Paris, to have a new name of their choosing; whereupon Procureur Manuel, like an antithetic literary man, recommends *Equality,* Egalité. A Philippe Egalité therefore will sit; seen of the Earth and Heaven.

Such a Convention is gathering itself together. Mere angry poultry in moulting season; whom Brunswick's grenadiers and cannoneers will give short account of. Would the weather only mend a little![554]

In vain, O Bertrand! The weather will not mend a whit:—nay even if it did? Dumouriez Polymetis, though Bertrand knows it not, started from brief slumber at Sedan, on that morning of the 29th of August; with stealthiness, with promptitude, audacity. Some three mornings after that, Brunswick, opening wide eyes, perceives the Passes of the Argonne all seized; blocked with felled trees, fortified with camps; and that it is a most shifty swift Dumouriez this, who has outwitted him!

The manœuvre may cost Brunswick "a loss of three weeks," very fatal in these circumstances. A Mountain-wall of forty miles lying between him and Paris: which he should have preoccupied;—which how now to get possession of? Also the rain it raineth every day; and we are in a hungry Champagne Pouilleuse, a land flowing only with ditch-water. How to cross this Mountain-wall of the Argonne; or what in the world to do with it?— there are marchings and wet splashings by steep paths, with *sackerments* and guttural interjections; forcings of Argonne Passes,—which unhappily will not force. Through the woods, volleying War reverberates, like huge gong-music, or Moloch's kettledrum, borne by the echoes; swoln torrents boil angrily round the foot of rocks, floating pale carcasses of men. In vain! Islettes Village, with its church-steeple, rises intact in the Mountain-pass, between the embosoming heights; your forced marchings and climbings have become forced slidings, and tumblings back. From the hill-tops thou seest nothing but dumb crags, and endless wet moaning woods; the Clermont *Vache* (huge Cow that she is) disclosing herself[555] at intervals; flinging off her cloud-blanket, and soon taking it on again, drowned in the pouring Heaven. The Argonne Passes will not force: you must *skirt* the Argonne; go round by the end of it.

But fancy whether the Emigrant Seigneurs have not got their brilliancy dulled a little; whether that "Foot Regiment in red-facings with nankeen trousers" could be in field-day order! In place of gasconading, a sort of desperation, and hydrophobia from *excess* of water, is threatening to supervene. Young Prince de Ligne, son of that brave literary De Ligne the Thundergod of Dandies, fell backwards; shot dead in Grand-Pré, the

Northmost of the Passes: Brunswick is skirting and rounding, laboriously, by the extremity of the South. Four days; days of a rain as of Noah,—without fire, without food! For fire you cut down green trees, and produce smoke; for food you eat green grapes, and produce colic, pestilential dysentery, ὀλέκοντο δὲ λαοί. And the Peasants assassinate us, they do not join us; shrill women cry shame on us, threaten to draw their very scissors on us! O ye hapless dulled-bright Seigneurs, and hydrophobic splashed Nankeens;— but O, ten times more, ye poor *sackerment*ing ghastly-visaged Hessians and Hulans, fallen on your backs; who had no call to die there, except compulsion and three-halfpence a-day! Nor has Mrs. Le Blanc of the Golden Arm a good time of it, in her bower of dripping rushes. Assassinating Peasants are hanged; Old-Constituent Honourable members, though of venerable age, ride in carts with their hands tied; these are the woes of war.

Thus they; sprawling and wriggling, far and wide, on the slopes and passes of the Argonne;—a loss to Brunswick of five-and-twenty disastrous days. There is wriggling and struggling; facing, backing, and right-about facing; as the positions shift, and the Argonne gets partly rounded, partly forced:—but still Dumouriez, force him, round him as you will, sticks like a rooted fixture on the ground; fixture with many *hinges;* wheeling now this way, now that; shewing always new front, in the most unexpected manner: nowise consenting to take himself away. Recruits stream up on him: full of heart; yet rather difficult to deal with. Behind Grand-Pré, for example, Grand-Pré which is on the wrong-side of the Argonne, for we are now forced and rounded,—the full heart, in one of those wheelings and shewings of new front, did as it were overset itself, as full hearts are liable to do; and there rose a shriek of *sauve qui peut,* and a death-panic which had nigh ruined all! So that the General had to come galloping; and, with thunder-words, with gesture, stroke of drawn sword even, check and rally, and bring back the sense of shame;[556] —nay to seize the first shriekers and ringleaders; "shave their heads and eyebrows," and pack them forth into the world as a sign. Thus too (for really the rations are short, and wet camping with hungry stomach brings bad humour) there is like to be mutiny. Whereupon again Dumouriez "arrives at the head of their line, with his staff, and an escort of a hundred huzzars. He had placed some squadrons behind them, the artillery in front; he said to them: 'As for you, for I will neither call you citizens, nor soldiers, nor my men (*ni mes enfans*), you see before you this artillery, behind you this cavalry. You have dishonoured yourselves by crimes. If you amend, and grow to behave like this brave Army which you have the honour of belonging to, you will find in me a good father. But plunderers and assassins I do not suffer here. At the smallest mutiny I will have you shivered in pieces (*hacher en pièces*). Seek out the scoundrels that are among you, and dismiss them yourselves; I hold you responsible for them.'"[557]

Patience, O Dumouriez! This uncertain heap of shriekers, mutineers, were they once drilled and inured, will become a phalanxed mass of Fighters; and wheel and whirl, to order, swiftly like the wind or the whirlwind: tanned mustachio-figures; often barefoot, even bare-backed; with sinews of iron; who require only bread and gunpowder: very Sons of Fire, the adroitest, hastiest, hottest ever seen perhaps since Attila's time. They may conquer and overrun amazingly, much as that same Attila did;—whose Attila's-Camp and Battlefield thou now seest, on this very ground;[558] who, after sweeping bare the world, was, with difficulty, and days of tough fighting, checked *here* by Roman Ætius and Fortune; and his dust-cloud made to vanish in the East again!—

Strangely enough, in this shrieking Confusion of a Soldiery, which we saw long since fallen all suicidally out of square in suicidal collision,—at Nanci, or on the streets of Metz, where brave Bouillé stood with drawn sword; and which has collided and ground itself to pieces worse and worse ever since, down now to such a state: in this shrieking Confusion, and not elsewhere, lies the first germ of returning Order for France! Round which, we say, poor France nearly all ground down suicidally likewise into rubbish and Chaos, will be glad to rally; to begin growing, and new-shaping her inorganic dust: very slowly, through centuries, through Napoleons, Louis Philippes, and other the like media and phases,—into a new, infinitely preferable France, we can hope!—

These wheelings and movements in the region of the Argonne, which are all faithfully described by Dumouriez himself, and more interesting to us than Hoyle's or Philidor's best Game of Chess, let us, nevertheless, O Reader, entirely omit;—and hasten to remark two things: the first a minute private, the second a large public thing. Our minute private thing is: the presence, in the Prussian host, in that war-game of the Argonne, of a certain Man, belonging to the sort called Immortal; who, in days since then, is becoming visible more and more, in that character, as the Transitory more and more vanishes; for from of old it was remarked that when the Gods appear among men, it is seldom in recognisable shape; thus Admetus" neatherds give Apollo a draught of their goatskin whey-bottle (well if they do not give him strokes with their ox-rungs), not dreaming that he is the Sungod! This man's name is *Johann Wolfgang von Goethe.* He is Herzog Weimar's Minister, come with the small contingent of Weimar; to do insignificant unmilitary duty here; very irrecognizable to nearly all! He stands at present, with drawn bridle, on the height near Saint-Menehould, making an experiment on the "cannon-fever;" having ridden thither against persuasion, into the dance and firing of the cannon-balls, with a scientific desire to understand what that same cannon-fever may be: "The sound of them," says he, "is curious enough; as if it were compounded of the humming of tops, the gurgling of water and the whistle of birds. By degrees you get a very uncommon sensation; which can only be described by similitude. It seems as if you were in some place extremely hot, and at the same time were completely penetrated by the heat of it; so that you feel as if you and this element you are in were perfectly on a par. The eyesight loses nothing of its strength or distinctness; and yet it is as if all things had got a kind of brown-red colour, which makes the situation and the objects still more impressive on you."[559]

This is the cannon-fever, as a World-Poet feels it.—A man entirely irrecognisable! In whose irrecognisable head, meanwhile, there verily is the spiritual counterpart (and call it complement) of this same huge Death-Birth of the World; which now effectuates itself, outwardly in the Argonne, in such cannon-thunder; inwardly, in the irrecognisable head, quite otherwise than by thunder! Mark that man, O Reader, as the memorablest of all the memorable in this Argonne Campaign. What we say of him is not dream, nor flourish of rhetoric; but scientific historic fact; as many men, now at this distance, see or begin to see.

But the large public thing we had to remark is this: That the Twentieth of September, 1792, was a raw morning covered with mist; that from three in the morning Sainte-Menehould, and those Villages and homesteads we know of old were stirred by the rumble of artillery-wagons, by the clatter of hoofs, and many footed tramp of men: all manner of military, Patriot and Prussian, taking up positions, on the Heights of La Lune and other Heights; shifting and shoving,—seemingly in some dread chess-game; which may the Heavens turn to good! The Miller of Valmy has fled dusty under ground; his Mill, were it never so windy, will have rest today. At seven in the morning the mist clears off: see Kellermann, Dumouriez' second in command, with "eighteen pieces of cannon," and deep-serried ranks, drawn up round that same silent Windmill, on his knoll of strength; Brunswick, also, with serried ranks and cannon, glooming over to him from the height of La Lune; only the little brook and its little dell now parting them.

So that the much-longed-for has come at last! Instead of hunger and dysentery, we shall have sharp shot; and then!—Dumouriez, with force and firm front, looks on from a neighbouring height; can help only with his wishes, in silence. Lo, the eighteen pieces do bluster and bark, responsive to the bluster of La Lune; and thunder-clouds mount into the air; and echoes roar through all dells, far into the depths of Argonne Wood (deserted now); and limbs and lives of men fly dissipated, this way and that. Can Brunswick make an impression on them? The dull-bright Seigneurs stand biting their thumbs: these Sansculottes seem not to fly like poultry! Towards noontide a cannon-shot blows Kellermann's horse from under him; there bursts a powder-cart high into the air, with knell heard over all: some swagging and swaying observable;—Brunswick will try! '*Camarades,*' cries Kellermann, '*Vive la Patrie! Allons vaincre pour elle,* Let us conquer.' 'Live the Fatherland!' rings responsive, to the welkin, like rolling-fire from side to side: our ranks are as firm as rocks; and Brunswick may recross the dell, ineffectual; regain his old position on La Lune; not unbattered by the way. And so, for the length of a September day,—with bluster and bark; with bellow far echoing! The cannonade lasts till sunset; and no impression made. Till an hour after sunset, the few remaining Clocks of the District striking Seven; at this late time of day Brunswick tries again. With not a whit better fortune! He is met by rock-ranks, by shouts of *Vive la Patrie;* and driven back, not unbattered. Whereupon he ceases; retires "to the Tavern of La Lune;" and sets to raising a redoute lest *he* be attacked!

Verily so: ye dulled-bright Seigneurs, make of it what ye may. Ah, and France does not rise round us in mass; and the Peasants do not join us, but assassinate us: neither hanging nor any persuasion will induce them! They have lost their old distinguishing love of King, and King's-cloak,—I fear, altogether; and will even fight to be rid of it: that seems now their humour. Nor does Austria prosper, nor the siege of Thionville. The Thionvillers, carrying their insolence to the epigrammatic pitch, have put a Wooden Horse on their walls, with a bundle of hay hung from him, and this Inscription: "When I finish my hay, you will take Thionville."[560] To such height has the frenzy of mankind risen.

The trenches of Thionville may shut: and what though those of Lille open? The Earth smiles not on us, nor the Heaven; but weeps and blears itself, in sour rain, and worse. Our very friends insult us; we are wounded in the house of our friends: 'His Majesty of Prussia had a greatcoat, when the rain came; and (contrary to all known laws) he put it on, though our two French Princes, the hope of their country, had none!' To which indeed, as Goethe admits, what answer could be made?[561] —Cold and Hunger and Affront, Colic and Dysentery and Death; and we here, cowering *redouted,* most unredoubtable, amid the "tattered corn-shocks and deformed stubble," on the splashy Height of La Lune, round the mean Tavern de La Lune!—

This is the Cannonade of Valmy; wherein the World-Poet experimented on the cannon-fever; wherein the French Sansculottes did not fly like poultry. Precious to France! Every soldier did his duty, and Alsatian Kellermann (how preferable to old Lückner the dismissed!) began to become greater; and *Égalité Fils,* Equality Junior, a light gallant Field-Officer, distinguished himself by intrepidity:—it is the same intrepid individual who now, as Louis-Philippe, without the Equality, struggles, under sad circumstances, to be called King of the French for a season.

Chapter 3.1.VIII.
Exeunt

But this Twentieth of September is otherwise a great day. For, observe, while Kellermann's horse was flying blown from under him at the Mill of Valmy, our new National Deputies, that shall be a NATIONAL CONVENTION, are hovering and gathering about the Hall of the Hundred Swiss; with intent to constitute themselves!

On the morrow, about noontide, Camus the Archivist is busy "verifying their powers;" several hundreds of them already here. Whereupon the Old Legislative comes solemnly over, to merge its old ashes phœnix-like in the body of the new;—and so forthwith, returning all solemnly back to the Salle de Manége, there sits a National Convention, Seven Hundred and Forty-nine complete, or complete enough; presided by Pétion;—which proceeds directly to do business. Read that reported afternoon's-debate, O Reader; there are few debates like it: dull reporting *Moniteur* itself becomes more dramatic than a very Shakespeare. For epigrammatic Manuel rises, speaks strange things; how the President shall have a guard of honour, and lodge in the Tuileries:—*rejected*. And Danton rises and speaks; and Collot d'Herbois rises, and Curate Gregoire, and lame Couthon of the Mountain rises; and in rapid Melibœan stanzas, only a few lines each, they propose motions not a few: That the corner-stone of our new Constitution is Sovereignty of the People; that our Constitution shall be accepted by the People or be null; further that the People ought to be avenged, and have right Judges; that the Imposts must continue till new order; that Landed and other Property be sacred forever; finally that "Royalty from this day is abolished in France:"— *Decreed* all, before four o'clock strike, with acclamation of the world![562] The tree was all so ripe; only shake it and there fall such yellow cart-loads.

And so over in the Valmy Region, as soon as the news come, what stir is this, audible, visible from our muddy heights of La Lune?[563] Universal shouting of the French on their opposite hillside; caps raised on bayonets; and a sound as of *République; Vive la République* borne dubious on the winds!—On the morrow morning, so to speak, Brunswick slings his knapsacks before day, lights any fires he has; and marches without tap of drum. Dumouriez finds ghastly symptoms in that camp; "*latrines* full of blood!"[564] The chivalrous King of Prussia, for he as we saw is here in person, may long rue the day; may look colder than ever on these dulled-bright Seigneurs, and French Princes their Country's hope;—and, on the whole, put on his great-coat without ceremony, happy that he has one. They retire, all retire with convenient despatch, through a Champagne trodden into a quagmire, the wild weather pouring on them; Dumouriez through his Kellermanns and Dillons pricking them a little in the hinder parts. A little, not much; now pricking, now negotiating: for Brunswick has his eyes opened; and the Majesty of Prussia is a repentant Majesty.

Nor has Austria prospered, nor the Wooden Horse of Thionville bitten his hay; nor Lille City surrendered itself. The Lille trenches opened, on the 29th of the month; with balls and shells, and redhot balls; as if not trenches but Vesuvius and the Pit had opened. It was frightful, say all eye-witnesses; but it is ineffectual. The Lillers have risen to such temper; especially after these news from Argonne and the East. Not a Sans-indispensables in Lille that would surrender for a King's ransom. Redhot balls rain, day and night; "six-thousand," or so, and bombs "filled internally with oil of turpentine which splashes up in flame;"—mainly on the dwellings of the Sansculottes and Poor; the streets of the Rich being spared. But the Sansculottes get water-pails; form quenching-regulations, 'The ball is in Peter's house!' 'The ball is in John's!' They divide their lodging and substance with each other; shout *Vive la République*; and faint not in heart. A ball thunders through the main chamber of the Hôtel-de-Ville, while the Commune is there assembled: 'We are in permanence,' says one, coldly, proceeding with his business; and the ball remains permanent too, sticking in the wall, probably to this day.[565]

The Austrian Archduchess (Queen's Sister) will herself see red artillery fired; in their over-haste to satisfy an Archduchess "two mortars explode and kill thirty persons." It is in vain; Lille, often burning, is always quenched again; Lille will not yield. The very boys deftly wrench the matches out of fallen bombs: "a man clutches a rolling ball with his hat, which takes fire; when cool, they crown it with a *bonnet rouge*." Memorable also be that nimble Barber, who when the bomb burst beside him, snatched up a shred of it, introduced soap and lather into it, crying, '*Voilà mon plat à barbe*, My new shaving-dish!' and shaved "fourteen people" on the spot. Bravo, thou nimble Shaver; worthy to shave old spectral Redcloak, and find treasures!— On the eighth day of this desperate siege, the sixth day of October, Austria finding it fruitless, draws off, with no pleasurable consciousness; rapidly, Dumouriez tending thitherward; and Lille too, black with ashes and smoulder, but jubilant skyhigh, flings its gates open. The *Plat à barbe* became fashionable; "no Patriot of an elegant turn," says Mercier several years afterwards, "but shaves himself out of the splinter of a Lille bomb."

Quid multa, Why many words? The Invaders are in flight; Brunswick's Host, the third part of it gone to death, staggers disastrous along the deep highways of Champagne; spreading out also into "the fields, of a tough spongy red-coloured clay;—like Pharaoh through a Red Sea of mud," says Goethe; "for he also lay broken chariots, and riders and foot seemed sinking around."[566] On the eleventh morning of October, the World-Poet, struggling Northwards out of Verdun, which he had entered Southwards, some five weeks ago, in quite other order, discerned the following Phenomenon and formed part of it:

"Towards three in the morning, without having had any sleep, we were about mounting our carriage, drawn up at the door; when an insuperable obstacle disclosed itself: for there rolled on already, between the pavement-stones which were crushed up into a ridge on each side, an uninterrupted column of sick-wagons through the Town, and all was trodden as into a morass. While we stood waiting what could be made of it, our Landlord the Knight of Saint-Louis pressed past us, without salutation." He had been a Calonne's Notable in 1787, an Emigrant since; had returned to his home, jubilant, with the Prussians; but must now forth again into the wide world, "followed by a servant carrying a little bundle on his stick.

"The activity of our alert Lisieux shone eminent; and, on this occasion too, brought us on: for he struck into a small gap of the wagon-row; and held the advancing team back till we, with our six and our four horses, got intercalated; after which, in my light little coachlet, I could breathe freer. We were now under way; at a funeral pace, but still under way. The day broke; we found ourselves at the outlet of the Town, in a tumult and turmoil without measure. All sorts of vehicles, few horsemen, innumerable foot-people, were crossing each other on the great esplanade before the Gate. We turned to the right, with our Column, towards Estain, on a limited highway, with ditches at each side. Self-preservation, in so monstrous a press, knew now no pity, no respect of aught. Not far before us there fell down a horse of an ammunition-wagon: they cut the traces, and let it lie. And now as the three others could not bring their load along, they cut them also loose, tumbled the heavy-packed vehicle into the ditch; and, with the smallest retardation, we had to drive on, right over the horse, which was just about to rise; and I saw too clearly how its legs, under the wheels, went crashing and quivering.

"Horse and foot endeavoured to escape from the narrow laborious highway into the meadows: but these too were rained to ruin; overflowed by full ditches, the connexion of the footpaths every where interrupted. Four gentlemanlike, handsome, well-dressed French soldiers waded for a time beside our carriage; wonderfully clean and neat: and had such art of picking their steps, that their foot-gear testified no higher than the ancle to the muddy pilgrimage these good people found themselves engaged in.

"That under such circumstances one saw, in ditches, in meadows, in fields and crofts, dead horses enough, was natural to the case: by and by, however, you found them also flayed, the fleshy parts even cut away; sad token of the universal distress.

"Thus we fared on; every moment in danger, at the smallest stoppage on our own part, of being ourselves tumbled overboard; under which circumstances, truly, the careful dexterity of our Lisieux could not be sufficiently praised. The same talent shewed itself at Estain; where we arrived towards noon; and descried, over the beautiful well-built little Town, through streets and on squares, around and beside us, one sense-confusing tumult: the mass rolled this way and that; and, all struggling forward, each hindered the other. Unexpectedly our carriage drew up before a stately house in the market-place; master and mistress of the mansion saluted us in reverent distance." Dexterous Lisieux, though we knew it not, had said we were the King of Prussia's Brother!

"But now, from the ground-floor windows, looking over the whole market-place, we had the endless tumult lying, as it were, palpable. All sorts of walkers, soldiers in uniform, marauders, stout but sorrowing citizens and peasants, women and children, crushed and jostled each other, amid vehicles of all forms: ammunition-wagons, baggage-wagons; carriages, single, double, and multiplex; such hundredfold miscellany of teams, requisitioned or lawfully owned, making way, hitting together, hindering each other, rolled here to right and to left. Horned-cattle too were struggling on; probably herds that had been put in requisition. Riders you saw few; but the elegant carriages of the Emigrants, many-coloured, lackered, gilt and silvered, evidently by the best builders, caught your eye.[567]

"The crisis of the strait however arose further on a little; where the crowded market-place had to introduce itself into a street,—straight indeed and good, but proportionably far too narrow. I have, in my life, seen nothing like it: the aspect of it might perhaps be compared to that of a swoln river which has been raging over meadows and fields, and is now again obliged to press itself through a narrow bridge, and flow on in its bounded channel. Down the long street, all visible from our windows, there swelled continually the strangest tide: a high double-seated travelling-coach towered visible over the flood of things. We thought of the fair Frenchwomen we had seen in the morning. It was not they, however, it was Count Haugwitz; him you could look at, with a kind of sardonic malice, rocking onwards, step by step, there."[568]

In such untriumphant Procession has the Brunswick Manifesto issued! Nay in worse, "in Negotiation with these miscreants,"—the first news of which produced such a revulsion in the Emigrant nature, as put our scientific World-Poet "in fear for the wits of several."[569] There is no help: they must fare on, these poor Emigrants, angry with all persons and things, and making all persons angry, in the hapless course they struck into. Landlord and landlady testify to you, at *tables-d'hôte*, how insupportable these Frenchmen are: how, in spite of such humiliation, of poverty and probable beggary, there is ever the same struggle for precedence, the same forwardness, and want of discretion. High in honour, at the head of the table, you with your own eyes observe not a Seigneur but the automaton of a Seigneur, fallen into dotage; still worshipped, reverently waited on, and fed. In miscellaneous seats, is a miscellany of soldiers, commissaries, adventurers; consuming silently their barbarian victuals. "On all brows is to be read a hard destiny; all are silent, for each has his own sufferings to bear, and looks forth into misery without bounds." One hasty wanderer, coming in, and eating without ungraciousness what is set before him, the landlord lets off almost scot-free. 'He is,' whispered the landlord to me, 'the first of these cursed people I have seen condescend to taste our German black bread.'[570]

And Dumouriez is in Paris; lauded and feasted; paraded in glittering saloons, floods of beautifullest blond-dresses and broadcloth-coats flowing past him, endless, in admiring joy. One night, nevertheless, in the splendour of one such scene, he sees himself suddenly apostrophised by a squalid unjoyful Figure, who has come in *un*invited, nay despite of all lackeys; an unjoyful Figure! The Figure is come 'in express mission from the Jacobins,' to inquire sharply, better then than later, touching certain things: 'Shaven eyebrows of Volunteer Patriots, for instance?' Also 'your threats of shivering in pieces?' Also, 'why you have not chased Brunswick hotly enough?' Thus, with sharp croak, inquires the Figure.—'*Ah, c'est vous qu'on appelle Marat*, You are he they call Marat!' answers the General, and turns coldly on his heel.[571] —'Marat!' The blonde-gowns quiver like aspens; the dress-coats gather round; Actor Talma (for it is his house), and almost the very chandelier-lights, are blue: till this obscene Spectrum, or visual Appearance, vanish back into native Night.

General Dumouriez, in few brief days, is gone again, towards the Netherlands; will attack the Netherlands, winter though it be. And General Montesquiou, on the South-East, has driven in the Sardinian Majesty; nay, almost without a shot fired, has taken Savoy from him, which longs to become a piece of the Republic. And General Custine, on the North-East, has dashed forth on Spires and its Arsenal; and then on Electoral Mentz, not uninvited, wherein are German Democrats and no shadow of an Elector now:—so that in the last days of October, Frau Forster, a daughter of Heyne's, somewhat democratic, walking out of the Gate of Mentz with her Husband, finds French Soldiers playing at bowls with cannon-balls there. Forster trips cheerfully over one iron bomb, with 'Live the Republic!' A black-bearded National Guard answers: '*Elle vivra bien sans vous*, It will probably live independently of you!'[572]

BOOK 3.II.
REGICIDE

Chapter 3.2.I.
The Deliberative

France therefore has done two things very completely: she has hurled back her Cimmerian Invaders far over the marches; and likewise she has shattered her own internal Social Constitution, even to the minutest fibre of it, into wreck and dissolution. Utterly it is all altered: from King down to Parish Constable, all Authorities, Magistrates, Judges, persons that bore rule, have had, on the sudden, to alter themselves, so far as needful; or else, on the sudden, and not without violence, to be altered: a Patriot "Executive Council of Ministers," with a Patriot Danton in it, and then a whole Nation and National Convention, have taken care of that. Not a Parish Constable, in the furthest hamlet, who has said *De Par le Roi*, and shewn loyalty, but must retire, making way for a new improved Parish Constable who can say *De par la République*.

It is a change such as History must beg her readers to imagine, *un*described. An instantaneous change of the whole body-politic, the soul-politic being all changed; such a change as few bodies, politic or other, can experience in this world. Say perhaps, such as poor Nymph Semele's body did experience, when she would needs, with woman's humour, see her Olympian Jove as very Jove;—and so stood, poor Nymph, this moment Semele, next moment not Semele, but Flame and a Statue of red-hot Ashes! France has looked upon Democracy; seen it face to face.—The Cimmerian Invaders will rally, in humbler temper, with better or worse luck: the wreck and dissolution must reshape itself into a social Arrangement as it can and may. But as for this National Convention, which is to settle every thing, if it do, as Deputy Paine and France generally expects, get all finished "in a few months," we shall call it a most deft Convention.

In truth, it is very singular to see how this mercurial French People plunges suddenly from *Vive le Roi* to *Vive la République;* and goes simmering and dancing; shaking off daily (so to speak), and trampling into the dust, its old social garnitures, ways of thinking, rules of existing; and cheerfully dances towards the Ruleless, Unknown, with such hope in its heart, and nothing but *Freedom, Equality and Brotherhood* in its mouth. Is it two centuries, or is it only two years, since all France roared simultaneously to the welkin, bursting forth into sound and smoke at its *Feast of Pikes,* 'Live the Restorer of French Liberty?' Three short years ago there was still Versailles and an Œil-de-Bœuf: now there is that watched Circuit of the Temple, girt with dragon-eyed Municipals, where, as in its final limbo, Royalty lies extinct. In the year 1789, Constituent Deputy Barrère "wept," in his *Break-of-Day* Newspaper, at sight of a reconciled King Louis; and now in 1792, Convention Deputy Barrère, perfectly tearless, may be considering, whether the reconciled King Louis shall be guillotined or not.

Old garnitures and social vestures drop off (we say) so fast, being indeed quite decayed, and are trodden under the National dance. And the new vestures, where are they; the new modes and rules? Liberty, Equality, Fraternity: not vestures but the wish for vestures! The Nation is for the present, figuratively speaking, *naked!* It has no rule or vesture; but is naked,—a Sansculottic Nation.

So far, therefore, in such manner have our Patriot Brissots, Guadets triumphed. Vergniaud's Ezekiel-visions of the fall of thrones and crowns, which he spake hypothetically and prophetically in the Spring of the year, have suddenly come to fulfilment in the Autumn. Our eloquent Patriots of the Legislative, like strong Conjurors, by the word of their mouth, have swept Royalism with its old modes and formulas to the winds; and shall now govern a France free of formulas. Free of formulas! And yet man lives not except with formulas; with customs, *ways* of doing and living: no text truer than this; which will hold true from the Tea-table and Tailor's shopboard up to the High Senate-houses, Solemn Temples; nay through all provinces of Mind and Imagination, onwards to the outmost confines of articulate Being,—*Ubi homines sunt modi sunt.* There are modes wherever there are men. It is the deepest law of man's nature; whereby man is a craftsman and "tool-using animal;" not the slave of Impulse, Chance, and Brute Nature, but in some measure their lord. Twenty-five millions of men, suddenly stript bare of their *modi,* and dancing them down in that manner, are a terrible thing to govern!

Eloquent Patriots of the Legislative, meanwhile, have precisely this problem to solve. Under the name and nickname of "statesmen, *hommes d'état,*" of "moderate-men, *modérantins,*" of Brissotins, Rolandins, finally of

Girondins, they shall become world-famous in solving it. For the Twenty-five millions are Gallic effervescent too;—filled both with hope of the unutterable, of universal Fraternity and Golden Age; and with terror of the unutterable, Cimmerian Europe all rallying on us. It is a problem like few. Truly, if man, as the Philosophers brag, did to any extent look before and after, what, one may ask, in many cases would become of him? What, in this case, would become of these Seven Hundred and Forty-nine men? The Convention, seeing clearly before and after, were a paralysed Convention. Seeing clearly to the length of its own nose, it is not paralysed.

To the Convention itself neither the work nor the method of doing it is doubtful: To make the Constitution; to defend the Republic till that be made. Speedily enough, accordingly, there has been a "Committee of the Constitution" got together. Sieyes, Old-Constituent, Constitution-builder by trade; Condorcet, fit for better things; Deputy Paine, foreign Benefactor of the Species, with that "red carbuncled face, and the black beaming eyes;" Hérault de Séchelles, Ex-Parlementeer, one of the handsomest men in France: these, with inferior guild-brethren, are girt cheerfully to the work; will once more "make the Constitution;" let us hope, more effectually than last time. For that the Constitution can be made, who doubts,—unless the Gospel of Jean Jacques came into the world in vain? True, our last Constitution did tumble within the year, so lamentably. But what then, except sort the rubbish and boulders, and build them up again better? "Widen your basis," for one thing,—to Universal Suffrage, if need be; exclude rotten materials, Royalism and such like, for another thing. And in brief, *build*, O unspeakable Sieyes and Company, unwearied! Frequent perilous downrushing of scaffolding and rubble-work, be that an irritation, no discouragement. Start ye always again, clearing aside the wreck; if with broken limbs, yet with whole hearts; and build, we say, in the name of Heaven,—till either the work do stand; or else mankind abandon it, and the Constitution-builders be paid off, with laughter and tears! One good time, in the course of Eternity, it was appointed that this of Social Contract too should try itself out. And so the Committee of Constitution shall toil: with hope and faith;—with no disturbance from any reader of these pages.

To make the Constitution, then, and return home joyfully in a few months: this is the prophecy our National Convention gives of itself; by this scientific program shall its operations and events go on. But from the best scientific program, in such a case, to the actual fulfilment, what a difference! Every reunion of men, is it not, as we often say, a reunion of incalculable Influences; every unit of it a microcosm of Influences;—of which how shall Science calculate or prophesy! Science, which cannot, with all its calculuses, differential, integral, and of variations, calculate the

Problem of Three gravitating Bodies, ought to hold her peace here, and say only: In this National Convention there are Seven Hundred and Forty-nine very singular Bodies, that gravitate and do much else;—who, probably in an amazing manner, will work the appointment of Heaven.

Of National Assemblages, Parliaments, Congresses, which have long sat; which are of saturnine temperament; above all, which are not "dreadfully in earnest," something may be computed or conjectured: yet even these are a kind of Mystery in progress,—whereby we see the Journalist Reporter find livelihood: even these jolt madly out of the ruts, from time to time. How much more a poor National Convention, of French vehemence; urged on at such velocity; without routine, without rut, track or landmark; and dreadfully in earnest every man of them! It is a Parliament literally such as there was never elsewhere in the world. Themselves are new, unarranged; they are the Heart and presiding centre of a France fallen wholly into maddest disarrangement. From all cities, hamlets, from the utmost ends of this France with its Twenty-five million vehement souls, thick-streaming influences storm in on that same Heart, in the Salle de Manége, and storm out again: such fiery venous-arterial circulation is the function of that Heart. Seven Hundred and Forty-nine human individuals, we say, never sat together on Earth, under more original circumstances. Common individuals most of them, or not far from common; yet in virtue of the position they occupied, so notable. How, in this wild piping of the whirlwind of human passions, with death, victory, terror, valour, and all height and all depth pealing and piping, these men, left to their own guidance, will speak and act?

Readers know well that this French National Convention (quite contrary to its own Program) became the astonishment and horror of mankind; a kind of Apocalyptic Convention, or black *Dream become real;* concerning which History seldom speaks except in the way of interjection: how it covered France with woe, delusion, and delirium; and from its bosom there went forth Death on the pale Horse. To hate this poor National Convention is easy; to praise and love it has not been found impossible. It is, as we say, a Parliament in the most original circumstances. To us, in these pages, be it as a fuliginous fiery mystery, where Upper has met Nether, and in such alternate glare and blackness of darkness poor bedazzled mortals know not which is Upper, which is Nether; but rage and plunge distractedly, as mortals, in that case, will do. A Convention which has to consume itself, suicidally; and become dead ashes—with its World! Behoves us, not to enter exploratively its dim embroiled deeps; yet to stand with unwavering eyes, looking how it welters; what notable phases and occurrences it will successively throw up.

One general superficial circumstance we remark with praise: the force of Politeness. To such depth has the sense of civilisation penetrated man's life; no Drouet, no Legendre, in the maddest tug of war, can altogether shake it off. Debates of Senates dreadfully in earnest are seldom given frankly to the world; else perhaps they would surprise it. Did not the Grand Monarque himself once chase his Louvois with a pair of brandished tongs? But reading long volumes of these Convention Debates, all in a foam with furious earnestness, earnest many times to the extent of life and death, one is struck rather with the degree of continence they manifest in speech; and how in such wild ebullition, there is still a kind of polite rule struggling for mastery, and the forms of social life never altogether disappear. These men, though they menace with clenched right-hands, do not clench one another by the collar; they draw no daggers, except for oratorical purposes, and this not often: profane swearing is almost unknown, though the Reports are frank enough; we find only one or two oaths, oaths by Marat, reported in all.

For the rest, that there is "effervescence" who doubts? Effervescence enough; Decrees passed by acclamation today, repealed by vociferation tomorrow; temper fitful, most rotatory changeful, always headlong! The "voice of the orator is covered with rumours;" a hundred "honourable Members rush with menaces towards the Left side of the Hall;" President has "broken three bells in succession," — claps on his hat, as signal that the country is near ruined. A fiercely effervescent Old-Gallic Assemblage! — Ah, how the loud sick sounds of Debate, and of Life, which is a *debate*, sink silent one after another: so loud now, and in a little while so low! Brennus, and those antique Gael Captains, in their way to Rome, to Galatia, and such places, whither they were in the habit of marching in the most fiery manner, had Debates as effervescent, doubt it not; though no *Moniteur* has reported them. They scolded in Celtic Welsh, those Brennuses; neither were they Sansculotte; nay rather breeches (*braccæ*, say of felt or rough-leather) were the only thing they had; being, as Livy testifies, naked down *to* the haunches: — and, see, it is the same sort of work and of men still, now when they have got coats, and speak nasally a kind of broken Latin! But on the whole does not TIME envelop this present National Convention; as it did those Brennuses, and ancient August Senates in felt breeches? Time surely; and also Eternity. Dim dusk of Time, — or noon which will be dusk; and then there is night, and silence; and Time with all its sick noises is swallowed in the still sea. Pity thy brother, O Son of Adam! The angriest frothy jargon that he utters, is it not properly the whimpering of an infant which cannot *speak* what ails it, but is in distress clearly, in the inwards of it; and so must squall and whimper continually, till its Mother take it, and it get — to sleep!

This Convention is not four days old, and the melodious Melibœan stanzas that shook down Royalty are still fresh in our ear, when there bursts out a new diapason,—unhappily, of Discord, this time. For speech has been made of a thing difficult to speak of well: the September Massacres. How deal with these September Massacres; with the Paris Commune that presided over them? A Paris Commune hateful-terrible; before which the poor effete Legislative had to quail, and sit quiet. And now if a young omnipotent Convention will not so quail and sit, what steps shall it take? Have a Departmental Guard in its pay, answer the Girondins, and Friends of Order! A Guard of National Volunteers, missioned from all the Eighty-three or Eighty-five Departments, for that express end; these will keep Septemberers, tumultuous Communes in a due state of submissiveness, the Convention in a due state of sovereignty. So have the Friends of Order answered, sitting in Committee, and reporting; and even a Decree has been passed of the required tenour. Nay certain Departments, as the Var or Marseilles, in mere expectation and assurance of a Decree, have their contingent of Volunteers already on march: brave Marseillese, foremost on the Tenth of August, will not be hindmost here; "fathers gave their sons a musket and twenty-five louis," says Barbaroux, "and bade them march."

Can any thing be properer? A Republic that will found itself on justice must needs investigate September Massacres; a Convention calling itself National, ought it not to be guarded by a National force?—Alas, Reader, it seems so to the eye: and yet there is much to be said and argued. Thou beholdest here the small beginning of a Controversy, which mere logic will not settle. Two small well-springs, September, Departmental Guard, or rather at bottom they are but one and the same small well-spring; which will swell and widen into waters of bitterness; all manner of subsidiary streams and brooks of bitterness flowing in, from this side and that; till it become a wide river of bitterness, of rage and separation,—which can subside only into the Catacombs. This Departmental Guard, decreed by overwhelming majorities, and then repealed for peace's sake, and not to insult Paris, is again decreed more than once; nay it is partially executed, and the very men that are to be of it are seen visibly parading the Paris streets,—shouting once, being overtaken with liquor: '*À bas Marat*, Down with Marat!'[573] Nevertheless, decreed never so often, it is repealed just as often; and continues, for some seven months, an angry noisy Hypothesis only: a fair Possibility struggling to become a Reality, but which shall never be one; which, after endless struggling, shall, in February next, sink into sad rest,—dragging much along with it. So singular are the ways of men and honourable Members.

But on this fourth day of the Convention's existence, as we said, which is the 25th of September 1792, there comes Committee Report on that Decree of the Departmental Guard, and speech of repealing it; there come denunciations of anarchy, of a Dictatorship,—which let the incorruptible Robespierre consider: there come denunciations of a certain *Journal de la République*, once called *Ami du Peuple*; and so thereupon there comes, visibly stepping up, visibly standing aloft on the Tribune, ready to speak, the Bodily Spectrum of People's-Friend Marat! Shriek, ye Seven Hundred and Forty-nine; it is verily Marat, he and not another. Marat is no phantasm of the brain, or mere lying impress of Printer's Types; but a thing material, of joint and sinew, and a certain small stature: ye behold him there, in his blackness in his dingy squalor, a living fraction of Chaos and Old Night; visibly incarnate, desirous to speak. 'It appears,' says Marat to the shrieking Assembly, 'that a great many persons here are enemies of mine.' 'All! All!' shriek hundreds of voices: enough to drown any People's-Friend. But Marat will not drown: he speaks and croaks explanation; croaks with such reasonableness, air of sincerity, that repentant pity smothers anger, and the shrieks subside or even become applauses. For this Convention is unfortunately the crankest of machines: it shall be pointing eastward, with stiff violence, this moment; and then do but touch some spring dexterously, the whole machine, clattering and jerking seven-hundred-fold, will whirl with huge crash, and, next moment, is pointing westward! Thus Marat, absolved and applauded, victorious in this turn of fence, is, as the Debate goes on, prickt at again by some dexterous Girondin; and then the shrieks rise anew, and Decree of Accusation is on the point of passing; till the dingy People's-Friend bobs aloft once more; croaks once more persuasive stillness, and the Decree of Accusation sinks, Whereupon he draws forth—a Pistol; and setting it to his Head, the seat of such thought and prophecy, says: 'If they had passed their Accusation Decree, he, the People's-Friend, would have blown his brains out.' A People's Friend has that faculty in him. For the rest, as to this of the two hundred and sixty thousand Aristocrat Heads, Marat candidly says, *'C'est là mon avis*, such is my opinion.' Also it is not indisputable: 'No power on Earth can prevent me from seeing into traitors, and unmasking them,'— by my superior originality of mind?[574] An honourable member like this Friend of the People few terrestrial Parliaments have had.

We observe, however, that this first onslaught by the Friends of Order, as sharp and prompt as it was, has failed. For neither can Robespierre, summoned out by talk of Dictatorship, and greeted with the like rumour on shewing himself, be thrown into Prison, into Accusation;—not though Barbaroux openly bear testimony against him, and sign it on paper. With such sanctified meekness does the Incorruptible lift his seagreen cheek to the smiter; lift his thin voice, and with jesuitic dexterity plead, and prosper: asking at last, in a prosperous manner: 'But what witnesses has the Citoyen Barbaroux to support his testimony?' *'Moi!'* cries hot Rebecqui, standing up, striking his breast with both hands, and answering, 'Me!'[575] Nevertheless the Seagreen pleads again, and makes it good: the long hurlyburly, "personal merely," while so much public matter lies fallow, has ended in the order of the day. O Friends of the Gironde, why will you occupy our august sessions with mere paltry Personalities, while the grand Nationality lies in such a state?—The Gironde has touched, this day, on the foul black-spot of its fair Convention Domain; has trodden on it, and yet *not* trodden it down. Alas, it is a *well-spring*, as we said, this black-spot; and will not tread down!

Chapter 3.2.II.
The Executive

May we not conjecture therefore that round this grand enterprise of Making the Constitution there will, as heretofore, very strange embroilments gather, and questions and interests complicate themselves; so that after a few or even several months, the Convention will not have settled every thing? Alas, a whole tide of questions comes rolling, boiling; growing ever wider, without end! Among which, apart from this question of September and Anarchy, let us notice those, which emerge oftener than the others, and promise to become Leading Questions: of the Armies; of the Subsistences; thirdly, of the Dethroned King.

As to the Armies, Public Defence must evidently be put on a proper footing; for Europe seems coalising itself again; one is apprehensive even England will join it. Happily Dumouriez prospers in the North;—nay what if he should prove too prosperous, and become *Liberticide*, Murderer of Freedom!—Dumouriez prospers, through this winter season; yet not without lamentable complaints. Sleek Pache, the Swiss Schoolmaster, he that sat frugal in his Alley, the wonder of neighbours, has got lately—whither thinks the Reader? To be Minister of war! Madame Roland, struck with his sleek ways, recommended him to her Husband as Clerk: the sleek Clerk had no need of salary, being of true Patriotic temper; he would come with a bit of bread in his pocket, to save dinner and time; and, munching incidentally, do three men's work in a day, punctual, silent, frugal,—the sleek Tartuffe that he was. Wherefore Roland, in the late Overturn, recommended him to be War-Minister. And now, it would seem, he is secretly undermining Roland; playing into the hands of your hotter Jacobins and September Commune; and cannot, like strict Roland, be the *Veto des Coquins!* [576]

How the sleek Pache might mine and undermine, one knows not well; this however one does know: that his War-Office has become a den of thieves and confusion, such as all men shudder to behold. That the Citizen Hassenfratz, as Head-Clerk, sits there in *bonnet rouge*, in rapine, in violence, and some Mathematical calculation; a most insolent, red-nightcapped man.

That Pache munches his pocket-loaf, amid head-clerks and sub-clerks, and has spent all the War-Estimates: that Furnishers scour in gigs, over all districts of France, and drive bargains;—and lastly that the Army gets next to no furniture. No shoes, though it is winter; no clothes; some have not even arms: "In the Army of the South," complains an honourable Member, "there are thirty thousand pairs of breeches wanting,"—a most scandalous want.

Roland's strict soul is sick to see the course things take: but what can he do? Keep his own Department strict; rebuke, and repress wheresoever possible; at lowest, complain. He can complain in Letter after Letter, to a National Convention, to France, to Posterity, the Universe; grow ever more querulous indignant;—till at last may he not grow wearisome? For is not this continual text of his, at bottom a rather barren one: How astonishing that in a time of Revolt and abrogation of all Law but Cannon Law, there should be such Unlawfulness? Intrepid Veto-of-Scoundrels, narrow-faithful, respectable, methodic man, work thou in that manner, since happily it is thy manner, and wear thyself away; though ineffectual, not profitless in it—then nor *now!*—The brave Dame Roland, bravest of all French women, begins to have misgivings: the figure of Danton has too much of the "Sardanapalus character," at a Republican Rolandin Dinner-table: Clootz, Speaker of Mankind, proses sad stuff about a Universal Republic, or union of all Peoples and Kindreds in one and the same Fraternal Bond; of which Bond, how it is to be *tied*, one unhappily sees not.

It is also an indisputable, unaccountable or accountable fact that Grains are becoming scarcer and scarcer. Riots for grain, tumultuous Assemblages demanding to have the price of grain fixed abound far and near. The Mayor of Paris and other poor Mayors are like to have their difficulties. Pétion was re-elected Mayor of Paris; but has declined; being now a Convention Legislator. Wise surely to decline: for, besides this of Grains and all the rest, there is in these times an Improvised insurrectionary Commune passing into an Elected legal one; getting their accounts settled,—not without irritancy! Pétion has declined: nevertheless many do covet and canvass. After months of scrutinising, balloting, arguing and jargoning, one Doctor Chambon gets the post of honour: who will not long keep it; but be, as we shall see, literally *crushed* out of it.[577]

Think also if the private Sansculotte has not his difficulties, in a time of dearth! Bread, according to the People's-Friend, may be some "six sous per pound, a day's wages some fifteen;" and grim winter here. How the Poor Man continues living, and so seldom starves, by miracle! Happily, in these days, he can enlist, and have himself shot by the Austrians, in an unusually satisfactory manner: for the Rights of Man.—But Commandant Santerre, in this so straitened condition of the flour-market, and state of Equality and Liberty, proposes, through the Newspapers, two remedies, or at least palliatives: *First*, that all classes of men should live, two days of the week, on potatoes; then *second*, that every man should hang his dog. Hereby, as the Commandant thinks, the saving, which indeed he computes to so many sacks, would be very considerable. A cheerfuller form of inventive-stupidity than Commandant Santerre's dwells in no human soul. Inventive-stupidity, imbedded in health, courage and good-nature: much to be commended. 'My whole strength,' he tells the Convention once, 'is, day and night, at the service of my fellow-Citizens: if they find me worthless, they will dismiss me; I will return and brew beer.'[578]

Or figure what correspondences a poor Roland, Minister of the Interior, must have, on this of Grains alone! Free-trade in Grain, impossibility to fix the Prices of Grain; on the other hand, clamour and necessity to fix them: Political Economy lecturing from the Home Office, with demonstration clear as Scripture;—ineffectual for the empty National Stomach. The Mayor of Chartres, like to be eaten himself, cries to the Convention: the Convention sends honourable Members in Deputation; who endeavour to feed the multitude by miraculous spiritual methods; but cannot. The multitude, in spite of all Eloquence, come bellowing round; will have the Grain-Prices fixed, and at a moderate elevation; or else—the honourable Deputies hanged on the spot! The honourable Deputies, reporting this business, admit that, on the edge of horrid death, they did fix, or affect to fix the Price of Grain: for which, be it also noted, the Convention, a Convention that will not be trifled with, sees good to reprimand them.[579]

But as to the origin of these Grain Riots, is it not most probably your secret Royalists again? Glimpses of Priests were discernible in this of Chartres,—to the eye of Patriotism. Or indeed may not "the root of it all lie in the Temple Prison, in the heart of a perjured King," well as we guard him?[580] Unhappy perjured King!—And so there shall be Baker's Queues, by and by, more sharp-tempered than ever: on every Baker's door-rabbet an iron ring, and coil of rope; whereon, with firm grip, on this side and that, we form our Queue: but mischievous deceitful persons cut the rope, and our Queue becomes a ravelment; wherefore the coil must be made of iron chain.[581] Also there shall be Prices of Grain well fixed; but then no grain purchasable by them: bread not to be had except by Ticket from the Mayor, few ounces per mouth daily; after long swaying, with firm grip, on the chain of the Queue. And Hunger shall stalk direful; and Wrath and Suspicion, whetted to the Preternatural pitch, shall stalk;—as those other preternatural "shapes of Gods in their wrathfulness" were discerned stalking, "in glare and gloom of that fire-ocean," when Troy Town fell!—

Chapter 3.2.III.
Discrowned

But the question more pressing than all on the Legislator, as yet, is this third: What shall be done with King Louis?

King Louis, now King and Majesty to his own family alone, in their own Prison Apartment alone, has been Louis Capet and the Traitor Veto with the rest of France. Shut in his Circuit of the Temple, he has heard and seen the loud whirl of things; yells of September Massacres, Brunswick war-thunders dying off in disaster and discomfiture; he passive, a spectator merely;—waiting whither it would please to whirl with him. From the neighbouring windows, the curious, not without pity, might see him walk daily, at a certain hour, in the Temple Garden, with his Queen, Sister and two Children, all that now belongs to him in this Earth.[582] Quietly he walks and waits; for he is not of lively feelings, and is of a devout heart. The wearied Irresolute has, at least, no need of resolving now. His daily meals, lessons to his Son, daily walk in the Garden, daily game at ombre or drafts, fill up the day: the morrow will provide for itself.

The morrow indeed; and yet How? Louis asks, How? France, with perhaps still more solicitude, asks, How? A King dethroned by insurrection is verily not easy to dispose of. Keep him prisoner, he is a secret centre for the Disaffected, for endless plots, attempts and hopes of theirs. Banish him, he is an open centre for them; his royal war-standard, with what of divinity it has, unrolls itself, summoning the world. Put him to death? A cruel questionable extremity that too: and yet the likeliest in these extreme circumstances, of insurrectionary men, whose own life and death lies staked: accordingly it is said, from the last step of the throne to the first of the scaffold there is short distance.

But, on the whole, we will remark here that this business of Louis looks altogether different now, as seen over Seas and at the distance of forty-four years, than it looked then, in France, and struggling, confused all round one! For indeed it is a most lying thing that same Past Tense always: so beautiful, sad, almost Elysian-sacred, "in the moonlight of Memory," it seems; and *seems* only. For observe: always, one most important element is surreptitiously (we not noticing it) withdrawn from the Past Time: the haggard element of Fear! Not *there* does Fear dwell, nor Uncertainty, nor Anxiety; but it dwells *here;* haunting us, tracking us; running like an accursed ground-discord through all the music-tones of our Existence;—making the Tense a mere Present one! Just so is it with this of Louis. Why smite the fallen? asks Magnanimity, out of danger now. He is fallen so low this once-high man; no criminal nor traitor, how far from it; but the unhappiest of Human Solecisms: whom if abstract Justice had to pronounce upon, she might well become concrete Pity, and pronounce only sobs and dismissal!

So argues retrospective Magnanimity: but Pusillanimity, present, prospective? Reader, thou hast never lived, for months, under the rustle of Prussian gallows-ropes; never wert thou portion of a National Sahara-waltz, Twenty-five millions running distracted to fight Brunswick! Knights Errant themselves, when they conquered Giants, usually slew the Giants: quarter was only for other Knights Errant, who knew courtesy and the laws of battle. The French Nation, in simultaneous, desperate dead-pull, and as if by miracle of madness, has pulled down the most dread Goliath, huge with the growth of ten centuries; and cannot believe, though his giant bulk, covering acres, lies prostrate, bound with peg and packthread, that he will not rise again, man-devouring; that the victory is not partly a dream. Terror has its scepticism; miraculous victory its rage of vengeance. Then as to criminalty, is the prostrated Giant, who will devour us if he rise, an innocent Giant? Curate Gregoire, who indeed is now Constitutional Bishop Gregoire, asserts, in the heat of eloquence, that Kingship by the very nature of it is a crime capital; that Kings' Houses are as wild-beasts' dens.[583] Lastly consider this: that there is on record a Trial of Charles First! This printed *Trial of Charles First* is sold and read every where at present:[584] *—Quelle spectacle!* Thus did the English People judge their Tyrant, and become the first of Free Peoples: which feat, by the grace of Destiny, may not France now rival? Scepticism of terror, rage of miraculous victory, sublime spectacle to the universe,—all things point one fatal way.

Such leading questions, and their endless incidental ones: of September Anarchists and Departmental Guard; of Grain Riots, plaintiff Interior Ministers; of Armies, Hassenfratz dilapidations; and what is to be done with Louis,—beleaguer and embroil this Convention; which would so gladly make the Constitution rather. All which questions too, as we often urge of such things, are in *growth;* they grow in every French head; and can be *seen* growing also, very curiously, in this mighty welter of Parliamentary Debate, of Public Business which the Convention has to do. A question emerges, so small at first; is put off, submerged; but always re-emerges bigger than before. It is a curious, indeed an indescribable sort of growth which such things have.

We perceive, however, both by its frequent re-emergence and by its rapid enlargement of bulk, that this Question of King Louis will take the lead of all the rest. And truly, in that case, it will take the *lead* in a much deeper sense. For as Aaron's Rod swallowed all the other Serpents; so will the Foremost Question, whichever may get foremost, absorb all other questions and interests; and from it and the decision of it will they all, so to speak, be *born*, or new-born, and have shape, physiognomy and destiny corresponding. It was appointed of Fate that, in this wide-weltering, strangely growing, monstrous stupendous imbroglio of Convention Business, the grand First-Parent of all the questions, controversies, measures and enterprises which were to be evolved there to the world's astonishment, should be this Question of King Louis.

Chapter 3.2.IV.
The Loser Pays

The Sixth of November, 1792, was a great day for the Republic: outwardly, over the Frontiers; inwardly, in the *Salle de Manége*.

Outwardly: for Dumouriez, overrunning the Netherlands, did, on that day, come in contact with Saxe-Teschen and the Austrians; Dumouriez wide-winged, they wide-winged; at and around the village of Jemappes, near Mons. And fire-hail is whistling far and wide there, the great guns playing, and the small; so many green Heights getting fringed and maned with red Fire. And Dumouriez is swept back on this wing, and swept back on that, and is like to be swept back utterly; when he rushes up in person, the prompt Polymetis; speaks a prompt word or two; and then, with clear tenor-pipe, "uplifts the Hymn of the Marseillese, *entonna la Marseillaise*,"[585] ten thousand tenor or bass pipes joining; or say, some Forty Thousand in all; for every heart leaps at the sound: and so with rhythmic march-melody, waxing ever quicker, to double and to treble quick, they rally, they advance, they rush, death-defying, man-devouring; carry batteries, redoutes, whatsoever is to be carried; and, like the fire-whirlwind, sweep all manner of Austrians from the scene of action. Thus, through the hands of Dumouriez, may Rouget de Lille, in figurative speech, be said to have gained, miraculously, like another Orpheus, by his Marseillese fiddle-strings (*fidibus canoris*) a Victory of Jemappes; and conquered the Low Countries.

Young General Egalité, it would seem, shone brave among the bravest on this occasion. Doubtless a brave Egalité;—whom however does not Dumouriez rather talk of oftener than need were? The Mother Society has her own thoughts. As for the Elder Egalité he flies low at this time; appears in the Convention for some half-hour daily, with rubicund, pre-occupied, or impressive quasi-contemptuous countenance; and then takes himself away. [586] The Netherlands are conquered, at least overrun. Jacobin missionaries, your Prolys, Pereiras, follow in the train of the Armies; also Convention Commissioners, melting church-plate, revolutionising and remodelling— among whom Danton, in brief space, does immensities of business; not neglecting his own wages and trade-profits, it is thought. Hassenfratz dilapidates at home; Dumouriez grumbles and they dilapidate abroad: within the walls there is sinning, and without the walls there is sinning.

But in the Hall of the Convention, at the same hour with this victory of Jemappes, there went another thing forward: Report, of great length, from the proper appointed Committee, on the Crimes of Louis. The Galleries listen breathless; take comfort, ye Galleries: Deputy Valazé, Reporter on this occasion, thinks Louis very criminal; and that, if convenient, he should be tried;—poor Girondin Valazé, who may be tried himself, one day! Comfortable so far. Nay here comes a second Committee-reporter, Deputy Mailhe, with a Legal Argument, very prosy to read now, very refreshing to hear then, That, by the Law of the Country, Louis Capet was only called Inviolable by a figure of rhetoric; but at bottom was perfectly violable, triable; that he can, and even should be tried. This Question of Louis, emerging so often as an angry confused possibility, and submerging again, has emerged now in an articulate shape.

Patriotism growls indignant joy. The so-called reign of Equality is not to be a mere name, then, but a thing! Try Louis Capet? scornfully ejaculates Patriotism: Mean criminals go to the gallows for a purse cut; and this chief criminal, guilty of a France cut; of a France slashed asunder with Clotho-scissors and Civil war; with his victims "twelve hundred on the Tenth of August alone" lying low in the Catacombs, fattening the passes of Argonne Wood, of Valmy and far Fields; *he*, such chief criminal, shall not even come to the bar?—For, alas, O Patriotism! add we, it was from of old said, *The loser pays!* It is he who has to pay *all* scores, run up by whomsoever; on him must all breakages and charges fall; and the twelve hundred on the Tenth of August are not rebel traitors, but victims and martyrs: such is the law of quarrel.

Patriotism, nothing doubting, watches over this Question of the Trial, now happily emerged in an articulate shape; and will see it to maturity, if the gods permit. With a keen solicitude Patriotism watches; getting ever keener, at every new difficulty, as Girondins and false brothers interpose delays; till it get a keenness as of fixed-idea, and will have this Trial and no earthly thing instead of it,—if Equality be not a name. Love of Equality; then scepticism of terror, rage of victory, sublime spectacle of the universe: all these things are strong.

But indeed this Question of the Trial, is it not to all persons a most grave one; filling with dubiety many a Legislative head! Regicide? asks the

Gironde Respectability: To kill a king, and become the horror of respectable nations and persons? But then also, to save a king; to lose one's footing with the decided Patriot; and undecided Patriot, though never so respectable, being mere hypothetic froth and no footing?—The dilemma presses sore; and between the horns of it you wriggle round and round. Decision is nowhere, save in the Mother Society and her Sons. These have decided, and go forward: the others wriggle round uneasily within their dilemma-horns, and make way nowhither.

Chapter 3.2.V.
Stretching of Formulas

But how this Question of the Trial grew laboriously, through the weeks of gestation, now that it has been articulated or conceived, were superfluous to trace here. It emerged and submerged among the infinite of questions and embroilments. The Veto of Scoundrels writes plaintive Letters as to Anarchy; "concealed Royalists," aided by Hunger, produce Riots about Grain. Alas, it is but a week ago, these Girondins made a new fierce onslaught on the September Massacres!

For, one day, among the last of October, Robespierre, being summoned to the tribune by some new hint of that old calumny of the Dictatorship, was speaking and pleading there, with more and more comfort to himself; till, rising high in heart, he cried out valiantly: Is there any man here that dare specifically accuse me? '*Moi!*' exclaimed one. Pause of deep silence: a lean angry little Figure, with broad bald brow, strode swiftly towards the tribune, taking papers from its pocket: 'I accuse thee, Robespierre,'—I, Jean Baptiste Louvet! The Seagreen became tallow-green; shrinking to a corner of the tribune: Danton cried, 'Speak, Robespierre, there are many good citizens that listen;' but the tongue refused its office. And so Louvet, with a shrill tone, read and recited crime after crime: dictatorial temper, exclusive popularity, bullying at elections, mob-retinue, September Massacres;—till all the Convention shrieked again, and had almost indicted the Incorruptible there on the spot. Never did the Incorruptible run such a risk. Louvet, to his dying day, will regret that the Gironde did not take a bolder attitude, and extinguish him there and then.

Not so, however: the Incorruptible, about to be indicted in this sudden manner, could not be refused a week of delay. That week, he is not idle; nor is the Mother Society idle,—fierce-tremulous for her chosen son. He is ready at the day with his written Speech; smooth as a Jesuit Doctor's; and convinces some. And now? Why, now lazy Vergniaud does not rise with Demosthenic thunder; poor Louvet, unprepared, can do little or nothing: Barrère proposes that these comparatively despicable "personalities" be dismissed by order of the day! Order of the day it accordingly is. Barbaroux cannot even get a hearing; not though he rush down to the Bar, and demand to be heard there as a petitioner.[587] The convention, eager for public business (with that first articulate emergence of the Trial just coming on), dismisses these comparative *misères* and despicabilities: splenetic Louvet must digest his spleen, regretfully for ever: Robespierre, dear to Patriotism, is dearer for the dangers he has run.

This is the second grand attempt by our Girondin Friends of Order, to extinguish that black-spot in their domain; and we see they have made it far blacker and wider than before! Anarchy, September Massacre: it is a thing that lies hideous in the general imagination; very detestable to the undecided Patriot, of Respectability: a thing to be harped on as often as need is. Harp on it, denounce it, trample it, ye Girondin Patriots:—and yet behold, the black-spot will not trample down; it will only, as we say, trample blacker and wider: fools, it is no black-spot of the surface, but a well-spring of the deep! Consider rightly, it is the apex of the everlasting Abyss, this black-spot, looking up as water through thin ice;—say, as the region of Nether Darkness through your thin film of Gironde Regulation and Respectability; trample it *not*, lest the film break, and then—!

The truth is, if our Gironde Friends had an understanding of it, where were French Patriotism, with all its eloquence, at this moment, had *not* that same great Nether Deep, of Bedlam, Fanaticism and Popular wrath and madness, risen unfathomable on the Tenth of August? French Patriotism were an eloquent Reminiscence; swinging on Prussian gibbets. Nay, where, in few months, were it still, should the same great Nether Deep subside?— Nay, as readers of Newspapers pretend to recollect, this hatefulness of the September Massacre is itself partly an after-thought: readers of Newspapers can quote Gorsas and various Brissotins approving of the September Massacre, at the time it happened; and calling it a salutary vengeance![588] So that the real grief, after all, were not so much righteous horror, as grief that one's own power was departing? Unhappy Girondins!

In the Jacobin Society, therefore, the decided Patriot complains that here are men who with their private ambitions and animosities, will ruin Liberty, Equality, and Brotherhood, all three: they check the spirit of Patriotism, throw stumbling-blocks in its way; and instead of pushing on, all shoulders at the wheel, will stand idle there, spitefully clamouring what foul ruts there are, what rude jolts we give! To which the Jacobin Society answers with angry roar;—with angry shriek, for there are Citoyennes too, thick crowded in the galleries here. Citoyennes who bring their seam with them, or their knitting-needles; and shriek or knit as the case needs; famed *Tricoteuses*, Patriot Knitters;—*Mère Duchesse*, or the like Deborah and Mother of the Faubourgs, giving the keynote. It is a changed Jacobin Society; and a still changing. Where Mother Duchess now sits, authentic Duchesses have sat. High-rouged dames went once in jewels and spangles; now, instead of jewels, you may take the knitting-needles and leave the rouge: the rouge will gradually give place to natural brown, clean washed or even unwashed; and Demoiselle Théroigne herself get scandalously fustigated. Strange enough: it is the same tribune raised in mid-air, where a high Mirabeau, a high Barnave and Aristocrat Lameths once thundered: whom gradually your Brissots, Guadets, Vergniauds, a hotter style of Patriots in *bonnet rouge*, did displace; red heat, as one may say, superseding light. And now your Brissots in turn, and Brissotins, Rolandins, Girondins, are becoming supernumerary; must desert the sittings, or be expelled: the light of the Mighty Mother is burning not red but blue!—Provincial Daughter-Societies loudly disapprove these things; loudly demand the swift reinstatement of such eloquent Girondins, the swift "erasure of Marat, *radiation de Marat.*" The Mother Society, so far as natural reason can predict, seems ruining herself. Nevertheless she has, at all crises, seemed so; she has a *preter*natural life in her, and will not ruin.

But, in a fortnight more, this great Question of the Trial, while the fit Committee is assiduously but silently working on it, receives an unexpected stimulus. Our readers remember poor Louis's turn for smithwork: how, in old happier days, a certain Sieur Gamain of Versailles was wont to come over, and instruct him in lock-making;—often scolding him, they say for his numbness. By whom, nevertheless, the royal Apprentice had learned something of that craft. Hapless Apprentice; perfidious Master-Smith! For now, on this 20th of November 1792, dingy Smith Gamain comes over to the Paris Municipality, over to Minister Roland, with hints that he, Smith Gamain, knows a thing; that, in May last, when traitorous Correspondence was so brisk, he and the royal Apprentice fabricated an "Iron Press, *Armoire de Fer,*" cunningly inserting the same in a wall of the royal chamber in the Tuileries; invisible under the wainscot; where doubtless it still sticks! Perfidious Gamain, attended by the proper Authorities, finds the wainscot panel which none else can find; wrenches it up; discloses the Iron Press,—full of Letters and Papers! Roland clutches them out; conveys them over in towels to the fit assiduous Committee, which sits hard by. In towels, we say, and without notarial inventory; an oversight on the part of Roland.

Here, however, are Letters enough: which disclose to a demonstration the Correspondence of a traitorous self-preserving Court; and this not with Traitors only, but even with Patriots, so-called! Barnave's treason, of Correspondence with the Queen, and friendly advice to her, ever since that Varennes Business, is hereby manifest: how happy that we have him, this Barnave, lying safe in the Prison of Grenoble, since September last, for he had long been suspect! Talleyrand's treason, many a man's treason, if not manifest hereby, is next to it. Mirabeau's treason: wherefore his Bust in the Hall of the Convention "is veiled with gauze," till we ascertain. Alas, it is too ascertainable! His Bust in the Hall of the Jacobins, denounced by Robespierre from the tribune in mid-air, is not veiled, it is instantly broken to sherds; a Patriot mounting swiftly with a ladder, and shivering it down on the floor;—it and others: amid shouts.[589] Such is *their* recompense and amount of wages, at this date: on the principle of supply and demand! Smith Gamain, inadequately recompensed for the present, comes, some fifteen months after, with a humble Petition; setting forth that no sooner was that important Iron Press finished off by him, than (as he now bethinks himself) Louis gave him a large glass of wine. Which large glass of wine did produce in the stomach of Sieur Gamain the terriblest effects, evidently tending towards death, and was then brought up by an emetic; but has, notwithstanding, entirely ruined the constitution of Sieur Gamain; so that he cannot work for his family (as he now bethinks himself). The recompense of *which* is "Pension of Twelve Hundred Francs," and "honourable mention." So different is the ratio of demand and supply at different times.

Thus, amid obstructions and stimulating furtherances, has the Question of the Trial to grow; emerging and submerging; fostered by solicitous Patriotism. Of the Orations that were spoken on it, of the painfully devised Forms of Process for managing it, the Law Arguments to prove it lawful, and all the infinite floods of Juridical and other ingenuity and oratory, be no syllable reported in this History. Lawyer ingenuity is good: but what can it profit here? If the truth must be spoken, O august Senators, the only Law in this case is: *Væ victis*, the loser pays! Seldom did Robespierre say a wiser word than the hint he gave to that effect, in his oration, that it was needless to speak of Law, that here, if never elsewhere, our Right was Might. An oration admired almost to ecstasy by the Jacobin Patriot: who shall say that Robespierre is not a thorough-going man; bold in Logic at least? To the like effect, or still more plainly, spake young Saint-Just, the black-haired, mild-toned youth. Danton is on mission, in the Netherlands, during this preliminary work. The rest, far as one reads, welter amid Law of Nations, Social Contract, Juristics, Syllogistics; to us barren as the East wind. In fact, what can be more unprofitable than the sight of Seven Hundred and Forty-nine ingenious men, struggling with their whole force and industry, for a long course of weeks, to do at bottom this: To stretch out the old Formula and Law Phraseology, so that it may cover the new, contradictory, entirely *un*coverable Thing? Whereby the poor Formula does but *crack*, and one's honesty along with it! The thing that is palpably *hot*, burning, wilt thou prove it, by syllogism, to be a freezing-mixture? This of stretching out Formulas till they crack is, especially in times of swift change, one of the sorrowfullest tasks poor Humanity has.

Chapter 3.2.VI.
At the Bar

Meanwhile, in a space of some five weeks, we have got to another emerging of the Trial, and a more practical one than ever.

On Tuesday, eleventh of December, the King's Trial has *emerged*, very decidedly: into the streets of Paris; in the shape of that green Carriage of Mayor Chambon, within which sits the King himself, with attendants, on his way to the Convention Hall! Attended, in that green Carriage, by Mayors Chambon, Procureurs Chaumette; and outside of it by Commandants Santerre, with cannon, cavalry and double row of infantry; all Sections under arms, strong Patrols scouring all streets; so fares he, slowly through the dull drizzling weather: and about two o'clock we behold him, "in walnut-coloured great-coat, *redingote noisette*," descending through the Place Vendôme, towards that Salle de Manége; to be indicted, and judicially interrogated. The mysterious Temple Circuit has given up its secret; which now, in this walnut-coloured coat, men behold with eyes. The same bodily Louis who was once Louis the Desired, fares there: hapless King, he is getting now towards port; his deplorable farings and voyagings draw to a close. What duty remains to him henceforth, that of placidly enduring, he is fit to do.

The singular Procession fares on; in silence, says Prudhomme, or amid growlings of the Marseillese Hymn; in silence, ushers itself into the Hall of the Convention, Santerre holding Louis's arm with his hand. Louis looks round him, with composed air, to see what kind of Convention and Parliament it is. Much changed indeed:—since February gone two years, when our Constituent, then busy, spread fleur-de-lys velvet for us; and we came over to say a kind word here, and they all started up swearing Fidelity; and all France started up swearing, and made it a Feast of Pikes; which has ended in this! Barrère, who once "wept" looking up from his Editor's-Desk, looks down now from his President's-Chair, with a list of Fifty-seven Questions; and says, dry-eyed: 'Louis, you may sit down.' Louis sits down: it is the very seat, they say, same timber and stuffing, from which he accepted the Constitution, amid dancing and illumination, autumn gone a year. So much woodwork remains identical; so much else is not identical. Louis sits and listens, with a composed look and mind.

Of the Fifty-seven Questions we shall not give so much as one. They are questions captiously embracing all the main Documents seized on the Tenth of August, or found lately in the Iron Press; embracing all the main incidents of the Revolution History; and they ask, in substance, this: Louis, who wert King, art thou not guilty to a certain extent, by act and written document, of trying to continue King? Neither in the Answers is there much notable. Mere quiet negations, for most part; an accused man standing on the simple basis of *No:* I do not recognise that document; I did not do that act; or did it according to the law that then was. Whereupon the Fifty-seven Questions, and Documents to the number of a Hundred and Sixty-two, being exhausted in this manner, Barrère finishes, after some three hours, with his: 'Louis, I invite you to withdraw.'

Louis withdraws, under Municipal escort, into a neighbouring Committee-room; having first, in leaving the bar, demanded to have Legal Counsel. He declines refreshment, in this Committee-room, then, seeing Chaumette busy with a small loaf which a grenadier had divided with him, says, he will take a bit of bread. It is five o'clock; and he had breakfasted but slightly in a morning of such drumming and alarm. Chaumette breaks his half-loaf: the King eats of the crust; mounts the green Carriage, eating; asks now what he shall do with the crumb? Chaumette's clerk takes it from him; flings it out into the street. Louis says, It is pity to fling out bread, in a time of dearth. 'My grandmother,' remarks Chaumette, 'used to say to me, Little boy, never waste a crumb of bread, you cannot make one.' 'Monsieur Chaumette,' answers Louis, 'your grandmother seems to have been a sensible woman.'[590] Poor innocent mortal: so quietly he waits the drawing of the lot;—fit to do this at least well; Passivity alone, without Activity, sufficing for it! He talks once of travelling over France by and by, to have a geographical and topographical view of it; being from of old fond of geography.—The Temple Circuit again receives him, closes on him; gazing Paris may retire to its hearths and coffee-houses, to its clubs and theatres: the damp Darkness has sunk, and with it the drumming and patrolling of this strange Day.

Louis is now separated from his Queen and Family; given up to his simple reflections and resources. Dull lie these stone walls round him; of his loved ones none with him. In this state of "uncertainty," providing for the worst, he writes his Will: a Paper which can still be read; full of placidity, simplicity, pious sweetness. The Convention, after debate, has granted him Legal Counsel, of his own choosing. Advocate Target feels himself "too old," being turned of fifty-four; and declines. He had gained great honour once, defending Rohan the Necklace-Cardinal; but will gain none here. Advocate Tronchet, some ten years older, does not decline. Nay behold, good old Malesherbes steps forward voluntarily; to the last of his fields, the good old hero! He is grey with seventy years: he says, "I was twice called to the Council of him who was my Master, when all the world coveted that honour; and I owe him the same service now, when it has become one which many reckon dangerous." These two, with a younger Desèze, whom they will select for pleading, are busy over that Fifty-and-sevenfold Indictment, over the Hundred and Sixty-two Documents; Louis aiding them as he can.

A great Thing is now therefore in open progress; all men, in all lands, watching it. By what Forms and Methods shall the Convention acquit itself, in such manner that there rest not on it even the suspicion of blame? Difficult that will be! The Convention, really much at a loss, discusses and deliberates. All day from morning to night, day after day, the Tribune drones with oratory on this matter; one must stretch the old Formula to cover the new Thing. The Patriots of the Mountain, whetted ever keener, clamour for despatch above all; the only good Form will be a swift one. Nevertheless the Convention deliberates; the Tribune drones,—drowned indeed in tenor, and even in treble, from time to time; the whole Hall shrilling up round it into pretty frequent wrath and provocation. It has droned and shrilled wellnigh a fortnight, before we can decide, this shrillness getting ever shriller, That on Wednesday 26th of December, Louis shall appear, and plead. His Advocates complain that it is fatally soon; which they well might as Advocates: but without remedy; to Patriotism it seems endlessly late.

On Wednesday, therefore, at the cold dark hour of eight in the morning, all Senators are at their post. Indeed they warm the cold hour, as we find, by a violent effervescence, such as is too common now; some Louvet or Buzot attacking some Tallien, Chabot; and so the whole Mountain effervescing against the whole Gironde. Scarcely is this done, at nine, when Louis and his three Advocates, escorted by the clang of arms and Santerre's National force, enter the Hall.

Desèze unfolds his papers; honourably fulfilling his perilous office, pleads for the space of three hours. An honourable Pleading, "composed almost overnight;" courageous yet discreet; not without ingenuity, and soft pathetic eloquence: Louis fell on his neck, when they had withdrawn, and said with tears, *Mon pauvre Desèze*. Louis himself, before withdrawing, had added a few words, 'perhaps the last he would utter to them:' how it pained his heart, above all things, to be held guilty of that bloodshed on the Tenth of August; or of ever shedding or wishing to shed French blood. So saying, he withdrew from that Hall;—having indeed finished his work there. Many are the strange errands he has had thither; but this strange one is the last.

And now, why will the Convention loiter? Here is the Indictment and Evidence; here is the Pleading: does not the rest follow of itself? The Mountain, and Patriotism in general, clamours still louder for despatch; for Permanent-session, till the task be done. Nevertheless a doubting, apprehensive Convention decides that it will still deliberate first; that all Members, who desire it, shall have leave to speak.—To your desks, therefore, ye eloquent Members! Down with your thoughts, your echoes and hearsays of thoughts: now is the time to shew oneself; France and the Universe listens! Members are not wanting: Oration spoken Pamphlet follows spoken Pamphlet, with what eloquence it can: President's List swells ever higher with names claiming to speak; from day to day, all days and all hours, the constant Tribune drones;—shrill Galleries supplying, very variably, the tenor and treble. It were a dull tune otherwise.

The Patriots, in Mountain and Galleries, or taking counsel nightly in Section-house, in Mother Society, amid their shrill *Tricoteuses*, have to watch lynx-eyed; to give voice when needful; occasionally very loud. Deputy Thuriot, he who was Advocate Thuriot, who was Elector Thuriot, and from the top of the Bastille, saw Saint-Antoine rising like the ocean; this Thuriot can stretch a Formula as heartily as most men. Cruel Billaud is not silent, if you incite him. Nor is cruel Jean-Bon silent; a kind of Jesuit he too;—write him not, as the Dictionaries too often do, *Jambon*, which signifies mere *Ham*.

But, on the whole, let no man conceive it possible that Louis is not guilty. The only question for a reasonable man is, or was: Can the Convention judge Louis? Or must it be the whole People: in Primary Assembly, and with delay? Always delay, ye Girondins, false *hommes d'état!* so bellows Patriotism, its patience almost failing.—But indeed, if we consider it, what shall these poor Girondins do? Speak their convictions that Louis is a Prisoner of War; and cannot be put to death without injustice, solecism, peril? Speak such conviction; and lose utterly your footing with the decided Patriot? Nay properly it is not even a conviction, but a conjecture and dim puzzle. How many poor Girondins are sure of but one thing: That a man and Girondin ought to *have* footing somewhere, and to stand firmly on it; keeping well with the Respectable Classes! *This* is what conviction and assurance of faith they have. They must wriggle painfully between their dilemma-horns.[591]

Nor is France idle, nor Europe. It is a Heart this Convention, as we said, which sends out influences, and receives them. A King's Execution, call it

Martyrdom, call it Punishment, were an influence! Two notable influences this Convention has already sent forth, over all Nations; much to its own detriment. On the 19th of November, it emitted a Decree, and has since confirmed and unfolded the details of it. That any Nation which might see good to shake off the fetters of Despotism was thereby, so to speak, the Sister of France, and should have help and countenance. A Decree much noised of by Diplomatists, Editors, International Lawyers; such a Decree as no living Fetter of Despotism, nor Person in Authority anywhere, can approve of! It was Deputy Chambon the Girondin who propounded this Decree;—at bottom perhaps as a flourish of rhetoric.

The second influence we speak of had a still poorer origin: in the restless loud-rattling slightly-furnished head of one Jacob Dupont from the Loire country. The Convention is speculating on a plan of National Education: Deputy Dupont in his speech says, 'I am free to avow, M. le Président, that I for my part am an Atheist,'[592] —thinking the world might like to know that. The French world received it without commentary; or with no audible commentary, so *loud* was France otherwise. The Foreign world received it with confutation, with horror and astonishment;[593] a most miserable influence this! And now if to these two were added a third influence, and sent pulsing abroad over all the Earth: that of Regicide?

Foreign Courts interfere in this Trial of Louis; Spain, England: not to be listened to; though they come, as it were, at least Spain comes, with the olive-branch in one hand, and the sword without scabbard in the other. But at home too, from out of this circumambient Paris and France, what influences come thick-pulsing! Petitions flow in; pleading for equal justice, in a reign of so-called Equality. The living Patriot pleads;—O ye National Deputies, do not the dead Patriots plead? The Twelve Hundred that lie in cold obstruction, do not they plead; and petition, in Death's dumb-show, from their narrow house there, more eloquently than speech? Crippled Patriots hop on crutches round the Salle de Manége, demanding justice. The Wounded of the Tenth of August, the Widows and Orphans of the Killed petition in a body; and hop and defile, eloquently mute, through the Hall: one wounded Patriot, unable to hop, is borne on his bed thither, and passes shoulder-high, in the horizontal posture.[594] The Convention Tribune, which has paused at such sight, commences again,—droning mere Juristic Oratory. But out of doors Paris is piping ever higher. Bull-voiced St. Huruge is heard; and the hysteric eloquence of Mother Duchesse: "Varlet, Apostle of Liberty," with pike and red cap, flies hastily, carrying his oratorical folding-stool. Justice on the Traitor! cries all the Patriot world. Consider also this other cry, heard loud on the streets: 'Give us Bread, or else kill us!' Bread and Equality; Justice on the Traitor, that we may have Bread!

The Limited or undecided Patriot is set against the Decided. Mayor Chambon heard of dreadful rioting at the *Théâtre de la Nation:* it had come to rioting, and even to fist-work, between the Decided and the Undecided, touching a new Drama called *Ami des Lois* (Friend of the Laws). One of the poorest Dramas ever written; but which had didactic applications in it; wherefore powdered wigs of Friends of Order and black hair of Jacobin heads are flying there; and Mayor Chambon hastens with Santerre, in hopes to quell it. Far from quelling it, our poor Mayor gets so "squeezed," says the Report, and likewise so blamed and bullied, say we,—that he, with regret, quits the brief Mayoralty altogether, "his lungs being affected." This miserable *Amis des Lois* is debated of in the Convention itself; so violent, mutually-enraged, are the Limited Patriots and the Unlimited.[595]

Between which two classes, are not Aristocrats enough, and Crypto-Aristocrats, busy? Spies running over from London with important Packets; spies pretending to run! One of these latter, Viard was the name of him, pretended to accuse Roland, and even the Wife of Roland; to the joy of Chabot and the Mountain. But the Wife of Roland came, being summoned, on the instant, to the Convention Hall; came, in her high clearness; and, with few clear words, dissipated this Viard into despicability and air; all Friends of Order applauding.[596] So, with Theatre-riots, and "Bread, or else kill us;" with Rage, Hunger, preternatural Suspicion, does this wild Paris pipe. Roland grows ever more querulous, in his Messages and Letters; rising almost to the hysterical pitch. Marat, whom no power on Earth can prevent seeing into traitors and Rolands, takes to bed for three days; almost dead, the invaluable People's-Friend, with heartbreak, with fever and headache: "*O, Peuple babillard, si tu savais agir,* People of Babblers, if thou couldst but act!*"

To crown all, victorious Dumouriez, in these New-year's days, is arrived in Paris;—one fears, for no good. He pretends to be complaining of Minister Pache, and Hassenfratz dilapidations; to be concerting measures for the spring campaign: one finds him much in the company of the Girondins. Plotting with them against Jacobinism, against Equality, and the Punishment of Louis! We have Letters of his to the Convention itself. Will he act the old Lafayette part, this new victorious General? Let him withdraw again; not undenounced.[597]

And still, in the Convention Tribune, it drones continually, mere Juristic Eloquence, and Hypothesis without Action; and there are still fifties on the President's List. Nay these Gironde Presidents give their own party preference: we suspect they play foul with the List; men of the Mountain cannot be heard. And still it drones, all through December into January and a New year; and there is no end! Paris pipes round it; multitudinous; ever higher, to the note of the whirlwind. Paris will "bring cannon from Saint-Denis;" there is talk of "shutting the Barriers," — to Roland's horror.

Whereupon, behold, the Convention Tribune suddenly ceases droning: we cut short, be on the List who likes; and make end. On Tuesday next, the Fifteenth of January 1793, it shall go to the Vote, name by name; and, one way or other, this great game play itself out!

Chapter 3.2.VII.
The Three Votings

Is Louis Capet guilty of conspiring against Liberty? Shall our Sentence be itself final, or need ratifying by Appeal to the People? If guilty, what Punishment? This is the form agreed to, after uproar and "several hours of tumultuous indecision:" these are the Three successive Questions, whereon the Convention shall now pronounce. Paris floods round their Hall; multitudinous, many sounding. Europe and all Nations listen for their answer. Deputy after Deputy shall answer to his name: Guilty or Not guilty?

As to the Guilt, there is, as above hinted, no doubt in the mind of Patriot man. Overwhelming majority pronounces Guilt; the unanimous Convention votes for Guilt, only some feeble twenty-eight voting not Innocence, but refusing to vote at all. Neither does the Second Question prove doubtful, whatever the Girondins might calculate. Would not Appeal to the People be another name for civil war? Majority of two to one answers that there shall be no Appeal: this also is settled. Loud Patriotism, now at ten o'clock, may hush itself for the night; and retire to its bed not without hope. Tuesday has gone well. On the morrow comes, What Punishment? On the morrow is the tug of war.

Consider therefore if, on this Wednesday morning, there is an affluence of Patriotism; if Paris stands a-tiptoe, and all Deputies are at their post! Seven Hundred and Forty-nine honourable Deputies; only some twenty absent on mission, Duchâtel and some seven others absent by sickness. Meanwhile expectant Patriotism and Paris standing a-tiptoe, have need of patience. For this Wednesday again passes in debate and effervescence; Girondins proposing that a "majority of three-fourths" shall be required; Patriots fiercely resisting them. Danton, who has just got back from mission in the Netherlands, does obtain "order of the day" on this Girondin proposal; nay he obtains further that we decide *sans désemparer*, in Permanent-session, till we have done.

And so, finally, at eight in the evening this Third stupendous Voting, by roll-call or *appel nominal*, does begin. What Punishment? Girondins undecided, Patriots decided, men afraid of Royalty, men afraid of Anarchy, must answer here and now. Infinite Patriotism, dusky in the lamp-light, floods all corridors, crowds all galleries, sternly waiting to hear. Shrill-sounding Ushers summon you by Name and Department; you must rise to the Tribune and say.

Eye-witnesses have represented this scene of the Third Voting, and of the votings that grew out of it; a scene protracted, like to be endless, lasting, with few brief intervals, from Wednesday till Sunday morning,—as one of the strangest seen in the Revolution. Long night wears itself into day, morning's paleness is spread over all faces; and again the wintry shadows sink, and the dim lamps are lit: but through day and night and the vicissitude of hours, Member after Member is mounting continually those Tribune-steps; pausing aloft there, in the clearer upper light, to speak his Fate-word; then diving down into the dusk and throng again. Like Phantoms in the hour of midnight; most spectral, pandemonial! Never did President Vergniaud, or any terrestrial President, superintend the like. A King's Life, and so much else that depends thereon, hangs trembling in the balance. Man after man mounts; the buzz hushes itself till he have spoken: Death; Banishment: Imprisonment till the Peace. Many say, Death; with what cautious well-studied phrases and paragraphs they could devise, of explanation, of enforcement, of faint recommendation to mercy. Many too say, Banishment; something short of Death. The balance trembles, none can yet guess whitherward. Whereat anxious Patriotism bellows; irrepressible by Ushers.

The poor Girondins, many of them, under such fierce bellowing of Patriotism, say Death; justifying, *motivant*, that most miserable word of theirs by some brief casuistry and jesuitry. Vergniaud himself says, Death; justifying by jesuitry. Rich Lepelletier Saint-Fargeau had been of the Noblesse, and then of the Patriot Left Side, in the Constituent; and had argued and reported, there and elsewhere, not a little, *against* Capital Punishment: nevertheless he now says, Death; a word which may cost him dear. Manuel did surely rank with the Decided in August last; but he has been sinking and backsliding ever since September, and the scenes of September. In this Convention, above all, no word he could speak would find favour; he says now, Banishment; and in mute wrath quits the place for ever,—much hustled in the corridors. Philippe Egalité votes in his soul and conscience, Death, at the sound of which, and of whom, even Patriotism shakes its head; and there runs a groan and shudder through this Hall of Doom. Robespierre's vote cannot be doubtful; his speech is long. Men see the figure of shrill Sieyes ascend; hardly pausing, passing merely, this figure says, '*La Mort sans phrase*, Death without phrases;' and fares onward and downward. Most spectral, pandemonial!

And yet if the Reader fancy it of a funereal, sorrowful or even grave character, he is far mistaken. "The Ushers in the Mountain quarter," says Mercier, "had become as Box-openers at the Opera;" opening and shutting of Galleries for privileged persons, for "d'Orléans Egalité's mistresses," or other high-dizened women of condition, rustling with laces and tricolor. Gallant Deputies pass and repass thitherward, treating them with ices, refreshments and small-talk; the high-dizened heads beck responsive; some have their card and pin, pricking down the Ayes and Noes, as at a game of *Rouge-et-Noir*. Further aloft reigns Mère Duchesse with her unrouged Amazons; she cannot be prevented making long *Hahas*, when the vote is not *La Mort*. In these Galleries there is refection, drinking of wine and brandy "as in open tavern, *en pleine tabagie*." Betting goes on in all coffeehouses of the neighbourhood. But within doors, fatigue, impatience, uttermost weariness sits now on all visages; lighted up only from time to time, by turns of the game. Members have fallen asleep; Ushers come and awaken them to vote: other Members calculate whether they shall not have time to run and dine. Figures rise, like phantoms, pale in the dusky lamp-light; utter from this Tribune, only one word: Death. "*Tout est optique*," says Mercier, "the world is all an optical shadow."[598] Deep in the Thursday night, when the Voting is done, and Secretaries are summing it up, sick Duchâtel, more spectral than another, comes borne on a chair, wrapt in blankets, "in nightgown and nightcap," to vote for Mercy: one vote it is thought may turn the scale.

Ah no! In profoundest silence, President Vergniaud, with a voice full of sorrow, has to say: 'I declare, in the name of the Convention, that the Punishment it pronounces on Louis Capet is that of Death.' Death by a small majority of Fifty-three. Nay, if we deduct from the one side, and add to the other, a certain Twenty-six, who said Death but coupled some faintest ineffectual surmise of mercy with it, the majority will be but *One*.

Death is the sentence: but its execution? It is not executed yet! Scarcely is the vote declared when Louis's Three Advocates enter; with Protest in his name, with demand for Delay, for Appeal to the People. For this do Desèze and Tronchet plead, with brief eloquence: brave old Malesherbes pleads for it with eloquent want of eloquence, in broken sentences, in embarrassment and sobs; that brave time-honoured face, with its grey strength, its broad sagacity and honesty, is mastered with emotion, melts into dumb tears.[599] —They reject the Appeal to the People; that having been already settled. But as to the Delay, what they call *Sursis*, it *shall* be considered; shall be voted for tomorrow: at present we adjourn. Whereupon Patriotism "hisses" from the Mountain: but a "tyrannical majority" has so decided, and adjourns.

There is still this *fourth* Vote then, growls indignant Patriotism:—this vote, and who knows what other votes, and adjournments of voting; and the whole matter still hovering hypothetical! And at every new vote those Jesuit Girondins, even they who voted for Death, would so fain find a loophole! Patriotism must watch and rage. Tyrannical adjournments there have been; one, and now another at midnight on plea of fatigue, — all Friday wasted in hesitation and higgling; in re-counting of the votes, which are found correct as they stood! Patriotism bays fiercer than ever; Patriotism, by long-watching, has become red-eyed, almost rabid.

'Delay: yes or no?' men do vote it finally, all Saturday, all day and night. Men's nerves are worn out, men's hearts are desperate; now it shall end. Vergniaud, spite of the baying, ventures to say Yes, Delay; though he had voted Death. Philippe Egalité says, in his soul and conscience, No. The next Member mounting: 'Since Philippe says No, I for my part say Yes, *Moi je dis Oui.*' The balance still trembles. Till finally, at three o'clock on Sunday morning, we have: *No Delay*, by a majority of Seventy; *Death within four-and-twenty hours!*

Garat Minister of Justice has to go to the Temple, with this stern message: he ejaculates repeatedly, '*Quelle commission affreuse*, What a frightful function!'[600] Louis begs for a Confessor; for yet three days of life, to prepare himself to die. The Confessor is granted; the three days and all respite are refused.

There is no deliverance, then? Thick stone walls answer, None—Has King Louis no friends? Men of action, of courage grown desperate, in this his extreme need? King Louis's friends are feeble and far. Not even a voice in the coffeehouses rises for him. At Méot the Restaurateur's no Captain Dampmartin now dines; or sees death-doing whiskerandoes on furlough exhibit daggers of improved structure! Méot's gallant Royalists on furlough are far across the Marches; they are wandering distracted over the world: or their bones lie whitening Argonne Wood. Only some weak Priests "leave Pamphlets on all the bournestones," this night, calling for a rescue; calling for the pious women to rise; or are taken distributing Pamphlets, and sent to prison.[601]

Nay there is one death-doer, of the ancient Méot sort, who, with effort, has done even less and worse: slain a Deputy, and set all the Patriotism of Paris on edge! It was five on Saturday evening when Lepelletier St. Fargeau, having given his vote, *No Delay*, ran over to Février's in the Palais Royal to snatch a morsel of dinner. He had dined, and was paying. A thickset man "with black hair and blue beard," in a loose kind of frock, stept up to him; it was, as Février and the bystanders bethought them, one Pâris of the old King's-Guard. 'Are you Lepelletier?' asks he.—'Yes.'—'You voted in the

King's Business?'—'I voted Death.'—'*Scélérat*, take that!' cries Pâris, flashing out a sabre from under his frock, and plunging it deep in Lepelletier's side. Février clutches him; but he breaks off; is gone.

The voter Lepelletier lies dead; he has expired in great pain, at one in the morning;—two hours before that Vote of *No Delay* was fully summed up! Guardsman Pâris is flying over France; cannot be taken; will be found some months after, self-shot in a remote inn.[602] —Robespierre sees reason to think that Prince d'Artois himself is privately in Town; that the Convention will be butchered in the lump. Patriotism sounds mere wail and vengeance: Santerre doubles and trebles all his patrols. Pity is lost in rage and fear; the Convention has refused the three days of life and all respite.

Chapter 3.2.VIII.
Place de la Révolution

To this conclusion, then, hast thou come, O hapless Louis! The Son of Sixty Kings is to die on the Scaffold by form of law. Under Sixty Kings this same form of Law, form of Society, has been fashioning itself together, these thousand years; and has become, one way and other, a most strange Machine. Surely, if needful, it is also frightful this Machine; dead, blind; not what it should be; which, with swift stroke, or by cold slow torture, has wasted the lives and souls of innumerable men. And behold now a King himself, or say rather Kinghood in his person, is to expire here in cruel tortures;—like a Phalaris shut in the belly of his own red-heated Brazen Bull! It is ever so; and thou shouldst know it, O haughty tyrannous man: injustice breeds injustice; curses and falsehoods do verily "return always home," wide as they may wander. Innocent Louis bears the sins of many generations: he too experiences that man's tribunal is not in this Earth; that if he had no Higher one, it were not well with him.

A King dying by such violence appeals impressively to the imagination; as the like must do, and ought to do. And yet at bottom it is not the King dying, but the Man! Kingship is a coat; the grand loss is of the skin. The man from whom you take his Life, to him can the whole combined world do *more?* Lally went on his hurdle, his mouth filled with a gag. Miserablest mortals, doomed for picking pockets, have a whole five-act Tragedy in them, in that dumb pain, as they go to the gallows, unregarded; they consume the cup of trembling down to the lees. For Kings and for Beggars, for the justly doomed and the unjustly, it is a hard thing to die. Pity them all: thy utmost pity with all aids and appliances and throne-and-scaffold contrasts, how far short is it of the thing pitied!

A Confessor has come; Abbé Edgeworth, of Irish extraction, whom the King knew by good report, has come promptly on this solemn mission. Leave the Earth alone, then, thou hapless King; it with its malice will go its way, thou also canst go thine. A hard scene yet remains: the parting with our loved ones. Kind hearts, environed in the same grim peril with us; to be left *here!* Let the Reader look with the eyes of Valet Cléry, through these glass-doors, where also the Municipality watches; and see the cruellest of scenes:

"At half-past eight, the door of the ante-room opened: the Queen appeared first, leading her Son by the hand; then Madame Royale and Madame Elizabeth: they all flung themselves into the arms of the King. Silence reigned for some minutes; interrupted only by sobs. The Queen made a movement to lead his Majesty towards the inner room, where M. Edgeworth was waiting unknown to them: 'No,' said the King, 'let us go into the dining-room, it is there only that I can see you.' They entered there; I shut the door of it, which was of glass. The King sat down, the Queen on his left hand, Madame Elizabeth on his right, Madame Royale almost in front; the young Prince remained standing between his Father's legs. They all leaned towards him, and often held him embraced. This scene of woe lasted an hour and three-quarters; during which we could hear nothing; we could see only that always when the King spoke, the sobbings of the Princesses redoubled, continued for some minutes; and that then the King began again to speak."[603] —And so our meetings and our partings do now end! The sorrows we gave each other; the poor joys we faithfully shared, and all our lovings and our sufferings, and confused toilings under the earthly Sun, are over. Thou good soul, I shall never, never through all ages of Time, see thee any more!—NEVER! O Reader, knowest thou that hard word?

For nearly two hours this agony lasts; then they tear themselves asunder. 'Promise that you will see us on the morrow.' He promises:—Ah yes, yes; yet once; and go now, ye loved ones; cry to God for yourselves and me!—It was a hard scene, but it is over. He will not see them on the morrow. The Queen in passing through the ante-room glanced at the Cerberus Municipals; and with woman's vehemence, said through her tears, '*Vous êtes tous des scélérats.*'

King Louis slept sound, till five in the morning, when Cléry, as he had been ordered, awoke him. Cléry dressed his hair. While this went forward, Louis took a ring from his watch, and kept trying it on his finger; it was his wedding-ring, which he is now to return to the Queen as a mute farewell. At half-past six, he took the Sacrament; and continued in devotion, and conference with Abbé Edgeworth. He will not see his Family: it were too hard to bear.

At eight, the Municipals enter: the King gives them his Will and messages and effects; which they, at first, brutally refuse to take charge of: he gives them a roll of gold pieces, a hundred and twenty-five louis; these are to be returned to Malesherbes, who had lent them. At nine, Santerre says the hour is come. The King begs yet to retire for three minutes. At the end of three minutes, Santerre again says the hour is come. "Stamping on the ground with his right foot, Louis answers: '*Partons*, let us go.'"—How the rolling of those drums comes in, through the Temple bastions and bulwarks, on the heart of a queenly wife; soon to be a widow! He is gone, then, and has not seen us? A Queen weeps bitterly; a King's Sister and Children. Over all these Four does Death also hover: all shall perish miserably save one; she, as Duchesse d'Angouleme, will live,—not happily.

At the Temple Gate were some faint cries, perhaps from voices of pitiful women: '*Grâce! Grâce!*' Through the rest of the streets there is silence as of the grave. No man not armed is allowed to be there: the armed, did any even pity, dare not express it, each man overawed by all his neighbours. All windows are down, none seen looking through them. All shops are shut. No wheel-carriage rolls this morning, in these streets but one only. Eighty thousand armed men stand ranked, like armed statues of men; cannons bristle, cannoneers with match burning, but no word or movement: it is as a city enchanted into silence and stone; one carriage with its escort, slowly rumbling, is the only sound. Louis reads, in his Book of Devotion, the Prayers of the Dying: clatter of this death-march falls sharp on the ear, in the great silence; but the thought would fain struggle heavenward, and forget the Earth.

As the clocks strike ten, behold the Place de la Révolution, once Place de Louis Quinze: the Guillotine, mounted near the old Pedestal where once stood the Statue of that Louis! Far round, all bristles with cannons and armed men: spectators crowding in the rear; d'Orléans Egalité there in cabriolet. Swift messengers, *hoquetons*, speed to the Townhall, every three minutes: near by is the Convention sitting,—vengeful for Lepelletier. Heedless of all, Louis reads his Prayers of the Dying; not till five minutes yet has he finished; then the Carriage opens. What temper he is in? Ten different witnesses will give ten different accounts of it. He is in the collision of all tempers; arrived now at the black Mahlstrom and descent of Death: in sorrow, in indignation, in resignation struggling to be resigned. 'Take care of M. Edgeworth,' he straitly charges the Lieutenant who is sitting with them: then they two descend.

The drums are beating: '*Taisez-vous*, Silence!' he cries "in a terrible voice, *d'une voix terrible*." He mounts the scaffold, not without delay; he is in puce coat, breeches of grey, white stockings. He strips off the coat; stands disclosed in a sleeve-waistcoat of white flannel. The Executioners approach to bind him: he spurns, resists; Abbé Edgeworth has to remind him how the Saviour, in whom men trust, submitted to be bound. His hands are tied, his head bare; the fatal moment is come. He advances to the edge of the Scaffold, "his face very red," and says: 'Frenchmen, I die innocent: it is from the Scaffold and near appearing before God that I tell you so. I pardon my enemies; I desire that France—' A General on horseback, Santerre or another, prances out with uplifted hand: '*Tambours!*' The drums drown the voice. 'Executioners do your duty!' The Executioners, desperate lest themselves be murdered (for Santerre and his Armed Ranks will strike, if they do not), seize the hapless Louis: six of them desperate, him singly desperate, struggling there; and bind him to their plank. Abbé Edgeworth, stooping, bespeaks him: 'Son of Saint Louis, ascend to Heaven.' The Axe clanks down; a King's Life is shorn away. It is Monday the 21st of January 1793. He was aged Thirty-eight years four months and twenty-eight days. [604]

Executioner Samson shews the Head: fierce shout of *Vive la République* rises, and swells; caps raised on bayonets, hats waving: students of the College of Four Nations take it up, on the far Quais; fling it over Paris. Orleans drives off in his cabriolet; the Townhall Councillors rub their hands, saying, 'It is done, It is done.' There is dipping of handkerchiefs, of pike-points in the blood. Headsman Samson, though he afterwards denied it,[605] sells locks of the hair: fractions of the puce coat are long after worn in rings.[606] —And so, in some half-hour it is done; and the multitude has all departed. Pastrycooks, coffee-sellers, milkmen sing out their trivial quotidian cries: the world wags on, as if this were a common day. In the coffeehouses that evening, says Prudhomme, Patriot shook hands with Patriot in a more cordial manner than usual. Not till some days after, according to Mercier, did public men see what a grave thing it was.

A grave thing it indisputably is; and will have consequences. On the morrow morning, Roland, so long steeped to the lips in disgust and chagrin, sends in his demission. His accounts lie all ready, correct in black-on-white to the uttermost farthing: these he wants but to have audited, that he might retire to remote obscurity to the country and his books. They will never be audited those accounts; he will never get retired thither.

It was on Tuesday that Roland demitted. On Thursday comes Lepelletier St. Fargeau's Funeral, and passage to the Pantheon of Great Men. Notable as the wild pageant of a winter day. The Body is borne aloft, half-bare; the winding sheet disclosing the death-wound: sabre and bloody clothes parade themselves; a "lugubrious music" wailing harsh *næniæ*. Oak-crowns shower down from windows; President Vergniaud walks there, with Convention, with Jacobin Society, and all Patriots of every colour, all mourning brotherlike.

Notable also for another thing, this Burial of Lepelletier: it was the last act these men ever did with concert! All Parties and figures of Opinion, that agitate this distracted France and its Convention, now stand, as it were, face to face, and dagger to dagger; the King's Life, round which they all struck and battled, being hurled down. Dumouriez, conquering Holland, growls ominous discontent, at the head of Armies. Men say Dumouriez will have a King; that young d'Orléans Egalité shall be his King. Deputy Fauchet, in the *Journal des Amis*, curses his day, more bitterly than Job did; invokes the poniards of Regicides, of "Arras Vipers" or Robespierres, of Pluto Dantons, of horrid Butchers Legendre and Simulacra d'Herbois, to send him swiftly to another world than *theirs*.[607] This is *Te-Deum* Fauchet, of the Bastille Victory, of the *Cercle Social*. Sharp was the death-hail rattling round one's Flag-of-truce, on that Bastille day: but it was soft to such wreckage of high Hope as this; one's New Golden Era going down in leaden dross, and sulphurous black of the Everlasting Darkness!

At home this Killing of a King has divided all friends; and abroad it has united all enemies. Fraternity of Peoples, Revolutionary Propagandism; Atheism, Regicide; total destruction of social order in this world! All Kings, and lovers of Kings, and haters of Anarchy, rank in coalition; as in a war for life. England signifies to Citizen Chauvelin, the Ambassador or rather Ambassador's-Cloak, that he must quit the country in eight days. Ambassador's-Cloak and Ambassador, Chauvelin and Talleyrand, depart accordingly.[608] Talleyrand, implicated in that Iron Press of the Tuileries, thinks it safest to make for America.

England has cast out the Embassy: England declares war,—being shocked principally, it would seem, at the condition of the River Scheldt. Spain declares war; being shocked principally at some other thing; which doubtless the Manifesto indicates.[609] Nay we find it was not England that declared war first, or Spain first; but that France herself declared war first on both of them;[610] —a point of immense Parliamentary and Journalistic interest in those days, but which has become of no interest whatever in these. They all declare war. The sword is drawn, the scabbard thrown away. It is even as Danton said, in one of his all-too gigantic figures: 'The coalised Kings threaten us; we hurl at their feet, as gage of battle, the Head of a King.'

BOOK 3.III.
THE GIRONDINS

Chapter 3.3.I.
Cause and Effect

This huge Insurrectionary Movement, which we liken to a breaking out of Tophet and the Abyss, has swept away Royalty, Aristocracy, and a King's life. The question is, What will it next do; how will it henceforth shape itself? Settle down into a reign of Law and Liberty; according as the habits, persuasions and endeavours of the educated, monied, respectable class prescribe? That is to say: the volcanic lava-flood, bursting up in the manner described, will explode and flow according to Girondin Formula and pre-established rule of Philosophy? If so, for our Girondin friends it will be well.

Meanwhile were not the prophecy rather that as no external force, Royal or other, now remains which could control this Movement, the Movement will follow a course of its own; probably a very original one? Further, that whatsoever man or men can best interpret the inward tendencies it has, and give them voice and activity, will obtain the lead of it? For the rest, that as a thing *without* order, a thing proceeding from beyond and beneath the region of order, it must work and welter, not as a Regularity but as a Chaos; destructive and self-destructive; always till something that *has* order arise, strong enough to bind it into subjection again? Which something, we may further conjecture, will not be a Formula, with philosophical propositions and forensic eloquence; but a Reality, probably with a sword in its hand!

As for the Girondin Formula, of a respectable Republic for the Middle Classes, all manner of Aristocracies being now sufficiently demolished, there seems little reason to expect that the business will stop there. *Liberty,*

Equality, Fraternity, these are the words; enunciative and prophetic. Republic for the respectable washed Middle Classes, how can that be the fulfilment thereof? Hunger and nakedness, and nightmare oppression lying heavy on Twenty-five million hearts; this, not the wounded vanities or contradicted philosophies of philosophical Advocates, rich Shopkeepers, rural Noblesse, was the prime mover in the French Revolution; as the like will be in all such Revolutions, in all countries. Feudal Fleur-de-lys had become an insupportably bad marching banner, and needed to be torn and trampled: but Moneybag of Mammon (for that, in these times, is what the respectable Republic for the Middle Classes will signify) is a still worse, while it lasts. Properly, indeed, it is the worst and basest of all banners, and symbols of dominion among men; and indeed is possible only in a time of general Atheism, and Unbelief in any thing save in brute Force and Sensualism; pride of birth, pride of office, any known kind of pride being a degree better than purse-pride. Freedom, Equality, Brotherhood: not in the Moneybag, but far elsewhere, will Sansculottism seek these things.

We say therefore that an Insurrectionary France, loose of control from without, destitute of supreme order from within, will form one of the most tumultuous Activities ever seen on this Earth; such as no Girondin Formula can regulate. An immeasurable force, made up of forces manifold, heterogeneous, compatible and incompatible. In plainer words, this France must needs split into Parties; each of which seeking to make itself good, contradiction, exasperation will arise; and Parties on Parties find that they cannot work together, cannot exist together.

As for the number of Parties, there will, strictly counting, be as many Parties as there are Opinions. According to which rule, in this National Convention itself, to say nothing of France generally, the number of Parties ought to be Seven Hundred and Forty-Nine; for every unit entertains his opinion. But now as every unit has at once an individual nature, or necessity to follow his own road, and a gregarious nature or necessity to see himself travelling by the side of others,—what can there be but dissolutions, precipitations, endless turbulence of attracting and repelling; till once the master-element get evolved, and this wild alchemy arrange itself again?

To the length of Seven Hundred and Forty-nine Parties, however, no Nation was ever yet seen to go. Nor indeed much beyond the length of Two Parties; two at a time;—so invincible is man's tendency to unite, with all the invincible divisiveness he has! Two Parties, we say, are the usual number at one time: let these two fight it out, all minor shades of party rallying under the shade likest them; when the one has fought down the other, then it, in its turn, may divide, self-destructive; and so the process continue, as far as needful. This is the way of Revolutions, which spring up as the French one has done; when the so-called Bonds of Society snap asunder; and all Laws that are not Laws of Nature become naught and Formulas merely.

But quitting these somewhat abstract considerations, let History note this concrete reality which the streets of Paris exhibit, on Monday the 25th of February 1793. Long before daylight that morning, these streets are noisy and angry. Petitioning enough there has been; a Convention often solicited. It was but yesterday there came a Deputation of Washerwomen with Petition; complaining that not so much as soap could be had; to say nothing of bread, and condiments of bread. The cry of women, round the Salle de Manége, was heard plaintive: '*Du pain et du savon*, Bread and Soap.'[611]

And now from six o'clock, this Monday morning, one perceives the Baker's Queues unusually expanded, angrily agitating themselves. Not the Baker alone, but two Section Commissioners to help him, manage with difficulty the daily distribution of loaves. Soft-spoken assiduous, in the early candle-light, are Baker and Commissioners: and yet the pale chill February sunrise discloses an unpromising scene. Indignant Female Patriots, partly supplied with bread, rush now to the shops, declaring that they will have groceries. Groceries enough: sugar-barrels rolled forth into the street, Patriot Citoyennes weighing it out at a just rate of eleven-pence a pound; likewise coffee-chests, soap-chests, nay cinnamon and cloves-chests, with *aquavitæ* and other forms of alcohol,—at a just rate, which some do not pay; the pale-faced Grocer silently wringing his hands! What help? The distributive Citoyennes are of violent speech and gesture, their long Eumenides' hair hanging out of curl; nay in their girdles pistols are seen sticking: some, it is even said, have *beards*,—male Patriots in petticoats and mob-cap. Thus, in the streets of Lombards, in the street of Five-Diamonds, street of Pullies, in most streets of Paris does it effervesce, the livelong day; no Municipality, no Mayor Pache, though he was War-Minister lately, sends military against it, or aught against it but persuasive-eloquence, till seven at night, or later.

On Monday gone five weeks, which was the twenty-first of January, we saw Paris, beheading its King, stand silent, like a petrified City of Enchantment: and now on this Monday it is so noisy, selling sugar! Cities, especially Cities in Revolution, are subject to these alternations; the secret courses of civic business and existence effervescing and efflorescing, in this manner, as a concrete Phenomenon to the eye. Of which Phenomenon, when secret existence becoming public effloresces on the street, the philosophical cause-and-effect is not so easy to find. What, for example, may be the accurate philosophical meaning, and meanings, of this sale of sugar? These things that have become visible in the street of Pullies and over Paris, whence are they, we say; and whither?—

That Pitt has a hand in it, the gold of Pitt: so much, to all reasonable Patriot men, may seem clear. But then, through what agents of Pitt? Varlet, Apostle of Liberty, was discerned again of late, with his pike and his red nightcap. Deputy Marat published in his journal, this very day, complaining of the bitter scarcity, and sufferings of the people, till he seemed to get wroth: "If your Rights of Man were anything but a piece of written paper, the plunder of a few shops, and a forestaller or two hung up at the door-lintels, would put an end to such things."[612] Are not these, say the Girondins, pregnant indications? Pitt has bribed the Anarchists; Marat is the agent of Pitt: hence this sale of sugar. To the Mother Society, again, it is clear that the scarcity is factitious; is the work of Girondins, and such like; a set of men sold partly to Pitt; sold wholly to their own ambitions, and hard-hearted pedantries; who will not fix the grain-prices, but prate pedantically of free-trade; wishing to starve Paris into violence, and embroil it with the Departments: *hence* this sale of sugar.

And, alas, if to these two notabilities, of a Phenomenon and such Theories of a Phenomenon, we add this third notability, That the French Nation has believed, for several years now, in the possibility, nay certainty and near advent, of a universal Millennium, or reign of Freedom, Equality, Fraternity, wherein man should be the brother of man, and sorrow and sin flee away? Not bread to eat, nor soap to wash with; and the reign of perfect Felicity ready to arrive, due always since the Bastille fell! How did our hearts burn within us, at that Feast of Pikes, when brother flung himself on brother's bosom; and in sunny jubilee, Twenty-five millions burst forth into sound and cannon-smoke! Bright was our Hope then, as sunlight; red-angry is our Hope grown now, as consuming fire. But, O Heavens, what enchantment is it, or devilish legerdemain, of such effect, that Perfect Felicity, always within arm's length, could never be laid hold of, but only in her stead Controversy and Scarcity? This set of traitors after that set! Tremble, ye traitors; dread a People which calls itself patient, long-suffering; but which cannot always submit to have its pocket picked, in this way,—of a Millennium!

Yes, Reader, here is a miracle. Out of that putrescent rubbish of Scepticism, Sensualism, Sentimentalism, hollow Machiavelism, such a Faith has verily risen; flaming in the heart of a People. A whole People, awakening as it were to consciousness in deep misery, believes that it is within reach of a Fraternal Heaven-on-Earth. With longing arms, it struggles to embrace the Unspeakable; cannot embrace it, owing to certain causes.— Seldom do we find that a whole People can be said to have any Faith at all; except in things which it can eat and handle. Whensoever it gets any Faith, its history becomes spirit-stirring, note-worthy. But since the time when steel Europe shook itself simultaneously, at the word of Hermit Peter, and rushed towards the Sepulchre where God had lain, there was no universal impulse of Faith that one could note. Since Protestantism went silent, no Luther's voice, no Zisca's drum any longer proclaiming that God's Truth was *not* the Devil's Lie; and the last of the Cameronians (Renwick was the name of him; honour to the name of the brave!) sank, shot, on the Castle Hill of Edinburgh, there was no partial impulse of Faith among Nations. Till now, behold, once more this French Nation believes! Herein, we say, in that astonishing Faith of theirs, lies the miracle. It is a Faith undoubtedly of the more prodigious sort, even among Faiths; and will embody itself in prodigies. It is the soul of that world-prodigy named French Revolution; whereat the world still gazes and shudders.

But, for the rest, let no man ask History to explain by cause-and-effect how the business proceeded henceforth. This battle of Mountain and Gironde, and what follows, is the battle of Fanaticisms and Miracles; unsuitable for cause-and-effect. The sound of it, to the mind, is as a hubbub of voices in distraction; little of articulate is to be gathered by long listening and studying; only battle-tumult, shouts of triumph, shrieks of despair. The Mountain has left no Memoirs; the Girondins have left Memoirs, which are too often little other than long-drawn Interjections, of *Woe is me and Cursed be ye.* So soon as History can philosophically delineate the conflagration of a kindled Fireship, she may try this other task. Here lay the bitumen-stratum, there the brimstone one; so ran the vein of gunpowder, of nitre, terebinth and foul grease: this, were she inquisitive enough, History might partly know. But how they acted and reacted below decks, one fire-stratum playing into the other, by its nature and the art of man, now when all hands ran raging, and the flames lashed high over shrouds and topmast: this let not History attempt.

The Fireship is old France, the old French Form of Life; her creed a Generation of men. Wild are their cries and their ragings there, like spirits tormented in that flame. But, on the whole, are they not *gone*, O Reader? Their Fireship and they, frightening the world, have sailed away; its flames and its thunders quite away, into the Deep of Time. One thing therefore History will do: pity them all; for it went hard with them all. Not even the seagreen Incorruptible but shall have some pity, some human love, though it takes an effort. And now, so much once thoroughly attained, the rest will become easier. To the eye of equal brotherly pity, innumerable perversions dissipate themselves; exaggerations and execrations fall off, of their own accord. Standing wistfully on the safe shore, we will look, and see, what is of interest to us, what is adapted to us.

Chapter 3.3.II.
Culottic and Sansculottic

Gironde and Mountain are now in full quarrel; their mutual rage, says Toulongeon, is growing a "pale" rage. Curious, lamentable: all these men have the word Republic on their lips; in the heart of every one of them is a passionate wish for something which he calls Republic: yet see their death-quarrel! So, however, are men made. Creatures who live in confusion; who, once thrown together, can readily fall into that confusion of confusions which quarrel is, simply because their confusions differ from one another; still more because they seem to differ! Men's words are a poor exponent of their thought; nay their thought itself is a poor exponent of the inward unnamed Mystery, wherefrom both thought and action have their birth. No man can explain himself, can get himself explained; men see not one another but distorted phantasms which they call one another; which they hate and go to battle with: for all battle is well said to be *misunderstanding*.

But indeed that similitude of the Fireship; of our poor French brethren, so fiery themselves, working also in an *element* of fire, was not insignificant. Consider it well, there is a shade of the truth in it. For a man, once committed headlong to republican or any other Transcendentalism, and fighting and fanaticising amid a Nation of his like, becomes as it were enveloped in an ambient atmosphere of Transcendentalism and Delirium: his individual self is lost in something that is not himself, but foreign though inseparable from him. Strange to think of, the man's cloak still seems to hold the same man: and yet the man is not there, his volition is not there; nor the source of what he will do and devise; instead of the man and his volition there is a piece of Fanaticism and Fatalism incarnated in the shape of him. He, the hapless incarnated Fanaticism, goes his road; no man can help him, he himself least of all. It is a wonderful tragical predicament;—such as human language, unused to deal with these things, being contrived for the uses of common life, struggles to shadow out in figures. The ambient element of material fire is not wilder than this of Fanaticism; nor, though visible to the eye, is it more real. Volition bursts forth involuntary; rapt along; the movement of free human minds becomes a raging tornado of fatalism, blind as the winds; and

Mountain and Gironde, when they recover themselves, are alike astounded to see *where* it has flung and dropt them. To such height of miracle can men work on men; the Conscious and the Unconscious blended inscrutably in this our inscrutable Life; endless Necessity environing Freewill!

The weapons of the Girondins are Political Philosophy, Respectability and Eloquence. Eloquence, or call it rhetoric, really of a superior order; Vergniaud, for instance, turns a period as sweetly as any man of that generation. The weapons of the Mountain are those of mere nature: Audacity and Impetuosity which may become Ferocity, as of men complete in their determination, in their conviction; nay of men, in some cases, who as Septemberers must either prevail or perish. The ground to be fought for is Popularity: further you may either seek Popularity with the friends of Freedom and Order, or with the friends of Freedom Simple; to seek it with both has unhappily become impossible. With the former sort, and generally with the Authorities of the Departments, and such as read Parliamentary Debates, and are of Respectability, and of a peace-loving monied nature, the Girondins carry it. With the extreme Patriot again, with the indigent millions, especially with the Population of Paris who do not read so much as hear and see, the Girondins altogether lose it, and the Mountain carries it.

Egoism, nor meanness of mind, is not wanting on either side. Surely not on the Girondin side; where in fact the instinct of self-preservation, too prominently unfolded by circumstances, cuts almost a sorry figure; where also a certain finesse, to the length even of shuffling and shamming, now and then shews itself. They are men skilful in Advocate-fence. They have been called the Jesuits of the Revolution;[613] but that is too hard a name. It must be owned likewise that this rude blustering Mountain has a sense in it of what the Revolution means; which these eloquent Girondins are totally void of. Was the Revolution made, and fought for, against the world, these four weary years, that a Formula might be substantiated; that Society might become *methodic*, demonstrable by logic; and the old Noblesse with their pretensions vanish? Or ought it not withal to bring some glimmering of light and alleviation to the Twenty-five Millions, who sat in darkness, heavy-laden, till they rose with pikes in their hands? At least and lowest, one would think, it should bring them a proportion of bread to live on? There is in the Mountain here and there; in Marat People's-friend; in the incorruptible Seagreen himself, though otherwise so lean and formularly, a heartfelt knowledge of this latter fact;—without which knowledge all other knowledge here is naught, and the choicest forensic eloquence is as sounding brass and a tinkling cymbal. Most cold, on the other hand, most patronising, unsubstantial is the tone of the Girondins towards "our poorer brethren;"—those brethren whom one often hears of under the collective name of "the masses," as if they were not persons at all, but mounds of combustible explosive material, for blowing down Bastilles with! In very truth, a Revolutionist of this kind, is he not a Solecism? Disowned by Nature and Art; deserving only to be erased, and disappear! Surely, to our poorer brethren of Paris, all this Girondin patronage sounds deadening and killing: if fine-spoken and incontrovertible in logic, then all the falser, all the hatefuller in fact.

Nay doubtless, pleading for Popularity, here among our poorer brethren of Paris, the Girondin has a hard game to play. If he gain the ear of the Respectable at a distance, it is by insisting on September and such like; it is at the expense of this Paris where he dwells and perorates. Hard to perorate in such an auditory! Wherefore the question arises: Could we not get ourselves out of this Paris? Twice or oftener such an attempt is made. If not we ourselves, thinks Guadet, then at least our *Suppléans* might do it. For every Deputy has his *Suppléant*, or Substitute, who will take his place if need be: might not these assemble, say at Bourges, which is a quiet episcopal Town, in quiet Berri, forty good leagues off? In that case, what profit were it for the Paris Sansculottery to insult us; our *Suppléans* sitting quiet in Bourges, to whom we could run? Nay even the Primary electoral Assemblies, thinks Guadet, might be reconvoked, and a New Convention got, with new orders from the Sovereign people; and right glad were Lyons, were Bourdeaux, Rouen, Marseilles, as yet Provincial Towns, to welcome us in their turn, and become a sort of Capital Towns; and teach these Parisians reason.

Fond schemes; which all misgo! If decreed, in heat of eloquent logic, today, they are repealed, by clamour, and passionate wider considerations, on the morrow.[614] Will you, O Girondins, parcel us into separate Republics, then; like the Swiss, like your Americans; so that there be no Metropolis or indivisible French Nation any more? Your Departmental Guard seemed to point that way! Federal Republic? Federalist? Men and Knitting-women repeat *Fédéraliste*, with or without much Dictionary-meaning; but go on repeating it, as is usual in such cases, till the meaning of it becomes almost magical, fit to designate all mystery of Iniquity; and *Fédéraliste* has grown a word of Exorcism and *Apage-Satanas*. But furthermore, consider what "poisoning of public opinion" in the Departments, by these Brissot, Gorsas, Caritat-Condorcet Newspapers! And then also what counter-poisoning, still feller in quality, by a *Père Duchesne* of Hébert, brutallest Newspaper yet published on Earth; by a *Rougiff* of Guffroy; by the "incendiary leaves of Marat!" More than once, on complaint given and effervescence rising, it is decreed that a man cannot both be Legislator and Editor; that he shall choose between the one function and the other.[615] But this too, which indeed could help little, is revoked or eluded; remains a pious wish mainly.

Meanwhile, as the sad fruit of such strife, behold, O ye National Representatives, how between the friends of Law and the friends of Freedom everywhere, mere heats and jealousies have arisen; fevering the whole Republic! Department, Provincial Town is set against Metropolis, Rich against Poor, Culottic against Sansculottic, man against man. From the Southern Cities come Addresses of an almost inculpatory character; for Paris has long suffered Newspaper calumny. Bourdeaux demands a reign of Law and Respectability, meaning Girondism, with emphasis. With emphasis Marseilles demands the like. Nay from Marseilles there come *two* Addresses: one Girondin; one Jacobin Sansculottic. Hot Rebecqui, sick of this Convention-work, has given place to his Substitute, and gone home; where also, with such jarrings, there is work to be sick of.

Lyons, a place of Capitalists and Aristocrats, is in still worse state; almost in revolt. Chalier the Jacobin Town-Councillor has got, too literally, to daggers-drawn with Nièvre-Chol the *Modératin* Mayor; one of your Moderate, perhaps Aristocrat, Royalist or Federalist Mayors! Chalier, who pilgrimed to Paris "to behold Marat and the Mountain," has verily kindled himself at their sacred urn: for on the 6th of February last, History or Rumour has seen him haranguing his Lyons Jacobins in a quite transcendental manner, with a drawn dagger in his hand; recommending (they say) sheer September-methods, patience being worn out; and that the Jacobin Brethren should, impromptu, work the Guillotine themselves! One sees him still, in Engravings: mounted on a table; foot advanced, body contorted; a bald, rude, slope-browed, infuriated visage of the canine species, the eyes starting from their sockets; in his puissant right-hand the brandished dagger, or horse-pistol, as some give it; other dog-visages kindling under him:—a man not likely to end well! However, the Guillotine was *not* got together impromptu, that day, "on the Pont Saint-Clair," or elsewhere; but indeed continued lying rusty in its loft:[616] Nièvre-Chol with military went about, rumbling cannon, in the most confused manner; and the "nine hundred prisoners" received no hurt. So distracted is Lyons grown, with its cannon rumbling. Convention Commissioners must be sent thither forthwith: if even they can appease it, and keep the Guillotine in its loft?

Consider finally if, on all these mad jarrings of the Southern Cities, and of France generally, a traitorous Crypto-Royalist class is not looking and watching; ready to strike in, at the right season! Neither is there bread; neither is there soap: see the Patriot women selling out sugar, at a just rate of twenty-two sous per pound! Citizen Representatives, it were verily well that your quarrels finished, and the reign of Perfect Felicity began.

Chapter 3.3.III.
Growing Shrill

On the whole, one cannot say that the Girondins are wanting to themselves, so far as good-will might go. They prick assiduously into the sore-places of the Mountain; from principle, and also from jesuitism.

Besides September, of which there is now little to be made except effervescence, we discern two sore-places where the Mountain often suffers: Marat and Orléans Egalité. Squalid Marat, for his own sake and for the Mountain's, is assaulted ever and anon; held up to France, as a squalid bloodthirsty Portent, inciting to the pillage of shops; of whom let the Mountain have the credit! The Mountain murmurs, ill at ease: this "Maximum of Patriotism," how shall they either own him or disown him? As for Marat personally, he, with his fixed-idea, remains invulnerable to such things: nay the People's-friend is very evidently rising in importance, as his befriended People rises. No shrieks now, when he goes to speak; occasional applauses rather, furtherance which breeds confidence. The day when the Girondins proposed to "decree him accused" (*décréter d'accusation*, as they phrase it) for that February Paragraph, of "hanging up a Forestaller or two at the door-lintels," Marat proposes to have *them* "decreed insane;" and, descending the Tribune-steps, is heard to articulate these most unsenatorial ejaculations: '*Les Cochons, les imbecilles*, Pigs, idiots!' Oftentimes he croaks harsh sarcasm, having really a rough rasping tongue, and a very deep fund of contempt for fine outsides; and once or twice, he even laughs, nay "explodes into laughter, *rit aux éclats*," at the gentilities and superfine airs of these Girondin 'men of statesmanship,' with their pedantries, plausibilities, pusillanimities: 'these two years,' says he, 'you have been whining about attacks, and plots, and danger from Paris; and you have not a scratch to shew for yourselves.'[617] —Danton gruffly rebukes him, from time to time: a Maximum of Patriotism, whom one can neither own nor disown!

But the second sore-place of the Mountain is this anomalous Monseigneur Equality Prince d'Orléans. Behold these men, says the Gironde; with a whilom Bourbon Prince among them: they are creatures of the D'Orléans

Faction; they will have Philippe made King; one King no sooner guillotined than another made in his stead! Girondins have moved, Buzot moved long ago, from principle and also from jesuitism, that the whole race of Bourbons should be marched forth from the soil of France; this Prince Egalité to bring up the rear. Motions which might produce some effect on the public;— which the Mountain, ill at ease, knows not what to do with.

And poor Orléans Egalité himself, for one begins to pity even him, what does he do with them? The disowned of all parties, the rejected and foolishly be-drifted hither and hither, to what corner of Nature can he now drift with advantage? Feasible hope remains not for him: unfeasible hope, in pallid doubtful glimmers, there may still come, bewildering, not cheering or illuminating,—from the Dumouriez quarter; and how, if not the timewasted Orléans Egalité, then perhaps the young unworn Chartres Egalité might rise to be a kind of King? Sheltered, if shelter it be, in the clefts of the Mountain, poor Egalité will wait: one refuge in Jacobinism, one in Dumouriez and Counter-Revolution, are there not two chances? However, the look of him, Dame Genlis says, is grown gloomy; sad to see. Sillery also, the Genlis's Husband, who hovers about the Mountain, not on it, is in a bad way. Dame Genlis has come to Raincy, out of England and Bury St. Edmunds, in these days; being summoned by Egalité, with her young charge, Mademoiselle Egalité, that so Mademoiselle might not be counted among Emigrants and hardly dealt with. But it proves a ravelled business: Genlis and charge find that they must retire to the Netherlands; must wait on the Frontiers for a week or two; till Monseigneur, by Jacobin help, get it wound up. "Next morning," says Dame Genlis, "Monseigneur, gloomier than ever, gave me his arm, to lead me to the carriage. I was greatly troubled; Mademoiselle burst into tears; her Father was pale and trembling. After I had got seated, he stood immovable at the carriage-door, with his eyes fixed on me; his mournful and painful look seemed to implore pity;—'Adieu, Madame!' said he. The altered sound of his voice completely overcame me; not able to utter a word, I held out my hand; he grasped it close; then turning, and advancing sharply towards the postillions, he gave them a sign, and we rolled away."[618]

Nor are Peace-makers wanting; of whom likewise we mention two; one fast on the crown of the Mountain, the other not yet alighted anywhere: Danton and Barrère. Ingenious Barrère, Old-Constituent and Editor from the slopes of the Pyrenees, is one of the usefullest men of this Convention, in his way. Truth may lie on both sides, on either side, or on neither side; my friends, ye must give and take: for the rest, success to the winning side! This is the motto of Barrère. Ingenious, almost genial; quick-sighted, supple, graceful; a man that will prosper. Scarcely Belial in the assembled

Pandemonium was plausibler to ear and eye. An indispensable man: in the great *Art of Varnish* he may be said to seek his fellow. Has there an explosion arisen, as many do arise, a confusion, unsightliness, which no tongue can speak of, nor eye look on; give it to Barrère; Barrère shall be Committee-Reporter of it; you shall see it transmute itself into a regularity, into the very beauty and improvement that was needed. Without one such man, we say, how were this Convention bested? Call him not, as exaggerative Mercier does, "the greatest liar in France:" nay it may be argued there is not truth enough in him to make a real lie of. Call him, with Burke, Anacreon of the Guillotine, and a man serviceable to this Convention.

The other Peace-maker whom we name is Danton. Peace, O peace with one another! cries Danton often enough: Are we not alone against the world; a little band of brothers? Broad Danton is loved by all the Mountain; but they think him too easy-tempered, deficient in suspicion: he has stood between Dumouriez and much censure, anxious not to exasperate our only General: in the shrill tumult Danton's strong voice reverberates, for union and pacification. Meetings there are; dinings with the Girondins: it is so pressingly essential that there be union. But the Girondins are haughty and respectable; this Titan Danton is not a man of Formulas, and there rests on him a shadow of September. 'Your Girondins have no confidence in me:' this is the answer a conciliatory Meillan gets from him; to all the arguments and pleadings this conciliatory Meillan can bring, the repeated answer is, '*Ils n'ont point de confiance.*'[619] —The tumult will get ever shriller; rage is growing pale.

In fact, what a pang is it to the heart of a Girondin, this first withering probability that the despicable unphilosophic anarchic Mountain, after all, may triumph! Brutal Septemberers, a fifth-floor Tallien, "a Robespierre without an idea in his head," as Condorcet says, "or a feeling in his heart:" and yet we, the flower of France, cannot stand against them; behold the sceptre departs from us; from us and goes to them! Eloquence, Philosophism, Respectability avail not: "against Stupidity the very gods fight to no purpose,

"Mit der Dummheit kämpfen Götter selbst vergebens!"

Shrill are the plaints of Louvet; his thin existence all acidified into rage, and preternatural insight of suspicion. Wroth is young Barbaroux; wroth and scornful. Silent, like a Queen with the aspic on her bosom, sits the wife of Roland; Roland's Accounts never yet got audited, his name become a byword. Such is the fortune of war, especially of revolution. The great gulf of Tophet, and Tenth of August, opened itself at the magic of your eloquent voice; and lo now, it will not close at your voice! It is a dangerous thing such magic. The Magician's Famulus got hold of the forbidden Book, and summoned a goblin: *Plait-il*, What is your will? said the Goblin. The Famulus, somewhat struck, bade him fetch water: the swift goblin fetched it, pail in each hand; but lo, would not cease fetching it! Desperate, the Famulus shrieks at him, smites at him, cuts him in two; lo, *two* goblin water-carriers ply; and the house will be swum away in Deucalion Deluges.

Chapter 3.3.IV.
Fatherland in Danger

Or rather we will say, this Senatorial war might have lasted long; and Party tugging and throttling with Party might have suppressed and smothered one another, in the ordinary bloodless Parliamentary way; on one condition: that France had been at least able to exist, all the while. But this Sovereign People has a digestive faculty, and cannot do without bread. Also we are at war, and must have victory; at war with Europe, with Fate and Famine: and behold, in the spring of the year, all victory deserts us.

Dumouriez had his outposts stretched as far as Aix-la-Chapelle, and the beautifullest plan for pouncing on Holland, by stratagem, flat-bottomed boats and rapid intrepidity; wherein too he had prospered so far; but unhappily could prosper no further. Aix-la-Chapelle is lost; Maestricht will not surrender to mere smoke and noise: the flat-bottomed boats must launch themselves again, and return the way they came. Steady now, ye rapidly intrepid men; retreat with firmness, Parthian-like! Alas, were it General Miranda's fault; were it the War-minister's fault; or were it Dumouriez's own fault and that of Fortune: enough, there is nothing for it but retreat,—well if it be not even flight; for already terror-stricken cohorts and stragglers pour off, not waiting for order; flow disastrous, as many as ten thousand of them, without halt till they see France again.[620] Nay worse: Dumouriez himself is perhaps secretly turning traitor? Very sharp is the tone in which he writes to our Committees. Commissioners and Jacobin Pillagers have done such incalculable mischief; Hassenfratz sends neither cartridges nor clothing; shoes we have, deceptively "soled with wood and pasteboard." Nothing in short is right. Danton and Lacroix, when it was they that were Commissioners, would needs join Belgium to France;—of which Dumouriez might have made the prettiest little Duchy for his own secret behoof! With all these things the General is wroth; and writes to us in a sharp tone. Who knows what this hot little General is meditating? Dumouriez Duke of Belgium or Brabant; and say, Egalité the Younger King of France: there were an end for our Revolution!—Committee of Defence gazes, and shakes its head: who except Danton, defective in suspicion, could still struggle to be of hope?

And General Custine is rolling back from the Rhine Country; conquered Mentz will be reconquered, the Prussians gathering round to bombard it with shot and shell. Mentz may resist, Commissioner Merlin, the Thionviller, "making sallies, at the head of the besieged;"—resist to the death; but not longer than that. How sad a reverse for Mentz! Brave Foster, brave Lux planted Liberty-trees, amid *ça-ira*-ing music, in the snow-slush of last winter, there: and made Jacobin Societies; and got the Territory incorporated with France: they came hither to Paris, as Deputies or Delegates, and have their eighteen francs a-day: but see, before once the Liberty-Tree is got rightly in leaf, Mentz is changing into an explosive crater; vomiting fire, bevomited with fire!

Neither of these men shall again see Mentz; they have come hither only to die. Foster has been round the Globe; he saw Cook perish under Owyhee clubs; but like this Paris he has yet seen or suffered nothing. Poverty escorts him: from home there can nothing come, except Job's-news; the eighteen daily francs, which we here as Deputy or Delegate with difficulty "touch," are in paper *assignats*, and sink fast in value. Poverty, disappointment, inaction, obloquy; the brave heart slowly breaking! Such is Foster's lot. For the rest, Demoiselle Théroigne smiles on you in the Soirees; "a beautiful brownlocked face," of an exalted temper; and contrives to keep her carriage. Prussian Trenck, the poor subterranean Baron, jargons and jangles in an unmelodious manner. Thomas Paine's face is red-pustuled, "but the eyes uncommonly bright." Convention Deputies ask you to dinner: very courteous; and "we all play at *plumsack*."[621] "It is the Explosion and New-creation of a World," says Foster; "and the actors in it, such small mean objects, buzzing round one like a handful of flies."—

Likewise there is war with Spain. Spain will advance through the gorges of the Pyrenees; rustling with Bourbon banners; jingling with artillery and menace. And England has donned the red coat; and marches, with Royal Highness of York,—whom some once spake of inviting to be our King. Changed that humour now: and ever more changing; till no hatefuller thing walk this Earth than a denizen of that tyrannous Island; and Pitt be declared and decreed, with effervescence, "*L'ennemi du genre humain*, The enemy of mankind;" and, very singular to say, you make an order that no Soldier of Liberty give quarter to an Englishman. Which order however, the Soldier of Liberty does but partially obey. We will take no Prisoners then, say the Soldiers of Liberty; they shall all be "Deserters" that we take.[622] It is a frantic order; and attended with inconvenience. For surely, if you give no quarter, the plain issue is that you will get none; and so the business become as broad as it was long.—Our "recruitment of Three Hundred Thousand men," which was the decreed force for this year, is like to have work enough laid to its hand.

So many enemies come wending on; penetrating through throats of Mountains, steering over the salt sea; towards all points of our territory; rattling chains at us. Nay worst of all: there is an enemy within our own territory itself. In the early days of March, the Nantes Postbags do not arrive; there arrive only instead of them Conjecture, Apprehension, bodeful wind of Rumour. The bodefullest proves true! Those fanatic Peoples of La Vendée will no longer keep under: their fire of insurrection, heretofore dissipated with difficulty, blazes out anew, after the King's Death, as a wide conflagration; not riot, but civil war. Your Cathelineaus, your Stofflets, Charettes, are other men than was thought: behold how their Peasants, in mere russet and hodden, with their rude arms, rude array, with their fanatic Gaelic frenzy and wild-yelling battle-cry of *God and the King,* dash at us like a dark whirlwind; and blow the best-disciplined Nationals we can get into panic and *sauve-qui-peut!* Field after field is theirs; one sees not where it will end. Commandant Santerre may be sent thither; but with non-effect; he might as well have returned and brewed beer.

It has become peremptorily necessary that a National Convention cease arguing, and begin acting. Yield one party of you to the other, and do it swiftly. No theoretic outlook is here, but the close certainty of ruin; the very day that is passing over must be provided for.

It was Friday the eighth of March when this Job's-post from Dumouriez, thickly preceded and escorted by so many other Job's-posts, reached the National Convention. Blank enough are most faces. Little will it avail whether our Septemberers be punished or go unpunished; if Pitt and Cobourg are coming in, with one punishment for us all; nothing now between Paris itself and the Tyrants but a doubtful Dumouriez, and hosts in loose-flowing loud retreat!—Danton the Titan rises in this hour, as always in the hour of need. Great is his voice, reverberating from the domes:—Citizen-Representatives, shall we not, in such crisis of Fate, lay aside discords? Reputation: O what is the reputation of this man or of that? *Que mon nom soit flétri, que la France soit libre,* Let my name be blighted; let France be free! It is necessary now again that France rise, in swift vengeance, with her million right-hands, with her heart as of one man. Instantaneous recruitment in Paris; let every Section of Paris furnish its thousands; every section of France! Ninety-six Commissioners of us, two for each Section of the Forty-eight, they must go forthwith, and tell Paris what the Country needs of her. Let Eighty more of us be sent, post-haste, over France; to spread the fire-cross, to call forth the might of men. Let the Eighty also be on the road, before this sitting rise. Let them go, and think what their errand is. Speedy Camp of Fifty thousand between Paris and the North Frontier; for Paris will pour forth her volunteers! Shoulder to shoulder; one strong universal death-defiant rising and rushing; we shall hurl back these Sons of Night yet again; and France, in spite of the world, be free![623] —So sounds the Titan's voice: into all Section-houses; into all French hearts. Sections sit in Permanence, for recruitment, enrolment, that very night. Convention Commissioners, on swift wheels, are carrying the fire-cross from Town to Town, till all France blaze.

And so there is Flag of *Fatherland in Danger* waving from the Townhall, Black Flag from the top of Notre-Dame Cathedral; there is Proclamation, hot eloquence; Paris rushing out once again to strike its enemies down. That, in such circumstances, Paris was in no mild humour can be conjectured. Agitated streets; still more agitated round the Salle de Manége! Feuillans-Terrace crowds itself with angry Citizens, angrier Citizenesses; Varlet perambulates with portable-chair: ejaculations of no measured kind, as to perfidious fine-spoken *Hommes d'état*, friends of Dumouriez, secret-friends of Pitt and Cobourg, burst from the hearts and lips of men. To fight the enemy? Yes, and even to 'freeze him with terror, *glacer d'effroi;*' but first to have domestic Traitors punished! Who are they that, carping and quarrelling, in their jesuitic most *moderate* way, seek to shackle the Patriotic movement? That divide France against Paris, and poison public opinion in the Departments? That when we ask for bread, and a Maximum fixed-price, treat us with lectures on Free-trade in grains? Can the human stomach satisfy itself with lectures on Free-trade; and are we to fight the Austrians in a moderate manner, or in an immoderate? This Convention must be *purged*.

'Set up a swift Tribunal for Traitors, a Maximum for Grains:' thus speak with energy the Patriot Volunteers, as they defile through the Convention Hall, just on the wing to the Frontiers;—perorating in that heroical Cambyses' vein of theirs: beshouted by the Galleries and Mountain; bemurmured by the Right-side and Plain. Nor are prodigies wanting: lo, while a Captain of the Section Poissonnière perorates with vehemence about Dumouriez, Maximum, and Crypto-Royalist Traitors, and his troop beat chorus with him, waving their Banner overhead, the eye of a Deputy discerns, in this same Banner, that the *cravates* or streamers of it have Royal fleurs-de-lys! The Section-Captain shrieks; his troop shriek, horror-struck, and "trample the Banner under foot:"·seemingly the work of some Crypto-Royalist Plotter? Most probable;[62] —or perhaps at bottom, only the *old* Banner of the Section, manufactured prior to the Tenth of August, when such streamers were according to rule![625]

History, looking over the Girondin Memoirs, anxious to disentangle the truth of them from the hysterics, finds these days of March, especially this Sunday the Tenth of March, play a great part. Plots, plots: a plot for murdering the Girondin Deputies; Anarchists and Secret-Royalists plotting, in hellish concert, for that end! The far greater part of which is hysterics. What we do find indisputable is that Louvet and certain Girondins were apprehensive they might be murdered on Saturday, and did not go to the evening sitting: but held council with one another, each inciting his fellow to do something resolute, and end these Anarchists: to which, however, Pétion, opening the window, and finding the night very wet, answered only, '*Ils ne feront rien,*' and "composedly resumed his violin," says Louvet:[626] thereby, with soft Lydian tweedledeeing, to wrap himself against eating cares. Also that Louvet felt especially liable to being killed; that several Girondins went abroad to seek beds: liable to being killed; but were not. Further that, in very truth, Journalist Deputy Gorsas, poisoner of the Departments, he and his Printer had their houses broken into (by a tumult of Patriots, among whom red-capped Varlet, American Fournier loom forth, in the darkness of the rain and riot); had their wives put in fear; their presses, types and circumjacent equipments beaten to ruin; no Mayor interfering in time; Gorsas himself escaping, pistol in hand, "along the coping of the back wall." Further that Sunday, the morrow, was not a workday; and the streets were more agitated than ever: Is it a new September, then, that these Anarchists intend? Finally, that no September came;—and also that hysterics, not unnaturally, had reached almost their acme.[627]

Vergniaud denounces and deplores; in sweetly turned periods. Section Bonconseil, *Good-counsel* so-named, not Mauconseil or *Ill-counsel* as it once was,—does a far notabler thing: demands that Vergniaud, Brissot, Guadet, and other denunciatory fine-spoken Girondins, to the number of Twenty-two, be put under arrest! Section Good-counsel, so named ever since the Tenth of August, is sharply rebuked, like a Section of Ill-counsel;[628] but its word is spoken, and will not fall to the ground.

In fact, one thing strikes us in these poor Girondins; their fatal shortness of vision; nay fatal poorness of character, for that is the root of it. They are as strangers to the People they would govern; to the thing they have come to work in. Formulas, Philosophies, Respectabilities, what has been written in Books, and admitted by the Cultivated Classes; *this* inadequate *Scheme* of Nature's working is all that Nature, let her work as she will, can reveal to these men. So they perorate and speculate; and call on the Friends of Law, when the question is not Law or No-Law, but Life or No-Life. Pedants of the Revolution, if not Jesuits of it! Their Formalism is great; great also is their Egoism. France rising to fight Austria has been raised only by Plot of the Tenth of March, to kill Twenty-two of *them!* This Revolution Prodigy, unfolding itself into terrific stature and articulation, by its own laws and Nature's, not by the laws of Formula, has become unintelligible, incredible as an impossibility, the waste chaos of a Dream." A Republic founded on what they call the Virtues; on what we call the Decencies and Respectabilities: this they will have, and nothing but this. Whatsoever other Republic Nature and

Reality send, shall be considered as not sent; as a kind of Nightmare Vision, and thing non-extant; disowned by the Laws of Nature, and of Formula. Alas! Dim for the best eyes is this Reality; and as for these men, they will not look at it with eyes at all, but only through "facetted spectacles" of Pedantry, wounded Vanity; which yield the most portentous fallacious spectrum. Carping and complaining forever of Plots and Anarchy, they will do one thing: prove, to demonstration, that the Reality will not translate into their Formula; that they and their Formula are incompatible with the Reality: and, in its dark wrath, the Reality will extinguish it and them! What a man *kens* he *cans*. But the beginning of a man's doom is that vision be withdrawn from him; that he see not the reality, but a false spectrum of the reality; and, following that, step darkly, with more or less velocity, downwards to the utter Dark; to Ruin, which is the great Sea of Darkness, whither all falsehoods, winding or direct, continually flow!

This Tenth of March we may mark as an epoch in the Girondin destinies; the rage so exasperated itself, the misconception so darkened itself. Many desert the sittings; many come to them armed.[629] An honourable Deputy, setting out after breakfast, must now, besides taking his Notes, see whether his Priming is in order.

Meanwhile with Dumouriez in Belgium it fares ever worse. Were it again General Miranda's fault, or some other's fault, there is no doubt whatever but the "Battle of Nerwinden," on the 18th of March, is lost; and our rapid retreat has become a far too rapid one. Victorious Cobourg, with his Austrian prickers, hangs like a dark cloud on the rear of us: Dumouriez never off horseback night or day; engagement every three hours; our whole discomfited Host rolling rapidly inwards, full of rage, suspicion, and *sauve-qui-peut*! And then Dumouriez himself, what his intents may be? Wicked seemingly and not charitable! His despatches to Committee openly denounce a factious Convention, for the woes it has brought on France and him. And his speeches—for the General has no reticence! The Execution of the Tyrant this Dumouriez calls the Murder of the King. Danton and Lacroix, flying thither as Commissioners once more, return very doubtful; even Danton now doubts.

Three Jacobin Missionaries, Proly, Dubuisson, Pereyra, have flown forth; sped by a wakeful Mother Society: they are struck dumb to hear the General speak. The Convention, according to this General, consists of three hundred scoundrels and four hundred imbeciles: France cannot do without a King. 'But we have executed our King.' 'And what is it to me,' hastily cries Dumouriez, a General of no reticence, 'whether the King's name be *Ludovicus* or *Jacobus?*' 'Or *Philippus!*' rejoins Proly;—and hastens to report progress. Over the Frontiers such hope is there.

Chapter 3.3.V.
Sansculottism Accoutred

Let us look, however, at the grand internal Sansculottism and Revolution Prodigy, whether it stirs and waxes: there and not elsewhere hope may still be for France. The Revolution Prodigy, as Decree after Decree issues from the Mountain, like creative *fiats*, accordant with the nature of the Thing, — is shaping itself rapidly, in these days, into terrific stature and articulation, limb after limb. Last March, 1792, we saw all France flowing in blind terror; shutting town-barriers, boiling pitch for Brigands: happier, this March, that it is a seeing terror; that a creative Mountain exists, which can say *fiat!* Recruitment proceeds with fierce celerity: nevertheless our Volunteers hesitate to set out, till Treason be punished at home; they do not fly to the frontiers; but only fly hither and thither, demanding and denouncing. The Mountain must speak new *fiat*, and new *fiats*.

And does it not speak such? Take, as first example, those *Comités Révolutionnaires* for the arrestment of Persons Suspect. Revolutionary Committee, of Twelve chosen Patriots, sits in every Township of France; examining the Suspect, seeking arms, making domiciliary visits and arrestments; — caring, generally, that the Republic suffer no detriment. Chosen by universal suffrage, each in its Section, they are a kind of elixir of Jacobinism; some Forty-four Thousand of them awake and alive over France! In Paris and all Towns, every house-door must have the names of the inmates legibly printed on it, "at a height not exceeding five feet from the ground;" every Citizen must produce his certificatory *Carte de Civisme*, signed by Section-President; every man be ready to give account of the faith that is in him. Persons Suspect had as well depart this soil of Liberty! And yet departure too is bad: all Emigrants are declared Traitors, their property become National; they are "dead in Law," — save indeed that for *our* behoof they shall "live yet fifty years in Law," and what heritages may fall to them in ‡hat time become National too! A mad vitality of Jacobinism, with Forty-four Thousand centres of activity, circulates through all fibres of France.

Very notable also is the *Tribunal Extraordinaire:* [630] decreed by the Mountain; some Girondins dissenting, for surely such a Court contradicts every formula;—other Girondins assenting, nay co-operating, for do not we all hate Traitors, O ye people of Paris?—Tribunal of the Seventeenth in Autumn last was swift; but this shall be swifter. Five Judges; a standing Jury, which is named from Paris and the Neighbourhood, that there be not delay in naming it: they are subject to no Appeal; to hardly any Law-forms, but must "get themselves convinced" in all readiest ways; and for security are bound "to vote audibly;" audibly, in the hearing of a Paris Public. This is the *Tribunal Extraordinaire;* which, in few months, getting into most lively action, shall be entitled *Tribunal Revolutionnaire;* as indeed it from the very first has entitled itself: with a Herman or a Dumas for Judge President, with a Fouquier-Tinville for Attorney-General, and a Jury of such as Citizen Leroi, who has surnamed himself *Dix-Août,* "Leroi *August-Tenth,*" it will become the wonder of the world. Herein has Sansculottism fashioned for itself a Sword of Sharpness: a weapon magical; tempered in the Stygian hell-waters; to the edge of it all armour, and defence of strength or of cunning shall be soft; it shall mow down Lives and Brazen-gates; and the waving of it shed terror through the souls of men.

But speaking of an amorphous Sansculottism taking form, ought we not above all things to specify how the Amorphous gets itself a Head? Without metaphor, this Revolution Government continues hitherto in a very anarchic state. Executive Council of Ministers, Six in number, there is; but they, especially since Roland's retreat, have hardly known whether they were Ministers or not. Convention Committees sit supreme over them; but then each Committee as supreme as the others: Committee of Twenty-one, of Defence, of General Surety; simultaneous or successive, for specific purposes. The Convention alone is all-powerful,—especially if the Commune go with it; but is too numerous for an administrative body. Wherefore, in this perilous quick-whirling condition of the Republic, before the end of March, we obtain our small *Comité de Salut Public;* [631] as it were, for miscellaneous accidental purposes, requiring despatch;—as it proves, for a sort of universal supervision, and universal subjection. They are to report weekly, these new Committee-men; but to deliberate in secret. Their number is Nine, firm Patriots all, Danton one of them: Renewable every month;—yet why not reelect them if they turn out well? The flower of the matter is that they are but nine; that they sit in secret. An insignificant-looking thing at first, this Committee; but with a principle of growth in it! Forwarded by fortune, by internal Jacobin energy, it will reduce all Committees and the Convention itself to mute obedience, the Six Ministers to Six assiduous Clerks; and work its will on the Earth and under Heaven, for a season. "A Committee of Public Salvation," whereat the world still shrieks and shudders.

If we call that Revolutionary Tribunal a Sword, which Sansculottism has provided for itself, then let us call the "Law of the Maximum," a Provender-scrip, or Haversack, wherein better or worse some ration of bread may be found. It is true, Political Economy, Girondin free-trade, and all law of supply and demand, are hereby hurled topsyturvy: but what help? Patriotism must live; the "cupidity of farmers" seems to have no bowels. Wherefore this Law of the Maximum, fixing the highest price of grains, is, with infinite effort, got passed;[632] and shall gradually extend itself into a Maximum for all manner of *comestibles* and commodities: with such scrambling and topsyturvying as may be fancied! For now, if, for example, the farmer will not sell? The farmer shall be forced to sell. An accurate Account of what grain he has shall be delivered in to the Constituted Authorities: let him see that he say not too much; for in that case, his rents, taxes and contributions will rise proportionally: let him see that he say not too little; for, on or before a set day, we shall suppose in April, *less* than one-third of this declared quantity, must remain in his barns, more than two-thirds of it must have been thrashed and sold. One can denounce him, and raise penalties.

By such inextricable overturning of all Commercial relation will Sansculottism keep life in; since not otherwise. On the whole, as Camille Desmoulins says once, 'while the Sansculottes fight, the Monsieurs must pay.' So there come *Impôts Progressifs*, Ascending Taxes; which consume, with fast-increasing voracity, and "superfluous-revenue' of men: beyond fifty-pounds a-year you are not exempt; rising into the hundreds you bleed freely; into the thousands and tens of thousands, you bleed gushing. Also there come Requisitions; there comes "Forced-Loan of a Milliard," some Fifty-Millions Sterling; which of course they that *have* must lend. Unexampled enough: it has grown to be no country for the Rich, this; but a country for the Poor! And then if one fly, what steads it? Dead in Law; nay kept alive fifty years yet, for *their* accursed behoof! In this manner, therefore, it goes; topsyturvying, *ça-ira*-ing;—and withal there is endless sale of Emigrant National-Property, there is Cambon with endless cornucopia of Assignats. The Trade and Finance of Sansculottism; and how, with Maximum and Bakers'-queues, with Cupidity, Hunger, Denunciation and Paper-money, it led its galvanic-life, and began and ended,—remains the most interesting of all Chapters in Political Economy: still to be written.

All which things are they not clean against Formula? O Girondin Friends, it is not a Republic of the Virtues we are getting; but only a Republic of the Strengths, virtuous and other!

Chapter 3.3.VI.
The Traitor

But Dumouriez, with his fugitive Host, with his King *Ludovicus* or King *Philippus?* There lies the crisis; there hangs the question: Revolution Prodigy, or Counter-Revolution?—One wide shriek covers that North-East region. Soldiers, full of rage, suspicion and terror, flock hither and thither; Dumouriez the many-counselled, never off horseback, knows now no counsel that were not worse than none: the counsel, namely, of joining himself with Cobourg; marching to Paris, extinguishing Jacobinism, and, with some new King Ludovicus or King Philippus, resting the Constitution of 1791![633]

Is Wisdom quitting Dumouriez; the herald of Fortune quitting him? Principle, faith political or other, beyond a certain faith of mess-rooms, and honour of an officer, had him not to quit. At any rate, his quarters in the Burgh of Saint-Amand; his headquarters in the Village of Saint-Amand des Boues, a short way off,—have become a Bedlam. National Representatives, Jacobin Missionaries are riding and running: of the "three Towns," Lille, Valenciennes or even Condé, which Dumouriez wanted to snatch for himself, not one can be snatched: your Captain is admitted, but the Town-gate is closed on him, and then the Prison gate, and "his men wander about the ramparts." Couriers gallop breathless; men wait, or seem waiting, to assassinate, to be assassinated; Battalions nigh frantic with such suspicion and uncertainty, with *Vive-la-République* and *Sauve-qui-peut*, rush this way and that;—Ruin and Desperation in the shape of Cobourg lying entrenched close by.

Dame Genlis and her fair Princess d'Orléans find this Burgh of Saint-Amand no fit place for them; Dumouriez's protection is grown worse than none. Tough Genlis one of the toughest women; a woman, as it were, with nine lives in her; whom nothing will beat: she packs her bandboxes; clear for flight in a private manner. Her beloved Princess she will—leave here, with the Prince Chartres Egalité her Brother. In the cold grey of the April morning, we find her accordingly established in her hired vehicle, on the street of Saint-Amand; postilions just cracking their whips to go,—when behold the young Princely Brother, struggling hitherward, hastily calling; bearing the Princess in his arms! Hastily he has clutched the poor young lady up, in her very night-gown, nothing saved of her goods except the watch from the pillow: with brotherly despair he flings her in, among the bandboxes, into Genlis's chaise, into Genlis's arms: Leave her not, in the name of Mercy and Heaven! A shrill scene, but a brief one:—the postilions crack and go. Ah, whither? Through by-roads and broken hill-passes: seeking their way with lanterns after nightfall; through perils, and Cobourg Austrians, and suspicious French Nationals; finally, into Switzerland; safe though nigh moneyless.[634] The brave young Egalité has a most wild Morrow to look for; but now only himself to carry through it.

For indeed over at that Village named *of the Mudbaths*, Saint-Amand des Boues, matters are still worse. About four o'clock on Tuesday afternoon, the 2d of April 1793, two Couriers come galloping as if for life: *Mon Général!* Four National Representatives, War-Minister at their head, are posting hitherward, from Valenciennes: are close at hand,—with what intents one may guess! While the Couriers are yet speaking, War-Minister and National Representatives, old Camus the Archivist for chief speaker of them, arrive. Hardly has *Mon Général* had time to order out the Huzzar Regiment de Berchigny; that it take rank and wait near by, in case of accident. And so, enter War-Minister Beurnonville, with an embrace of friendship, for he is an old friend; enter Archivist Camus and the other three, following him.

They produce Papers, invite the General to the bar of the Convention: merely to give an explanation or two. The General finds it unsuitable, not to say impossible, and that 'the service will suffer.' Then comes reasoning; the voice of the old Archivist getting loud. Vain to reason loud with this Dumouriez; he answers mere angry irreverences. And so, amid plumed staff-officers, very gloomy-looking; in jeopardy and uncertainty, these poor National messengers debate and consult, retire and re-enter, for the space of some two hours: without effect. Whereupon Archivist Camus, getting quite loud, proclaims, in the name of the National Convention, for he has the power to do it, That General Dumouriez is *arrested*: 'Will you obey the National Mandate, General!' '*Pas dans ce moment-ci*, Not at this particular moment,' answers the General also aloud; then glancing the other way, utters certain unknown vocables, in a mandatory manner; seemingly a German word-of-command.[635] Hussars clutch the Four National Representatives, and Beurnonville the War-minister; pack them out of the apartment; out of the Village, over the lines to Cobourg, in two chaises that very night,—as hostages, prisoners; to lie long in Maestricht and Austrian strongholds![636] *Jacta est alea.*

This night Dumouriez prints his "Proclamation;" this night and the morrow the Dumouriez Army, in such darkness visible, and rage of semi-desperation as there is, shall meditate what the General is doing, what they themselves will do in it. Judge whether this Wednesday was of halcyon nature, for any one! But, on the Thursday morning, we discern Dumouriez with small escort, with Chartres Egalité and a few staff-officers, ambling along the Condé Highway: perhaps they are for Condé, and trying to persuade the Garrison there; at all events, they are for an interview with Cobourg, who waits in the woods by appointment, in that quarter. Nigh the Village of Doumet, three National Battalions, a set of men always full of Jacobinism, sweep past us; marching rather swiftly,—seemingly in mistake, by a way we had not ordered. The General dismounts, steps into a cottage, a little from the wayside; will give them right order in writing. Hark! what strange growling is heard: what barkings are heard, loud yells of 'Traitors,' of 'Arrest:' the National Battalions have wheeled round, are emitting shot! Mount, Dumouriez, and spring for life! Dumouriez and Staff strike the spurs in, deep; vault over ditches, into the fields, which prove to be morasses; sprawl and plunge for life; bewhistled with curses and lead. Sunk to the middle, with or without horses, several servants killed, they escape out of shot-range, to General Mack the Austrian's quarters. Nay they return on the morrow, to Saint-Amand and faithful foreign Berchigny; but what boots it? The Artillery has all revolted, is jingling off to Valenciennes: all have revolted, are revolting; except only foreign Berchigny, to the extent of some poor fifteen hundred, none will follow Dumouriez against France and Indivisible Republic: Dumouriez's occupation's gone.[637]

Such an instinct of Frenehhood and Sansculottism dwells in these men: they will follow no Dumouriez nor Lafayette, nor any mortal on such errand. Shriek may be of *Sauve-qui-peut*, but will also be of *Vive-la-République*. New National Representatives arrive; new General Dampierre, soon killed in battle; new General Custine; the agitated Hosts draw back to some Camp of Famars; make head against Cobourg as they can.

And so Dumouriez is in the Austrian quarters; his drama ended, in this rather sorry manner. A most shifty, wiry man; one of Heaven's Swiss that wanted only work. Fifty years of unnoticed toil and valour; one year of toil and valour, not unnoticed, but seen of all countries and centuries; then thirty other years again unnoticed, of Memoir-writing, English Pension, scheming and projecting to no purpose: Adieu thou Swiss of Heaven, worthy to have been something else!

His Staff go different ways. Brave young Egalité reaches Switzerland and the Genlis Cottage; with a strong crabstick in his hand, a strong heart in his body: his Princedom in now reduced to that. Egalité the Father sat playing whist, in his Palais Egalité, at Paris, on the 6th day of this same month of April, when a catchpole entered: Citoyen Egalité is wanted at the Convention Committee![638] Examination, requiring Arrestment; finally requiring Imprisonment, transference to Marseilles and the Castle of If! Orléansdom has sunk in the black waters; Palais Egalité, which was Palais Royal, is like to become Palais National.

Chapter 3.3.VII.

In Fight

Our Republic, by paper Decree, may be "One and Indivisible;" but what profits it while these things are? Federalists in the Senate, renegadoes in the Army, traitors everywhere! France, all in desperate recruitment since the Tenth of March, does not fly to the frontier, but only flies hither and thither. This defection of contemptuous diplomatic Dumouriez falls heavy on the fine-spoken high-sniffing *Hommes d'état*, whom he consorted with; forms a second epoch in their destinies.

Or perhaps more strictly we might say, the second Girondin epoch, though little noticed then, began on the day when, in reference to this defection, the Girondins broke with Danton. It was the first day of April; Dumouriez had not yet plunged across the morasses to Cobourg, but was evidently meaning to do it, and our Commissioners were off to arrest him; when what does the Girondin Lasource see good to do, but rise, and jesuitically question and insinuate at great length, whether a main accomplice of Dumouriez had not probably been—Danton? Gironde grins sardonic assent; Mountain holds its breath. The figure of Danton, Levasseur says, while this speech went on, was noteworthy. He sat erect, with a kind of internal convulsion struggling to keep itself motionless; his eye from time to time flashing wilder, his lip curling in Titanic scorn.[639] Lasource, in a fine-spoken attorney-manner, proceeds: there is this probability to his mind, and there is that; probabilities which press painfully on him, which cast the Patriotism of Danton under a painful shade; which painful shade he, Lasource, will hope that Danton may find it not impossible to dispel.

'*Les Scélérats!*' cries Danton, starting up, with clenched right-hand, Lasource having done: and descends from the Mountain, like a lava-flood; his answer not unready. Lasource's probabilities fly like idle dust; but leave a result behind them. 'Ye were right, friends of the Mountain,' begins Danton, 'and I was wrong: there is no peace possible with these men. Let it be war then! They will not save the Republic with us: it shall be saved without them; saved in spite of them.' Really a burst of rude Parliamentary eloquence this; which is still worth reading, in the old *Moniteur!* With fire-words the exasperated rude Titan rives and smites these Girondins; at every hit the glad Mountain utters chorus: Marat, like a musical *bis*, repeating the last phrase.[640] Lasource's probabilities are gone: but Danton's pledge of battle remains lying.

A third epoch, or scene in the Girondin Drama, or rather it is but the completion of this second epoch, we reckon from the day when the patience of virtuous Pétion finally boiled over; and the Girondins, so to speak, took up this battle-pledge of Danton's and decreed Marat accused. It was the eleventh of the same month of April, on some effervescence rising, such as often rose; and President had covered himself, mere Bedlam now ruling; and Mountain and Gironde were rushing on one another with clenched right-hands, and even with pistols in them; when, behold, the Girondin Duperret drew a sword! Shriek of horror rose, instantly quenching all other effervescence, at sight of the clear murderous steel; whereupon Duperret returned it to the leather again;—confessing that he did indeed draw it, being instigated by a kind of sacred madness, '*sainte fureur*,' and pistols held at him; but that if he parricidally had chanced to scratch the outmost skin of National Representation with it, he too carried pistols, and would have blown his brains out on the spot.[641]

But now in such posture of affairs, virtuous Pétion rose, next morning, to lament these effervescences, this endless Anarchy invading the Legislative Sanctuary itself; and here, being growled at and howled at by the Mountain, his patience, long tried, did, as we say, boil over; and he spake vehemently, in high key, with foam on his lips; "whence," says Marat, "I concluded he had got "*la rage*," the rabidity, or dog-madness. Rabidity smites others rabid: so there rises new foam-lipped demand to have Anarchists extinguished; and specially to have Marat put under Accusation. Send a Representative to the Revolutionary Tribunal? Violate the inviolability of a Representative? Have a care, O Friends! This poor Marat has faults enough; but against Liberty or Equality, what fault? That he has loved and fought for it, not wisely but too well. In dungeons and cellars, in pinching poverty, under anathema of men; even so, in such fight, has he grown so dingy, bleared; even so has his head become a Stylites one! Him you will fling to your Sword of Sharpness; while Cobourg and Pitt advance on us, fire-spitting?

The Mountain is loud, the Gironde is loud and deaf; all lips are foamy. With "Permanent-Session of twenty-four hours," with vote by rollcall, and a dead-lift effort, the Gironde carries it: Marat is ordered to the Revolutionary Tribunal, to answer for that February Paragraph of Forestallers at the door-lintel, with other offences; and, after a little hesitation, he obeys.[642]

Thus is Danton's battle-pledge taken up: there is, as he said there would be, "war without truce or treaty, *ni trève ni composition*." Wherefore, close now with one another, Formula and Reality, in death-grips, and wrestle it out; both of you cannot live, but only one!

Chapter 3.3.VIII.
In Death-Grips

It proves what strength, were it only of inertia, there is in established Formulas, what weakness in nascent Realities, and illustrates several things, that this death-wrestle should still have lasted some six weeks or more. National business, discussion of the Constitutional Act, for our Constitution should decidedly be got ready, proceeds along with it. We even change our Locality; we shift, on the Tenth of May, from the old Salle de Manége, into our new Hall, in the Palace, once a King's but now the Republic's, of the Tuileries. Hope and ruth, flickering against despair and rage, still struggles in the minds of men.

It is a most dark confused death-wrestle, this of the six weeks. Formalist frenzy against Realist frenzy; Patriotism, Egoism, Pride, Anger, Vanity, Hope and Despair, all raised to the frenetic pitch: Frenzy meets Frenzy, like dark clashing whirlwinds; neither understands the other; the weaker, one day, will understand that *it* is verily swept down! Girondism is strong as established Formula and Respectability: do not as many as Seventy-two of the Departments, or say respectable Heads of Departments, declare for us? Calvados, which loves its Buzot, will even rise in revolt, so hint the Addresses; Marseilles, cradle of Patriotism, will rise; Bourdeaux will rise, and the Gironde Department, as one man; in a word, who will *not* rise, were our *Représentation Nationale* to be insulted, or one hair of a Deputy's head harmed! The Mountain, again, is strong as Reality and Audacity. To the Reality of the Mountain are not all furthersome things possible? A new Tenth of August, if needful; nay a new Second of September! —

But, on Wednesday afternoon, twenty-fourth day of April, year 1793, what tumult as of fierce jubilee is this? It is Marat returning from Revolutionary Tribunal! A week or more of death-peril: and now there is triumphant acquittal; Revolutionary Tribunal can find no accusation against this man. And so the eye of History beholds Patriotism, which had gloomed unutterable things all week, break into loud jubilee, embrace its Marat; lift him into a chair of triumph, bear him shoulder-high through the streets. Shoulder-high is the injured People's-friend, crowned with an oak-garland; amid the wavy sea of red nightcaps, carmagnole jackets, grenadier bonnets and female mob-caps; far-sounding like a sea! The injured People's-friend has here reached his culminating-point; he too strikes the stars with his sublime head.

But the Reader can judge with what face President Lasource, he of the "painful probabilities," who presides in this Convention Hall, might welcome such jubilee-tide, when it got thither, and the Decreed of Accusation floating on the top of it! A National Sapper, spokesman on the occasion, says, the People know their Friend, and love his life as their own; 'whosoever wants Marat's head must get the Sapper's first.'[643] Lasource answered with some vague painful mumblement,—which, says Levasseur, one could not help tittering at.[644] Patriot Sections, Volunteers not yet gone to the Frontiers, come demanding the 'purgation of traitors from your own bosom;' the expulsion, or even the trial and sentence, of a factious Twenty-two.

Nevertheless the Gironde has got its Commission of Twelve; a Commission specially appointed for investigating these troubles of the Legislative Sanctuary: let Sansculottism say what it will, Law shall triumph. Old-Constituent Rabaut Saint-Etienne presides over this Commission: 'it is the last plank whereon a wrecked Republic may perhaps still save herself.' Rabaut and they therefore sit, intent; examining witnesses; launching arrestments; looking out into a waste dim sea of troubles.—the womb of *Formula*, or perhaps her grave! Enter not that sea, O Reader! There are dim desolation and confusion; raging women and raging men. Sections come demanding Twenty-two; for the *number* first given by Section Bonconseil still holds, though the names should even vary. Other Sections, of the wealthier kind, come denouncing such demand; nay the same Section will demand today, and denounce the demand tomorrow, according as the wealthier sit, or the poorer. Wherefore, indeed, the Girondins decree that all Sections shall close "at ten in the evening;" before the working people come: which Decree remains without effect. And nightly the Mother of Patriotism wails doleful; doleful, but her eye kindling! And Fournier l'Americain is busy, and the two Banker Freys, and Varlet Apostle of Liberty; the bull-voice of Marquis Saint-Huruge is heard. And shrill women vociferate from all Galleries, the Convention ones and downwards. Nay a "Central Committee" of all the Forty-eight Sections, looms forth huge and dubious; sitting dim in the *Archevêché*, sending Resolutions, receiving them: a Centre of the Sections; in dread deliberation as to a New Tenth of August!

One thing we will specify to throw light on many: the aspect under which, seen through the eyes of these Girondin Twelve, or even seen through one's own eyes, the Patriotism of the softer sex presents itself. There are Female Patriots, whom the Girondins call Megaeras, and count to the extent of eight thousand; with serpent-hair, all out of curl; who have changed the distaff for the dagger. They are of "the Society called Brotherly," *Fraternelle*, say *Sisterly*, which meets under the roof of the Jacobins. "Two thousand daggers," or so, have been ordered,—doubtless, for them. They rush to Versailles, to raise more women; but the Versailles women will not rise.[645]

Nay, behold, in National Garden of Tuileries,—Demoiselle Théroigne herself is become as a brownlocked Diana (were that possible) attacked by her own dogs, or she-dogs! The Demoiselle, keeping her carriage, is for Liberty indeed, as she has full well shewn; but then for Liberty with Respectability: whereupon these serpent-haired Extreme She-Patriots now do fasten on her, tatter her, shamefully fustigate her, in their shameful way; almost fling her into the Garden-ponds, had not help intervened. Help, alas, to small purpose. The poor Demoiselle's head and nervous-system, none of the soundest, is so tattered and fluttered that it will never recover; but flutter worse and worse, till it crack; and within year and day we hear of her in madhouse, and straitwaistcoat, which proves permanent!—Such brownlocked Figure did flutter, and inarticulately jabber and gesticulate, little able to *speak* the obscure meaning it had, through some segment of that Eighteenth Century of Time. She disappears here from the Revolution and Public History, for evermore.[646]

Another thing we will not again specify, yet again beseech the Reader to imagine: the reign of Fraternity and Perfection. Imagine, we say, O Reader, that the Millennium were struggling on the threshold, and yet not so much as groceries could be had,—owing to traitors. With what impetus would a man strike traitors, in that case? Ah, thou canst not imagine it: thou hast thy groceries safe in the shops, and little or no hope of a Millennium ever coming!—But, indeed, as to the temper there was in men and women, does not this one fact say enough: the height SUSPICION had risen to? Preternatural we often called it; seemingly in the language of exaggeration: but listen to the cold deposition of witnesses. Not a musical Patriot can blow himself a snatch of melody from the French Horn, sitting mildly pensive on the housetop, but Mercier will recognise it to be a signal which one Plotting Committee is making to another. Distraction has possessed Harmony herself; lurks in the sound of *Marseillese* and *ça-ira*.[647] Louvet, who can see as deep into a millstone as the most, discerns that we shall be invited back to our old Hall of the Manege, by a Deputation; and then the Anarchists will massacre Twenty-two of us, as we walk over. It is Pitt and Cobourg; the gold of Pitt.—Poor Pitt! They little know what work he has with his own Friends of the People; getting them bespied, beheaded, their habeas-corpuses suspended, and his own Social Order and strong-boxes kept tight,—to fancy him raising mobs among his neighbours!

But the strangest fact connected with French or indeed with human Suspicion, is perhaps this of Camille Desmoulins. Camille's head, one of the clearest in France, has got itself so saturated through every fibre with Preternaturalism of Suspicion, that looking back on that Twelfth of July 1789, when the thousands rose round him, yelling responsive at his word in the Palais Royal Garden, and took cockades, he finds it explicable only on this hypothesis, That they were all hired to do it, and set on by the Foreign and other Plotters. "It was not for nothing," says Camille with insight, "that this multitude burst up round me when I spoke!" No, not for nothing. Behind, around, before, it is one huge Preternatural Puppet-play of Plots; Pitt pulling the wires.[648] Almost I conjecture that I Camille myself am a Plot, and wooden with wires.—The force of insight could no further go.

Be this as it will, History remarks that the Commission of Twelve, now clear enough as to the Plots; and luckily having "got the threads of them all by the end," as they say,—are launching Mandates of Arrest rapidly in these May days; and carrying matters with a high hand; resolute that the sea of troubles shall be restrained. What chief Patriot, Section-President even, is safe? They can arrest him; tear him from his warm bed, because he has made irregular Section Arrestments! They arrest Varlet Apostle of Liberty. They arrest Procureur-Substitute Hébert, *Père Duchesne;* a Magistrate of the People, sitting in Townhall; who, with high solemnity of martyrdom, takes leave of his colleagues; prompt he, to obey the Law; and solemnly acquiescent, disappears into prison.

The swifter fly the Sections, energetically demanding him back; demanding not arrestment of Popular Magistrates, but of a traitorous Twenty-two. Section comes flying after Section;—defiling energetic, with their Cambyses' vein of oratory: nay the Commune itself comes, with Mayor Pache at its head; and with question not of Hébert and the Twenty-two alone, but with this ominous old question made new, 'Can you save the Republic, or must we do it?' To whom President Max Isnard makes fiery answer: If by fatal chance, in any of those tumults which since the Tenth of March are ever returning, Paris were to lift a sacrilegious finger against the National Representation, France would rise as one man, in never-imagined vengeance, and shortly 'the traveller would ask, on which side of the Seine Paris had stood!'[649] Whereat the Mountain bellows only louder, and every Gallery; Patriot Paris boiling round.

And Girondin Valazé has nightly conclaves at his house; sends billets; "Come punctually, and well armed, for there is to be business." And

Megaera women perambulate the streets, with flags, with lamentable *alleleu*. [650] And the Convention-doors are obstructed by roaring multitudes: find-spoken *Hommes d'état* are hustled, maltreated, as they pass; Marat will apostrophise you, in such death-peril, and say, Thou too art of them. If Roland ask leave to quit Paris, there is order of the day. What help? Substitute Hébert, Apostle Varlet, must be given back; to be crowned with oak-garlands. The Commission of Twelve, in a Convention overwhelmed with roaring Sections, is broken; then on the morrow, in a Convention of rallied Girondins, is reinstated. Dim Chaos, or the sea of troubles, is struggling through all its elements; writhing and chafing towards some creation.

Chapter 3.3.IX.
Extinct

Accordingly, on Friday, the Thirty-first of May 1793, there comes forth into the summer sunlight one of the strangest scenes. Mayor Pache with Municipality arrives at the Tuileries Hall of Convention; sent for, Paris being in visible ferment; and gives the strangest news.

How, in the grey of this morning, while we sat Permanent in Townhall, watchful for the commonweal, there entered, precisely as on a Tenth of August, some Ninety-six extraneous persons; who declared themselves to be in a state of Insurrection; to be plenipotentiary Commissioners from the Forty-eight Sections, sections or members of the Sovereign People, all in a state of Insurrection; and further that we, in the name of said Sovereign in Insurrection, were dismissed from office. How we thereupon laid off our sashes, and withdrew into the adjacent Saloon of Liberty. How in a moment or two, we were called back; and reinstated; the Sovereign pleasing to think us still worthy of confidence. Whereby, having taken new oath of office, we on a sudden find ourselves Insurrectionary Magistrates, with extraneous Committee of Ninety-six sitting by us; and a Citoyen Henriot, one whom some accuse of Septemberism, is made Generalissimo of the National Guard; and, since six o'clock, the tocsins ring and the drums beat:—Under which peculiar circumstances, what would an august National Convention please to direct us to do?[651]

Yes, there is the question! 'Break the Insurrectionary Authorities,' answers some with vehemence. Vergniaud at least will have 'the National Representatives all die at their post;' this is sworn to, with ready loud acclaim. But as to breaking the Insurrectionary Authorities,—alas, while we yet debate, what sound is that? Sound of the Alarm-Cannon on the Pont Neuf; which it is death by the Law to fire without order from us!

It does boom off there, nevertheless; sending a sound through all hearts. And the tocsins discourse stern music; and Henriot with his Armed Force has enveloped us! And Section succeeds Section, the livelong day; demanding with Cambyses'-oratory, with the rattle of muskets, That traitors, Twenty-two or more, be punished; that the Commission of Twelve be irrecoverably broken. The heart of the Gironde dies within it; distant are the Seventy-two respectable Departments, this fiery Municipality is near! Barrère is for a middle course; granting something. The Commission of Twelve declares that, not waiting to be broken, it hereby breaks itself, and is no more. Fain would Reporter Rabaut speak his and its last-words; but he is bellowed off. Too happy that the Twenty-two are still left unviolated!—Vergniaud, carrying the laws of refinement to a great length, moves, to the amazement of some, that "the Sections of Paris have deserved well of their country." Whereupon, at a late hour of the evening, the deserving Sections retire to their respective places of abode. Barrère shall report on it. With busy quill and brain he sits, secluded; for him no sleep tonight. Friday the last of May has ended in this manner.

The Sections have deserved well: but ought they not to deserve better? Faction and Girondism is struck down for the moment, and consents to be a nullity; but will it not, at another favourabler moment rise, still feller; and the Republic have to be saved in spite of it? So reasons Patriotism, still Permanent; so reasons the Figure of Marat, visible in the dim Section-world, on the morrow. To the conviction of men!—And so at eventide of Saturday, when Barrère had just got it all varnished in the course of the day, and his Report was setting off in the evening mail-bags, tocsin peals out *again!* *Générale* is beating; armed men taking station in the Place Vendôme and elsewhere for the night; supplied with provisions and liquor. There under the summer stars will they wait, this night, what is to be seen and to be done, Henriot and Townhall giving due signal.

The Convention, at sound of *générale*, hastens back to its Hall; but to the number only of a Hundred; and does little business, puts off business till the morrow. The Girondins do not stir out thither, the Girondins are abroad seeking beds. Poor Rabaut, on the morrow morning, returning to his post, with Louvet and some others, through streets all in ferment, wrings his hands, ejaculating, '*Illa suprema dies!*'[652] It has become Sunday, the second day of June, year 1793, by the old style; by the new style, year One of Liberty, Equality, Fraternity. We have got to the last scene of all, that ends this history of the Girondin Senatorship.

It seems doubtful whether any terrestrial Convention had ever met in such circumstances as this National one now does. Tocsin is pealing; Barriers shut; all Paris is on the gaze, or under arms. As many as a Hundred Thousand under arms they count: National Force; and the Armed Volunteers, who should have flown to the Frontiers and La Vendée; but would not, treason being unpunished; and only flew hither and thither! So many, steady under arms, environ the National Tuileries and Garden. There are horse, foot, artillery, sappers with beards: the artillery one can see with their camp-furnaces in this National Garden, heating bullets red, and their match is lighted. Henriot in plumes rides, amid a plumed Staff: all posts and issues are safe; reserves lie out, as far as the Wood of Boulogne; the choicest Patriots nearest the scene. One other circumstance we will note: that a careful Municipality, liberal of camp-furnaces, has not forgotten provision-carts. No member of the Sovereign need now go home to dinner; but can keep rank, —plentiful victual circulating unsought. Does not this People understand Insurrection? Ye, *not* uninventive, *Gualches!* —

Therefore let a National Representation, "mandatories of the Sovereign," take thought of it. Expulsion of your Twenty-two, and your Commission of Twelve: we stand here till it be done! Deputation after Deputation, in ever stronger language, comes with that message. Barrère proposes a middle course:—Will not perhaps the inculpated Deputies consent to withdraw voluntarily; to make a generous demission, and self-sacrifice for the sake of one's country? Isnard, repentant of that search on which river-bank Paris stood, declares himself ready to demit. Ready also is *Te-Deum* Fauchet; old Dusaulx of the Bastille, "*vieux radoteur,* old dotard," as Marat calls him, is still readier. On the contrary, Lanjuinais the Breton declares that there is one man who never will demit voluntarily; but will protest to the uttermost, while a voice is left him. And he accordingly goes on protesting; amid rage and clangor; Legendre crying at last: 'Lanjuinais, come down from the Tribune, or I will fling thee down, *ou je te jette en bas!*' For matters are come to extremity. Nay they do clutch hold of Lanjuinais, certain zealous Mountain-men; but cannot fling him down, for he "cramps himself on the railing;" and "his clothes get torn." Brave Senator, worthy of pity! Neither will Barbaroux demit; he 'has sworn to die at his post, and will keep that oath.' Whereupon the Galleries all rise with explosion; brandishing weapons, some of them; and rush out saying: '*Allons,* then; we must save our country!' Such a Session is this of Sunday the second of June.

Churches fill, over Christian Europe, and then empty themselves; but this Convention empties not, the while: a day of shrieking contention, of agony, humiliation and tearing of coatskirts; *illa suprema dies!* Round stand Henriot and his Hundred Thousand, copiously refreshed from tray and basket: nay he is "distributing five francs a-piece;" we Girondins saw it with our eyes; five francs to keep them in heart! And distraction of armed riot encumbers our borders, jangles at our Bar; we are prisoners in our own Hall: Bishop Grégoire could not get out for a *besoin actuel* without four gendarmes to wait on him! What is the character of a National Representative become? And now the sunlight falls yellower on western windows, and the chimney-tops are flinging longer shadows; the refreshed Hundred Thousand, nor their shadows, stir not! What to resolve on? Motion rises, superfluous one would think, That the Convention go forth in a body; ascertain with its own eyes whether it is free or not. Lo, therefore, from the Eastern Gate of the Tuileries, a distressed Convention issuing; handsome Hérault Séchelles at their head; he with hat on, in sign of public calamity, the rest bareheaded,—towards the Gate of the Carrousel; wondrous to see: towards Henriot and his plumed staff. 'In the name of the National Convention, make way!' Not an inch of the way does Henriot make: 'I receive no orders, till the Sovereign, yours and mine, has been obeyed.' The Convention presses on; Henriot prances back, with his staff, some fifteen paces, 'To arms! Cannoneers to your guns!'—flashes out his puissant sword, as the Staff all do, and the Hussars all do. Cannoneers brandish the lit match; Infantry present arms,—alas, in the level way, as if for firing! Hatted Herault leads his distressed flock, through their pinfold of a Tuileries again; across the Garden, to the Gate on the opposite side. Here is Feuillans Terrace, alas, there is our old Salle de Manége; but neither at this Gate of the Pont Tournant is there egress. Try the other; and the other: no egress! We wander disconsolate through armed ranks; who indeed salute with *Live the Republic*, but also with *Die the Gironde*. Other such sight, in the year One of Liberty, the westering sun never saw.

And now behold Marat meets us; for he lagged in this Suppliant Procession of ours: he has got some hundred elect Patriots at his heels: he orders us in the Sovereign's name to return to our place, and do as we are bidden and bound. The Convention returns. 'Does not the Convention,' says Couthon with a singular power of face, 'see that it is free?'—none but friends round it? The Convention, overflowing with friends and armed Sectioners, proceeds to vote as bidden. Many will not vote, but remain silent; some one or two protest, in words: the Mountain has a clear unanimity. Commission of Twelve, and the denounced Twenty-two, to whom we add Ex-Ministers Clavière and Lebrun: these, with some slight extempore alterations (this or that orator proposing, but Marat disposing), are voted to be under "Arrestment in their own houses." Brissot, Buzot, Vergniaud, Guadet, Louvet, Gensonné, Barbaroux, Lasource, Lanjuinais, Rabaut,—Thirty-two, by the tale; all that we have known as Girondins, and more than we have known. They, "under the safeguard of the French People;" by and by, under the safeguard of two Gendarmes each, shall dwell peaceably in their own houses; as Non-Senators; till further order. Herewith ends *Séance* of Sunday the second of June 1793.

At ten o'clock, under mild stars, the Hundred Thousand, their work well finished, turn homewards. This same day, Central Insurrection Committee has arrested Madame Roland; imprisoned her in the Abbaye. Roland has fled, no one knows whither.

Thus fell the Girondins, by Insurrection; and became extinct as a Party: not without a sigh from most Historians. The men were men of parts, of Philosophic culture, decent behaviour; not condemnable in that they were Pedants and had not better parts; not condemnable, but most unfortunate. They wanted a Republic of the Virtues, wherein themselves should be head; and they could only get a Republic of the Strengths, wherein others than they were head.

For the rest, Barrère shall make Report of it. The night concludes with a "civic promenade by torchlight:"[653] surely the true reign of Fraternity is now not far?

BOOK 3.IV.
TERROR

Chapter 3.4.I.
Charlotte Corday

In the leafy months of June and July, several French Departments germinate a set of rebellious *paper*-leaves, named Proclamations, Resolutions, Journals, or Diurnals "of the Union for Resistance to Oppression." In particular, the Town of Caen, in Calvados, sees its paper-leaf of *Bulletin de Caen* suddenly bud, suddenly establish itself as Newspaper there; under the Editorship of Girondin National Representatives!

For among the proscribed Girondins are certain of a more desperate humour. Some, as Vergniaud, Valazé, Gensonné, "arrested in their own houses" will await with stoical resignation what the issue may be. Some, as Brissot, Rabaut, will take to flight, to concealment; which, as the Paris Barriers are opened again in a day or two, is not yet difficult. But others there are who will rush, with Buzot, to Calvados; or far over France, to Lyons, Toulon, Nantes and elsewhither, and then rendezvous at Caen: to awaken as with war-trumpet the respectable Departments; and strike down an anarchic Mountain Faction; at least not yield without a stroke at it. Of this latter temper we count some score or more, of the Arrested, and of the Not-yet-arrested; a Buzot, a Barbaroux, Louvet, Guadet, Pétion, who have escaped from Arrestment in their own homes; a Salles, a Pythagorean Valady, a Duchâtel, the Duchâtel that came in blanket and nightcap to vote for the life of Louis, who have escaped from danger and likelihood of Arrestment. These, to the number at one time of Twenty-seven, do accordingly lodge here, at the "*Intendance*, or Departmental Mansion," of the Town of Caen; welcomed by Persons in Authority; welcomed and defrayed, having no money of their own. And the *Bulletin de Caen* comes forth, with the most animating paragraphs: How the Bourdeaux Department, the Lyons Department, this Department after the other is declaring itself; sixty, or say sixty-nine, or seventy-two[654] respectable Departments either declaring, or ready to declare. Nay Marseilles, it seems, will march on Paris by itself, if need be. So has Marseilles Town said, That she will march. But on the other hand, that Montélimart Town has said, No thoroughfare; and means even to "bury herself" under her own stone and mortar first—of this be no mention in *Bulletin of Caen.*

Such animating paragraphs we read in this Newspaper; and fervours, and eloquent sarcasm: tirades against the Mountain, frame pen of Deputy Salles; which resemble, say friends, Pascal's *Provincials.* What is more to the purpose, these Girondins have got a General in chief, one Wimpfen, formerly under Dumouriez; also a secondary questionable General Puisaye, and others; and are doing their best to raise a force for war. National Volunteers, whosoever is of right heart: gather in, ye National Volunteers, friends of Liberty; from our Calvados Townships, from the Eure, from Brittany, from far and near; forward to Paris, and extinguish Anarchy! Thus at Caen, in the early July days, there is a drumming and parading, a perorating and consulting: Staff and Army; Council; Club of *Carabots*, Anti-jacobin friends of Freedom, to denounce atrocious Marat. With all which, and the editing of *Bulletins*, a National Representative has his hands full.

At Caen it is most animated; and, as one hopes, more or less animated in the "Seventy-two Departments that adhere to us." And in a France begirt with Cimmerian invading Coalitions, and torn with an internal La Vendée, *this* is the conclusion we have arrived at: to put down Anarchy by Civil War! *Durum et durum*, the Proverb says, *non faciunt murum.* La Vendée burns: Santerre can do nothing there; he may return home and brew beer. Cimmerian bombshells fly all along the North. That Siege of Mentz is become famed;—lovers of the Picturesque (as Goethe will testify), washed country-people of both sexes, stroll thither on Sundays, to see the artillery work and counterwork; "you only duck a little while the shot whizzes past."[655] Condé is capitulating to the Austrians; Royal Highness of York, these several weeks, fiercely batters Valenciennes. For, alas, our fortified Camp of Famars was stormed; General Dampierre was killed; General Custine was blamed,—and indeed is now come to Paris to give "explanations."

Against all which the Mountain and atrocious Marat must even make head as they can. They, anarchic Convention as they are, publish Decrees, expostulatory, explanatory, yet not without severity; they ray forth Commissioners, singly or in pairs, the olive-branch in one hand, yet the sword in the other. Commissioners come even to Caen; but without effect.

Mathematical Romme, and Prieur named of the Côte d'Or, venturing thither, with their olive and sword, are packed into prison: there may Romme lie, under lock and key, "for fifty days;" and meditate his New Calendar, if he please. Cimmeria and Civil War! Never was Republic One and Indivisible at a lower ebb.—

Amid which dim ferment of Caen and the World, History specially notices one thing: in the lobby of the Mansion *de l'Intendance*, where busy Deputies are coming and going, a young Lady with an aged valet, taking grave graceful leave of Deputy Barbaroux.[656] She is of stately Norman figure; in her twenty-fifth year; of beautiful still countenance: her name is Charlotte Corday, heretofore styled d'Armans, while Nobility still was. Barbaroux has given her a Note to Deputy Duperret,—him who once drew his sword in the effervescence. Apparently she will to Paris on some errand? "She was a Republican before the Revolution, and never wanted energy." A completeness, a decision is in this fair female Figure: "by energy she means the spirit that will prompt one to sacrifice himself for his country." What if she, this fair young Charlotte, had emerged from her secluded stillness, suddenly like a Star; cruel-lovely, with half-angelic, half-demonic splendour; to gleam for a moment, and in a moment be extinguished: to be held in memory, so bright complete was she, through long centuries!— Quitting Cimmerian Coalitions without, and the dim-simmering Twenty-five millions within, History will look fixedly at this one fair Apparition of a Charlotte Corday; will note whither Charlotte moves, how the little Life burns forth so radiant, then vanishes swallowed of the Night.

With Barbaroux's Note of Introduction, and slight stock of luggage, we see Charlotte, on Tuesday the ninth of July, seated in the Caen Diligence, with a place for Paris. None takes farewell of her, wishes her Good-journey: her Father will find a line left, signifying that she is gone to England, that he must pardon her and forget her. The drowsy Diligence lumbers along; amid drowsy talk of Politics, and praise of the Mountain; in which she mingles not; all night, all day, and again all night. On Thursday, not long before none, we are at the Bridge of Neuilly; here is Paris with her thousand black domes,—the goal and purpose of thy journey! Arrived at the Inn de la Providence in the Rue des Vieux Augustins, Charlotte demands a room; hastens to bed; sleeps all afternoon and night, till the morrow morning.

On the morrow morning, she delivers her Note to Duperret. It relates to certain Family Papers which are in the Minister of the Interior's hand; which a Nun at Caen, an old Convent-friend of Charlotte's, has need of; which Duperret shall assist her in getting: this then was Charlotte's errand to Paris? She has finished this, in the course of Friday;—yet says nothing of returning. She has seen and silently investigated several things. The

Convention, in bodily reality, she has seen; what the Mountain is like. The living physiognomy of Marat she could not see; he is sick at present, and confined to home.

About eight on the Saturday morning, she purchases a large sheath-knife in the Palais Royal; then straightway, in the Place des Victoires, takes a hackney-coach: 'To the Rue de l'Ecole de Médecine, No. 44.' It is the residence of the Citoyen Marat!—The Citoyen Marat is ill, and cannot be seen; which seems to disappoint her much. Her business is with Marat, then? Hapless beautiful Charlotte; hapless squalid Marat! From Caen in the utmost West, from Neuchâtel in the utmost East, they two are drawing nigh each other; they two have, very strangely, business together.—Charlotte, returning to her Inn, despatches a short Note to Marat; signifying that she is from Caen, the seat of rebellion; that she desires earnestly to see him, and "will put it in his power to do France a great service." No answer. Charlotte writes another Note, still more pressing; sets out with it by coach, about seven in the evening, herself. Tired day-labourers have again finished their Week; huge Paris is circling and simmering, manifold, according to its vague wont: this one fair Figure has decision in it; drives straight,—towards a purpose.

It is yellow July evening, we say, the thirteenth of the month; eve of the Bastille day,—when "M. Marat," four years ago, in the crowd of the Pont Neuf, shrewdly required of that Besenval Hussar-party, which had such friendly dispositions, 'to dismount, and give up their arms, then;' and became notable among Patriot men! Four years: what a road he has travelled;—and sits now, about half-past seven of the clock, stewing in slipper-bath; sore afflicted; ill of Revolution Fever,—of what other malady this History had rather not name. Excessively sick and worn, poor man: with precisely elevenpence-halfpenny of ready money, in paper; with slipper-bath; strong three-footed stool for writing on, the while; and a squalid—Washerwoman, one may call her: that is his civic establishment in Medical-School Street; thither and not elsewhither has his road led him. Not to the reign of Brotherhood and Perfect Felicity; yet surely on the way towards that?—Hark, a rap again! A musical woman's-voice, refusing to be rejected: it is the Citoyenne who would do France a service. Marat, recognising from within, cries, Admit her. Charlotte Corday is admitted.

Citoyen Marat, I am from Caen the seat of rebellion, and wished to speak with you.—Be seated, *mon enfant*. Now what are the Traitors doing at Caen? What Deputies are at Caen?—Charlotte names some Deputies. 'Their heads shall fall within a fortnight,' croaks the eager People's-Friend, clutching his tablets to write: *Barbaroux, Pétion*, writes he with bare shrunk arm, turning aside in the bath: *Pétion*, and *Louvet*, and—Charlotte has drawn her knife from the sheath; plunges it, with one sure stroke, into the writer's heart. '*À moi, chère amie,* Help, dear!' No more could the Death-choked say or shriek. The helpful Washerwoman running in, there is no Friend of the People, or Friend of the Washerwoman, left; but his life with a groan gushes out, indignant, to the shades below.[657]

And so Marat People's-Friend is ended; the lone Stylites has got hurled down suddenly from his Pillar,—*whitherward* He that made him does know. Patriot Paris may sound triple and tenfold, in dole and wail; re-echoed by Patriot France; and the Convention, "Chabot pale with terror declaring that they are to be all assassinated," may decree him Pantheon Honours, Public Funeral, Mirabeau's dust making way for him; and Jacobin Societies, in lamentable oratory, summing up his character, parallel him to One, whom they think it honour to call "the good Sansculotte,"—whom we name not here.[658] Also a Chapel may be made, for the urn that holds his Heart, in the Place du Carrousel; and new-born children be named Marat; and Lago-de-Como Hawkers bake mountains of stucco into unbeautiful Busts; and David paint his Picture, or Death-scene; and such other Apotheosis take place as the human genius, in these circumstances, can devise: but Marat returns no more to the light of this Sun. One sole circumstance we have read with clear sympathy, in the old *Moniteur* Newspaper: how Marat's brother comes from Neuchâtel to ask of the Convention "that the deceased Jean-Paul Marat's musket be given him."[659] For Marat too had a brother, and natural affections; and was wrapt once in swaddling-clothes, and slept safe in a cradle like the rest of us. Ye children of men!—A sister of his, they say, lives still to this day in Paris.

As for Charlotte Corday her work is accomplished; the recompense of it is near and sure. The *chère amie,* and neighbours of the house, flying at her, she "overturns some movables," entrenches herself till the gendarmes arrive; then quietly surrenders; goes quietly to the Abbaye Prison: she alone quiet, all Paris sounding in wonder, in rage or admiration, round her. Duperret is put in arrest, on account of her; his Papers sealed,—which may lead to consequences. Fauchet, in like manner; though Fauchet had not so much as heard of her. Charlotte, confronted with these two Deputies, praises the grave firmness of Duperret, censures the dejection of Fauchet.

On Wednesday morning, the thronged Palais de Justice and Revolutionary Tribunal can see her face; beautiful and calm: she dates it "fourth day of the Preparation of Peace." A strange murmur ran through the Hall, at sight of her; you could not say of what character.[660] Tinville has his indictments and tape-papers the cutler of the Palais Royal will testify that he sold her the sheath-knife; 'all these details are needless,' interrupted Charlotte; 'it is I that killed Marat.' By whose instigation?—'By no one's.' What tempted you, then? His crimes. 'I killed one man,' added she, raising her voice extremely (*extrêmement*), as they went on with their questions, 'I killed one man to save a hundred thousand; a villain to save innocents; a savage wild-beast to give repose to my country. I was a Republican before the Revolution; I never wanted energy.' There is therefore nothing to be said. The public gazes astonished: the hasty limners sketch her features, Charlotte not disapproving; the men of law proceed with their formalities. The doom is Death as a murderess. To her Advocate she gives thanks; in gentle phrase, in high-flown classical spirit. To the Priest they send her she gives thanks; but needs not any shriving, or ghostly or other aid from him.

On this same evening, therefore, about half-past seven o'clock, from the gate of the Conciergerie, to a City all on tiptoe, the fatal Cart issues: seated on it a fair young creature, sheeted in red smock of Murderess; so beautiful, serene, so full of life; journeying towards death,—alone amid the world. Many take off their hats, saluting reverently; for what heart but must be touched?[661] Others growl and howl. Adam Lux, of Mentz, declares that she is greater than Brutus; that it were beautiful to die with her: the head of this young man seems turned. At the Place de la Révolution, the countenance of Charlotte wears the same still smile. The executioners proceed to bind her feet; she resists, thinking it meant as an insult; on a word of explanation, she submits with cheerful apology. As the last act, all being now ready, they take the neckerchief from her neck: a blush of maidenly shame overspreads that fair face and neck; the cheeks were still tinged with it, when the executioner lifted the severed head, to shew it to the people. "It is most true," says Foster, "that he struck the cheek insultingly; for I saw it with my eyes: the Police imprisoned him for it."[662]

In this manner have the Beautifullest and the Squalidest come in collision, and extinguished one another. Jean-Paul Marat and Marie-Anne Charlotte Corday both, suddenly, are no more. "Day of the Preparation of Peace?" Alas, how were peace possible or preparable, while, for example, the hearts of lovely Maidens, in their convent-stillness, are dreaming not of Love-paradises, and the light of Life; but of Codrus'-sacrifices, and death well earned? That Twenty-five million hearts have got to such temper, this *is* the Anarchy; the soul of it lies in this: whereof not peace can be the embodiment! The death of Marat, whetting old animosities tenfold, will be worse than any life. O ye hapless Two, mutually extinctive, the Beautiful and the Squalid, sleep ye well,—in the Mother's bosom that bore you both!

This was the History of Charlotte Corday; most definite, most complete; angelic-demonic: like a Star! Adam Lux goes home, half-delirious; to pour forth his Apotheosis of her, in paper and print; to propose that she have a statue with this inscription, *Greater than Brutus*. Friends represent his danger; Lux is reckless; thinks it were beautiful to die with her.

Chapter 3.4.II.
In Civil War

But during these same hours, another guillotine is at work, on another: Charlotte, for the Girondins, dies at Paris today; Chalier, by the Girondins, dies at Lyons tomorrow.

From rumbling of cannon along the streets of that City, it has come to firing of them, to rabid fighting: Nièvre-Chol and the Girondins triumph;— behind whom there is, as everywhere, a Royalist Faction waiting to strike in. Trouble enough at Lyons; and the dominant party carrying it with a high hand! For indeed, the whole South is astir; incarcerating Jacobins; arming for Girondins: wherefore we have got a "Congress of Lyons;" also a "Revolutionary Tribunal of Lyons," and Anarchists shall tremble. So Chalier was soon found guilty, of Jacobinism, of murderous Plot, "address with drawn dagger on the sixth of February last;" and, on the morrow, he also travels his final road, along the streets of Lyons, "by the side of an ecclesiastic, with whom he seems to speak earnestly,"—the axe now glittering high. He could weep, in old years, this man, and "fall on his knees on the pavement," blessing Heaven at sight of Federation Programs or like; then he pilgrimed to Paris, to worship Marat and the Mountain: now Marat and he are both gone;—we said he could not end well. Jacobinism groans inwardly, at Lyons; but dare not outwardly. Chalier, when the Tribunal sentenced him, made answer: 'My death will cost this City dear.'

Montélimart Town is not buried under its ruins; yet Marseilles is actually marching, under order of a "Lyons Congress;" is incarcerating Patriots; the very Royalists now shewing face. Against which a General Cartaux fights, though in small force; and with him an Artillery Major, of the name of— Napoleon Buonaparte. This Napoleon, to prove that the Marseillese have no chance ultimately, not only fights but writes; publishes his *Supper of Beaucaire*, a Dialogue which has become curious.[663] Unfortunate Cities, with their actions and their reactions! Violence to be paid with violence in geometrical ratio; Royalism and Anarchism both striking in;—the final net-amount of which geometrical series, what man shall sum?

The Bar of Iron has never yet floated in Marseilles Harbour; but the Body of Rebecqui was found floating, self-drowned there. Hot Rebecqui seeing how confusion deepened, and Respectability grew poisoned with Royalism, felt that there was no refuge for a Republican but death. Rebecqui disappeared: no one knew whither; till, one morning, they found the empty case or body of him risen to the top, tumbling on the salt waves;[664] and perceived that Rebecqui had withdrawn forever.—Toulon likewise is incarcerating Patriots; sending delegates to Congress; intriguing, in case of necessity, with the Royalists and English. Montpellier, Bourdeaux, Nantes: all France, that is not under the swoop of Austria and Cimmeria, seems rushing into madness, and suicidal ruin. The Mountain labours; like a volcano in a burning volcanic Land. Convention Committees, of Surety, of Salvation, are busy night and day: Convention Commissioners whirl on all highways; bearing olive-branch and sword, or now perhaps sword only. Chaumette and Municipals come daily to the Tuileries demanding a Constitution: it is some weeks now since he resolved, in Townhall, that a Deputation "should go every day" and demand a Constitution, till one were got;[665] whereby suicidal France might rally and pacify itself; a thing inexpressibly desirable.

This then is the fruit your Anti-anarchic Girondins have got from that Levying of War in Calvados? This fruit, we may say; and no other whatsoever. For indeed, before either Charlotte's or Chalier's head had fallen, the Calvados War itself had, as it were, vanished, dreamlike, in a shriek! With "seventy-two Departments" on one's side, one might have hoped better things. But it turns out that Respectabilities, though they will vote, will not fight. Possession is always nine points in Law; but in Lawsuits of *this* kind, one may say, it is ninety-and-nine points. Men do what they were wont to do; and have immense irresolution and inertia: they obey him who has the symbols that claim obedience. Consider what, in modern society, this one fact means: the Metropolis is with our enemies! Metropolis, *Mother-city;* rightly so named: all the rest are but as her children, her nurselings. Why, there is not a leathern Diligence, with its post-bags and luggage-boots, that lumbers out from her, but is as a huge life-pulse; she is the heart of all. Cut short that one leathern Diligence, how much is cut short!—General Wimpfen, looking practically into the matter, can see nothing for it but that one should fall back on Royalism; get into communication with Pitt! Dark innuendoes he flings out, to that effect: whereat we Girondins start, horrorstruck. He produces as his Second in command a certain "*Ci-devant,*" one Comte Puisaye; entirely unknown to Louvet; greatly suspected by him.

Few wars, accordingly, were ever levied of a more insufficient character than this of Calvados. He that is curious in such things may read the details of it in the Memoirs of that same *Ci-devant* Puisaye, the much-enduring man and Royalist: How our Girondin National Forces, marching off with plenty of wind-music, were drawn out about the old Château of Brecourt, in the wood-country near Vernon, to meet the Mountain National forces advancing from Paris. How on the fifteenth afternoon of July, they did meet,—and, as it were, shrieked mutually, and took mutually to flight without loss. How Puisaye thereafter, for the Mountain Nationals fled first, and we thought ourselves the victors,—was roused from his warm bed in the Castle of Brecourt; and had to gallop without boots; our Nationals, in the night-watches, having fallen unexpectedly into *sauve qui peut:*—and in brief the Calvados War had burnt priming; and the only question now was, Whitherward to vanish, in what hole to hide oneself![666]

The National Volunteers rush homewards, faster than they came. The Seventy-two Respectable Departments, says Meillan, "all turned round, and forsook us, in the space of four-and-twenty hours." Unhappy those who, as at Lyons for instance, have gone too far for turning! "One morning," we find placarded on our Intendance Mansion, the Decree of Convention which casts us *Hors la loi,* into Outlawry: placarded by our Caen Magistrates;—clear hint that we also are to vanish. Vanish, indeed: but whitherward? Gorsas has friends in Rennes; he will hide there,—unhappily will not lie hid. Guadet, Lanjuinais are on cross roads; making for Bourdeaux. To Bourdeaux! cries the general voice, of Valour alike and of Despair. Some flag of Respectability still floats there, or is thought to float.

Thitherward therefore; each as he can! Eleven of these ill-fated Deputies, among whom we may count, as twelfth, Friend Riouffe the Man of Letters, do an original thing. Take the uniform of National Volunteers, and retreat southward with the Breton Battalion, as private soldiers of that corps. These brave Bretons had stood truer by us than any other. Nevertheless, at the end of a day or two, they also do now get dubious, self-divided; we must part from them; and, with some half-dozen as convoy or guide, retreat by ourselves,—a solitary marching detachment, through waste regions of the West.[667]

Chapter 3.4.III.
Retreat of the Eleven

It is one of the notablest Retreats, this of the Eleven, that History presents: The handful of forlorn Legislators retreating there, continually, with shouldered firelock and well-filled cartridge-box, in the yellow autumn; long hundreds of miles between them and Bourdeaux; the country all getting hostile, suspicious of the truth; simmering and buzzing on all sides, more and more. Louvet has preserved the Itinerary of it; a piece worth all the rest he ever wrote.

O virtuous Pétion, with thy early-white head, O brave young Barbaroux, has it come to this? Weary ways, worn shoes, light purse;—encompassed with perils as with a sea! Revolutionary Committees are in every Township; of Jacobin temper; our friends all cowed, our cause the losing one. In the Borough of Moncontour, by ill chance, it is market-day: to the gaping public such transit of a solitary Marching Detachment is suspicious; we have need of energy, of promptitude and luck, to be allowed to march through. Hasten, ye weary pilgrims! The country is getting up; noise of you is bruited day after day, a solitary Twelve retreating in this mysterious manner: with every new day, a wider wave of inquisitive pursuing tumult is stirred up till the whole West will be in motion. "Cussy is tormented with gout, Buzot is too fat for marching." Riouffe, blistered, bleeding, marching only on tiptoe; Barbaroux limps with sprained ancle, yet ever cheery, full of hope and valour. Light Louvet glances hare-eyed, not hare-hearted: only virtuous Pétion's serenity "was but once seen ruffled."[668] They lie in straw-lofts, in woody brakes; rudest paillasse on the floor of a secret friend is luxury. They are seized in the dead of night by Jacobin mayors and tap of drum; get off by firm countenance, rattle of muskets, and ready wit.

Of Bourdeaux, through fiery La Vendée and the long geographical spaces that remain, it were madness to think: well, if you can get to Quimper on the sea-coast, and take shipping there. Faster, ever faster! Before the end of the march, so hot has the country grown, it is found advisable to march all night. They do it; under the still night-canopy they plod along;—and yet behold, Rumour has outplodded them. In the paltry Village of Carhaix (be its thatched huts, and bottomless peat-bogs, long notable to the Traveller), one is astonished to find light still glimmering: citizens are awake, with rush-lights burning, in that nook of the terrestrial Planet; as we traverse swiftly the one poor street, a voice is heard saying, 'There they are, *Les voilà qui passent!*'[669] Swifter, ye doomed lame Twelve: speed ere they can arm; gain the Woods of Quimper before day, and lie squatted there!

The doomed Twelve do it; though with difficulty, with loss of road, with peril, and the mistakes of a night. In Quimper are Girondin friends, who perhaps will harbour the homeless, till a Bourdeaux ship weigh. Wayworn, heartworn, in agony of suspense, till Quimper friendship get warning, they lie there, squatted under the thick wet boscage; suspicious of the face of man. Some pity to the brave; to the unhappy! Unhappiest of all Legislators, O when ye packed your luggage, some score, or two-score months ago; and mounted this or the other leathern vehicle, to be Conscript Fathers of a regenerated France, and reap deathless laurels,—did ye think your journey was to lead *hither?* The Quimper Samaritans find them squatted; lift them up to help and comfort; will hide them in sure places. Thence let them dissipate gradually; or there they can lie quiet, and write *Memoirs*, till a Bourdeaux ship sail.

And thus, in Calvados all is dissipated; Romme is out of prison, meditating his Calendar; ringleaders are locked in his room. At Caen the Corday family mourns in silence; Buzot's House is a heap of dust and demolition; and amid the rubbish sticks a Gallows, with this inscription, *Here dwelt the Traitor Buzot who conspired against the Republic.* Buzot and the other vanished Deputies are *hors la loi*, as we saw; their lives free to take where they can be found. The worse fares it with the poor Arrested visible Deputies at Paris. "Arrestment at home" threatens to become "Confinement in the Luxembourg;" to end: *where?* For example, what pale-visaged thin man is this, journeying towards Switzerland as a Merchant of Neuchâtel, whom they arrest in the town of Moulins? To Revolutionary Committee he is suspect. To Revolutionary Committee, on probing the matter, he is evidently: Deputy Brissot! Back to thy Arrestment, poor Brissot; or indeed to strait confinement,—whither others are fared to follow. Rabaut has built himself a false-partition, in a friend's house; lives, in invisible darkness, between two walls. It will end, this same Arrestment business, in Prison, and the Revolutionary Tribunal.

Nor must we forget Duperret, and the seal put on his papers by reason of Charlotte. One Paper is there, fit to breed woe enough: A secret solemn Protest against that *suprema dies* of the Second of June! This Secret Protest our poor Duperret had drawn up, the same week, in all plainness of speech;

waiting the time for publishing it: to which Secret Protest his signature, and that of other honourable Deputies not a few, stands legibly appended. And now, if the seals were once broken, the Mountain still victorious? Such Protestors, your Merciers, Bailleuls, Seventy-three by the tale, what yet remains of Respectable Girondism in the Convention, may tremble to think!—These are the fruits of levying civil war.

Also we find, that, in these last days of July, the famed Siege of Mentz is *finished*; the Garrison to march out with honours of war; not to serve against the Coalition for a year! Lovers of the Picturesque, and Goethe standing on the Chaussée of Mentz, saw, with due interest, the Procession issuing forth, in all solemnity:

"Escorted by Prussian horse came first the French Garrison. Nothing could look stranger than this latter: a column of Marseillese, slight, swarthy, party-coloured, in patched clothes, came tripping on;—as if King Edwin had opened the Dwarf Hill, and sent out his nimble Host of Dwarfs. Next followed regular troops; serious, sullen; not as if downcast or ashamed. But the remarkablest appearance, which struck every one, was that of the Chasers (*Chasseurs*) coming out mounted: they had advanced quite silent to where we stood, when their Band struck up the *Marseillaise*. This Revolutionary *Te-Deum* has in itself something mournful and bodeful, however briskly played; but at present they gave it in altogether slow time, proportionate to the creeping step they rode at. It was piercing and fearful, and a most serious-looking thing, as these cavaliers, long, lean men, of a certain age, with mien suitable to the music, came pacing on: singly you might have likened them to Don Quixote; in mass, they were highly dignified.

"But now a single troop became notable: that of the Commissioners or *Représentans*. Merlin of Thionville, in hussar uniform, distinguishing himself by wild beard and look, had another person in similar costume on his left; the crowd shouted out, with rage, at sight of this latter, the name of a Jacobin Townsman and Clubbist; and shook itself to seize him. Merlin drew bridle; referred to his dignity as French Representative, to the vengeance that should follow any injury done; he would advise every one to compose himself, for this was not the *last time* they would see him here.[670] Thus rode Merlin; threatening in defeat. But what now shall stem that tide of Prussians setting in through the open North-East?" Lucky, if fortified Lines of Weissembourg, and impassibilities of Vosges Mountains, confine it to French Alsace, keep it from submerging the very heart of the country!

Furthermore, precisely in the same days, Valenciennes Siege is finished, in the North-West:—fallen, under the red hail of York! Condé fell some fortnight since. Cimmerian Coalition presses on. What seems very notable too, on all these captured French Towns there flies not the Royalist fleur-de-lys, in the name of a new Louis the Pretender; but the Austrian flag flies; as if Austria meant to keep them for herself! Perhaps General Custines, still in Paris, can give some explanation of the fall of these strong-places? Mother Society, from tribune and gallery, growls loud that he ought to do it;— remarks, however, in a splenetic manner that "the *Monsieurs* of the Palais Royal" are calling, Long-life to this General.

The Mother Society, purged now, by successive "scrutinies or *épurations*," from all taint of Girondism, has become a great Authority: what we can call shield-bearer, or bottle-holder, nay call it fugleman, to the purged National Convention itself. The Jacobins Debates are reported in the *Moniteur*, like Parliamentary ones.

Chapter 3.4.IV.

O Nature

But looking more specially into Paris City, what is this that History, on the 10th of August, Year One of Liberty, "by old-style, year 1793," discerns there? Praised be the Heavens, a new Feast of Pikes!

For Chaumette's "Deputation every day" has worked out its result: a Constitution. It was one of the rapidest Constitutions ever put together; made, some say in eight days, by Hérault Séchelles and others: probably a workmanlike, roadworthy Constitution enough;—on which point, however, we are, for some reasons, little called to form a judgment. Workmanlike or not, the Forty-four Thousand Communes of France, by overwhelming majorities, did hasten to accept it; glad of any Constitution whatsoever. Nay Departmental Deputies have come, the venerablest Republicans of each Department, with solemn message of Acceptance; and now what remains but that our new Final Constitution be proclaimed, and sworn to, in Feast of Pikes? The Departmental Deputies, we say, are come some time ago;— Chaumette very anxious about them, lest Girondin *Monsieurs*, Agio-jobbers, or were it even *Filles de joie* of a Girondin temper, corrupt their morals.[671] Tenth of August, immortal Anniversary, greater almost than Bastille July, is the Day.

Painter David has not been idle. Thanks to David and the French genius, there steps forth into the sunlight, this day, a Scenic Phantasmagory unexampled:—whereof History, so occupied with Real-Phantasmagories, will say but little.

For one thing, History can notice with satisfaction, on the ruins of the Bastille, a *Statue of Nature*; gigantic, spouting water from her two *mammelles*. Not a Dream this; but a Fact, palpable visible. There she spouts, great Nature; dim, before daybreak. But as the coming Sun ruddies the East, come countless Multitudes, regulated and unregulated; come Departmental Deputies, come Mother Society and Daughters; comes National Convention, led on by handsome Herault; soft wind-music breathing note of expectation. Lo, as great Sol scatters his first fire-handful, tipping the hills and chimney-heads with gold, Herault is at great Nature's feet (she is Plaster of Paris merely); Herault lifts, in an iron saucer, water spouted from the sacred breasts; drinks of it, with an eloquent Pagan Prayer, beginning, 'O Nature!' and all the Departmental Deputies drink, each with what best suitable ejaculation or prophetic-utterance is in him;—amid breathings, which become blasts, of wind-music; and the roar of artillery and human throats: finishing well the first act of this solemnity.

Next are processionings along the Boulevards: Deputies or Officials bound together by long indivisible tricolor riband; general "members of the Sovereign" walking pellmell, with pikes, with hammers, with the tools and emblems of their crafts; among which we notice a Plough, and ancient Baucis and Philemon seated on it, drawn by their children. Many-voiced harmony and dissonance filling the air. Through Triumphal Arches enough: at the basis of the first of which, we descry—whom thinkest thou?—the Heroines of the Insurrection of Women. Strong Dames of the Market, they sit there (Théroigne too ill to attend, one fears), with oak-branches, tricolor bedizenment; firm-seated on their Cannons. To whom handsome Herault, making pause of admiration, addresses soothing eloquence; whereupon they rise and fall into the march.

And now mark, in the Place de la Révolution, what other August Statue may this be; veiled in canvas,—which swiftly we shear off by pulley and cord? The *Statue of Liberty!* She too is of plaster, hoping to become of metal; stands where a Tyrant Louis Quinze once stood. "Three thousand birds" are let loose, into the whole world, with labels round their neck, *We are free; imitate us.* Holocaust of Royalist and *ci-devant* trumpery, such as one could still gather, is burnt; pontifical eloquence must be uttered, by handsome Herault, and Pagan orisons offered up.

And then forward across the River; where is new enormous Statuary; enormous plaster Mountain; Hercules-*Peuple*, with uplifted all-conquering club; "many-headed Dragon of Girondin Federalism rising from fetid marsh;"—needing new eloquence from Herault. To say nothing of Champ-de-Mars, and Fatherland's Altar there; with urn of slain Defenders, Carpenter's-level of the Law; and such exploding, gesticulating and perorating, that Herault's lips must be growing white, and his tongue cleaving to the roof of his mouth.[672]

Towards six-o'clock let the wearied President, let Paris Patriotism generally sit down to what repast, and social repasts, can be had; and with flowing tankard or light-mantling glass, usher in this New and Newest Era. In fact, is not Romme's New Calendar getting ready? On all housetops flicker little tricolor Flags, their flagstaff a Pike and Liberty-Cap. On all house-walls, for no Patriot, not suspect, will be behind another, there stand printed these words: *Republic one and indivisible, Liberty, Equality, Fraternity, or Death.*

As to the New Calendar, we may say here rather than elsewhere that speculative men have long been struck with the inequalities and incongruities of the Old Calendar; that a New one has long been as good as determined on. Maréchal the Atheist, almost ten years ago, proposed a New Calendar, free at least from superstition: this the Paris Municipality would now adopt, in defect of a better; at all events, let us have either this of Maréchal's or a better, —the New Era being come. Petitions, more than once, have been sent to that effect; and indeed, for a year past, all Public Bodies, Journalists, and Patriots in general, have dated *First Year of the Republic.* It is a subject not without difficulties. But the Convention has taken it up; and Romme, as we say, has been meditating it; not Maréchal's New Calendar, but a better New one of Romme's and our own. Romme, aided by a Monge, a Lagrange and others, furnishes mathematics; Fabre d'Eglantine furnishes poetic nomenclature: and so, on the 5th of October 1793, after trouble enough, they bring forth this New Republican Calendar of theirs, in a complete state; and by Law, get it put in action.

Four equal Seasons, Twelve equal Months of thirty days each: this makes three hundred and sixty days; and five odd days remain to be disposed of. The five odd days we will make Festivals, and name the five *Sansculottides,* or Days without Breeches. Festival of Genius; Festival of Labour; of Actions; of Rewards; of Opinion: these are the five Sansculottides. Whereby the great Circle, or Year, is made complete: solely every fourth year, whilom called Leap-year, we introduce a sixth Sansculottide; and name it Festival of the Revolution. Now as to the day of commencement, which offers difficulties, is it not one of the luckiest coincidences that the Republic herself commenced on the 21st of September; close on the Vernal Equinox? Vernal Equinox, at midnight for the meridian of Paris, in the year whilom Christian 1792, from that moment shall the New Era reckon itself to begin. *Vendémiaire, Brumaire, Frimaire;* or as one might say, in mixed English, *Vintagearious, Fogarious, Frostarious:* these are our three Autumn months. *Nivose, Pluviose, Ventose,* or say *Snowous, Rainous, Windous,* make our Winter season. *Germinal, Floréal, Prairial,* or *Buddal, Floweral, Meadowal,* are our Spring season. *Messidor, Thermidor, Fructidor,* that is to say (*dor* being Greek for *gift*), *Reapidor, Heatidor, Fruitidor,* are Republican Summer. These Twelve, in a singular manner, divide the Republican Year. Then as to minuter subdivisions, let us venture at once on a bold stroke: adopt your decimal subdivision; and instead of world-old Week, or *Se'ennight,* make it a *Tennight* or *Décade;* —not without results. There are three Decades, then, in each of the months; which is very regular; and the *Decadi*, or Tenth-day, shall always be "the Day of Rest." And the Christian Sabbath, in that case? Shall shift for itself!

This, in brief, in this New Calendar of Romme and the Convention; calculated for the meridian of Paris, and Gospel of Jean-Jacques: not one of the least afflicting occurrences for the actual British reader of French History;—confusing the soul with *Messidors, Meadowals;* till at last, in self-defence, one is forced to construct some ground-scheme, or rule of Commutation from New-style to Old-style, and have it lying by him. Such ground-scheme, almost worn out in our service, but still legible and printable, we shall now, in a Note, present to the reader. For the Romme Calendar, in so many Newspapers, Memoirs, Public Acts, has stamped itself deep into that section of Time: a New Era that lasts some Twelve years and odd is not to be despised.[673] Let the reader, therefore, with such ground-scheme, help himself, where needful, out of New-style into Old-style, called also "slave-style, *stile-esclave;*"—whereof we, in these pages, shall as much as possible use the latter only.

Thus with new Feast of Pikes, and New Era or New Calendar, did France accept her New Constitution: the most Democratic Constitution ever committed to paper. How it will work in practice? Patriot Deputations from time to time solicit fruition of it; that it be set a-going. Always, however, this seems questionable; for the moment, unsuitable. Till, in some weeks, *Salut Public*, through the organ of Saint-Just, makes report, that, in the present alarming circumstances, the state of France is Revolutionary; that her "Government must be Revolutionary till the Peace!" Solely as Paper, then, and as a Hope, must this poor New Constitution exist;—in which shape we may conceive it lying; even now, with an infinity of other things, in that Limbo near the Moon. Further than paper it never got, nor ever will get.

Chapter 3.4.V.
Sword of Sharpness

In fact it is something quite other than paper theorems, it is iron and audacity that France now needs.

Is not La Vendée still blazing;—alas too literally; rogue Rossignol burning the very corn-mills? General Santerre could do nothing there; General Rossignol, in blind fury, often in liquor, can do less than nothing. Rebellion spreads, grows ever madder. Happily those lean Quixote-figures, whom we saw retreating out of Mentz, "bound not to serve against the Coalition for a year," have got to Paris. National Convention packs them into post-vehicles and conveyances; sends them swiftly, by post, into La Vendée! There valiantly struggling, in obscure battle and skirmish, under rogue Rossignol, let them, unlaurelled, save the Republic, and "be cut down gradually to the last man."[674]

Does not the Coalition, like a fire-tide, pour in; Prussia through the opened North-East; Austria, England through the North-West? General Houchard prospers no better there than General Custine did: let him look to it! Through the Eastern and the Western Pyrenees Spain has deployed itself; spreads, rustling with Bourbon banners, over the face of the South. Ashes and embers of confused Girondin civil war covered that region already. Marseilles is damped down, not quenched; to be quenched in blood. Toulon, terrorstruck, too far gone for turning, has flung itself, ye righteous Powers,—into the hands of the English! On Toulon Arsenal there flies a Flag,—nay not even the Fleur-de-lys of a Louis Pretender; there flies that accursed St. George's Cross of the English and Admiral Hood! What remnants of sea-craft, arsenals, roperies, war-navy France had, has given itself to these enemies of human nature, "*ennemis du genre humain.*" Beleaguer it, bombard it, ye Commissioners Barras, Fréron, Robespierre Junior; thou General Cartaux, General Dugommier; above all, thou remarkable Artillery-Major, Napoleon Buonaparte! Hood is fortifying himself, victualling himself; means, apparently, to make a new Gibraltar of it.

But lo, in the Autumn night, late night, among the last of August, what sudden red sunblaze is this that has risen over Lyons City; with a noise to deafen the world? It is the Powder-tower of Lyons, nay the Arsenal with four Powder-towers, which has caught fire in the Bombardment; and sprung into the air, carrying "a hundred and seventeen houses" after it. With a light, one fancies, as of the noon sun; with a roar second only to the Last Trumpet! All living sleepers far and wide it has awakened. What a sight was that, which the eye of History saw, in the sudden nocturnal sunblaze! The roofs of hapless Lyons, and all its domes and steeples made momentarily clear; Rhone and Saone streams flashing suddenly visible; and height and hollow, hamlet and smooth stubblefield, and all the region round;—heights, alas, all scarped and counterscarped, into trenches, curtains, redouts; blue Artillery-men, little Powder-devilkins, plying their hell-trade there, through the *not* ambrosial night! Let the darkness cover it again; for it pains the eye. Of a truth, Chalier's death is costing this City dear. Convention Commissioners, Lyons Congresses have come and gone; and action there was and reaction; bad ever growing worse; till it has come to this: Commissioner Dubois-Crancé, "with seventy thousand men, and all the Artillery of several Provinces," bombarding Lyons day and night.

Worse things still are in store. Famine is in Lyons, and ruin, and fire. Desperate are the sallies of the besieged; brave Précy, their National Colonel and Commandant, doing what is in man: desperate but ineffectual. Provisions cut off; nothing entering our city but shot and shells! The Arsenal has roared aloft; the very Hospital will be battered down, and the sick buried alive. A Black Flag hung on this latter noble Edifice, appealing to the pity of the beseigers; for though maddened, were they not still our brethren? In their blind wrath, they took it for a flag of defiance, and aimed thitherward the more. Bad is growing ever worse here: and how will the worse stop, till it have grown worst of all? Commissioner Dubois will listen to no pleading, to no speech, save this only, "We surrender at discretion." Lyons contains in it subdued Jacobins; dominant Girondins; secret Royalists. And now, mere deaf madness and cannon-shot enveloping them, will not the desperate Municipality fly, at last, into the arms of Royalism itself? Majesty of Sardinia was to bring help, but it failed. Emigrant Autichamp, in name of the Two Pretender Royal Highnesses, is coming through Switzerland with help; coming, not yet come: Précy hoists the Fleur-de-lys!

At sight of which, all true Girondins sorrowfully fling down their arms:—Let our Tricolor brethren storm us, then, and slay us in their wrath: with *you* we conquer not. The famishing women and children are sent forth: deaf Dubois sends them back;—rains in mere fire and madness. Our "redouts of cotton-bags" are taken, retaken; Précy under his Fleur-de-lys is valiant as Despair. What will become of Lyons? It is a siege of seventy days. [675]

Or see, in these same weeks, far in the Western waters: breasting through the Bay of Biscay, a greasy dingy little Merchantship, with Scotch skipper; under hatches whereof sit, disconsolate,—the last forlorn nucleus of Girondism, the Deputies from Quimper! Several have dissipated themselves, whithersoever they could. Poor Riouffe fell into the talons of Revolutionary Committee, and Paris Prison. The rest sit here under hatches; reverend Pétion with his grey hair, angry Buzot, suspicious Louvet, brave young Barbaroux, and others. They have escaped from Quimper, in this sad craft; are now tacking and struggling; in danger from the waves, in danger from the English, in still worse danger from the French;—banished by Heaven and Earth to the greasy belly of this Scotch skipper's Merchant-vessel, unfruitful Atlantic raving round. They are for Bourdeaux, if peradventure hope yet linger there. Enter not Bourdeaux, O Friends! Bloody Convention Representatives, Tallien and such like, with their Edicts, with their Guillotine, have arrived there; Respectability is driven under ground; Jacobinism lords it on high. From that Réole landingplace, or *Beak of Ambès*, as it were, Pale Death, waving his Revolutionary Sword of sharpness, waves you elsewhither!

On one side or the other of that Bec d'Ambès, the Scotch Skipper with difficulty moors, a dexterous greasy man; with difficulty lands his Girondins;—who, after reconnoitring, must rapidly burrow in the Earth; and so, in subterranean ways, in friends' back-closets, in cellars, barn-lofts, in Caves of Saint-Emilion and Libourne, stave off cruel Death.[676] Unhappiest of all Senators!

Chapter 3.4.VI.
Risen against Tyrants

Against all which incalculable impediments, horrors and disasters, what can a Jacobin Convention oppose? The uncalculating Spirit of Jacobinism, and Sansculottic sans-formulistic Frenzy! Our Enemies press in on us, says Danton, but they shall not conquer us, 'we will burn France to ashes rather, *nous brûlerons la France.*'

Committees, of *Sureté* or *Salut*, have raised themselves "*à la hauteur*, to the height of circumstances." Let all mortals raise themselves *à la hauteur*. Let the Forty-four thousand Sections and their Revolutionary Committees stir every fibre of the Republic; and every Frenchman feel that he is to do or die. They are the life-circulation of Jacobinism, these Sections and Committees: Danton, through the organ of Barrère and *Salut Public*, gets decreed, That there be in Paris, by law, two meetings of Section weekly; also, that the Poorer Citizen be *paid* for attending, and have his day's-wages of Forty Sous.[677] This is the celebrated "Law of the Forty Sous;" fiercely stimulant to Sansculottism, to the life-circulation of Jacobinism.

On the twenty-third of August, Committee of Public Salvation, as usual through Barrère, had promulgated, in words not unworthy of remembering, their Report, which is soon made into a Law, of *Levy in Mass.* "All France, and whatsoever it contains of men or resources, is put under requisition," says Barrère; really in Tyrtæan words, the best we know of his. "The Republic is one vast besieged city." Two hundred and fifty Forges shall, in these days, be set up in the Luxembourg Garden, and round the outer wall of the Tuileries; to make gun-barrels; in sight of Earth and Heaven! From all hamlets, towards their Departmental Town; from all their Departmental Towns, towards the appointed Camp and seat of war, the Sons of Freedom shall march; their banner is to bear: "*Le Peuple Français debout contres les Tyrans*, The French People risen against Tyrants." "The young men shall go to the battle; it is their task to conquer: the married men shall forge arms, transport baggage and artillery; provide subsistence: the women shall work at soldiers' clothes, make tents; serve in the hospitals. The children shall scrape old-linen into surgeon's-lint: the aged men shall have themselves carried into public places; and there, by their words, excite the courage of the young; preach hatred to Kings and unity to the Republic."[678] Tyrtæan words, which tingle through all French hearts.

In this humour, then, since no other serves, will France rush against its enemies. Headlong, reckoning no cost or consequence; heeding no law or rule but that supreme law, Salvation of the People! The weapons are all the iron that is in France; the strength is that of all the men, women and children that are in France. There, in their two hundred and fifty shed-smithies, in Garden of Luxembourg or Tuileries, let them forge gun-barrels, in sight of Heaven and Earth.

Nor with heroic daring against the Foreign foe, can black vengeance against the Domestic be wanting. Life-circulation of the Revolutionary Committees being quickened by that *Law of the Forty Sous*, Deputy Merlin, not the Thionviller, whom we saw ride out of Mentz, but Merlin of Douai, named subsequently Merlin *Suspect*,—comes, about a week after, with his world-famous *Law of the Suspect:* ordering all Sections, by their Committees, instantly to arrest all Persons Suspect; and explaining withal who the Arrestable and Suspect specially are. 'Are Suspect,' says he, 'all who by their actions, by their connexions, speakings, writings have'—in short become Suspect.[679] Nay Chaumette, illuminating the matter still further, in his Municipal Placards and Proclamations, will bring it about that you may almost recognise a Suspect on the streets, and clutch him there,—off to Committee, and Prison. Watch well your words, watch well your looks: if Suspect of nothing else, you may grow, as came to be a saying, "Suspect of being Suspect!" For are we not in a State of Revolution?

No frightfuller Law ever ruled in a Nation of men. All Prisons and Houses of Arrest in French land are getting crowded to the ridge-tile: Forty-four thousand Committees, like as many companies of reapers or gleaners, gleaning France, are gathering their harvest, and storing it in these Houses. Harvest of Aristocrat tares! Nay, lest the Forty-four thousand, each on its own harvest-field, prove insufficient, we are to have an ambulant "Revolutionary Army:" six thousand strong, under right captains, this shall perambulate the country at large, and strike in wherever it finds such harvest-work slack. So have Municipality and Mother Society petitioned; so has Convention decreed.[680] Let Aristocrats, Federalists, Monsieurs vanish, and all men tremble: "The Soil of Liberty shall be purged,"—with a vengeance!

Neither hitherto has the Revolutionary Tribunal been keeping holyday. Blanchelande, for losing Saint-Domingo; "Conspirators of Orleans," for "assassinating," for assaulting the sacred Deputy Leonard-Bourdon: these with many Nameless, to whom life was sweet, have died. Daily the great Guillotine has its due. Like a black Spectre, daily at eventide, glides the Death-tumbril through the variegated throng of things. The variegated street shudders at it, for the moment; next moment forgets it: The Aristocrats! They were guilty against the Republic; their death, were it only that their goods are confiscated, will be useful to the Republic; *Vive la République!*

In the last days of August, fell a notabler head: General Custine's. Custine was accused of harshness, of unskilfulness, perfidiousness; accused of many things: found guilty, we may say, of one thing, unsuccessfulness. Hearing his unexpected Sentence, "Custine fell down before the Crucifix," silent for the space of two hours: he fared, with moist eyes and a book of prayer, towards the Place de la Révolution; glanced upwards at the clear suspended axe; then mounted swiftly aloft,[681] swiftly was struck away from the lists of the Living. He had fought in America; he was a proud, brave man; and his fortune led him *hither*.

On the 2nd of this same month, at three in the morning, a vehicle rolled off, with closed blinds, from the Temple to the Conciergerie. Within it were two Municipals; and Marie-Antoinette, once Queen of France! There in that Conciergerie, in ignominious dreary cell, she, cut off from children, kindred, friend and hope, sits long weeks; expecting when the end will be.[682]

The Guillotine, we find, gets always a quicker motion, as other things are quickening. The Guillotine, by its speed of going, will give index of the general velocity of the Republic. The clanking of its huge axe, rising and falling there, in horrid systole-diastole, is portion of the whole enormous Life-movement and pulsation of the Sansculottic System!—"Orléans Conspirators" and Assaulters had to die, in spite of much weeping and entreating; so sacred is the person of a Deputy. Yet the sacred can become desecrated: your very Deputy is not greater than the Guillotine. Poor Deputy Journalist Gorsas: we saw him hide at Rennes, when the Calvados War burnt priming. He stole afterwards, in August, to Paris; lurked several weeks about the Palais *ci-devant* Royal; was seen there, one day; was clutched, identified, and without ceremony, being already "out of the Law," was sent to the Place de la Révolution. He died, recommending his wife and children to the pity of the Republic. It is the ninth day of October 1793. Gorsas is the first Deputy that dies on the scaffold; he will not be the last.

Ex-Mayor Bailly is in prison; Ex-Procureur Manuel. Brissot and our poor Arrested Girondins have become Incarcerated Indicted Girondins; universal Jacobinism clamouring for their punishment. Duperret's Seals are *broken!* Those Seventy-three Secret Protesters, suddenly one day, are reported upon, are decreed accused; the Convention-doors being "previously shut," that none implicated might escape. They were marched, in a very rough manner, to Prison that evening. Happy those of them who chanced to be absent! Condorcet has vanished into darkness; perhaps, like Rabaut, sits between two walls, in the house of a friend.

Chapter 3.4.VII.
Marie-Antoinette

On Monday the Fourteenth of October, 1793, a Cause is pending in the Palais de Justice, in the new Revolutionary Court, such as these old stone-walls never witnessed: the Trial of Marie-Antoinette. The once brightest of Queens, now tarnished, defaced, forsaken, stands here at Fouquier Tinville's Judgment-bar; answering for her life! The Indictment was delivered her last night.[683] To such changes of human fortune what words are adequate? Silence alone is adequate.

There are few Printed things one meets with, of such tragic almost ghastly significance as those bald Pages of the *Bulletin du Tribunal Révolutionnaire*, which bear title, *Trial of the Widow Capet*. Dim, dim, as if in disastrous eclipse; like the pale kingdoms of Dis! Plutonic Judges, Plutonic Tinville; encircled, nine times, with Styx and Lethe, with Fire-Phlegethon and Cocytus named of Lamentation! The very witnesses summoned are like Ghosts: exculpatory, inculpatory, they themselves are all hovering over death and doom; they are known, in our imagination, as the prey of the Guillotine. Tall *ci-devant* Count d'Estaing, anxious to shew himself Patriot, cannot escape; nor Bailly, who, when asked If he knows the Accused, answers with a reverent inclination towards her, 'Ah, yes, I know Madame.' Ex-Patriots are here, sharply dealt with, as Procureur Manuel; Ex-Ministers, shorn of their splendour. We have cold Aristocratic impassivity, faithful to itself even in Tartarus; rabid stupidity, of Patriot Corporals, Patriot Washerwomen, who have much to say of Plots, Treasons, August Tenth, old Insurrection of Women. For all now has become a crime, in her who has *lost*.

Marie-Antoinette, in this her utter abandonment and hour of extreme need, is not wanting to herself, the imperial woman. Her look, they say, as that hideous Indictment was reading, continued calm; "she was sometimes observed moving her fingers, as when one plays on the Piano." You discern, not without interest, across that dim Revolutionary Bulletin itself, how she bears herself queenlike. Her answers are prompt, clear, often of Laconic brevity; resolution, which has grown contemptuous without ceasing to be dignified, veils itself in calm words. 'You persist then in denial?'—'My plan is not denial: it is the truth I have said, and I persist in that.' Scandalous Hébert has borne his testimony as to many things: as to one thing, concerning Marie-Antoinette and her little Son,—wherewith Human Speech had better not further be soiled. She has answered Hébert; a Juryman begs to observe that she has not answered as to this. 'I have not answered,' she exclaims with noble emotion, 'because Nature refuses to answer such a charge brought against a Mother. I appeal to all the Mothers that are here.' Robespierre, when he heard of it, broke out into something almost like swearing at the brutish blockheadism of this Hébert;[684] on whose foul head his foul lie has recoiled. At four o'clock on Wednesday morning, after two days and two nights of interrogating, jury-charging, and other darkening of counsel, the result comes out: Sentence of Death. 'Have you anything to say?' The Accused shook her head, without speech. Night's candles are burning out; and with her too Time is finishing, and it will be Eternity and Day. This Hall of Tinville's is dark, ill-lighted except where she stands. Silently she withdraws from it, to die.

Two Processions, or Royal Progresses, three-and-twenty years apart, have often struck us with a strange feeling of contrast. The first is of a beautiful Archduchess and Dauphiness, quitting her Mother's City, at the age of Fifteen; towards hopes such as no other Daughter of Eve then had: "On the morrow," says Weber an eye witness, "the Dauphiness left Vienna. The whole City crowded out; at first with a sorrow which was silent. She appeared: you saw her sunk back into her carriage; her face bathed in tears; hiding her eyes now with her handkerchief, now with her hands; several times putting out her head to see yet again this Palace of her Fathers, whither she was to return no more. She motioned her regret, her gratitude to the good Nation, which was crowding here to bid her farewell. Then arose not only tears; but piercing cries, on all sides. Men and women alike abandoned themselves to such expression of their sorrow. It was an audible sound of wail, in the streets and avenues of Vienna. The last Courier that followed her disappeared, and the crowd melted away."[685]

The young imperial Maiden of Fifteen has now become a worn discrowned Widow of Thirty-eight; grey before her time: this is the last Procession: "Few minutes after the Trial ended, the drums were beating to arms in all Sections; at sunrise the armed force was on foot, cannons getting placed at the extremities of the Bridges, in the Squares, Crossways, all along from the Palais de Justice to the Place de la Révolution. By ten o'clock, numerous patrols were circulating in the Streets; thirty thousand foot and horse drawn up under arms. At eleven, Marie-Antoinette was brought out. She had on an undress of *piqué blanc*: she was led to the place of execution, in the same manner as an ordinary criminal; bound, on a Cart; accompanied by a Constitutional Priest in Lay dress; escorted by numerous detachments of infantry and cavalry. These, and the double row of troops all along her road, she appeared to regard with indifference. On her countenance there was visible neither abashment nor pride. To the cries of *Vive la République* and *Down with Tyranny*, which attended her all the way, she seemed to pay no heed. She spoke little to her Confessor. The tricolor Streamers on the housetops occupied her attention, in the Streets du Roule and Saint-Honoré; she also noticed the Inscriptions on the house-fronts. On reaching the Place de la Révolution, her looks turned towards the *Jardin National*, whilom Tuileries; her face at that moment gave signs of lively emotion. She mounted the Scaffold with courage enough; at a quarter past Twelve, her head fell; the Executioner shewed it to the people, amid universal long-continued cries of *"Vive la République."* [686]

Chapter 3.4.VIII.
The Twenty-two

Whom next, O Tinville? The next are of a different colour: our poor Arrested Girondin Deputies. What of them could still be laid hold of; our Vergniaud, Brissot, Fauchet, Valazé, Gensonné; the once flower of French Patriotism, Twenty-two by the tale: *hither*, at Tinville's Bar, onward from "safeguard of the French People," from confinement in the Luxembourg, imprisonment in the Conciergerie, have they now, by the course of things, arrived. Fouquier Tinville must give what account of them he can.

Undoubtedly this Trial of the Girondins is the greatest that Fouquier has yet had to do. Twenty-two, all chief Republicans, ranged in a line there; the most eloquent in France; Lawyers too; not without friends in the auditory. How will Tinville prove these men guilty of Royalism, Federalism, Conspiracy against the Republic? Vergniaud's eloquence awakes once more; "draws tears," they say. And Journalists report, and the Trial lengthens itself out day after day; "threatens to become eternal," murmur many. Jacobinism and Municipality rise to the aid of Fouquier. On the 28th of the month, Hébert and others come in deputation to inform a Patriot Convention that the Revolutionary Tribunal is quite "shackled by forms of Law;" that a Patriot Jury ought to have "the power of cutting short, of *terminer les débats*, when they feel themselves convinced." Which pregnant suggestion, of cutting short, passes itself, with all despatch, into a Decree.

Accordingly, at ten o'clock on the night of the 30th of October, the Twenty-two, summoned back once more, receive this information, That the Jury feeling themselves convinced have cut short, have brought in their verdict; that the Accused are found guilty, and the Sentence on one and all of them is Death with confiscation of goods.

Loud natural clamour rises among the poor Girondins; tumult; which can only be repressed by the gendarmes. Valazé stabs himself; falls down dead on the spot. The rest, amid loud clamour and confusion, are driven back to their Conciergerie; Lasource exclaiming, 'I die on the day when the People have lost their reason; ye will die when they recover it.'[687] No help! Yielding to violence, the Doomed uplift the Hymn of the Marseillese; return singing to their dungeon.

Riouffe, who was their Prison-mate in these last days, has lovingly recorded what death they made. To our notions, it is not an edifying death. Gay satirical *Pot-pourri* by Ducos; rhymed Scenes of Tragedy, wherein Barrère and Robespierre discourse with Satan; death's eve spent in "singing" and "sallies of gaiety," with "discourses on the happiness of peoples:" these things, and the like of these, we have to accept for what they are worth. It is the manner in which the Girondins make *their* Last Supper. Valazé, with bloody breast, sleeps cold in death; hears not their singing. Vergniaud has his dose of poison; but it is not enough for his friends, it is enough only for himself; wherefore he flings it from him; presides at this Last Supper of the Girondins, with wild coruscations of eloquence, with song and mirth. Poor human Will struggles to assert itself; if not in this way, then in that.[688]

But on the morrow morning all Paris is out; such a crowd as no man had seen. The Death-carts, Valazé's cold corpse stretched among the yet living Twenty-one, roll along. Bareheaded, hands bound; in their shirt-sleeves, coat flung loosely round the neck: so fare the eloquent of France; bemurmured, beshouted. To the shouts of *Vive la République*, some of them keep answering with counter-shouts of *Vive la République*. Others, as Brissot, sit sunk in silence. At the foot of the scaffold they again strike up, with appropriate variations, the Hymn of the Marseillese. Such an act of music; conceive it well! The yet Living chant there; the chorus so rapidly wearing weak! Samson's axe is rapid; one head per minute, or little less. The chorus is worn out; farewell for evermore ye Girondins. Te-Deum Fauchet has become silent; Valazé's dead head is lopped: the sickle of the Guillotine has reaped the Girondins all away. "The eloquent, the young, the beautiful and brave!" exclaims Riouffe. O Death, what feast is toward in thy ghastly Halls?

Nor alas, in the far Bourdeaux region, will Girondism fare better. In caves of Saint-Emilion, in loft and cellar, the weariest months, roll on; apparel worn, purse empty; wintry November come; under Tallien and his Guillotine, all hope now gone. Danger drawing ever nigher, difficulty pressing ever straiter, they determine to separate. Not unpathetic the farewell; tall Barbaroux, cheeriest of brave men, stoops to clasp his Louvet: 'In what place soever thou findest my mother,' cries he, 'try to be instead of a son to her: no resource of mine but I will share with thy Wife, should chance ever lead me where she is.'[689]

Louvet went with Guadet, with Salles and Valady; Barbaroux with Buzot and Pétion. Valady soon went southward, on a way of his own. The two friends and Louvet had a miserable day and night; the 14th of November month, 1793. Sunk in wet, weariness and hunger, they knock, on the morrow, for help, at a friend's country-house; the fainthearted friend refuses to admit them. They stood therefore under trees, in the pouring rain. Flying desperate, Louvet thereupon will to Paris. He sets forth, there and then, splashing the mud on each side of him, with a fresh strength gathered from fury or frenzy. He passes villages, finding "the sentry asleep in his box in the thick rain;" he is gone, before the man can call after him. He bilks Revolutionary Committees; rides in carriers' carts, covered carts and open; lies hidden in one, under knapsacks and cloaks of soldiers' wives on the Street of Orléans, while men search for him: has hairbreadth escapes that would fill three romances: finally he gets to Paris to his fair Helpmate; gets to Switzerland, and waits better days.

Poor Guadet and Salles were both taken, ere long; they died by the Guillotine in Bourdeaux; drums beating to drown their voice. Valady also is caught, and guillotined. Barbaroux and his two comrades weathered it longer, into the summer of 1794; but not long enough. One July morning, changing their hiding place, as they have often to do, "about a league from Saint-Emilion, they observe a great crowd of country-people;" doubtless Jacobins come to take them? Barbaroux draws a pistol, shoots himself dead. Alas, and it was not Jacobins; it was harmless villagers going to a village wake. Two days afterwards, Buzot and Pétion were found in a Cornfield, their bodies half-eaten with dogs.[690]

Such was the end of Girondism. They arose to regenerate France, these men; and have accomplished *this*. Alas, whatever quarrel we had with them, has not their cruel fate abolished it? Pity only survives. So many excellent souls of heroes sent down to Hades; they themselves given as a prey of dogs and all manner of birds! But, here too, the will of the Supreme Power was accomplished. As Vergniaud said: "The Revolution, like Saturn, is devouring its own children."

BOOK 3.V.
TERROR THE ORDER OF THE DAY

Chapter 3.5.I.
Rushing down

We are now, therefore, got to that black precipitous Abyss; whither all things have long been tending; where, having now arrived on the giddy verge, they hurl down, in confused ruin; headlong, pellmell, down, down;— till Sansculottism have consummated itself; and in this wondrous French Revolution, as in a Doomsday, a World have been rapidly, if not born again, yet destroyed and engulphed. Terror has long been terrible: but to the actors themselves it has now become manifest that their appointed course is one of Terror; and they say, Be it so. '*Que la Terreur soit a l'ordre du jour.*'

So many centuries, say only from Hugh Capet downwards, had been adding together, century transmitting it with increase to century, the sum of Wickedness, of Falsehood, Oppression of man by man. Kings were sinners, and Priests were, and People. Open-Scoundrels rode triumphant, bediademed, becoronetted, bemitred; or the still fataller species of Secret-Scoundrels, in their fair-sounding formulas, speciosities, respectabilities, hollow within: the race of Quacks was grown many as the sands of the sea. Till at length such a sum of Quackery had accumulated itself as, in brief, the Earth and the Heavens were weary of. Slow seemed the Day of Settlement: coming on, all imperceptible, across the bluster and fanfaronade of Courtierisms, Conquering-Heroisms, Most-Christian *Grand Monarque*-isms. Well-beloved Pompadourisms: yet behold it was always coming; behold it has come, suddenly, unlooked for by any man! The harvest of long centuries was ripening and whitening so rapidly of late; and now it is grown *white*, and is reaped rapidly, as it were, in one day. Reaped, in this Reign of Terror; and carried home, to Hades and the Pit!—Unhappy Sons of Adam: it is ever so; and never do they know it, nor will they know it. With cheerfully smoothed countenances, day after day, and generation after generation, they, calling cheerfully to one another, 'Well-speed-ye,' are at work, *sowing the wind*. And yet, as God lives, they *shall reap the whirlwind*: no other thing, we say, is possible,—since God is a Truth and His World is a Truth.

History, however, in dealing with this Reign of Terror, has had her own difficulties. While the Phenomenon continued in its primary state, as mere "Horrors of the French Revolution," there was abundance to be said and shrieked. With and also without profit. Heaven knows there were terrors and horrors enough: yet that was not all the Phenomenon; nay, more properly, that was not the Phenomenon at all, but rather was the *shadow* of it, the negative part of it. And now, in a new stage of the business, when History, ceasing to shriek, would try rather to include under her old Forms of speech or speculation this new amazing Thing; that so some accredited scientific Law of Nature might suffice for the unexpected Product of Nature, and History might get to speak of it articulately, and draw inferences and profit from it; in this new stage, History, we must say, babbles and flounders perhaps in a still painfuller manner. Take, for example, the latest Form of speech we have seen propounded on the subject as adequate to it, almost in these months, by our worthy M. Roux, in his *Histoire Parlementaire*. The latest and the strangest: that the French Revolution was a dead-lift effort, after eighteen hundred years of preparation, to realise—the Christian Religion![691] *Unity, Indivisibility, Brotherhood or Death* did indeed stand printed on all Houses of the Living; also, on Cemeteries, or Houses of the Dead, stood printed, by order of Procureur Chaumette, Here is eternal Sleep:[692] but a Christian Religion realised by the Guillotine and Death-Eternal, "is suspect to me," as Robespierre was wont to say, "*m'est suspecte.*"

Alas, no, M. Roux! A Gospel of Brotherhood, not according to any of the Four old Evangelists, and calling on men to repent, and amend *each his own* wicked existence, that they might be saved; but a Gospel rather, as we often hint, according to a new Fifth Evangelist Jean-Jacques, calling on men to amend *each the whole world's* wicked existence, and be saved by making the Constitution. A thing different and distant *toto cœlo*, as they say: the whole breadth of the sky, and further if possible!—It is thus, however, that History, and indeed all human Speech and Reason does yet, what Father Adam began life by doing: strive to *name* the new Things it sees of Nature's producing,—often helplessly enough.

But what if History were to admit, for once, that all the Names and Theorems yet known to her fall short? That this grand Product of Nature was even grand, and new, in that it came not to range itself under old recorded Laws-of-Nature at all; but to disclose new ones? In that case, History renouncing the pretention to *name* it at present, will *look* honestly at it, and name what she can of it! Any approximation to the right Name has value: were the right name itself once here, the Thing is known thenceforth; the Thing is then ours, and can be dealt with.

Now surely not realization, of Christianity, or of aught earthly, do we discern in this Reign of Terror, in this French Revolution of which it is the consummating. Destruction rather we discern—of all that was destructible. It is as if Twenty-five millions, risen at length into the Pythian mood, had stood up simultaneously to say, with a sound which goes through far lands and times, that this Untruth of an Existence had become insupportable. O ye Hypocrisies and Speciosities, Royal mantles, Cardinal plushcloaks, ye Credos, Formulas, Respectabilities, fair-painted Sepulchres full of dead men's bones,—behold, ye appear to us to be altogether a Lie. Yet our Life is not a Lie; yet our Hunger and Misery is not a Lie! Behold we lift up, one and all, our Twenty-five million right-hands; and take the Heavens, and the Earth and also the Pit of Tophet to witness, that either ye shall be abolished, or else we shall be abolished!

No inconsiderable Oath, truly; forming, as has been often said, the most remarkable transaction in these last thousand years. Wherefrom likewise there follow, and will follow, results. The fulfilment of this Oath; that is to say, the black desperate battle of Men against their whole Condition and Environment,—a battle, alas, withal, against the Sin and Darkness that was in themselves as in others: this is the Reign of Terror. Transcendental despair was the purport of it, though not consciously so. False hopes, of Fraternity, Political Millennium, and what not, we have always seen: but the unseen heart of the whole, the transcendental despair, was not false; neither has it been of no effect. Despair, pushed far enough, completes the circle, so to speak; and becomes a kind of genuine productive hope again.

Doctrine of Fraternity, out of old Catholicism, does, it is true, very strangely in the vehicle of a Jean-Jacques Evangel, suddenly plump down out of its cloud-firmament; and from a theorem determine to make itself a practice. But just so do all creeds, intentions, customs, knowledges, thoughts and things, which the French have, suddenly plump down; Catholicism, Classicism, Sentimentalism, Cannibalism: all *isms* that make up Man in France, are rushing and roaring in that gulf; and the theorem has become a practice, and whatsoever cannot swim sinks. Not Evangelist Jean-Jacques alone; there is not a Village Schoolmaster but has contributed his quota: do we not *thou* one another, according to the Free Peoples of Antiquity? The French Patriot, in red phrygian nightcap of Liberty, christens his poor little red infant Cato,—Censor, or else of Utica. Gracchus has become Baboeuf and edits Newspapers; Mutius Scaevola, Cordwainer of that ilk, presides in the Section Mutius-Scaevola: and in brief, there is a world wholly jumbling itself, to try what will swim!

Wherefore we will, at all events, call this Reign of Terror a very strange one. Dominant Sansculottism makes, as it were, free arena; one of the strangest temporary states Humanity was ever seen in. A nation of men, full of wants and void of habits! The old habits are gone to wreck because they were old: men, driven forward by Necessity and fierce Pythian Madness, have, on the spur of the instant, to devise for the want the *way* of satisfying it. The wonted tumbles down; by imitation, by invention, the Unwonted hastily builds itself up. What the French National head has in it comes out: if not a great result, surely one of the strangest.

Neither shall the reader fancy that it was all blank, this Reign of Terror: far from it. How many hammermen and squaremen, bakers and brewers, washers and wringers, over this France, must ply their old daily work, let the Government be one of Terror or one of Joy! In this Paris there are Twenty-three Theatres nightly; some count as many as Sixty Places of Dancing.[693] The Playwright manufactures: pieces of a strictly Republican character. Ever fresh Novelgarbage, as of old, fodders the Circulating Libraries.[694] The "Cesspool of *Agio*," now in the time of Paper Money, works with a vivacity unexampled, unimagined; exhales from itself "sudden fortunes," like Alladin-Palaces: really a kind of miraculous Fata-Morganas, since you *can* live in them, for a time. Terror is as a sable ground, on which the most variegated of scenes paints itself. In startling transitions, in colours all intensated, the sublime, the ludicrous, the horrible succeed one another; or rather, in crowding tumult, accompany one another.

Here, accordingly, if anywhere, the "hundred tongues," which the old Poets often clamour for, were of supreme service! In defect of any such organ on our part, let the Reader stir up his own imaginative organ: let us snatch for him this or the other significant glimpse of things, in the fittest sequence we can.

Chapter 3.5.II.
Death

In the early days of November, there is one transient glimpse of things that is to be noted: the last transit to his long home of Philippe d'Orléans Egalité. Philippe was "decreed accused," along with the Girondins, much to his and their surprise; but not tried along with them. They are doomed and dead, some three days, when Philippe, after his long half-year of durance at Marseilles, arrives in Paris. It is, as we calculate, the third of November 1793.

On which same day, two notable Female Prisoners are also put in ward there: Dame Dubarry and Josephine Beauharnais! Dame whilom Countess Dubarry, Unfortunate-female, had returned from London; they snatched her, not only as Ex-harlot of a whilom Majesty, and therefore suspect; but as having "furnished the Emigrants with money." Contemporaneously with whom, there comes the wife of Beauharnais, soon to be the widow: she that is Josephine Tascher Beauharnais; that shall be Josephine Empress Buonaparte, for a black Divineress of the Tropics prophesied long since that she should be a Queen and more. Likewise, in the same hours, poor Adam Lux, nigh turned in the head, who, according to Foster, "has taken no food these three weeks," marches to the Guillotine for his Pamphlet on Charlotte Corday: he "sprang to the scaffold;" said he "died for her with great joy." Amid such fellow-travellers does Philippe arrive. For, be the month named Brumaire year 2 of Liberty, or November year 1793 of Slavery, the Guillotine goes always, *Guillotine va toujours.*

Enough, Philippe's indictment is soon drawn, his jury soon convinced. He finds himself made guilty of Royalism, Conspiracy and much else; nay, it is a guilt in him that he voted Louis's Death, though he answers, 'I voted in my soul and conscience.' The doom he finds is death forthwith; this present sixth dim day of November is the last day that Philippe is to see. Philippe, says Montgaillard, thereupon called for breakfast: sufficiency of "oysters, two cutlets, best part of an excellent bottle of claret;" and consumed the same with apparent relish. A Revolutionary Judge, or some official Convention Emissary, then arrived, to signify that he might still do the State some service by revealing the truth about a plot or two. Philippe answered that, on him, in the pass things had come to, the State had, he thought, small claim; that nevertheless, in the interest of Liberty, he, having still some leisure on his hands, was willing, were a reasonable question asked him, to give reasonable answer. And so, says Montgaillard, he lent his elbow on the mantel-piece, and conversed in an under-tone, with great seeming composure; till the leisure was done, or the Emissary went his ways.

At the door of the Conciergerie, Philippe's attitude was erect and easy, almost commanding. It is five years, all but a few days, since Philippe, within these same stone walls, stood up with an air of graciosity, and asked King Louis, 'Whether it was a Royal Session, then, or a Bed of Justice?' O Heaven!—Three poor blackguards were to ride and die with him: some say, they objected to such company, and had to be flung in, neck and heels;[695] but it seems not true. Objecting or not objecting, the gallows-vehicle gets under way. Philippe's dress is remarked for its elegance; greenfrock, waistcoat of white *piqué*, yellow buckskins, boots clear as Warren: his air, as before, entirely composed, impassive, not to say easy and Brummellean-polite. Through street after street; slowly, amid execrations;—past the Palais Egalité whilom Palais-Royal! The cruel Populace stopped him there, some minutes: Dame de Buffon, it is said, looked out on him, in Jezebel head-tire; along the ashlar Wall, there ran these words in huge tricolor print, REPUBLIC ONE AND INDIVISIBLE; LIBERTY, EQUALITY, FRATERNITY OR DEATH: *National Property.* Philippe's eyes flashed hellfire, one instant; but the next instant it was gone, and he sat impassive, Brummellean-polite. On the scaffold, Samson was for drawing of his boots: 'tush,' said Philippe, 'they will come better off *after;* let us have done, *dépêchons-nous!*'

So Philippe was not without virtue, then? God forbid that there should be any living man without it! He had the virtue to keep living for five-and-forty years;—other virtues perhaps more than we know of. Probably no mortal ever had such things recorded of him: such facts, and also such lies. For he was a *Jacobin Prince of the Blood;* consider what a combination! Also, unlike any Nero, any Borgia, he lived in the Age of Pamphlets. Enough for us: Chaos *has* reabsorbed him; may it late or never bear his like again!—Brave young Orleans Egalité, deprived of all, only not deprived of himself, is gone to Coire in the Grisons, under the name of Corby, to teach Mathematics. The Egalité Family is at the darkest depths of the Nadir.

A far nobler Victim follows; one who will claim remembrance from several centuries: Jeanne-Marie Phlipon, the Wife of Roland. Queenly, sublime in her uncomplaining sorrow, seemed she to Riouffe in her Prison.

"Something more than is usually found in the looks of women painted itself," says Riouffe,[696] "in those large black eyes of hers, full of expression and sweetness. She spoke to me often, at the Grate: we were all attentive round her, in a sort of admiration and astonishment; she expressed herself with a purity, with a harmony and prosody that made her language like music, of which the ear could never have enough. Her conversation was serious, not cold; coming from the mouth of a beautiful woman, it was frank and courageous as that of a great men." "And yet her maid said: 'Before you, she collects her strength; but in her own room, she will sit three hours sometimes, leaning on the window, and weeping.'" She had been in Prison, liberated once, but recaptured the same hour, ever since the first of June: in agitation and uncertainty; which has gradually settled down into the last stern certainty, that of death. In the Abbaye Prison, she occupied Charlotte Corday's apartment. Here in the Conciergerie, she speaks with Riouffe, with Ex-Minister Clavière; calls the beheaded Twenty-two 'Nos amis, our Friends,'—whom we are soon to follow. During these five months, those Memoirs of hers were written, which all the world still reads.

But now, on the 8th of November, "clad in white," says Riouffe, "with her long black hair hanging down to her girdle," she is gone to the Judgment Bar. She returned with a quick step; lifted her finger, to signify to us that she was doomed: her eyes seemed to have been wet. Fouquier-Tinville's questions had been "brutal;" offended female honour flung them back on him, with scorn, not without tears. And now, short preparation soon done, she shall go her last road. There went with her a certain Lamarche, "Director of Assignat printing;" whose dejection she endeavoured to cheer. Arrived at the foot of the scaffold, she asked for pen and paper, 'to write the strange thoughts that were rising in her;'[697] a remarkable request; which was refused. Looking at the Statue of Liberty which stands there, she says bitterly: 'O Liberty, what things are done in thy name!' For Lamarche's sake, she will die first; shew him how easy it is to die: 'Contrary to the order' said Samson.—'Pshaw, you cannot refuse the last request of a Lady;' and Samson yielded.

Noble white Vision, with its high queenly face, its soft proud eyes, long black hair flowing down to the girdle; and as brave a heart as ever beat in woman's bosom! Like a white Grecian Statue, serenely complete, she shines in that black wreck of things;—long memorable. Honour to great Nature who, in Paris City, in the Era of Noble-Sentiment and Pompadourism, can make a Jeanne Phlipon, and nourish her to clear perennial Womanhood, though but on Logics, Encyclopédies, and the Gospel according to Jean-Jacques! Biography will long remember that trait of asking for a pen 'to write the strange thoughts that were rising in her.' It is as a little light-beam, shedding softness, and a kind of sacredness, over all that preceded: so in her too there was an Unnameable; she too was a Daughter of the Infinite; there were mysteries which Philosophism had not dreamt of!—She left long written counsels to her little Girl; she said her Husband would not survive her.

Still crueller was the fate of poor Bailly, First National President, First Mayor of Paris: doomed now for Royalism, Fayettism; for that Red-Flag Business of the Champ-de-Mars;—one may say in general, for leaving his Astronomy to meddle with Revolution. It is the 10th of November 1793, a cold bitter drizzling rain, as poor Bailly is led through the streets; howling Populace covering him with curses, with mud; waving over his face a burning or smoking mockery of a Red Flag. Silent, unpitied, sits the innocent old man. Slow faring through the sleety drizzle, they have got to the Champ-de-Mars: Not there! vociferates the cursing Populace; Such blood ought not to stain an Altar of the Fatherland; not there; but on that dungheap by the River-side! So vociferates the cursing Populace; Officiality gives ear to them. The Guillotine is taken down, though with hands numbed by the sleety drizzle; is carried to the River-side, is there set up again, with slow numbness; pulse after pulse still counting itself out in the old man's weary heart. For hours long; amid curses and bitter frost-rain! 'Bailly, thou tremblest,' said one. '*Mon ami*, it is for cold,' said Bailly, '*c'est de froid*.' Crueller end had no mortal.[698]

Some days afterwards, Roland hearing the news of what happened on the 8th, embraces his kind Friends at Rouen, leaves their kind house which had given him refuge; goes forth, with farewell too sad for tears. On the morrow morning, 16th of the month, "some four leagues from Rouen, Paris-ward, near Bourg-Baudoin, in M. Normand's Avenue," there is seen sitting leant against a tree, the figure of rigorous wrinkled man; stiff now in the rigour of death; a cane-sword run through his heart; and at his feet this writing: "Whoever thou art that findest me lying, respect my remains: they are those of a man who consecrated all his life to being useful; and who has died as he lived, virtuous and honest." "Not fear, but indignation, made me quit my retreat, on learning that my Wife had been murdered. I wished not to remain longer on an Earth polluted with crimes."[699]

Barnave's appearance at the Revolutionary Tribunal was of the bravest; but it could not stead him. They have sent for him from Grenoble; to pay the common smart, Vain is eloquence, forensic or other, against the dumb Clotho-shears of Tinville. He is still but two-and-thirty, this Barnave, and has known such changes. Short while ago, we saw him at the top of Fortune's Wheel, his word a law to all Patriots: and now surely he is at the *bottom* of the Wheel; in stormful altercation with a Tinville Tribunal, which is dooming him to die![700] And Pétion, once also of the Extreme Left, and named *Pétion Virtue*, where is he? Civilly dead; in the Caves of Saint-Emilion; to be devoured of dogs. And Robespierre, who rode along with him on the shoulders of the people, is in Committee of *Salut;* civilly alive: not to live always. So giddy-swift whirls and spins this immeasurable *tormentum* of a Revolution; wild-booming; not to be followed by the eye. Barnave, on the Scaffold, stamped his foot; and looking upwards was heard to ejaculate, 'This then is my reward?'

Deputy Ex-Procureur Manuel is already gone; and Deputy Osselin, famed also in August and September, is about to go: and Rabaut, discovered treacherously between his two walls, and the Brother of Rabaut. National Deputies not a few! And Generals: the memory of General Custine cannot be defended by his Son; his Son is already guillotined. Custine the Ex-Noble was replaced by Houchard the Plebeian: he too could not prosper in the North; for him too there was no mercy; he has perished in the Place de la Revolution, after attempting suicide in Prison. And Generals Biron, Beauharnais, Brunet, whatsoever General prospers not; tough old Lückner, with his eyes grown rheumy; Alsatian Westermann, valiant and diligent in La Vendée: *none of them can,* as the Psalmist sings, *his soul from death deliver.*

How busy are the Revolutionary Committees; Sections with their Forty Halfpence a-day! Arrestment on arrestment falls quick, continual; followed by death. Ex-Minister Clavière has killed himself in Prison. Ex-Minister Lebrun, seized in a hayloft, under the disguise of a working man, is instantly conducted to death.[701] Nay, withal, is it not what Barrère calls "coining money on the Place de la Révolution?" For always the "property of the guilty, if property he have," is confiscated. To avoid accidents, we even make a Law that suicide shall not defraud us; that a criminal who kills himself does not the less incur forfeiture of goods. Let the guilty tremble, therefore, and the suspect, and the rich, and in a word all manner of culottic men! Luxembourg Palace, once Monsieur's, has become a huge loathsome Prison; Chantilly Palace too, once Condé's:—and their Landlords are at Blankenberg, on the wrong side of the Rhine. In Paris are now some Twelve Prisons; in France some Forty-four Thousand: thitherward, thick as brown leaves in Autumn, rustle and travel the suspect; shaken down by Revolutionary Committees, they are swept thitherward, as into their storehouse,—to be consumed by Samson and Tinville. "The Guillotine goes not ill, *La Guillotine ne va pas mal.*"

Chapter 3.5.III.
Destruction

The suspect may well tremble; but how much more the open rebels;— the Girondin Cities of the South! Revolutionary Army is gone forth, under Ronsin the Playwright; six thousand strong; in "red nightcap, in tricolor waistcoat, in black-shag trousers, black-shag spencer, with enormous moustachioes, enormous sabre,—in *carmagnole complète;*"[702] and has portable guillotines. Representative Carrier has got to Nantes, by the edge of blazing La Vendée, which Rossignol has literally set on fire: Carrier will try what captives you make, what accomplices they have, Royalist or Girondin: his guillotine goes always, *va toujours;* and his wool-capped "Company of Marat." Little children are guillotined, and aged men. Swift as the machine is, it will not serve; the Headsman and all his valets sink, worn down with work; declare that the human muscles can no more.[703] Whereupon you must try fusillading; to which perhaps still frightfuller methods may succeed.

In Brest, to like purpose, rules Jean-Bon Saint-André; with an Army of Red Nightcaps. In Bourdeaux rules Tallien, with his Isabeau and henchmen: Guadets, Cussys, Salleses, may fall; the bloody Pike and Nightcap bearing supreme sway; the Guillotine coining money. Bristly fox-haired Tallien, once Able Editor, still young in years, is now become most gloomy, potent; a Pluto on Earth, and has the keys of Tartarus. One remarks, however, that a certain Senhorina Cabarus, or call her rather *Senhora* and wedded not yet widowed *Dame de Fontenai,* brown beautiful woman, daughter of Cabarus the Spanish merchant,—has softened the red bristly countenance; pleading for herself and friends; and prevailing. The keys of Tartarus, or any kind of power, are something to a woman; gloomy Pluto himself is not insensible to love. Like a new Proserpine, she, by this red gloomy Dis, is gathered; and, they say, softens his stone heart a little.

Maignet, at Orange in the South; Lebon, at Arras in the North, become world's wonders. Jacobin Popular Tribunal, with its National Representative, perhaps where Girondin Popular Tribunal had lately been, rises here and rises there; wheresoever needed. Fouchés, Maignets, Barrases, Frérons scour the Southern Departments; like reapers, with their guillotine-sickle. Many are the labourers, great is the harvest. By the hundred and the thousand, men's lives are cropt; cast like brands into the burning.

Marseilles is taken, and put under martial law: lo, at Marseilles, what one besmutted red-bearded corn-ear is this which they cut;—one gross Man, we mean, with copper-studded face; plenteous beard, or beard-stubble, of a tile-colour? By Nemesis and the Fatal Sisters, it is Jourdan Coupe-tête! Him they have clutched, in these martial-law districts; him too, with their "national razor," their *rasoir national*, they sternly shave away. Low now is Jourdan the Headsman's own head;—low as Deshuttes's and Varigny's, which he sent on pikes, in the Insurrection of Women! No more shall he, as a copper Portent, be seen gyrating through the Cities of the South; no more sit judging, with pipes and brandy, in the Ice-tower of Avignon. The all-hiding Earth has received him, the bloated Tilebeard: may we never look upon his like again!—Jourdan one names; the other Hundreds are not named. Alas, they, like confused faggots, lie massed together for us; counted by the cartload: and yet not an individual faggot-twig of them but had a Life and History; and was cut, not without pangs as when a Kaiser dies!

Least of all cities can Lyons escape. Lyons, which we saw in dread sunblaze, that Autumn night when the Powder-tower sprang aloft, was clearly verging towards a sad end. Inevitable: what could desperate valour and Précy do; Dubois-Crancé, deaf as Destiny, stern as Doom, capturing their "redouts of cotton-bags;" hemming them in, ever closer, with his Artillery-lava? Never would that *ci-devant* d'Autichamp arrive; never any help from Blankenberg. The Lyons Jacobins were hidden in cellars; the Girondin Municipality waxed pale, in famine, treason and red fire. Précy drew his sword, and some Fifteen Hundred with him; sprang to saddle, to cut their way to Switzerland. They cut fiercely; and were fiercely cut, and cut down; not hundreds, hardly units of them ever saw Switzerland.[704] Lyons, on the 9th of October, surrenders at discretion; it is become a devoted Town. Abbé Lamourette, now Bishop Lamourette, whilom Legislator, he of the old *Baiser-l'Amourette* or Delilah-Kiss, is seized here, is sent to Paris to be guillotined: "he made the sign of the cross," they say when Tinville intimated his death-sentence to him; and died as an eloquent Constitutional Bishop. But wo now to all Bishops, Priests, Aristocrats and Federalists that are in Lyons! The *manes* of Chalier are to be appeased; the Republic, maddened to the Sibylline pitch, has bared her right arm. Behold! Representative Fouché, it is Fouché of Nantes, a name to become well known; he with a Patriot company goes duly, in wondrous Procession, to raise the corpse of Chalier. An Ass, housed in Priest's cloak, with a mitre on its head, and trailing the

Mass-Books, some say the very Bible, at its tail, paces through Lyons streets; escorted by multitudinous Patriotism, by clangour as of the Pit; towards the grave of Martyr Chalier. The body is dug up and burnt: the ashes are collected in an Urn; to be worshipped of Paris Patriotism. The Holy Books were part of the funeral pile; their ashes are scattered to the wind. Amid cries of 'Vengeance! Vengeance!'—which, writes Fouché, shall be satisfied. [705]

Lyons in fact is a Town to be abolished; not Lyons henceforth but *"Commune Affranchie,* Township Freed;" the very name of it shall perish. It is to be razed, this once great City, if Jacobinism prophesy right; and a Pillar to be erected on the ruins, with this Inscription, *Lyons rebelled against the Republic; Lyons is no more.* Fouché, Couthon, Collot, Convention Representatives succeed one another: there is work for the hangman; work for the hammerman, *not* in building. The very Houses of Aristocrats, we say, are doomed. Paralytic Couthon, borne in a chair, taps on the wall, with emblematic mallet, saying, *'La Loi te frappe,* The Law strikes thee;' masons, with wedge and crowbar, begin demolition. Crash of downfall, dim ruin and dust-clouds fly in the winter wind. Had Lyons been of soft stuff, it had all vanished in those weeks, and the Jacobin prophecy had been fulfilled. But Towns are not built of soap-froth; Lyons Town is built of stone. Lyons, though it rebelled against the Republic, *is* to this day.

Neither have the Lyons Girondins all one neck, that you could despatch it at one swoop. Revolutionary Tribunal here, and Military Commission, guillotining, fusillading, do what they can: the kennels of the Place des Terreaux run red; mangled corpses roll down the Rhone. Collot d'Herbois, they say, was once hissed on the Lyons stage: but with what sibilation, of world-catcall or hoarse Tartarean Trumpet, will ye hiss him now, in this his new character of Convention Representative,—not to be repeated! Two hundred and nine men are marched forth over the River, to be shot in mass, by musket and cannon, in the Promenade of the Brotteaux. It is the second of such scenes; the first was of some Seventy. The corpses of the first were flung into the Rhone, but the Rhone stranded some; so these now, of the second lot, are to be buried on land. Their one long grave is dug; they stand ranked, by the loose mould-ridge; the younger of them singing the Marseillaise. Jacobin National Guards give fire; but have again to give fire, and again; and to take the bayonet and the spade, for though the doomed all fall, they do not all die;—and it becomes a butchery too horrible for speech. So that the very Nationals, as they fire, turn away their faces. Collot, snatching the musket from one such National, and levelling it with unmoved countenance, says 'It is thus a Republican ought to fire.'

This is the second Fusillade, and happily the last: it is found too hideous; even inconvenient. They were Two hundred and nine marched out; one escaped at the end of the Bridge: yet behold, when you count the corpses, they are Two hundred and *ten*. Rede us this riddle, O Collot? After long guessing, it is called to mind that two individuals, here in the Brotteaux ground, did attempt to leave the rank, protesting with agony that they were not condemned men, that they were Police Commissaries: which two we repulsed, and disbelieved, and shot with the rest![706] Such is the vengeance of an enraged Republic. Surely this, according to Barrère's phrase, is Justice "under rough forms, *sous des formes acerbes*." But the Republic, as Fouché says, must 'march to Liberty over corpses.' Or again as Barrère has it: 'None but the dead do not come back, *Il n'y a que les morts qui ne reviennent pas*.' Terror hovers far and wide: "The Guillotine goes not ill."

But before quitting those Southern regions, over which History can cast only glances from aloft, she will alight for a moment, and look fixedly at one point: the Siege of Toulon. Much battering and bombarding, heating of balls in furnaces or farm-houses, serving of artillery well and ill, attacking of Ollioules Passes, Forts Malbosquet, there has been: as yet to small purpose. We have had General Cartaux here, a whilom Painter elevated in the troubles of Marseilles; General Doppet, a whilom Medical man elevated in the troubles of Piemont, who, under Crancé, took Lyons, but cannot take Toulon. Finally we have General Dugommier, a pupil of Washington. Convention *Représentans* also we have had; Barrases, Salicettis, Robespierres the Younger:—also an Artillery *Chef de brigade*, of extreme diligence, who often takes his nap of sleep among the guns; a short taciturn, olive-complexioned young man, not unknown to us, by name Buonaparte: one of the best Artillery-officers yet met with. And still Toulon is not taken. It is the fourth month now; December, in slave-style; *Frostarious* or *Frimaire*, in new-style: and still their cursed Red-Blue Flag flies there. They are provisioned from the Sea; they have seized all heights, felling wood, and fortifying themselves; like the coney, they have built their nest in the rocks.

Meanwhile, *Frostarious* is not yet become *Snowous* or *Nivose*, when a Council of War is called; Instructions have just arrived from Government and *Salut Public*. Carnot, in *Salut Public*, has sent us a plan of siege: on which plan General Dugommier has this criticism to make, Commissioner Salicetti has that; and criticisms and plans are very various; when that young Artillery Officer ventures to speak; the same whom we saw snatching sleep among the guns, who has emerged several times in this History,—the name of him Napoleon Buonaparte. It is his humble opinion, for he has been gliding about with spy-glasses, with thoughts, That a certain Fort l'Eguillette can be clutched, as with lion-spring, on the sudden; wherefrom, were it once ours, the very heart of Toulon might be battered, the English Lines were, so to speak, turned inside out, and Hood and our Natural Enemies must next day either put to sea, or be burnt to ashes. Commissioners arch their eyebrows, with negatory sniff: who is this young gentleman with more wit than we all? Brave veteran Dugommier, however, thinks the idea worth a word; questions the young gentleman; becomes convinced; and there is for issue, Try it.

On the taciturn bronze-countenance, therefore, things being now all ready, there sits a grimmer gravity than ever, compressing a hotter central-fire than ever. Yonder, thou seest, is Fort l'Eguillette; a desperate lion-spring, yet a possible one; this day to be tried!—Tried it is; and found *good.* By stratagem and valour, stealing through ravines, plunging fiery through the fire-tempest, Fort l'Eguillette is clutched at, is carried; the smoke having cleared, wiser the Tricolor fly on it: the bronze-complexioned young man was right. Next morning, Hood, finding the interior of his lines exposed, his defences turned inside out, makes for his shipping. Taking such Royalists as wished it on board with him, he weighs anchor: on this 19th of December 1793, Toulon is once more the Republic's!

Cannonading has ceased at Toulon; and now the guillotining and fusillading may begin. Civil horrors, truly: but at least that infamy of an English domination is purged away. Let there be Civic Feast universally over France: so reports Barrère, or Painter David; and the Convention assist in a body.[707] Nay, it is said, these infamous English (with an attention rather to their own interests than to ours) set fire to our store-houses, arsenals, warships in Toulon Harbour, before weighing; some score of brave warships, the only ones we now had! However, it did not prosper, though the flame spread far and high; some two ships were burnt, not more; the very galley-slaves ran with buckets to quench. These same proud Ships, Ships l'Orient and the rest, have to carry this same young Man to Egypt first: not yet can they be changed to ashes, or to Sea-Nymphs; not yet to sky-rockets, O Ship l'Orient, nor became the prey of England,—before their time!

And so, over France universally, there is Civic Feast and high-tide: and Toulon sees fusillading, grape-shotting in mass, as Lyons saw; and "death is poured out in great floods, *vomie à grands flots*" and Twelve thousand Masons are requisitioned from the neighbouring country, to raze Toulon from the face of the Earth. For it is to be razed, so reports Barrère; all but the National Shipping Establishments; and to be called henceforth not Toulon, but *Port of the Mountain.* There in black death-cloud we must leave it;— hoping only that Toulon too is built of stone; that perhaps even Twelve thousand Masons cannot pull it down, till the fit pass.

One begins to be sick of "death vomited in great floods." Nevertheless hearest thou not, O reader (for the sound reaches through centuries), in the dead December and January nights, over Nantes Town,—confused noises, as of musketry and tumult, as of rage and lamentation; mingling with the everlasting moan of the Loire waters there? Nantes Town is sunk in sleep; but *Représentant* Carrier is not sleeping, the wool-capped Company of Marat is not sleeping. Why unmoors that flatbottomed craft, that *gabarre;* about eleven at night; with Ninety Priests under hatches? They are going to Belle Isle? In the middle of the Loire stream, on signal given, the gabarre is scuttled; she sinks with all her cargo. "Sentence of Deportation," writes Carrier, "was executed *vertically.*" The Ninety Priests, with their gabarre-coffin, lie deep! It is the first of the *Noyades*, what we may call *Drownages*, of Carrier; which have become famous forever.

Guillotining there was at Nantes, till the Headsman sank worn out: then fusillading "in the Plain of Saint-Mauve;" little children fusilladed, and women with children at the breast; children and women, by the hundred and twenty; and by the five hundred, so hot is La Vendée: till the very Jacobins grew sick, and all but the Company of Marat cried, Hold! Wherefore now we have got Noyading; and on the 24th night of *Frostarious* year 2, which is 14th of December 1793, we have a second Noyade: consisting of "a Hundred and Thirty-eight persons."[708]

Or why waste a gabarre, sinking it with them? Fling them out; fling them out, with their hands tied: pour a continual hail of lead over all the space, till the last struggler of them be sunk! Unsound sleepers of Nantes, and the Sea-Villages thereabouts, hear the musketry amid the night-winds; wonder what the meaning of it is. And women were in that gabarre; whom the Red Nightcaps were stripping naked; who begged, in their agony, that their smocks might not be stript from them. And young children were thrown in, their mothers vainly pleading: 'Wolflings,' answered the Company of Marat, 'who would grow to be wolves.'

By degrees, daylight itself witnesses Noyades: women and men are tied together, feet and feet, hands and hands: and flung in: this they call *Mariage Républicain*, Republican Marriage. Cruel is the panther of the woods, the she-bear bereaved of her whelps: but there is in man a hatred crueller than that. Dumb, out of suffering now, as pale swoln corpses, the victims tumble confusedly seaward along the Loire stream; the tide rolling them back: clouds of ravens darken the River; wolves prowl on the shoal-places: Carrier writes, "*Quel torrent révolutionnaire*, What a torrent of Revolution!" For the man is rabid; and the Time is rabid. These are the Noyades of Carrier; twenty-five by the tale, for what is done in darkness comes to be investigated in sunlight:[709] not to be forgotten for centuries,—We will turn to another aspect of the Consummation of Sansculottism; leaving this as the blackest.

But indeed men are all rabid; as the Time is. Representative Lebon, at Arras, dashes his sword into the blood flowing from the Guillotine; exclaims, 'How I like it!' Mothers, they say, by his order, have to stand by while the Guillotine devours their children: a band of music is stationed near; and, at the fall of every head, strikes up its *ça-ira*.[710] In the Burgh of Bedouin, in the Orange region, the Liberty-tree has been cut down over night. Representative Maignet, at Orange, hears of it; burns Bedouin Burgh to the last dog-hutch; guillotines the inhabitants, or drives them into the caves and hills.[711] Republic One and Indivisible! She is the newest Birth of Nature's waste inorganic Deep, which men name Orcus, Chaos, primeval Night; and knows one law, that of self-preservation. *Tigresse Nationale:* meddle not with a whisker of her! Swift-crushing is her stroke; look what a paw she spreads;—pity has not entered her heart.

Prudhomme, the dull-blustering Printer and Able Editor, as yet a Jacobin Editor, will become a renegade one, and publish large volumes on these matters, *Crimes of the Revolution;* adding innumerable lies withal, as if the truth were not sufficient. We, for our part, find it more edifying to know, one good time, that this Republic and National Tigress *is* a New Birth; a Fact of Nature among Formulas, in an Age of Formulas; and to look, oftenest in silence, how the so genuine Nature-Fact will demean itself among these. For the Formulas are partly genuine, partly delusive, supposititious: we call them, in the language of metaphor, regulated modelled *shapes;* some of which have bodies and life still in them; most of which, according to a German Writer, have only emptiness, "glass-eyes glaring on you with a ghastly affectation of life, and in their interior unclean accumulation of beetles and spiders!" But the Fact, let all men observe, is a genuine and sincere one; the sincerest of Facts: terrible in its sincerity, as very Death. Whatsoever is equally sincere may front it, and beard it; but whatsoever is *not?*—

Chapter 3.5.IV.
Carmagnole complete

Simultaneously with this Tophet-black aspect, there unfolds itself another aspect, which one may call a Tophet-red aspect: the Destruction of the Catholic Religion; and indeed, for the time being of Religion itself. We saw Romme's New Calendar establish its *Tenth* Day of Rest; and asked, what would become of the Christian Sabbath? The Calendar is hardly a month old, till all this is set at rest. Very singular, as Mercier observes: last *Corpus-Christi* Day 1792, the whole world, and Sovereign Authority itself, walked in religious gala, with a quite devout air;—Butcher Legendre, supposed to be irreverent, was like to be massacred in his Gig, as the thing went by. A Gallican Hierarchy, and Church, and Church Formulas seemed to flourish, a little brown-leaved or so, but not browner than of late years or decades; to flourish, far and wide, in the sympathies of an unsophisticated People; defying Philosophism, Legislature and the Encyclopédie. Far and wide, alas, like a brown-leaved Vallombrosa; which waits but one whirlblast of the November wind, and in an hour stands bare! Since that *Corpus-Christi* Day, Brunswick has come, and the Emigrants, and La Vendée, and eighteen months of Time: to all flourishing, especially to brown-leaved flourishing, there comes, were it never so slowly, an end.

On the 7th of November, a certain Citoyen Parens, Curate of Boissise-le-Bertrand, writes to the Convention that he has all his life been preaching a lie, and is grown weary of doing it; wherefore he will now lay down his Curacy and stipend, and begs that an august Convention would give him something else to live upon. "*Mention honorable*," shall we give him? Or "reference to Committee of Finances?" Hardly is this got decided, when goose Gobel, Constitutional Bishop of Paris, with his Chapter, with Municipal and Departmental escort in red nightcaps, makes his appearance, to do as Parens has done. Goose Gobel will now acknowledge "no Religion but Liberty;" therefore he doffs his Priest-gear, and receives the Fraternal embrace. To the joy of Departmental Momoro, of Municipal Chaumettes and Héberts, of Vincent and the Revolutionary Army! Chaumette asks, Ought there not, in these circumstances, to be among our intercalary Days

Sans-breeches, a Feast of Reason?[712] Proper surely! Let Atheist Maréchal, Lalande, and little Atheist Naigeon rejoice; let Clootz, Speaker of Mankind, present to the Convention his *Evidences of the Mahometan Religion*, "a work evincing the nullity of all Religions," —with thanks. There shall be Universal Republic now, thinks Clootz; and "one God only, *Le Peuple*."

The French Nation is of gregarious imitative nature; it needed but a fugle-motion in this matter; and goose Gobel, driven by Municipality and force of circumstances, has given one. What Curé will be behind him of Boissise; what Bishop behind him of Paris? Bishop Grégoire, indeed, courageously declines; to the sound of 'We force no one; let Grégoire consult his conscience;' but Protestant and Romish by the hundred volunteer and assent. From far and near, all through November into December, till the work is accomplished, come Letters of renegation, come Curates who are "learning to be Carpenters," Curates with their new-wedded Nuns: has not the Day of Reason dawned, very swiftly, and become noon? From sequestered Townships comes Addresses, stating plainly, though in Patois dialect, That "they will have no more to do with the black animal called Curay, *animal noir, appellé Curay.*"[713]

Above all things there come Patriotic Gifts, of Church-furniture. The remnant of bells, except for tocsin, descend from their belfries, into the National meltingpot, to make cannon. Censers and all sacred vessels are beaten broad; of silver, they are fit for the poverty-stricken Mint; of pewter, let them become bullets to shoot the "enemies of *du genre humain.*" Dalmatics of plush make breeches for him who has none; linen stoles will clip into shirts for the Defenders of the Country: old-clothesmen, Jew or Heathen, drive the briskest trade. Chalier's Ass Procession, at Lyons, was but a type of what went on, in those same days, in all Towns. In all Towns and Townships as quick as the guillotine may go, so quick goes the axe and the wrench: sacristies, lutrins, altar-rails are pulled down; the Mass Books torn into cartridge papers: men dance the Carmagnole all night about the bonfire. All highways jingle with metallic Priest-tackle, beaten broad; sent to the Convention, to the poverty-stricken Mint. Good Sainte Geneviève's *Chasse* is let down: alas, to be burst open, this time, and burnt on the Place de Grève. Saint Louis's shirt is burnt;—might not a Defender of the Country have had it? At Saint-Denis Town, no longer Saint-Denis but *Franciade*, Patriotism has been down among the Tombs, rummaging; the Revolutionary Army has taken spoil. This, accordingly, is what the streets of Paris saw:

"Most of these persons were still drunk, with the brandy they had swallowed out of chalices;—eating mackerel on the patenas! Mounted on Asses, which were housed with Priests' cloaks, they reined them with Priests' stoles: they held clutched with the same hand communion-cup and sacred wafer. They stopped at the doors of Dramshops; held out ciboriums: and the landlord, stoop in hand, had to fill them thrice. Next came Mules high-laden with crosses, chandeliers, censers, holy-water vessels, hyssops;—recalling to mind the Priests of Cybele, whose panniers, filled with the instruments of their worship, served at once as storehouse, sacristy and temple. In such equipage did these profaners advance towards the Convention. They enter there, in an immense train, ranged in two rows; all masked like mummers in fantastic sacerdotal vestments; bearing on hand-barrows their heaped plunder,—ciboriums, suns, candelabras, plates of gold and silver."[714]

The Address we do not give; for indeed it was in strophes, sung *vivâ voce*, with all the parts;—Danton glooming considerably, in his place; and demanding that there be prose and decency in future.[715] Nevertheless the captors of such *spolia opima* crave, not untouched with liquor, permission to dance the Carmagnole also on the spot: whereto an exhilarated Convention cannot but accede. Nay, "several Members," continues the exaggerative Mercier, who was not there to witness, being in Limbo now, as one of Duperret's *Seventy-three*, "several Members, quitting their curule chairs, took the hand of girls flaunting in Priest's vestures, and danced the Carmagnole along with them." Such Old-Hallow-tide have they, in this year, once named of Grace, 1793.

Out of which strange fall of Formulas, tumbling there in confused welter, betrampled by the Patriotic dance, is it not passing strange to see a *new* Formula arise? For the human tongue is not adequate to speak what "triviality run distracted" there is in human nature. Black Mumbo-Jumbo of the woods, and most Indian Wau-waus, one can understand: but this of Procureur *Anaxagoras* whilom John-Peter Chaumette? We will say only: Man is a born idol-worshipper, *sight*-worshipper, so sensuous-imaginative is he; and also partakes much of the nature of the ape.

For the same day, while this brave Carmagnole dance has hardly jigged itself out, there arrive Procureur Chaumette and Municipals and Departmentals, and with them the strangest freightage: a New Religion! Demoiselle Candeille, of the Opera; a woman fair to look upon, when well rouged: she, borne on palanquin shoulder-high; with red woolen nightcap; in azure mantle; garlanded with oak; holding in her hand the Pike of the Jupiter-*Peuple*, sails in; heralded by white young women girt in tricolor. Let the world consider it! This, O National Convention wonder of the universe, is our New Divinity; *Goddess of Reason*, worthy, and alone worthy of revering. Nay, were it too much to ask of an august National Representation that it also went with us to the *ci-devant* Cathedral called of Notre-Dame, and executed a few strophes in worship of her?

President and Secretaries give Goddess Candeille, borne at due height round their platform, successively the fraternal kiss; whereupon she, by decree, sails to the right-hand of the President and there alights. And now, after due pause and flourishes of oratory, the Convention, gathering its limbs, does get under way in the required procession towards Notre-Dame;— Reason, again in her litter, sitting in the van of them, borne, as one judges, by men in the Roman costume; escorted by wind-music, red nightcaps, and the madness of the world. And so straightway, Reason taking seat on the high-altar of Notre-Dame, the requisite worship or quasi-worship is, say the Newspapers, *executed;* National Convention chanting "the *Hymn to Liberty,* words by Chénier, music by Gossec." It is the first of the *Feasts of Reason;* first communion-service of the New Religion of Chaumette.

"The corresponding Festival in the Church of Saint-Eustache," says Mercier, "offered the spectacle of a great tavern. The interior of the choir represented a landscape decorated with cottages and boskets of trees. Round the choir stood tables over-loaded with bottles, with sausages, pork-puddings, pastries and other meats. The guests flowed in and out through all doors: whosoever presented himself took part of the good things: children of eight, girls as well as boys, put hand to plate, in sign of Liberty; they drank also of the bottles, and their prompt intoxication created laughter. Reason sat in azure mantle aloft, in a serene manner; Cannoneers, pipe in mouth, serving her as acolytes. And out of doors," continues the exaggerative man, "were mad multitudes dancing round the bonfire of Chapel-balustrades, of Priests' and Canons' stalls; and the dancers, I exaggerate nothing, the dancers nigh bare of breeches, neck and breast naked, stockings down, went whirling and spinning, like those Dust-vortexes, forerunners of Tempest and Destruction."[716] At Saint-Gervais Church again there was a terrible "smell of herrings;" Section or Municipality having provided no food, no condiment, but left it to chance. Other mysteries, seemingly of a Cabiric or even Paphian character, we heave under the Veil, which appropriately stretches itself "along the pillars of the aisles," —not to be lifted aside by the hand of History.

But there is one thing we should like almost better to understand than any other: what Reason herself thought of it, all the while. What articulate words poor Mrs. Momoro, for example, uttered; when she had become ungoddessed again, and the Bibliopolist and she sat quiet at home, at supper? For he was an earnest man, Bookseller Momoro; and had notions of Agrarian Law. Mrs. Momoro, it is admitted, made one of the best Goddesses of Reason; though her teeth were a little defective. And now if the reader will represent to himself that such visible Adoration of Reason went on "all over the Republic," through these November and December weeks, till the

Church woodwork was burnt out, and the business otherwise completed, he will feel sufficiently what an adoring Republic it was, and without reluctance quit this part of the subject.

Such gifts of Church-spoil are chiefly the work of the *Armée Révolutionnaire;* raised, as we said, some time ago. It is an Army with portable guillotine: commanded by Playwright Ronsin in terrible moustachioes; and even by some uncertain shadow of Usher Maillard, the old Bastille Hero, Leader of the Menads, September Man in Grey! Clerk Vincent of the War-Office, one of Pache's old Clerks, "with a head heated by the ancient orators," had a main hand in the appointments, at least in the staff-appointments.

But of the marchings and retreatings of these Six Thousand no Xenophon exists. Nothing, but an inarticulate hum, of cursing and sooty frenzy, surviving dubious in the memory of ages! They scour the country round Paris; seeking Prisoners; raising Requisitions; seeing that Edicts are executed, that the Farmers have thrashed sufficiently; lowering Church-bells or metallic Virgins. Detachments shoot forth dim, towards remote parts of France; nay new Provincial Revolutionary Armies rise dim, here and there, as Carrier's Company of Marat, as Tallien's Bourdeaux Troop; like sympathetic clouds in an atmosphere all electric. Ronsin, they say, admitted, in candid moments, that his troops were the elixir of the Rascality of the Earth. One sees them drawn up in market-places; travel-plashed, rough-bearded, in *carmagnole complète:* the first exploit is to prostrate what Royal or Ecclesiastical monument, crucifix or the like, there may be; to plant a cannon at the steeple, fetch down the bell without climbing for it, bell and belfry together. This, however, it is said, depends somewhat on the size of the town: if the town contains much population, and these perhaps of a dubious choleric aspect, the Revolutionary Army will do its work gently, by ladder and wrench; nay perhaps will take its billet without work at all; and, refreshing itself with a little liquor and sleep, pass on to the next stage.[717] Pipe in cheek, sabre on thigh; in carmagnole complete!

Such things have been; and may again be. Charles Second sent out his Highland Host over the Western Scotch Whigs; Jamaica Planters got Dogs from the Spanish Main to hunt their Maroons with: France too is bescoured with a Devil's Pack, the baying of which, at this distance of half a century, still sounds in the mind's ear.

Chapter 3.5.V.
Like a Thunder-Cloud

But the grand, and indeed substantially primary and generic aspect of the Consummation of Terror remains still to be looked at; nay blinkard History has for most part all but *over*looked this aspect, the soul of the whole: that which makes it terrible to the Enemies of France. Let Despotism and Cimmerian Coalitions consider. All French men and French things are in a State of Requisition; Fourteen Armies are got on foot; Patriotism, with all that it has of faculty in heart or in head, in soul or body or breeches-pocket, is rushing to the frontiers, to prevail or die! Busy sits Carnot, in *Salut Public;* busy for his share, in "organising victory." Not swifter pulses that Guillotine, in dread systole-diastole in the Place de la Révolution, than smites the Sword of Patriotism, smiting Cimmeria back to its own borders, from the sacred soil.

In fact the Government is what we can call Revolutionary; and some men are "*à la hauteur,*" on a level with the circumstances; and others are not *à la hauteur,*—so much the worse for them. But the Anarchy, we may say, has *organised* itself: Society is literally overset; its old forces working with mad activity, but in the inverse order; destructive and self-destructive.

Curious to see how all still refers itself to some head and fountain; not even an Anarchy but must have a centre to revolve round. It is now some six months since the Committee of *Salut Public* came into existence: some three months since Danton proposed that all power should be given it and "a sum of fifty millions," and the "Government be declared Revolutionary." He himself, since that day, would take no hand in it, though again and again solicited; but sits private in his place on the Mountain. Since that day, the Nine, or if they should even rise to Twelve have become permanent, always re-elected when their term runs out; *Salut Public, Sûreté Générale* have assumed their ulterior form and mode of operating.

Committee of Public Salvation, as supreme; of General Surety, as subaltern: these like a Lesser and Greater Council, most harmonious hitherto, have become the centre of all things. They ride this Whirlwind; they, raised by force of circumstances, insensibly, very strangely, thither to that dread height;—and guide it, and seem to guide it. Stranger set of Cloud-Compellers the Earth never saw. A Robespierre, a Billaud, a Collot, Couthon, Saint-Just; not to mention still meaner Amars, Vadiers, in *Sûreté Générale*: these are your Cloud-Compellers. Small intellectual talent is necessary: indeed where among them, except in the head of Carnot, busied organising victory, would you find any? The talent is one of instinct rather. It is that of divining aright what this great dumb Whirlwind wishes and wills; that of willing, with more frenzy than any one, what all the world wills. To stand at no obstacles; to heed no considerations human or divine; to 'know well that, of divine or human, there is one thing needful, Triumph of the Republic, Destruction of the Enemies of the Republic! With this one spiritual endowment, and so few others, it is strange to see how a dumb inarticulately storming Whirlwind of things puts, as it were, its reins into your hand, and invites and compels you to be leader of it.

Hard by, sits a Municipality of Paris; all in red nightcaps since the fourth of November last: a set of men fully "on a level with circumstances," or even beyond it. Sleek Mayor Pache, studious to be safe in the middle; Chaumettes, Héberts, Varlets, and Henriot their great Commandant; not to speak of Vincent the War-clerk, of Momoros, Dobsents, and such like: all intent to have Churches plundered, to have Reason adored, Suspects cut down, and the Revolution triumph. Perhaps carrying the matter *too* far? Danton was heard to grumble at the civic strophes; and to recommend prose and decency. Robespierre also grumbles that in overturning Superstition we did not mean to make a religion of Atheism. In fact, your Chaumette and Company constitute a kind of Hyper-Jacobinism, or rabid "Faction *des Enragés;*" which has given orthodox Patriotism some umbrage, of late months. To "know a Suspect on the streets:" what is this but bringing the *Law of the Suspect* itself into ill odour? Men half-frantic, men zealous overmuch,—they toil there, in their red nightcaps, restlessly, rapidly, accomplishing what of Life is allotted them.

And the Forty-four Thousand other Townships, each with revolutionary Committee, based on Jacobin Daughter Society; enlightened by the spirit of Jacobinism; quickened by the Forty Sous a-day!—The French Constitution spurned always at any thing like Two Chambers; and yet behold, has it not verily got Two Chambers? National Convention, elected for one; Mother of Patriotism, self-elected, for another! Mother of Patriotism has her Debates reported in the *Moniteur*, as important state-procedures; which indisputably they are. A Second Chamber of Legislature we call this Mother Society;— if perhaps it were not rather comparable to that old Scotch Body named *Lords of the Articles*, without whose origination, and signal given, the so-called Parliament could introduce no bill, could do no work? Robespierre himself, whose words are a law, opens his incorruptible lips copiously in the Jacobins Hall. Smaller Council of *Salut Public*, Greater Council of *Sûreté Générale*, all active Parties, come here to plead; to shape beforehand what decision they must arrive at, what destiny they have to expect. Now if a question arose, Which of those Two Chambers, Convention, or Lords of the Articles, was the *stronger?* Happily they as yet go hand in hand.

As for the National Convention, truly it has become a most composed Body. Quenched now the old effervescence; the Seventy-three locked in ward; once noisy Friends of the Girondins sunk all into silent men of the Plain, called even "Frogs of the Marsh," *Crapauds du Marais!* Addresses come, Revolutionary Church-plunder comes; Deputations, with prose, or strophes: these the Convention receives. But beyond this, the Convention has one thing mainly to do: to listen what *Salut Public* proposes, and say, Yea.

Bazire followed by Chabot, with some impetuosity, declared, one morning, that this was not the way of a Free Assembly. 'There ought to be an Opposition side, a *Côté Droit*,' cried Chabot; 'if none else will form it, I will: people say to me, You will all get guillotined in your turn, first you and Bazire, then Danton, then Robespierre himself.'[718] So spake the Disfrocked, with a loud voice: next week, Bazire and he lie in the Abbaye; wending, one may fear, towards Tinville and the Axe; and "people say to me"—what seems to be proving true! Bazire's blood was all inflamed with Revolution fever; with coffee and spasmodic dreams.[719] Chabot, again, how happy with his rich Jew-Austrian wife, late Fraulein Frey! But he lies in Prison; and his two Jew-Austrian Brothers-in-Law, the Bankers Frey, lie with him; waiting the urn of doom. Let a National Convention, therefore, take warning, and know its function. Let the Convention, all as one man, set its shoulder to the work; not with bursts of Parliamentary eloquence, but in quite other and serviceable ways!

Convention Commissioners, what we ought to call Representatives, "*Représentans* on mission," fly, like the Herald Mercury, to all points of the Territory; carrying your behests far and wide. In their "round hat plumed with tricolor feathers, girt with flowing tricolor taffeta; in close frock, tricolor sash, sword and jack-boots," these men are powerfuller than King or Kaiser. They say to whomso they meet, Do; and he must do it: all men's goods are at their disposal; for France is as one huge City in Siege. They smite with Requisitions, and Forced-loan; they have the power of life and death. Saint-Just and Lebas order the rich classes of Strasburg to "strip off their shoes," and send them to the Armies where as many as "ten thousand pairs" are needed. Also, that within four and twenty hours, "a thousand beds" are to be got ready;[720] wrapt in matting, and sent under way. For the time presses!—Like swift bolts, issuing from the fuliginous Olympus of *Salut Public* rush these men, oftenest in pairs; scatter your thunder-orders over France; make France one enormous Revolutionary thunder-cloud.

Chapter 3.5.VI.
Do thy Duty

Accordingly alongside of these bonfires of Church balustrades, and sounds of fusillading and noyading, there rise quite another sort of fires and sounds: Smithy-fires and Proof-volleys for the manufacture of arms.

Cut off from Sweden and the world, the Republic must learn to make steel for itself; and, by aid of Chemists, she has learnt it. Towns that knew only iron, now know steel: from their new dungeons at Chantilly, Aristocrats may hear the rustle of our new steel furnace there. Do not bells transmute themselves into cannon; iron stancheons into the white-weapon (*arme blanche*), by sword-cutlery? The wheels of Langres scream, amid their sputtering fire halo; grinding mere swords. The stithies of Charleville ring with gun-making. What say we, Charleville? Two hundred and fifty-eight Forges stand in the open spaces of Paris itself; a hundred and forty of them in the Esplanade of the Invalides, fifty-four in the Luxembourg Garden: so many Forges stand; grim Smiths beating and forging at lock and barrel there. The Clockmakers have come, requisitioned, to do the touch-holes, the hard-solder and filework. Five great Barges swing at anchor on the Seine Stream, loud with boring; the great press-drills grating harsh thunder to the general ear and heart. And deft Stock-makers do gouge and rasp; and all men bestir themselves, according to their cunning:—in the language of hope, it is reckoned that a "thousand finished muskets can be delivered daily."[721] Chemists of the Republic have taught us miracles of swift tanning;[722] the cordwainer bores and stitches;—*not* of "wood and pasteboard," or he shall answer it to Tinville! The women sew tents and coats, the children scrape surgeon's-lint, the old men sit in the market-places; able men are on march; all men in requisition: from Town to Town flutters, on the Heaven's winds, this Banner, THE FRENCH PEOPLE RISEN AGAINST TYRANTS.

All which is well. But now arises the question: What is to be done for saltpetre? Interrupted Commerce and the English Navy shut us out from saltpetre; and without saltpetre there is no gunpowder. Republican Science again sits meditative; discovers that saltpetre exists here and there, though in attenuated quantity: that old plaster of walls holds a sprinkling of it;—that the earth of the Paris Cellars holds a sprinkling of it, diffused through the common rubbish; that were these dug up and washed, saltpetre might be had. Whereupon swiftly, see! the Citoyens, with upshoved *bonnet rouge,* or with doffed bonnet, and hair toil-wetted; digging fiercely, each in his own cellar, for saltpetre. The Earth-heap rises at every door; the Citoyennes with hod and bucket carrying it up; the Citoyens, pith in every muscle, shovelling and digging: for life and saltpetre. Dig my *braves;* and right well speed ye. What of saltpetre is essential the Republic shall not want.

Consummation of Sansculottism has many aspects and tints: but the brightest tint, really of a solar or stellar brightness, is this which the Armies give it. That same fervour of Jacobinism which internally fills France with hatred, suspicions, scaffolds and Reason-worship, does, on the Frontiers, shew itself as a glorious *Pro patria mori.* Ever since Dumouriez's defection, three Convention Representatives attend every General. Committee of *Salut* has sent them, often with this Laconic order only: 'Do thy duty, *Fais ton devoir.'* It is strange, under what impediments the fire of Jacobinism, like other such fires, will burn. These Soldiers have shoes of wood and pasteboard, or go booted in hayropes, in dead of winter; they skewer a bass mat round their shoulders, and are destitute of most things. What then? It is for Rights of Frenchhood, of Manhood, that they fight: the unquenchable spirit, here as elsewhere, works miracles. 'With steel and bread,' says the Convention Representative, 'one may get to China.' The Generals go fast to the guillotine; justly and unjustly. From which what inference? This among others: That ill-success is death; that in victory alone is life! To conquer or die is no theatrical palabra, in these circumstances: but a practical truth and necessity. All Girondism, Halfness, Compromise is swept away. Forward, ye Soldiers of the Republic, captain and man! Dash with your Gaelic impetuosity, on Austria, England, Prussia, Spain, Sardinia; Pitt, Cobourg, York, and the Devil and the World! Behind us is but the Guillotine; before us is Victory, Apotheosis and Millennium without end!

See accordingly, on all Frontiers, how the Sons of Night, astonished after short triumph, do recoil;—the Sons of the Republic flying at them, with wild *Ça-ira* or Marseillese *Aux armes,* with the temper of cat-o'-mountain, or demon incarnate; which no Son of Night can stand! Spain, which came bursting through the Pyrenees, rustling with Bourbon banners, and went conquering here and there for a season, falters at such cat-o'-mountain welcome; draws itself in again; too happy now were the Pyrenees impassable. Not only does Dugommier, conqueror of Toulon, drive Spain back; he invades Spain. General Dugommier invades it by the Eastern Pyrenees; General Muller shall invade it by the Western. *Shall*, that is the word: Committee of *Salut Public* has said it; Representative Cavaignac, on mission there, must see it done. Impossible! cries Muller,—Infallible! answers Cavaignac. Difficulty, impossibility, is to no purpose. 'The Committee is deaf on that side of its head,' answers Cavaignac, '*n'entend pas de cette oreille là*. How many wantest thou, of men, of horses, cannons? Thou shalt have them. Conquerors, conquered or hanged, forward we must.'[723]   Which things also, even as the Representative spake them, were *done*. The Spring of the new Year sees Spain invaded: and redoubts are carried, and Passes and Heights of the most scarped description; Spanish Field-officerism struck mute at such cat-o'-mountain spirit, the cannon forgetting to fire.[724]   Swept are the Pyrenees; Town after Town flies up, burst by terror or the petard. In the course of another year, Spain will crave Peace; acknowledge its sins and the Republic; nay, in Madrid, there will be joy as for a victory, that even Peace is got.

Few things, we repeat, can be notabler than these Convention Representatives, with their power more than kingly. Nay at bottom are they not Kings, *Able-men*, of a sort; chosen from the Seven Hundred and Forty-nine French Kings; with this order, Do thy duty? Representative Levasseur, of small stature, by trade a mere pacific Surgeon-Accoucheur, has mutinies to quell; mad hosts (mad at the Doom of Custine) bellowing far and wide; he alone amid them, the one small Representative,—small, but as hard as flint, which also carries *fire* in it! So too, at Hondschooten, far in the afternoon, he declares that the battle is not lost; that it must be gained; and fights, himself, with his own obstetric hand;—horse shot under him, or say on foot, "up to the haunches in tide-water;" cutting stoccado and passado there, in defiance of Water, Earth, Air and Fire, the choleric little Representative that he was! Whereby, as natural, Royal Highness of York had to withdraw,— occasionally at full gallop; like to be swallowed by the tide: and his Siege of Dunkirk became a dream, realising only much loss of beautiful siege-artillery and of brave lives.[725]

General Houchard, it would appear, stood behind a hedge, on this Hondschooten occasion; wherefore they have since guillotined him. A new General Jourdan, late Serjeant Jourdan, commands in his stead: he, in long-winded Battles of Watigny, "murderous artillery-fire mingling itself with sound of Revolutionary battle-hymns," forces Austria behind the Sambre again; has hopes of purging the soil of Liberty. With hard wrestling, with artillerying and *ça-ira*-ing, it shall be done. In the course of a new Summer, Valenciennes will see itself beleaguered; Condé beleaguered; whatsoever is yet in the hands of Austria beleaguered and bombarded: nay, by Convention Decree, we even summon them *all* "either to surrender in twenty-four hours, or else be put to the sword;"—a high saying, which, though it remains unfulfilled, may shew what spirit one is of.

Representative Drouet, as an Old-Dragoon, could fight by a kind of second nature; but he was unlucky. Him, in a night-foray at Maubeuge, the Austrians took alive, in October last. They stript him almost naked, he says; making a shew of him, as King-taker of Varennes. They flung him into carts; sent him far into the interior of Cimmeria, to "a Fortress called Spitzberg" on the Danube River; and left him there, at an elevation of perhaps a hundred and fifty feet, to his own bitter reflections. Reflections; and also devices! For the indomitable Old-dragoon constructs wing-machinery, of Paperkite; saws window-bars: determines to fly down. He will seize a boat, will follow the River's course: land somewhere in Crim Tartary, in the Black Sea or Constantinople region: à la Sindbad! Authentic History, accordingly, looking far into Cimmeria, discerns dimly a phenomenon. In the dead night-watches, the Spitzberg sentry is near fainting with terror: Is it a huge vague Portent descending through the night air? It is a huge National Representative Old-dragoon, descending by Paperkite; too rapidly, alas! For Drouet had taken with him "a small provision-store, twenty pounds weight or thereby;" which proved accelerative: so he fell, fracturing his leg; and lay there, moaning, till day dawned, till you could discern clearly that he was not a Portent but a Representative![726]

Or see Saint-Just, in the Lines of Weissembourg, though physically of a timid apprehensive nature, how he charges with his "Alsatian Peasants armed hastily" for the nonce; the solemn face of him blazing into flame; his black hair and tricolor hat-taffeta flowing in the breeze; These our Lines of Weissembourg were indeed forced, and Prussia and the Emigrants rolled through: but we re-force the Lines of Weissembourg; and Prussia and the Emigrants roll back again still faster,—hurled with bayonet charges and fiery ça-ira-ing.

Ci-devant Sergeant Pichegru, ci-devant Sergeant Hoche, risen now to be Generals, have done wonders here. Tall Pichegru was meant for the Church; was Teacher of Mathematics once, in Brienne School,—his remarkablest Pupil there was the Boy Napoleon Buonaparte. He then, not in the sweetest humour, enlisted exchanging ferula for musket; and had got the length of the halberd, beyond which nothing could be hoped; when the Bastille barriers falling made passage for him, and he is here. Hoche bore a hand at the literal overturn of the Bastille; he was, as we saw, a Serjeant of the *Gardes Françaises*, spending his pay in rushlights and cheap editions of books. How the Mountains are burst, and many an Enceladus is disemprisoned: and Captains founding on Four parchments of Nobility, are blown with their parchments across the Rhine, into Lunar Limbo!

What high feats of arms, therefore, were done in these Fourteen Armies; and how, for love of Liberty and hope of Promotion, low-born valour cut its desperate way to Generalship; and, from the central Carnot in *Salut Public* to the outmost drummer on the Frontiers, men strove for their Republic, let readers fancy. The snows of Winter, the flowers of Summer continue to be stained with warlike blood. Gaelic impetuosity mounts ever higher with victory; spirit of Jacobinism weds itself to national vanity: the Soldiers of the Republic are becoming, as we prophesied, very Sons of Fire. Barefooted, barebacked: but with bread and iron you can get to China! It is one Nation against the whole world; but the Nation has that within her which the whole world will not conquer. Cimmeria, astonished, recoils faster or slower; all round the Republic there rises fiery, as it were, a magic ring of musket-volleying and *ça-ira*-ing. Majesty of Prussia, as Majesty of Spain, will by and by acknowledge his sins and the Republic: and make a Peace of Bâle.

Foreign Commerce, Colonies, Factories in the East and in the West, are fallen or falling into the hands of sea-ruling Pitt, enemy of human nature. Nevertheless what sound is this that we hear, on the first of June, 1794; sound of as war-thunder borne from the Ocean too; of tone most piercing? War-thunder from off the Brest waters: Villaret-Joyeuse and English Howe, after long manœuvring have ranked themselves there; and are belching fire. The enemies of human nature are on their own element; cannot be conquered; cannot be kept from conquering. Twelve hours of raging cannonade; sun now sinking westward through the battle-smoke: six French Ships taken, the Battle lost; what Ship soever can still sail, making off! But how is it, then, with that *Vengeur* Ship, she neither strikes nor makes off? She is lamed, she cannot make off; strike she will not. Fire rakes her fore and aft, from victorious enemies; the *Vengeur* is sinking. Strong are ye, Tyrants of the Sea; yet we also, are we weak? Lo! all flags, streamers, jacks, every rag of tricolor that will yet run on rope, fly rustling aloft: the whole crew crowds to the upper deck; and, with universal soul-maddening yell, shouts *Vive la République*,—sinking, sinking. She staggers, she lurches, her last drunk whirl; Ocean yawns abysmal: down rushes the *Vengeur*, carrying *Vive la République* along with her, unconquerable, into Eternity![727] Let foreign Despots think of that. There is an Unconquerable in man, when he stands on his Rights of Man: let Despots and Slaves and all people know this, and only them that stand on the Wrongs of Man tremble to know it.—So has History written, nothing doubting, of the sunk *Vengeur*.

—Reader! Mendez Pinto, Münchausen, Cagliostro, Psalmanazar have been great; but they are not the greatest. O Barrère, Barrère, Anacreon of the Guillotine! must inquisitive pictorial History, in a new edition, ask again, "How *is* it with the *Vengeur*," in this its glorious suicidal sinking;

and, with resentful brush, dash a bend-sinister of contumelious lamp-black through thee and it? Alas, alas! The *Vengeur*, after fighting bravely, did sink altogether as other ships do, her captain and above two-hundred of her crew escaping gladly in British boats; and this same enormous inspiring Feat, and rumour "of sound most piercing," turns out to be an enormous inspiring Non-entity, extant nowhere save, as falsehood, in the brain of Barrère! Actually so.[728] Founded, like the World itself, on *Nothing;* proved by Convention Report, by solemn Convention Decree and Decrees, and wooden *"Model of the Vengeur;"* believed, bewept, besung by the whole French People to this hour, it may be regarded as Barrère's masterpiece; the largest, most inspiring piece of *blague* manufactured, for some centuries, by any man or nation. As such, and not otherwise, be it henceforth memorable.

Chapter 3.5.VII.
Flame-Picture

In this manner, mad-blazing with flame of all imaginable tints, from the red of Tophet to the stellar-bright, blazes off this Consummation of Sansculottism.

But the hundredth part of the things that were done, and the thousandth part of the things that were projected and decreed to be done, would tire the tongue of History. Statue of the *Peuple Souverain*, high as Strasburg Steeple; which shall fling its shadow from the Pont Neuf over Jardin National and Convention Hall;—enormous, in Painter David's head! With other the like enormous Statues not a few: realised in paper Decree. For, indeed, the Statue of Liberty herself is still but Plaster in the Place de la Révolution! Then Equalisation of Weights and Measures, with decimal division; Institutions, of Music and of much else; Institute in general; School of Arts, School of Mars, *Elèves de la Patrie*, Normal Schools: amid such Gun-boring, Altar-burning, Saltpetre-digging, and miraculous improvements in Tannery!

What, for example, is this that Engineer Chappe is doing, in the Park of Vincennes? In the Park of Vincennes; and onwards, they say, in the Park of Lepelletier Saint-Fargeau the assassinated Deputy; and still onwards to the Heights of Ecouen and further, he has scaffolding set up, has posts driven in; wooden arms with elbow joints are jerking and fugling in the air, in the most rapid mysterious manner! Citoyens ran up suspicious. Yes, O Citoyens, we are signaling: it is a device this, worthy of the Republic; a thing for what we will call *Far-writing* without the aid of postbags; in Greek, it shall be named Telegraph.—*Télégraphe sacré!* answers Citoyenism: For writing to Traitors, to Austria?—and tears it down. Chappe had to escape, and get a new Legislative Decree. Nevertheless he has accomplished it, the indefatigable Chappe: this his *Far-writer*, with its wooden arms and elbow-joints, can intelligibly signal; and lines of them are set up, to the North Frontiers and elsewhither. On an Autumn evening of the Year Two, Far-writer having just written that Condé Town has surrendered to us, we send from Tuileries Convention Hall this response in the shape of Decree: "The name of Condé is changed to *Nord-Libre*, North-Free. The Army of the North ceases not to merit well of the country." —To the admiration of men! For lo, in some half hour, while the Convention yet debates, there arrives this new answer: "I inform thee, *je t'annonce*, Citizen President, that the decree of Convention, ordering change of the name Condé into *North-Free*; and the other declaring that the Army of the North ceases not to merit well of the country, are transmitted and acknowledged by Telegraph. I have instructed my Officer at Lille to forward them to North-Free by express. *Signed*, CHAPPE."[729]

Or see, over Fleurus in the Netherlands, where General Jourdan, having now swept the soil of Liberty, and advanced thus far, is just about to fight, and sweep or be swept, things there not in the Heaven's Vault, some Prodigy, seen by Austrian eyes and spyglasses: in the similitude of an enormous Windbag, with netting and enormous Saucer depending from it? A Jove's Balance, O ye Austrian spyglasses? One saucer-hole of a Jove's Balance; *your* poor Austrian scale having kicked itself quite aloft, out of sight? By Heaven, answer the spyglasses, it is a Montgolfier, a Balloon, and they are making signals! Austrian cannon-battery barks at this Montgolfier; harmless as dog at the Moon: the Montgolfier makes its signals; detects what Austrian ambuscade there may be, and descends at its ease.[730] What will not these devils incarnate contrive?

On the whole, is it not, O Reader, one of the strangest Flame-Pictures that ever painted itself; flaming off there, on its ground of Guillotine-black? And the nightly Theatres are Twenty-three; and the *Salons de danse* are sixty: full of mere *Egalité, Fraternite* and *Carmagnole*. And Section Committee-rooms are Forty-eight; redolent of tobacco and brandy: vigorous with twenty-pence a-day, coercing the suspect. And the Houses of Arrest are Twelve for Paris alone; crowded and even crammed. And at all turns, you need your "Certificate of Civism;" be it for going out, or for coming in; nay without it you cannot, for money, get your daily ounces of bread. Dusky red-capped Baker's-queues; wagging themselves; not in silence! For we still live by Maximum, in all things; waited on by these two, Scarcity and Confusion. The faces of men are darkened with suspicion; with suspecting, or being suspect. The streets lie unswept; the ways unmended. Law has shut her Books; speaks little, save impromptu, through the throat of Tinville. Crimes go unpunished: not crimes against the Revolution.[731] "The number of foundling children," as some compute, "is doubled."

How silent now sits Royalism; sits all Aristocratism; Respectability that kept its Gig! The honour now, and the safety, is to Poverty, not to Wealth.

Your Citizen, who would be fashionable, walks abroad, with his Wife on his arm, in red wool nightcap, black shag spencer, and carmagnole complete. Aristocratism crouches low, in what shelter is still left; submitting to all requisitions, vexations; too happy to escape with life. Ghastly châteaus stare on you by the wayside; disroofed, diswindowed; which the National House-broker is peeling for the lead and ashlar. The old tenants hover disconsolate, over the Rhine with Condé; a spectacle to men. *Ci-devant* Seigneur, exquisite in palate, will become an exquisite Restaurateur Cook in Hamburg; Ci-devant Madame, exquisite in dress, a successful *Marchande des Modes* in London. In Newgate-Street, you meet M. le Marquis, with a rough deal on his shoulder, adze and jack-plane under arm; he has taken to the joiner trade; it being necessary to live *(faut vivre)*.[732] —Higher than all Frenchmen the domestic Stock-jobber flourishes,—in a day of Paper-money. The Farmer also flourishes: "Farmers' houses," says Mercier, "have become like Pawn-brokers' shops;" all manner of furniture, apparel, vessels of gold and silver accumulate themselves there: bread is precious. The Farmer's rent is Paper-money, and he alone of men has bread: Farmer is better than Landlord, and will himself become Landlord.

And daily, we say, like a black Spectre, silently through that Life-tumult, passes the Revolution Cart; writing on the walls its MENE, MENE, *Thou art weighed, and found wanting!* A Spectre with which one has grown familiar. Men have adjusted themselves: complaint issues not from that Death-tumbril. Weak women and *ci-devants,* their plumage and finery all tarnished, sit there; with a silent gaze, as if looking into the Infinite Black. The once light lip wears a curl of irony, uttering no word; and the Tumbril fares along. They may be guilty before Heaven, or not; they are guilty, we suppose, before the Revolution. Then, does not the Republic "coin money" of them, with its great axe? Red Nightcaps howl dire approval: the rest of Paris looks on; if with a sigh, that is much; Fellow-creatures whom sighing cannot help; whom black Necessity and Tinville have clutched.

One other thing, or rather two other things, we will still mention; and no more: The Blond Perukes; the Tannery at Meudon. Great talk is of these *Perruques blondes:* O Reader, they are made from the Heads of Guillotined women! The locks of a Duchess, in this way, may come to cover the scalp of a Cordwainer: her blond German Frankism his black Gaelic poll, if it be bald. Or they may be worn affectionately, as relics; rendering one suspect?[733] Citizens use them, not without mockery; of a rather cannibal sort.

Still deeper into one's heart goes that Tannery at Meudon; not mentioned among the other miracles of tanning! "At Meudon," says Montgaillard with considerable calmness, "there was a Tannery of Human Skins; such of the Guillotined as seemed worth flaying: of which perfectly good wash-leather was made:" for breeches, and other uses. The skin of the men, he remarks, was superior in toughness (*consistance*) and quality to shamoy; that of women was good for almost nothing, being so soft in texture![734] — History looking back over Cannibalism, through *Purchas's Pilgrims* and all early and late Records, will perhaps find no terrestrial Cannibalism of a sort on the whole so detestable. It is a manufactured, soft-feeling, quietly elegant sort; a sort *perfide!* Alas then, is man's civilisation only a wrappage, through which the savage nature of him can still burst, infernal as ever? Nature still makes him; and has an Infernal in her as well as a Celestial.

BOOK 3.VI.
THERMIDOR

Chapter 3.6.I.
The Gods are athirst

What then is this Thing, called *La Révolution*, which, like an Angel of Death, hangs over France, noyading, fusillading, fighting, gun-boring, tanning human skins? *La Révolution* is but so many Alphabetic Letters; a thing nowhere to be laid hands on, to be clapt under lock and key: where is it? what is it? It is the Madness that dwells in the hearts of men. In this man it is, and in that man; as a rage or as a terror, it is in all men. Invisible, impalpable; and yet no black Azrael, with wings spread over half a continent, with sword sweeping from sea to sea, could be a truer Reality.

To explain, what is called explaining, the march of this Revolutionary Government, be no task of ours. Men cannot explain it. A paralytic Couthon, asking in the Jacobins, "what hast thou done to be hanged if the Counter-Revolution should arrive;" a sombre Saint-Just, not yet six-and-twenty, declaring that "for Revolutionists there is no rest but in the tomb;" a seagreen Robespierre converted into vinegar and gall; much more an Amar and Vadier, a Collot and Billaud: to inquire what thoughts, predetermination or prevision, might be in the head of these men! Record of their thought remains not; Death and Darkness have swept it out utterly. Nay if we even had their thought, all they could have articulately spoken to us, how insignificant a fraction were that of the Thing which realised itself, which decreed itself, on signal given by them! As has been said more than once, this Revolutionary Government is not a self-conscious but a blind fatal one. Each man, enveloped in his ambient-atmosphere of revolutionary fanatic Madness, rushes on, impelled and impelling; and has become a blind brute Force; no rest for him but in the grave! Darkness and the mystery of horrid cruelty cover it for us, in History; as they did in Nature. The chaotic Thunder-cloud, with its pitchy black, and its tumult of dazzling jagged fire, in a world all electric: thou wilt not undertake to shew how that comported itself,—what the secrets of its dark womb were; from what sources, with what specialities, the lightning it held did, in confused brightness of terror, strike forth, destructive and self-destructive, till it ended? Like a Blackness naturally of Erebus, which by will of Providence had for once mounted itself into dominion and the Azure: is not this properly the nature of Sansculottism consummating itself? Of which Erebus Blackness be it enough to discern that this and the other dazzling fire-bolt, dazzling fire-torrent, does by small Volition and great Necessity, verily issue,—in such and such succession; destructive so and so, self-destructive so and so: till it end.

Royalism is extinct, "sunk," as they say, "in the mud of the Loire;" Republicanism dominates without and within: what, therefore, on the 15th day of March, 1794, is this? Arrestment, sudden really as a bolt out of the Blue, has hit strange victims: Hébert *Père Duchene*, Bibliopolist Momoro, Clerk Vincent, General Ronsin; high Cordelier Patriots, redcapped Magistrates of Paris, Worshippers of Reason, Commanders of Revolutionary Army! Eight short days ago, their Cordelier Club was loud, and louder than ever, with Patriot denunciations. Hébert *Père Duchene* had 'held his tongue and his heart these two months, at sight of Moderates, Crypto-Aristocrats, Camilles, *Scélérats* in the Convention itself: but could not do it any longer; would, if other remedy were not, invoke the Sacred right of Insurrection.' So spake Hébert in Cordelier Session; with vivats, till the roofs rang again.[735] Eight short days ago; and now already! They rub their eyes: it is no dream; they find themselves in the Luxembourg. Goose Gobel too; and they that burnt Churches! Chaumette himself, potent Procureur, *Agent National* as they now call it, who could "recognise the Suspect by the very face of them," he lingers but three days; on the third day he too is hurled in. Most chopfallen, blue, enters the National Agent this Limbo whither he has sent so many. Prisoners crowd round, jibing and jeering: 'Sublime National Agent,' says one, 'in virtue of thy immortal Proclamation, lo there! I am suspect, thou art suspect, he is suspect, we are suspect, ye are suspect, they are suspect!'

The meaning of these things? Meaning! It is a Plot; Plot of the most extensive ramifications; which, however, Barrère holds the threads of. Such Church-burning and scandalous masquerades of Atheism, fit to make the Revolution odious: where indeed could they originate but in the gold of Pitt? Pitt indubitably, as Preternatural Insight will teach one, did hire this Faction of *Enragés*, to play their fantastic tricks; to roar in their Cordeliers Club about Moderatism; to print their *Père Duchene;* worship skyblue Reason in red nightcap; rob all Altars,—and bring the spoil to *us!*

Still more indubitable, visible to the mere bodily sight, is this: that the Cordeliers Club sits pale, with anger and terror; and has "veiled the Rights of Man,"—without effect. Likewise that the Jacobins are in considerable confusion; busy "purging themselves, "s'épurant," as, in times of Plot and public Calamity, they have repeatedly had to do. Not even Camille Desmoulins but has given offence: nay there have risen murmurs against Danton himself; though he bellowed them down, and Robespierre finished the matter by "embracing him in the Tribune."

Whom shall the Republic and a jealous Mother Society trust? In these times of temptation, of Preternatural Insight! For there are Factions of the Stranger, "de l'étranger," Factions of Moderates, of Enraged; all manner of Factions: we walk in a world of Plots; strings, universally spread, of deadly gins and falltraps, baited by the gold of Pitt! Clootz, Speaker of Mankind so-called, with his *Evidences of Mahometan Religion*, and babble of Universal Republic, him an incorruptible Robespierre has purged away. Baron Clootz, and Paine rebellious Needleman lie, these two months, in the Luxembourg; limbs of the Faction *de l'étranger*. Representative Phélippeaux is purged out: he came back from La Vendée with an ill report in his mouth against rogue Rossignol, and our method of warfare there. Recant it, O Phélippeaux, we entreat thee! Phélippeaux will not recant; and is purged out. Representative Fabre d'Eglantine, famed Nomenclator of Romme's Calendar, is purged out; nay, is cast into the Luxembourg: accused of Legislative Swindling "in regard to monies of the India Company." There with his Chabots, Bazires, guilty of the like, let Fabre wait his destiny. And Westermann friend of Danton, he who led the Marseillese on the Tenth of August, and fought well in La Vendée, but spoke not well of rogue Rossignol, is purged out. Lucky, if he too go not to the Luxembourg. And your Prolys, Guzmans, of the Faction of the Stranger, they have gone; Peyreyra, though he fled is gone, "taken in the disguise of a Tavern Cook." I am suspect, thou art suspect, he is suspect!—

The great heart of Danton is weary of it. Danton is gone to native Arcis, for a little breathing time of peace: Away, black Arachne-webs, thou world of Fury, Terror, and Suspicion; welcome, thou everlasting Mother, with thy spring greenness, thy kind household loves and memories; true art thou, were all else untrue! The great Titan walks silent, by the banks of the murmuring Aube, in young native haunts that knew him when a boy; wonders what the end of these things may be.

But strangest of all, Camille Desmoulins is purged out. Couthon gave as a test in regard to Jacobin purgation the question, "What hast thou done to be hanged if Counter-Revolution should arrive?" Yet Camille, who could so well answer this question, is purged out! The truth is, Camille, early in

December last, began publishing a new Journal, or Series of Pamphlets, entitled the *Vieux Cordelier*, Old Cordelier. Camille, not afraid at one time to "embrace Liberty on a heap of dead bodies," begins to ask now, Whether among so many arresting and punishing Committees there ought not to be a "Committee of Mercy?" Saint-Just, he observes, is an extremely solemn young Republican, who "carries his head as if it were a *Saint-Sacrement*; adorable Hostie, or divine Real-Presence! Sharply enough, this *old* Cordelier, Danton and he were of the earliest primary Cordeliers,—shoots his glittering war-shafts into your *new* Cordeliers, your Héberts, Momoros, with their brawling brutalities and despicabilities: say, as the Sun-god (for poor Camille is a Poet) shot into that Python Serpent sprung of mud.

Whereat, as was natural, the Hébertist Python did hiss and writhe amazingly; and threaten "sacred right of Insurrection;"—and, as we saw, get cast into Prison. Nay, with all the old wit, dexterity, and light graceful poignancy, Camille, translating "out of *Tacitus*, from the Reign of Tiberius," pricks into the *Law of the Suspect* itself; making it odious! Twice, in the Decade, his wild Leaves issue; full of wit, nay of humour, of harmonious ingenuity and insight,—one of the strangest phenomenon of that dark time; and smite, in their wild-sparkling way, at various monstrosities, Saint-Sacrament heads, and Juggernaut idols, in a rather reckless manner. To the great joy of Josephine Beauharnais, and the other Five Thousand and odd Suspect, who fill the Twelve Houses of Arrest; on whom a ray of hope dawns! Robespierre, at first approbatory, knew not at last what to think; then thought, with his Jacobins, that Camille must be expelled. A man of true Revolutionary spirit, this Camille; but with the unwisest sallies; whom Aristocrats and Moderates have the art to corrupt! Jacobinism is in uttermost crisis and struggle: enmeshed wholly in plots, corruptibilities, neck-gins and baited falltraps of Pitt *Ennemi du Genre Humain*. Camille's First Number begins with "O Pitt!"—his last is dated 15 Pluviose Year 2, 3d February 1794; and ends with these words of Montezuma's, "*Les dieux ont soif*, The gods are athirst."

Be this as it may, the Hébertists lie in Prison only some nine days. On the 24th of March, therefore, the Revolution Tumbrils carry through that Life-tumult a new cargo: Hébert, Vincent, Momoro, Ronsin, Nineteen of them in all; with whom, curious enough, sits Clootz Speaker of Mankind. They have been massed swiftly into a lump, this miscellany of Nondescripts; and travel now their last road. No help. They too must "look through the little window;" they too "must sneeze into the sack," *éternuer dans le sac*; as they have done to others so is it done to them. *Sainte-Guillotine*, meseems, is worse than the old Saints of Superstition; a man-devouring Saint? Clootz, still with an air of polished sarcasm, endeavours to jest, to offer cheering "arguments of Materialism;" he requested to be executed last, "in order to establish certain principles," — which Philosophy has not retained. General Ronsin too, he still looks forth with some air of defiance, eye of command: the rest are sunk in a stony paleness of despair. Momoro, poor Bibliopolist, no Agrarian Law yet realised, — they might as well have hanged thee at Evreux, twenty months ago, when Girondin Buzot hindered them. Hébert *Père Duchesne* shall never in this world rise in sacred right of insurrection; he sits there low enough, head sunk on breast; Red Nightcaps shouting round him, in frightful parody of his Newspaper Articles, 'Grand choler of the Père Duchesne!' Thus perish they; the sack receives all their heads. Through some section of History, Nineteen spectre-chimeras shall flit, speaking and gibbering; till Oblivion swallow them.

In the course of a week, the Revolutionary Army itself is disbanded; the General having become spectral. This Faction of Rabids, therefore, is also purged from the Republican soil; here also the baited falltraps of that Pitt have been wrenched up harmless; and anew there is joy over a Plot Discovered. The Revolution then is verily devouring its own children. All Anarchy, by the nature of it, is not only destructive but self-destructive.

Chapter 3.6.II.
Danton, No Weakness

Danton, meanwhile, has been pressingly sent for from Arcis: he must return instantly, cried Camille, cried Phélippeaux and Friends, who scented danger in the wind. Danger enough! A Danton, a Robespierre, chief-products of a victorious Revolution, are now arrived in immediate front of one another; must ascertain how they will live together, rule together. One conceives easily the deep mutual incompatibility that divided these two: with what terror of feminine hatred the poor seagreen Formula looked at the monstrous colossal Reality, and grew greener to behold him;—the Reality, again, struggling to think no ill of a chief-product of the Revolution; yet feeling at bottom that such chief-product was little other than a chief wind-bag, blown large by Popular air; not a man with the heart of a man, but a poor spasmodic incorruptible pedant, with a logic-formula instead of heart; of Jesuit or Methodist-Parson nature; full of sincere-cant, incorruptibility, of virulence, poltroonery; barren as the east-wind! Two such chief-products are too much for one Revolution.

Friends, trembling at the results of a quarrel on their part, brought them to meet. 'It is right,' said Danton, swallowing much indignation, 'to repress the Royalists: but we should not strike except where it is useful to the Republic; we should not confound the innocent and the guilty.'— 'And who told you,' replied Robespierre with a poisonous look, 'that one innocent person had perished?'—'*Quoi,*' said Danton, turning round to Friend Paris self-named Fabricius, Juryman in the Revolutionary Tribunal: '*Quoi,* not one innocent? What sayest thou of it, Fabricius!'[736] —Friends, Westermann, this Pâris and others urged him to shew himself, to ascend the Tribune and act. The man Danton was not prone to shew himself; to act, or uproar for his own safety. A man of careless, large, hoping nature; a large nature that could rest: he would sit whole hours, they say, hearing Camille talk, and liked nothing so well. Friends urged him to fly; his Wife urged him: 'Whither fly?' answered he: 'If freed France cast me out, there are only dungeons for me elsewhere. One carries not his country with him at the sole of his shoe!' The man Danton sat still. Not even the arrestment of Friend

Herault, a member of *Salut*, yet arrested by *Salut*, can rouse Danton.—On the night of the 30th of March, Juryman Paris came rushing in; haste looking through his eyes: A clerk of the *Salut* Committee had told him Danton's warrant was made out, he is to be arrested this very night! Entreaties there are and trepidation, of poor Wife, of Paris and Friends: Danton sat silent for a while; then answered, '*Ils n'oseraient*, They dare not;' and would take no measures. Murmuring 'They dare not,' he goes to sleep as usual.

And yet, on the morrow morning, strange rumour spreads over Paris City: Danton, Camille, Phélippeaux, Lacroix have been arrested overnight! It is verily so: the corridors of the Luxembourg were all crowded, Prisoners crowding forth to see this giant of the Revolution among them. 'Messieurs,' said Danton politely, 'I hoped soon to have got you all out of this: but here I am myself; and one sees not where it will end.'—Rumour may spread over Paris: the Convention clusters itself into groups; wide-eyed, whispering, 'Danton arrested!' Who then is safe? Legendre, mounting the Tribune, utters, at his own peril, a feeble word for him; moving that he be heard at that Bar before indictment; but Robespierre frowns him down: 'Did you hear Chabot, or Bazire? Would you have two weights and measures?' Legendre cowers low; Danton, like the others, must take his doom.

Danton's Prison-thoughts were curious to have; but are not given in any quantity: indeed few such remarkable men have been left so obscure to us as this Titan of the Revolution. He was heard to ejaculate: 'This time twelvemonth, I was moving the creation of that same Revolutionary Tribunal. I crave pardon for it of God and man. They are all Brothers Cain: Brissot would have had me guillotined as Robespierre now will. I leave the whole business in a frightful welter (*gâchis épouvantable*): not one of them understands anything of government. Robespierre will follow me; I drag down Robespierre. O, it were better to be a poor fisherman than to meddle with governing of men.'—Camille's young beautiful Wife, who had made him rich not in money alone, hovers round the Luxembourg, like a disembodied spirit, day and night. Camille's stolen letters to her still exist; stained with the mark of his tears.[737] 'I carry my head like a Saint-Sacrament?' so Saint-Just was heard to mutter: 'Perhaps he will carry his like a Saint-Dennis.'

Unhappy Danton, thou still unhappier light Camille, once light *Procureur de la Lanterne*, ye also have arrived, then, at the Bourne of Creation, where, like Ulysses Polytlas at the limit and utmost Gades of his voyage, gazing into that dim Waste beyond Creation, a man does see *the Shade of his Mother*, pale, ineffectual;—and days when his Mother nursed and wrapped him are all-too sternly contrasted with this day! Danton, Camille, Herault, Westermann, and the others, very strangely massed up with Bazires,

Swindler Chabots, Fabre d'Eglantines, Banker Freys, a most motley Batch, "*Fournée*" as such things will be called, stand ranked at the Bar of Tinville. It is the 2d of April 1794. Danton has had but three days to lie in Prison; for the time presses.

What is your name? place of abode? and the like, Fouquier asks; according to formality. 'My name is Danton,' answers he; 'a name tolerably known in the Revolution: my abode will soon be Annihilation (*dans le Néant*); but I shall live in the Pantheon of History.' A man will endeavour to say something forcible, be it by nature or not! Herault mentions epigrammatically that he 'sat in this Hall, and was detested of Parlementeers.' Camille makes answer, 'My age is that of the *bon Sansculotte Jésus*; an age fatal to Revolutionists.' O Camille, Camille! And yet in that Divine Transaction, let us say, there did lie, among other things, the fatallest Reproof ever uttered here below to Worldly Right-honourableness; "the highest Fact," so devout Novalis calls it, "in the Rights of Man." Camille's real age, it would seem, is thirty-four. Danton is one year older.

Some five months ago, the Trial of the Twenty-two Girondins was the greatest that Fouquier had then done. But here is a still greater to do; a thing which tasks the whole faculty of Fouquier; which makes the very heart of him waver. For it is the voice of Danton that reverberates now from these domes; in passionate words, piercing with their wild sincerity, winged with wrath. Your best Witnesses he shivers into ruin at one stroke. He demands that the Committee-men themselves come as Witnesses, as Accusers; he 'will cover them with ignominy.' He raises his huge stature, he shakes his huge black head, fire flashes from the eyes of him,—piercing to all Republican hearts: so that the very Galleries, though we filled them by ticket, murmur sympathy; and are like to burst down, and raise the People, and deliver him! He complains loudly that he is classed with Chabots, with swindling Stockjobbers; that his Indictment is a list of platitudes and horrors. 'Danton hidden on the Tenth of August?' reverberates he, with the roar of a lion in the toils: 'Where are the men that had to press Danton to shew himself, that day? Where are these high-gifted souls of whom he borrowed energy? Let them appear, these Accusers of mine: I have all the clearness of my self-possession when I demand them. I will unmask the three shallow scoundrels,' *les trois plats coquins*, Saint-Just, Couthon, Lebas, 'who fawn on Robespierre, and lead him towards his destruction. Let them produce themselves here; I will plunge them into Nothingness, out of which they ought never to have risen.' The agitated President agitates his bell; enjoins calmness, in a vehement manner: 'What is it to thee how I defend myself?' cries the other: 'the right of *dooming* me is thine always. The voice of a man speaking for his honour and his life may well drown the jingling of thy bell!' Thus Danton, higher and higher; till the lion voice of him "dies away in his throat:" speech will not utter what is in that man. The Galleries murmur ominously; the first day's Session is over.

O Tinville, President Herman, what will ye do? They have two days more of it, by strictest Revolutionary Law. The Galleries already murmur. If this Danton were to burst your mesh-work!—Very curious indeed to consider. It turns on a hair: and what a Hoitytoity were *there*, Justice and Culprit changing places; and the whole History of France running changed! For in France there is this Danton only that could still try to govern France. He only, the wild amorphous Titan;—and perhaps that other olive-complexioned individual, the Artillery Officer at Toulon, whom we left pushing his fortune in the South?

On the evening of the second day, matters looking not better but worse and worse, Fouquier and Herman, distraction in their aspect, rush over to *Salut Public*. What is to be done? *Salut Public* rapidly concocts a new Decree; whereby if men "insult Justice," they may be "thrown out of the Debates." For indeed, withal, is there not "a Plot in the Luxembourg Prison?" *Ci-devant* General Dillon, and others of the Suspect, plotting with Camille's Wife to distribute *assignats;* to force the Prisons, overset the Republic? Citizen Laflotte, himself Suspect but desiring enfranchisement, has reported said Plot for us:—a report that may bear fruit! Enough, on the morrow morning, an obedient Convention passes this Decree. *Salut* rushes off with it to the aid of Tinville, reduced now almost to extremities. And so, *Hors des Débats*, Out of the Debates, ye insolents! Policemen do your duty! In such manner, with a deadlift effort, *Salut*, Tinville Herman, Leroi *Dix-Août*, and all stanch jurymen setting heart and shoulder to it, the Jury becomes "sufficiently instructed;" Sentence is passed, is sent by an Official, and torn and trampled on: *Death this day*. It is the 5th of April, 1794. Camille's poor Wife may cease hovering about this Prison. Nay let her kiss her poor children; and prepare to enter it, and to follow!—

Danton carried a high look in the Death-cart. Not so Camille: it is but one week, and all is so topsy-turvied; angel Wife left weeping; love, riches, Revolutionary fame, left all at the Prison-gate; carnivorous Rabble now howling round. Palpable, and yet incredible; like a madman's dream! Camille struggles and writhes; his shoulders shuffle the loose coat off them, which hangs knotted, the hands tied: 'Calm my friend,' said Danton; 'heed not that vile canaille (*laissez là cette vile canaille*).' At the foot of the Scaffold, Danton was heard to ejaculate: 'O my Wife, my well-beloved, I shall never see thee more then!'—but, interrupting himself: 'Danton, no weakness!'

He said to Hérault-Séchelles stepping forward to embrace him: 'Our heads will meet *there*,' in the Headsman's sack. His last words were to Samson the Headsman himself: 'Thou wilt shew my head to the people; it is worth shewing.'

So passes, like a gigantic mass, of valour, ostentation, fury, affection and wild revolutionary manhood, this Danton, to his unknown home. He was of Arcis-sur-Aube; born of "good farmer-people" there. He had many sins; but one worst sin he had not, that of Cant. No hollow Formalist, deceptive and self-deceptive, *ghastly* to the natural sense, was this; but a very Man: with all his dross he was a Man; fiery-real, from the great fire-bosom of Nature herself. He saved France from Brunswick; he walked straight his own wild road, whither it led him. He may live for some generations in the memory of men.

Chapter 3.6.III.

The Tumbrils

Next week, it is still but the 10th of April, there comes a new Nineteen; Chaumette, Gobel, Hébert's Widow, the Widow of Camille: these also roll their fated journey; black Death devours them. Mean Hébert's Widow was weeping, Camille's Widow tried to speak comfort to her. O ye kind Heavens, azure, beautiful, eternal behind your tempests and Time-clouds, is there not pity for all! Gobel, it seems, was repentant; he begged absolution of a Priest; did as a Gobel best could. For Anaxagoras Chaumette, the sleek head now stript of its *bonnet rouge*, what hope is there? Unless Death *were* "an eternal sleep?" Wretched Anaxagoras, God shall judge thee, not I.

Hébert, therefore, is gone, and the Hébertists; they that robbed Churches, and adored blue Reason in red nightcap. Great Danton, and the Dantonists; they also are gone. Down to the catacombs; they are become silent men! Let no Paris Municipality, no Sect or Party of this hue or that, resist the will of Robespierre and *Salut*. Mayor Pache, not prompt enough in denouncing these Pitts Plots, may congratulate about them now. Never so heartily; it skills not! His course likewise is to the Luxembourg. We appoint one Fleuriot-Lescot Interim-Mayor in his stead: an "architect from Belgium," they say, this Fleuriot; he is a man one can depend on. Our new Agent-National is Payan, lately Juryman; whose cynosure also is Robespierre.

Thus then, we perceive, this confusedly electric Erebus-cloud of Revolutionary Government has altered its shape somewhat. Two masses, or wings, belonging to it; an over-electric mass of Cordelier Rabids, and an under-electric of Dantonist Moderates and Clemency-men, — these two masses, shooting bolts at one another, so to speak, have annihilated one another. For the Erebus-cloud, as we often remark, is of suicidal nature; and, in jagged irregularity, darts its lightning withal into itself. But now these two discrepant masses being mutually annihilated, it is as if the Erebus-cloud had got to internal composure; and did only pour its hellfire lightning on the World that lay under it. In plain words, Terror of the Guillotine was never terrible till now. Systole, diastole, swift and ever swifter goes the Axe of Samson. Indictments cease by degrees to have so much as plausibility: Fouquier chooses from the Twelve houses of Arrest what he calls Batches, "*Fournées*," a score or more at a time; his Jurymen are charged to make *feu de file*, fire-filing till the ground be *clear*. Citizen Laflotte's report of Plot in the Luxembourg is verily bearing fruit! If no speakable charge exist against a man, or Batch of men, Fouquier has always this: a Plot in the Prison. Swift and ever swifter goes Samson; up, finally, to three score and more at a Batch! It is the highday of Death: none but the Dead return not.

O dusky d'Espréménil, what a day is this, the 22d of April, thy last day! The Palais Hall here is the same stone Hall, where thou, five years ago, stoodest perorating, amid endless pathos of rebellious Parlement, in the grey of the morning; bound to march with d'Agoust to the Isles of Hieres. The stones are the same stones: but the rest, Men, Rebellion, Pathos, Peroration, see! it has all fled, like a gibbering troop of ghosts, like the phantasms of a dying brain! With d'Espréménil, in the same line of Tumbrils, goes the mournfullest medley. Chapelier goes, *ci-devant* popular President of the Constituent; whom the Menads and Maillard met in his carriage, on the Versailles Road. Thouret likewise, *ci-devant* President, father of Constitutional Law-acts; he whom we heard saying, long since, with a loud voice, 'The Constituent Assembly has fulfilled its mission!' And the noble old Malesherbes, who defended Louis and could not speak, like a grey old rock dissolving into sudden water: he journeys here now, with his kindred, daughters, sons and grandsons, his Lamoignons, Châteaubriands; silent, towards Death.—One young Châteaubriand alone is wandering amid the Natchez, by the roar of Niagara Falls, the moan of endless forests: Welcome thou great Nature, savage, but not false, not unkind, unmotherly; no Formula thou, or rapid jangle of Hypothesis, Parliamentary Eloquence, Constitution-building and the Guillotine; speak thou to me, O Mother, and sing my sick heart thy mystic everlasting lullaby-song, and let all the rest be far!—

Another row of Tumbrils we must notice: that which holds Elizabeth, the Sister of Louis. Her Trial was like the rest; for Plots, for Plots. She was among the kindliest, most innocent of women. There sat with her, amid four-and-twenty others, a once timorous Marchioness de Crussol; courageous now; expressing towards her the liveliest loyalty. At the foot of the Scaffold, Elizabeth with tears in her eyes, thanked this Marchioness; said she was grieved she could not reward her. 'Ah, Madame, would your Royal Highness deign to embrace me, my wishes were complete!'— 'Right willingly, Marquise de Crussol, and with my whole heart.'[738]

Thus they: at the foot of the Scaffold. The Royal Family is now reduced to two: a girl and a little boy. The boy, once named Dauphin, was taken from his Mother while she yet lived; and given to one Simon, by trade a Cordwainer, on service then about the Temple-Prison, to bring him up in principles of Sansculottism. Simon taught him to drink, to swear, to sing the *carmagnole*. Simon is now gone to the Municipality: and the poor boy, hidden in a tower of the Temple, from which in his fright and bewilderment and early decrepitude he wishes not to stir out, lies perishing, "his shirt not changed for six months;" amid squalor and darkness, lamentably,[739] —so as none but poor Factory Children and the like are wont to perish, and *not* be lamented!

The Spring sends its green leaves and bright weather, bright May brighter than ever: Death pauses not. Lavoisier famed Chemist, shall die and not live: Chemist Lavoisier was Farmer-General Lavoisier too, and now "all the Farmers-General are arrested;" all, and shall give an account of their monies and incomings; and die for "putting water in the tobacco" they sold. [740] Lavoisier begged a fortnight more of life, to finish some experiments: but 'the Republic does not need such;' the axe must do its work. Cynic Chamfort, reading these Inscriptions of *Brotherhood or Death*, says 'it is a Brotherhood of Cain:' arrested, then liberated; then about to be arrested again, this Chamfort cuts and slashes himself with frantic uncertain hand; gains, not without difficulty, the refuge of death. Condorcet has lurked deep, these many months; Argus-eyes watching and searching for him. His concealment is become dangerous to others and himself; he has to fly again, to skulk, round Paris, in thickets and stone-quarries. And so at the Village of Clamars, one bleared May morning, there enters a Figure, ragged, rough-bearded, hunger-stricken; asks breakfast in the tavern there. Suspect, by the look of him! 'Servant out of place, sayest thou?' Committee-President of Forty-Sous finds a Latin Horace on him: 'Art thou not one of those *Ci-devants* that were wont to keep servants? Suspect!' He is haled forthwith, breakfast unfinished, towards Bourg-la-Reine, on foot: he faints with exhaustion; is set on a peasant's horse; is flung into his damp prison-cell: on the morrow, recollecting him, you enter; Condorcet lies dead on the floor. They die fast, and disappear: the Notabilities of France disappear, one after one, like lights in a Theatre, which you are snuffing out.

Under which circumstances, is it not singular, and almost touching, to see Paris City drawn out, in the meek May nights, in civic ceremony, which they call "*Souper Fraternel*," Brotherly Supper? Spontaneous, or partially spontaneous, in the twelfth, thirteenth, fourteenth nights of this May month, it is seen. Along the Rue Saint-Honoré, and main Streets and Spaces, each Citoyen brings forth what of supper the stingy *Maximum* has yielded him, to the open air; joins it to his neighbour's supper; and with common table, cheerful light burning frequent, and what due modicum of cut-glasses and other garnish and relish is convenient, they eat frugally together, under the kind stars.[741] See it O Night! With cheerfully pledged wine-cup, hobnobbing to the Reign of Liberty, Equality, Brotherhood, with their wives in best ribands, with their little ones romping round, the Citoyens, in frugal Love-feast, sit there. Night in her wide empire sees nothing similar. O my brothers, why is the reign of Brotherhood *not* come! It is come, it shall come, say the Citoyens frugally hobnobbing.—Ah me! these everlasting stars, do they not look down "like glistening eyes, bright with immortal pity, over the lot of man!"—

One lamentable thing, however, is, that individuals will attempt assassination—of Representatives of the People. Representative Collot, Member even of *Salut*, returning home, "about one in the morning," probably touched with liquor, as he is apt to be, meets on the stairs, the cry '*Scélérat!*' and also the snap of a pistol: which latter flashes in the pan; disclosing to him, momentarily, a pair of truculent saucer-eyes, swart grim-clenched countenance; recognisable as that of our little fellow-lodger, Citoyen Amiral, formerly "a clerk in the Lotteries!; Collot shouts *Murder*, with lungs fit to awaken all the *Rue Favart*; Amiral snaps a second time; a second time flashes in the pan; then darts up into his apartment; and, after there firing, still with inadequate effect, one musket at himself and another at his captor, is clutched and locked in Prison.[742] An indignant little man this Amiral, of Southern temper and complexion, of "considerable muscular force." He denies not that he meant to 'purge France of a tyrant;' nay avows that he had an eye to the Incorruptible himself, but took Collot as more convenient!

Rumour enough hereupon; heaven-high congratulation of Collot, fraternal embracing, at the Jacobins, and elsewhere. And yet, it would seem the assassin-mood proves catching. Two days more, it is still but the 23d of May, and towards nine in the evening, Cecile Renault, Paper-dealer's daughter, a young woman of soft blooming look, presents herself at the Cabinet-maker's in the Rue Saint-Honoré; desires to see Robespierre. Robespierre cannot be seen: she grumbles irreverently. They lay hold of her. She has left a basket in a shop hard by: in the basket are female change of raiment and two knives! Poor Cecile, examined by Committee, declares she 'wanted to see what a tyrant was like:' the change of raiment was 'for my own use in the place I am surely going to.'—'What place?'—'Prison; and then the Guillotine,' answered she.—Such things come of Charlotte Corday; in a people prone to imitation, and monomania! Swart choleric men try Charlotte's feat, and their pistols miss fire; soft blooming young women try it, and, only half-resolute, leave their knives in a shop.

O Pitt, and ye Faction of the Stranger, shall the Republic never have rest; but be torn continually by baited springs, by wires of explosive spring-guns? Swart Amiral, fair young Cecile, and all that knew them, and many that did not know them, lie locked, waiting the scrutiny of Tinville.

Chapter 3.6.IV.
Mumbo-Jumbo

But on the day they call *Décadi*, New-Sabbath, 20 *Prairial*, 8th June by old style, what thing is this going forward, in the Jardin National, whilom Tuileries Garden?

All the world is there, in holydays clothes:[743] foul linen went out with the Hébertists; nay Robespierre, for one, would never once countenance that; but went always elegant and frizzled, not without vanity even,—and had his room hung round with seagreen Portraits and Busts. In holyday clothes, we say, are the innumerable Citoyens and Citoyennes: the weather is of the brightest; cheerful expectation lights all countenances. Juryman Vilate gives breakfast to many a Deputy, in his official Apartment, in the Pavillon *ci-devant* of Flora; rejoices in the bright-looking multitudes, in the brightness of leafy June, in the auspicious *Décadi*, or New-Sabbath. This day, if it please Heaven, we are to have, on improved Anti-Chaumette principles: a New Religion.

Catholicism being burned out, and Reason-worship guillotined, was there not need of one? Incorruptible Robespierre, not unlike the Ancients, as Legislator of a free people will now also be Priest and Prophet. He has donned his sky-blue coat, made for the occasion; white silk waistcoat broidered with silver, black silk breeches, white stockings, shoe-buckles of gold. He is President of the Convention; he has made the Convention *decree*, so they name it, *décréter* the "Existence of the Supreme Being," and likewise *"ce principe consolateur* of the Immortality of the Soul." These consolatory principles, the basis of rational Republican Religion, are getting decreed; and here, on this blessed *Décadi*, by help of Heaven and Painter David, is to be our first act of worship.

See, accordingly, how after Decree passed, and what has been called "the scraggiest Prophetic Discourse ever uttered by man,"—Mahomet Robespierre, in sky-blue coat and black breeches, frizzled and powdered to perfection, bearing in his hand a bouquet of flowers and wheat-ears, issues proudly from the Convention Hall; Convention following him, yet, as is remarked, with an interval. Amphitheatre has been raised, or at least *Monticule* or Elevation; hideous Statues of Atheism, Anarchy and such like, thanks to Heaven and Painter David, strike abhorrence into the heart. Unluckily however, our Monticule is too small. On the top of it not half of us can stand; wherefore there arises indecent shoving, nay treasonous irreverent growling. Peace, thou Bourdon de l'Oise; peace, or it may be worse for thee!

The seagreen Pontiff takes a torch, Painter David handing it; mouths some other froth-rant of vocables, which happily one cannot hear; strides resolutely forward, in sight of expectant France; sets his torch to Atheism and Company, which are but made of pasteboard steeped in turpentine. They burn up rapidly; and, from within, there rises "by machinery" an incombustible Statue of Wisdom, which, by ill hap, gets besmoked a little; but does stand there visible in as serene attitude as it can.

And then? Why, then, there is other Processioning, scraggy Discoursing, and—this *is* our Feast of the *Être Suprême;* our new Religion, better or worse, is come!—Look at it one moment, O Reader, not two. The Shabbiest page of Human Annals: or is there, that thou wottest of, one shabbier? Mumbo-Jumbo of the African woods to me seems venerable beside this new Deity of Robespierre; for this is a *conscious* Mumbo-Jumbo, and *knows* that he is machinery. O seagreen Prophet, unhappiest of windbags blown nigh to bursting, what distracted Chimera among realities are thou growing to! This then, this common pitch-link for artificial fireworks of turpentine and pasteboard; *this* is the miraculous Aaron's Rod thou wilt stretch over a hag-ridden hell-ridden France, and bid her plagues cease? Vanish, thou and it!—'*Avec ton Être Suprême,*' said Billaud, '*tu commences à m'embêter:* With thy *Être Suprême* thou beginnest to be a bore to me.'[744]

Catherine Théot, on the other hand, "an ancient serving-maid seventy-nine years of age," inured to Prophecy and the Bastille from of old, sits, in an upper room in the Rue-de-Contrescarpe, poring over the Book of Revelations, with an eye to Robespierre; finds that this astonishing thrice-potent Maximilien really is the Man spoken of by Prophets, who is to make the Earth young again. With her sit devout old Marchionesses, *ci-devant* honourable women; among whom Old-Constituent Dom Gerle, with his addle head, cannot be wanting. They sit there, in the Rue-de-Contrescarpe; in mysterious adoration: Mumbo is Mumbo, and Robespierre is his Prophet. A conspicuous man this Robespierre. He has his volunteer Bodyguard of *Tappe-durs,* let us say *Strike-sharps,* fierce Patriots with feruled sticks; and Jacobins kissing the hem of his garment. He enjoys the admiration of many, the worship of some; and is well worth the wonder of one and all.

The grand question and hope, however, is: Will not this Feast of the Tuileries Mumbo-Jumbo be a sign perhaps that the Guillotine is to abate? Far enough from that! Precisely on the second day after it, Couthon, one of the "three shallow scoundrels," gets himself lifted into the Tribune; produces a bundle of papers. Couthon proposes that, as Plots still abound, the *Law of the Suspect* shall have extension, and Arrestment new vigour and facility. Further that, as in such case business is like to be heavy, our Revolutionary Tribunal too shall have extension; be divided, say, into Four Tribunals, each with its President, each with its Fouquier or Substitute of Fouquier, all labouring at once, and any remnant of shackle or dilatory formality be struck off: in this way it may perhaps still overtake the work. Such is Couthon's *Decree of the Twenty-second Prairial*, famed in those times. At hearing of which Decree the very Mountain gasped, awestruck; and one Ruamps ventured to say that if it passed without adjournment and discussion, he, as one Representative, 'would blow his brains out.' Vain saying! The Incorruptible knit his brows; spoke a prophetic fateful word or two: the *Law of Prairial* is Law; Ruamps glad to leave his rash brains where they are. Death, then, and always Death! Even so. Fouquier is enlarging his borders; making room for Batches of a Hundred and fifty at once;—getting a Guillotine set up, of improved velocity, and to work under cover, in the apartment close by. So that *Salut* itself has to intervene, and forbid him: 'Wilt thou *demoralise* the Guillotine,' asks Collot, reproachfully, '*démoraliser le supplice!*'

There is indeed danger of that; were not the Republican faith great, it were already done. See, for example, on the 17th of June, what a *Batch*, Fifty-four at once! Swart Amiral is here, he of the pistol that missed fire; young Cecile Renault, with her father, family, entire kith and kin; the widow of d'Espréménil; old M. de Sombreuil of the Invalides, with his Son,—poor old Sombreuil, seventy-three years old, his Daughter saved him in September, and it was but for *this*. Faction of the Stranger, fifty-four of them! In red shirts and smocks, as Assassins and Faction of the Stranger, they flit along there; red baleful Phantasmagory, towards the land of Phantoms.

Meanwhile will not the people of the Place de la Révolution, the inhabitants along the Rue Saint-Honoré, as these continual Tumbrils pass, begin to look gloomy? Republicans too have bowels. The Guillotine is shifted, then again shifted; finally set up at the remote extremity of the South-East:[745] Suburbs Saint-Antoine and Saint-Marceau it is to be hoped, if they have bowels, have very tough ones.

Chapter 3.6.V.
The Prisons

It is time now, however, to cast a glance into the Prisons. When Desmoulins moved for his Committee of Mercy, these Twelve Houses of Arrest held five thousand persons. Continually arriving since then, there have now accumulated twelve thousand. They are Ci-devants, Royalists; in far greater part, they are Republicans, of various Girondin, Fayettish, Un-Jacobin colour. Perhaps no human Habitation or Prison ever equalled in squalor, in noisome horror, these Twelve Houses of Arrest. There exist records of personal experience in them *Mémoires sur les Prisons;* one of the strangest Chapters in the Biography of Man.

Very singular to look into it: how a kind of order rises up in all conditions of human existence; and wherever two or three are gathered together, there are formed modes of existing together, habitudes, observances, nay gracefulnesses, joys! Citoyen Coitant will explain fully how our lean dinner, of herbs and carrion, was consumed not without politeness and *place-aux-dames:* how Seigneur and Shoeblack, Duchess and Doll-Tearsheet, flung pellmell into a heap, ranked themselves according to method: at what hour "the Citoyennes took to their needlework;" and we, yielding the chairs to them, endeavoured to talk gallantly in a standing posture, or even to sing and harp more or less. Jealousies, enmities are not wanting; nor flirtations, of an effective character.

Alas, by degrees, even needlework must cease: Plot in the Prison rises, by Citoyen Laflotte and Preternatural Suspicion. Suspicious Municipality snatches from us all implements; all money and possession, of means or metal, is ruthlessly searched for, in pocket, in pillow and paillasse, and snatched away; red-capped Commissaries entering every cell! Indignation, temporary desperation, at robbery of its very thimble, fills the gentle heart. Old Nuns shriek shrill discord; demand to be killed forthwith. No help from shrieking! Better was that of the two shifty male Citizens, who, eager to preserve an implement or two, were it but a pipe-picker, or needle to darn hose with, determined to defend themselves: by tobacco. Swift then, as your fell Red Caps are heard in the Corridor rummaging and slamming, the two Citoyens light their pipes and begin smoking. Thick darkness envelops them. The Red Nightcaps, opening the cell, breathe but one mouthful; burst forth into chorus of barking and coughing. '*Quoi, Messieurs,*' cry the two Citoyens, 'You don't smoke? Is the pipe disagreeable! *Est-ce que vous ne fumez pas?*' But the Red Nightcaps have fled, with slight search: '*Vous n'aimez pas la pipe?*' cry the Citoyens, as their door slams-to again.[746] My poor brother Citoyens, O surely, in a reign of Brotherhood, you are not the two I would guillotine!

Rigour grows, stiffens into horrid tyranny; Plot in the Prison getting ever riper. This Plot in the Prison, as we said, is now the stereotype formula of Tinville: against whomsoever he knows no crime, this is a ready-made crime. His Judgment-bar has become unspeakable; a recognised mockery; known only as the wicket one passes through, towards Death. His Indictments are drawn out in blank; you insert the Names after. He has his *moutons*, detestable traitor jackalls, who report and bear witness; that they themselves may be allowed to live, — for a time. His *Fournées*, says the reproachful Collot, "shall in no case exceed three-score;" that is his *maximum.* Nightly come his Tumbrils to the Luxembourg, with the fatal Roll-call; list of the *Fournée* of tomorrow. Men rush towards the Grate; listen, if their name be in it? One deep-drawn breath, when the name is not in: we live still one day! And yet some score or scores of names were in. Quick these; they clasp their loved ones to their heart, one last time; with brief adieu, wet-eyed or dry-eyed, they mount, and are away. This night to the Conciergerie; through the Palais misnamed *of Justice*, to the Guillotine tomorrow.

Recklessness, defiant levity, the Stoicism if not of strength yet of weakness, has possessed all hearts. Weak women and *Ci-devants*, their locks not yet made into blond perukes, their skins not yet tanned into breeches, are accustomed to "act the Guillotine" by way of pastime. In fantastic mummery, with towel-turbans, blanket-ermine, a mock Sanhedrim of Judges sits, a mock Tinville pleads; a culprit is doomed, is guillotined by the oversetting of two chairs. Sometimes we carry it farther: Tinville himself, in his turn, is doomed, and not to the Guillotine alone. With blackened face, hirsute, horned, a shaggy Satan snatches him not unshrieking; shews him, with outstretched arm and voice, the fire that is not quenched, the worm that dies not; the monotony of Hell-pain, and the *What hour?* answered by, *It is Eternity!* [747]

And still the Prisons fill fuller, and still the Guillotine goes faster. On all high roads march flights of Prisoners, wending towards Paris. Not *Ci-devants* now; they, the noisy of them, are mown down; it is Republicans now. Chained two and two they march; in exasperated moments, singing their *Marseillaise*. A hundred and thirty-two men of Nantes for instance, march towards Paris, in these same days: Republicans, or say even Jacobins to the marrow of the bone; but Jacobins who had not approved Noyading. [748] *Vive la République* rises from them in all streets of towns: they rest by night, in unutterable noisome dens, crowded to choking; one or two dead on the morrow. They are wayworn, weary of heart; can only shout: *Live the Republic;* we, as under horrid enchantment, dying in this way for it!

Some Four Hundred Priests, of whom also there is record, ride at anchor, "in the roads of the Isle of Aix," long months; looking out on misery, vacuity, waste Sands of Oleron and the ever-moaning brine. Ragged, sordid, hungry; wasted to shadows: eating their unclean ration on deck, circularly, in parties of a dozen, with finger and thumb; beating their scandalous clothes between two stones; choked in horrible miasmata, closed under hatches, seventy of them in a berth, through night; so that the "aged Priest is found lying dead in the morning, in the attitude of prayer!"[749] —How long, O Lord!

Not forever; no. All Anarchy, all Evil, Injustice, is, by the nature of it, *dragon's-teeth;* suicidal, and cannot endure.

Chapter 3.6.VI.
To Finish the Terror

It is very remarkable, indeed, that since the *Être-Suprême* Feast, and the sublime continued harangues on it, which Billaud feared would become a bore to him, Robespierre has gone little to Committee; but held himself apart, as if in a kind of pet. Nay they have made a Report on that old Catherine Théot, and her Regenerative Man spoken of by the Prophets; not in the best spirit. This Théot mystery they affect to regard as a Plot; but have evidently introduced a vein of satire, of irreverent banter, not against the Spinster alone, but obliquely against her Regenerative Man! Barrère's light pen was perhaps at the bottom of it: read through the solemn snuffling organs of old Vadier of the *Sûreté Générale*, the Théot Report had its effect; wrinkling the general Republican visage into an iron grin. Ought these things to be?

We note farther that among the Prisoners in the Twelve Houses of Arrest, there is one whom we have seen before. Senhora Fontenai, *born* Cabarus, the fair Proserpine whom Representative Tallien Pluto-like did gather at Bourdeaux, not without effect on himself! Tallien is home, by recall, long since, from Bourdeaux; and in the most alarming position. Vain that he sounded, louder even than ever, the note of Jacobinism, to hide past shortcomings: the Jacobins purged him out; two times has Robespierre growled at him words of omen from the Convention Tribune. And now his fair Cabarus, hit by denunciation, lies Arrested, Suspect, in spite of all he could do!—Shut in horrid pinfold of death, the Senhora smuggles out to her red-gloomy Tallien the most pressing entreaties and conjurings: Save me; save thyself. Seest thou not that thy own head is doomed; thou with a too fiery audacity; a Dantonist withal; against whom lie grudges? Are ye not all doomed, as in the Polyphemus Cavern; the fawningest slave of you will be but eaten last!—Tallien feels with a shudder that it is true. Tallien has had words of omen, Bourdon has had words, Fréron is hated and Barras: each man "feels his head if it yet stick on his shoulders."

Meanwhile Robespierre, we still observe, goes little to Convention, not at all to Committee; speaks nothing except to his Jacobin House of Lords, amid his bodyguard of *Tappe-durs*. These "forty-days," for we are now far in July, he has not shewed face in Committee; could only work there by his three shallow scoundrels, and the terror there was of him. The Incorruptible himself sits apart; or is seen stalking in solitary places in the fields, with an intensely meditative air; some say, "with eyes red-spotted,"[750] fruit of extreme bile: the lamentablest seagreen Chimera that walks the Earth that July! O hapless Chimera; for thou too hadst a life, and a heart of flesh,—what is this the stern gods, seeming to smile all the way, have led and let thee to! Art not thou he who, few years ago, was a young Advocate of promise; and gave up the Arras Judgeship rather than sentence one man to die?—

What his thoughts might be? His plans for finishing the Terror? One knows not. Dim vestiges there flit of Agrarian Law; a victorious Sansculottism become Landed Proprietor; old Soldiers sitting in National Mansions, in Hospital Palaces of Chambord and Chantilly; peace bought by victory; breaches healed by Feast of *Être Suprême;*—and so, through seas of blood, to Equality, Frugality, worksome Blessedness, Fraternity, and Republic of the virtues! Blessed shore, of such a sea of Aristocrat blood: but how to land on it? Through one last wave: blood of corrupt Sansculottists; traitorous or semi-traitorous Conventionals, rebellious Talliens, Billauds, to whom with my *Être Suprême* I have become a bore; with my Apocalyptic Old Woman a laughing-stock!—So stalks he, this poor Robespierre, like a seagreen ghost through the blooming July. Vestiges of schemes flit dim. But *what* his schemes or his thoughts were will never be known to man.

New Catacombs, some say, are digging for a huge simultaneous butchery. Convention to be butchered, down to the right pitch, by General Henriot and Company: Jacobin House of Lords made dominant; and Robespierre Dictator.[751] There is actually, or else there is not actually, a List made out; which the Hairdresser has got eye on, as he frizzled the Incorruptible locks. Each man asks himself, Is it I?

Nay, as Tradition and rumour of Anecdote still convey it, there was a remarkable bachelor's dinner one hot day at Barrère's. For doubt not, O Reader, this Barrère and others of them gave dinners; had "country-house at Clichy," with elegant enough sumptuosities, and pleasures high-rouged![752] But at this dinner we speak of, the day being so hot, it is said, the guests all stript their coats, and left them in the drawing-room: whereupon Carnot glided out; driven by a necessity, needing of all things *paper;* groped in Robespierre's pocket; found a list of Forty, his own name among them; and tarried not at the wine-cup that day!—Ye must bestir yourselves, O Friends; ye dull Frogs of the Marsh, mute ever since Girondism sank under, even ye now must croak or die! Councils are held, with word and beck; nocturnal, mysterious as death. Does not a feline Maximilien stalk there; voiceless as yet; his green eyes red-spotted; back bent, and hair up? Rash Tallien, with his rash temper and audacity of tongue; he shall *bell the cat*. Fix a day; and be it soon, lest never!

Lo, before the fixed day, on the day which they call Eighth of Thermidor, 26th July 1794, Robespierre himself reappears in Convention; mounts to the Tribune! The biliary face seems clouded with new gloom; judge whether your Talliens, Bourdons listened with interest. It is a voice bodeful of death or of life. Long-winded, unmelodious as the screech-owl's, sounds that prophetic voice: Degenerate condition of Republican spirit; corrupt moderatism; *Sûreté, Salut* Committees themselves infected; back-sliding on this hand and on that; I, Maximilien, alone left incorruptible, ready to die at a moment's warning. For all which what remedy is there? The Guillotine; new vigour to the all-healing Guillotine: death to traitors of every hue! So sings the prophetic voice; into its Convention sounding-board. The old song this: but today, O Heavens! has the sounding-board ceased to act? There is not resonance in this Convention; there is, so to speak, a gasp of silence; nay a certain grating of one knows not what!—Lecointre, our old Draper of Versailles, in these questionable circumstances, sees nothing he can do so safe as rise, "insidiously" or not insidiously, and move, according to established wont, that the Robespierre Speech be "printed and sent to the Departments." Hark: gratings, even of dissonance! Honourable Members hint dissonance; Committee-Members, inculpated in the Speech, utter dissonance; demand "delay in printing." Ever higher rises the note of dissonance; inquiry is even made by Editor Fréron: 'What has become of the Liberty of Opinions in this Convention?' The Order to print and transmit, which had got passed, is rescinded. Robespierre, greener than ever before, has to retire, foiled; discerning that it is mutiny, that evil is nigh.

Mutiny is a thing of the fatallest nature in all enterprises whatsoever; a thing so incalculable, swift-frightful; not to be dealt with in *fright*. But mutiny in a Robespierre Convention, above all,—it is like fire seen sputtering in the ship's powder-room! One death-defiant plunge at it, this moment, and you may still tread it out: hesitate till next moment,—ship and ship's captain, crew and cargo are shivered far; the ship's voyage has suddenly ended between sea and sky. If Robespierre can, tonight, produce his Henriot and Company, and get his work done by them, he and Sansculottism may still subsist some time; if not, probably not. Oliver Cromwell, when that Agitator Serjeant stept forth from the ranks, with plea of grievances, and began gesticulating and demonstrating, as the mouthpiece of Thousands expectant there,—discerned, with those truculent eyes of his, how the matter lay; plucked a pistol from his holsters; blew Agitator and Agitation instantly out. Noll was a man fit for such things.

Robespierre, for his part, glides over at evening to his Jacobin House of Lords; unfolds there, instead of some adequate resolution, his woes, his uncommon virtues, incorruptibilities; then, secondly, his rejected screech-owl Oration;—reads this latter over again; and declares that he is ready to die at a moment's warning. Thou shalt not die! shouts Jacobinism from its thousand throats. 'Robespierre, I will drink the hemlock with thee,' cries Painter David, '*Je boirai la cigue avec toi;*'—a thing not essential to *do*, but which, in the fire of the moment, can be said.

Our Jacobin sounding-board, therefore, does act! Applauses heaven-high cover the rejected Oration; fire-eyed fury lights all Jacobin features: Insurrection a sacred duty; the Convention to be purged; Sovereign People under Henriot and Municipality; we will make a new June-Second of it: to your tents, O Israel! In this key pipes Jacobinism; in sheer tumult of revolt. Let Tallien and all Opposition men make off. Collot d'Herbois, though of the supreme *Salut*, and so lately near shot, is elbowed, bullied; is glad to escape alive. Entering Committee-room of *Salut*, all dishevelled, he finds sleek sombre Saint-Just there, among the rest; who in his sleek way asks, 'What is passing at the Jacobins?'—'What is passing?' repeats Collot, in the unhistrionic Cambyses' vein: 'What is passing? Nothing but revolt and horrors are passing. Ye want our lives; ye shall not have them.' Saint-Just stutters at such Cambyses'-oratory; takes his hat to withdraw. That *Report* he had been speaking of, Report on Republican Things in General we may say, which is to be read in Convention on the morrow, he cannot shew it them this moment: a friend has it; he, Saint-Just, will get it, and send it, were he once home. Once home, he sends not it, but an answer that he will not send it; that they will hear it from the Tribune tomorrow.

Let every man, therefore, according to a well-known good-advice, "pray to Heaven, and keep his powder dry!" Paris, on the morrow, will see a thing. Swift scouts fly dim or invisible, all night, from *Sûreté* and *Salut;* from conclave to conclave; from Mother Society to Townhall. Sleep, can it fall on the eyes of Talliens, Frérons, Collots? Puissant Henriot, Mayor Fleuriot, Judge Coffinhal, Procureur Payan, Robespierre and all the Jacobins are getting ready.

Chapter 3.6.VII.
Go Down to

Tallien's eyes beamed bright, on the morrow, Ninth of Thermidor "about nine o'clock," to see that the Convention had actually met. Paris is in rumour: but at least we are met, in Legal Convention here; we have not been snatched seriatim; treated with a *Pride's Purge* at the door. 'Allons, brave men of the Plain,' late Frogs of the Marsh! cried Tallien with a squeeze of the hand, as he passed in; Saint-Just's sonorous organ being now audible from the Tribune, and the game of games begun.

Saint-Just is verily reading that Report of his; green Vengeance, in the shape of Robespierre, watching nigh. Behold, however, Saint-Just has read but few sentences, when interruption rises, rapid *crescendo;* when Tallien starts to his feet, and Billaud, and this man starts and that,—and Tallien, a second time, with his: 'Citoyens, at the Jacobins last night, I trembled for the Republic. I said to myself, if the Convention dare not strike the Tyrant, then I myself dare; and with this I will do it, if need be,' said he, whisking out a clear-gleaming Dagger, and brandishing it there: the Steel of Brutus, as we call it. Whereat we all bellow, and brandish, impetuous acclaim. 'Tyranny; Dictatorship! Triumvirat!' And the *Salut* Committee-men accuse, and all men accuse, and uproar, and impetuously acclaim. And Saint-Just is standing motionless, pale of face; Couthon ejaculating, 'Triumvir?' with a look at his paralytic legs. And Robespierre is struggling to speak, but President Thuriot is jingling the bell against him, but the Hall is sounding against him like an Æolus-Hall: and Robespierre is mounting the Tribune-steps and descending again; going and coming, like to choke with rage, terror, desperation:—and mutiny is the order of the day![753]

O President Thuriot, thou that wert Elector Thuriot, and from the Bastille battlements sawest Saint-Antoine rising like the Ocean-tide, and hast seen much since, sawest thou ever the like of this? Jingle of bell, which thou jinglest against Robespierre, is hardly audible amid the Bedlam-storm; and men rage for life. 'President of Assassins,' shrieks Robespierre, 'I demand speech of thee for the last time!' It cannot be had. 'To you, O virtuous men of the Plain,' cries he, finding audience one moment, 'I appeal to you!' The virtuous men of the Plain sit silent as stones. And Thuriot's bell jingles, and the Hall sounds like Aeolus's Hall. Robespierre's frothing lips are grown "blue;" his tongue dry, cleaving to the roof of his mouth. 'The blood of Danton chokes him,' cry they. 'Accusation! Decree of Accusation!' Thuriot swiftly puts that question. Accusation passes; the incorruptible Maximilien is decreed Accused.

'I demand to share my Brother's fate, as I have striven to share his virtues,' cries Augustin, the Younger Robespierre: Augustin also is decreed. And Couthon, and Saint-Just, and Lebas, they are all decreed; and packed forth,—not without difficulty, the Ushers almost trembling to obey. Triumvirat and Company are packed forth, into Salut Committee-room; their tongue cleaving to the roof of their mouth. You have but to summon the Municipality; to cashier Commandant Henriot, and launch Arrest at him; to regular formalities; hand Tinville his victims. It is noon: the Aeolus-Hall has delivered itself; blows now victorious, harmonious, as one irresistible wind.

And so the work is finished? One thinks so; and yet it is not so. Alas, there is yet but the first-act finished; three or four other acts still to come; and an uncertain catastrophe! A huge City holds in it so many confusions: seven hundred thousand human heads; not one of which knows what its neighbour is doing, nay not what itself is doing.—See, accordingly, about three in the afternoon, Commandant Henriot, how instead of sitting cashiered, arrested, he gallops along the Quais, followed by Municipal Gendarmes, "trampling down several persons!" For the Townhall sits deliberating, openly insurgent: Barriers to be shut; no Gaoler to admit any Prisoner this day;—and Henriot is galloping towards the Tuileries, to deliver Robespierre. On the Quai de la Ferraillerie, a young Citoyen, walking with his wife, says aloud: 'Gendarmes, that man is not your Commandant; he is under arrest.' The Gendarmes strike down the young Citoyen with the flat of their swords.[754]

Representatives themselves (as Merlin the Thionviller) who accost him, this puissant Henriot flings into guardhouses. He bursts towards the Tuileries Committee-room, 'to speak with Robespierre:' with difficulty, the Ushers and Tuileries Gendarmes, earnestly pleading and drawing sabre, seize this Henriot; get the Henriot Gendarmes persuaded not to fight; get Robespierre and Company packed into hackney-coaches, sent off under escort, to the Luxembourg and other Prisons. This then is the end? May not an exhausted Convention adjourn now, for a little repose and sustenance, "at five o'clock?"

An exhausted Convention did it; and repented it. The end was not come; only the end of the *second-act*. Hark, while exhausted Representatives sit at victuals, — tocsin bursting from all steeples, drums rolling, in the summer evening: Judge Coffinhal is galloping with new Gendarmes to deliver Henriot from Tuileries Committee-room; and does deliver him! Puissant Henriot vaults on horseback; sets to haranguing the Tuileries Gendarmes; corrupts the Tuileries Gendarmes too; trots off with them to Townhall. Alas, and Robespierre is not in Prison: the Gaoler shewed his Municipal order, durst not on pain of his life, admit any Prisoner; the Robespierre Hackney-coaches, in confused jangle and whirl of uncertain Gendarmes, have floated safe — into the Townhall! There sit Robespierre and Company, embraced by Municipals and Jacobins, in sacred right of Insurrection; redacting Proclamations; sounding tocsins; corresponding with Sections and Mother Society. Is not here a pretty enough third-act of a *natural* Greek Drama; catastrophe more uncertain than ever?

The hasty Convention rushes together again, in the ominous nightfall: President Collot, for the chair is his, enters with long strides, paleness on his face; claps on his hat; says with solemn tone: 'Citoyens, armed Villains have beset the Committee-rooms, and got possession of them. The hour is come, to die at our post!' '*Oui,*' answer one and all: 'We swear it!' It is no rhodomontade, this time, but a sad fact and necessity; unless we *do* at our posts, we must verily die! Swift therefore, Robespierre, Henriot, the Municipality, are declared Rebels; put *Hors la Loi,* Out of Law. Better still, we appoint Barras Commandant of what Armed-Force is to be had; send Missionary Representatives to all Sections and quarters, to preach, and raise force; will die at least with harness on our back.

What a distracted City; men riding and running, reporting and hearsaying; the Hour clearly in travail, — child not to be *named* till born! The poor Prisoners in the Luxembourg hear the rumour; tremble for a new September. They see men making signals to them, on skylights and roofs, apparently signals of hope; cannot in the least make out what it is.[755] We observe however, in the eventide, as usual, the Death-tumbrils faring South-eastward, through Saint-Antoine, towards their Barrier du Trône. Saint-Antoine's tough bowels melt; Saint-Antoine surrounds the Tumbrils; says, It shall not be. O Heavens, why should it! Henriot and Gendarmes, scouring the streets that way, bellow, with waved sabres, that it must. Quit hope, ye poor Doomed! The Tumbrils move on.

But in this set of Tumbrils there are two other things notable: one notable person; and one want of a notable person. The notable person is Lieutenant-General Loiserolles, a nobleman by birth, and by nature; laying down his life here for his son. In the Prison of Saint-Lazare, the night before last, hurrying to the Grate to hear the Death-list read, he caught the name of his son. The son was asleep at the moment. 'I am Loiserolles,' cried the old man: at Tinville's bar, an error in the Christian name is little; small objection was made. The want of the notable person, again, is that of Deputy Paine! Paine has sat in the Luxembourg since January; and seemed forgotten; but Fouquier had pricked him at last. The Turnkey, List in hand, is marking with chalk the outer doors of tomorrow's *Fournée*. Paine's outer door happened to be open, turned back on the wall; the Turnkey marked it on the side next him, and hurried on: another Turnkey came, and shut it; no chalk-mark now visible, the *Fournée* went without Paine. Paine's life lay not there.—

Our fifth-act, of this natural Greek Drama, with its natural unities, can only be painted in gross; somewhat as that antique Painter, driven desperate, did the *foam*. For through this blessed July night, there is clangour, confusion very great, of marching troops; of Sections going this way, Sections going that; of Missionary Representatives reading Proclamations by torchlight; Missionary Legendre, who has raised force somewhere, emptying out the Jacobins, and flinging their key on the Convention table: 'I have locked their door; it shall be Virtue that re-opens it.' Paris, we say, is set against itself, rushing confused, as Ocean-currents do; a huge Mahlstrom, sounding there, under cloud of night. Convention sits permanent on this hand; Municipality most permanent on that. The poor Prisoners hear tocsin and rumour; strive to bethink them of the signals apparently of hope. Meek continual Twilight streaming up, which will be Dawn and a Tomorrow, silvers the Northern hem of Night; it wends and wends there, that meek brightness, like a silent prophecy, along the great Ring-Dial of the Heaven. So still, eternal! And on Earth all is confused shadow and conflict; dissidence, tumultuous gloom and glare; and Destiny as yet shakes her doubtful urn.

About three in the morning, the dissident Armed-Forces have *met*. Henriot's Armed Force stood ranked in the Place de Grève; and now Barras's, which he has recruited, arrives there; and they front each other, cannon bristling against cannon. Citoyens! cries the voice of Discretion, loudly enough, Before coming to bloodshed, to endless civil-war, hear the Convention Decree read: "Robespierre and all rebels Out of Law!"—Out of Law? There is terror in the sound: unarmed Citoyens disperse rapidly home; Municipal Cannoneers range themselves on the Convention side, with shouting. At which shout, Henriot descends from his upper room, far gone in drink as some say; finds his Place de Grève empty; the cannons' mouth turned *towards* him; and, on the whole,—that it is now the catastrophe!

Stumbling in again, the wretched drunk-sobered Henriot announces: 'All is lost!' '*Misérable!* it is thou that hast lost it,' cry they: and fling him, or else he flings himself, out of window: far enough down; into masonwork and horror of cesspool; not into death but worse. Augustin Robespierre follows him; with the like fate. Saint-Just called on Lebas to kill him: who would not. Couthon crept under a table; attempting to kill himself; not doing it.—On entering that Sanhedrim of Insurrection, we find all as good as extinct; undone, ready for seizure. Robespierre was sitting on a chair, with pistol shot blown through, not his head, but his under jaw; the suicidal hand had failed.[756] With prompt zeal, not without trouble, we gather these wretched Conspirators; fish up even Henriot and Augustin, bleeding and foul; pack them all, rudely enough, into carts; and shall, before sunrise, have them safe under lock and key. Amid shoutings and embracings.

Robespierre lay in an anteroom of the Convention Hall, while his Prison-escort was getting ready; the mangled jaw bound up rudely with bloody linen: a spectacle to men. He lies stretched on a table, a deal-box his pillow; the sheath of the pistol is still clenched convulsively in his hand. Men bully him, insult him: his eyes still indicate intelligence; he speaks no word. "He had on the sky-blue coat he had got made for the Feast of the *Être Suprême"* —O reader, can thy hard heart hold out against that? His trousers were nankeen; the stockings had fallen down over the ankles. He spake no word more in this world.

And so, at six in the morning, a victorious Convention adjourns. Report flies over Paris as on golden wings; penetrates the Prisons; irradiates the faces of those that were ready to perish: turnkeys and *moutons*, fallen from their high estate, look mute and blue. It is the 28th day of July, called 10th of Thermidor, year 1794.

Fouquier had but to identify; his Prisoners being already Out of Law. At four in the afternoon, never before were the streets of Paris seen so crowded. From the Palais de Justice to the Place de la Révolution, for *thither* again go the Tumbrils this time, it is one dense stirring mass; all windows crammed; the very roofs and ridge-tiles budding forth human Curiosity, in strange gladness. The Death-tumbrils, with their motley Batch of Outlaws, some Twenty-three or so, from Maximilien to Mayor Fleuriot and Simon the Cordwainer, roll on. All eyes are on Robespierre's Tumbril, where he, his jaw bound in dirty linen, with his half-dead Brother, and half-dead Henriot, lie shattered; their "seventeen hours" of agony about to end. The Gendarmes point their swords at him, to shew the people which is he. A woman springs on the Tumbril; clutching the side of it with one hand; waving the other Sibyl-like; and exclaims: 'The death of thee gladdens my very heart, *m'enivre de joie;'* Robespierre opened his eyes; '*Scélérat*, go down to Hell, with the curses of all wives and mothers!' —At the foot of the scaffold, they stretched him on the ground till his turn came. Lifted aloft, his eyes again opened; caught the bloody axe. Samson wrenched the coat off him; wrenched the dirty linen from his jaw: the jaw fell powerless, there burst from him a cry;— hideous to hear and see. Samson, thou canst not be too quick!

Samson's work done, there burst forth shout on shout of applause. Shout, which prolongs itself not only over Paris, but over France, but over Europe, and down to this Generation. Deservedly, and also undeservedly. O unhappiest Advocate of Arras, wert thou worse than other Advocates? Stricter man, according to his Formula, to his Credo and his Cant, of probities, benevolences, pleasures-of-virtue, and such like, lived not in that age. A man fitted, in some luckier settled age, to have become one of those incorruptible barren Pattern-Figures, and have had marble-tablets and funeral-sermons! His poor landlord, the Cabinetmaker in the Rue Saint-Honoré, loved him; his Brother died for him. May God be merciful to him, and to us.

This is end of the Reign of Terror; new glorious *Revolution* named *of Thermidor;* of Thermidor 9th, year 2; which being interpreted into old slave-style means 27th of July, 1794. Terror is ended; and death in the Place de la Révolution, were the "*Tail* of Robespierre" once executed; which service Fouquier in large Batches is swiftly managing.

BOOK 3.VII.
VENDÉMIAIRE

Chapter 3.7.I.
Decadent

How little did any one suppose that here was the end not of Robespierre only, but of the Revolution System itself! Least of all did the mutinying Committee-men suppose it; who had mutinied with no view whatever except to continue the National Regeneration with their own heads on their shoulders. And yet so it verily was. The insignificant stone they had struck out, so insignificant anywhere else, proved to be the Keystone: the whole arch-work and edifice of Sansculottism began to loosen, to crack, to yawn; and tumbled, piecemeal, with considerable rapidity, plunge after plunge; till the Abyss had swallowed it all, and in this upper world Sansculottism was no more.

For despicable as Robespierre himself might be, the death of Robespierre was a signal at which great multitudes of men, struck dumb with terror heretofore, rose out of their hiding places: and, as it were, saw one another, how multitudinous they were; and began speaking and complaining. They are countable by the thousand and the million; who have suffered cruel wrong. Ever louder rises the plaint of such a multitude; into a universal sound, into a universal continuous peal, of what they call Public Opinion. Camille had demanded a "Committee of Mercy," and could not get it; but now the whole nation resolves itself into a Committee of Mercy: the Nation has tried Sansculottism, and is weary of it. Force of Public Opinion! What King or Convention can withstand it? You in vain struggle: the thing that is rejected as "calumnious" today must pass as veracious with triumph another day: gods and men have declared that Sansculottism cannot be. Sansculottism, on that Ninth night of Thermidor suicidally "fractured its under jaw;" and lies writhing, never to rise more.

Through the next fifteenth months, it is what we may call the death-agony of Sansculottism. Sansculottism, Anarchy of the Jean-Jacques Evangel, having now got deep enough, is to perish in a new singular system of Culottism and Arrangement. For Arrangement is indispensable to man; Arrangement, were it grounded only on that old primary Evangel of Force, with Sceptre in the shape of Hammer. Be there method, be there order, cry all men; were it that of the Drill-serjeant! More tolerable is the drilled Bayonet-rank, than that undrilled Guillotine, incalculable as the wind.— How Sansculottism, writhing in death-throes, strove some twice, or even three times, to get on its feet again; but fell always, and was flung resupine, the next instant; and finally breathed out the life of it, and stirred no more: this we are now, from a due distance, with due brevity, to glance at; and then—O Reader!—Courage, I see land!

Two of the first acts of the Convention, very natural for it after this Thermidor, are to be specified here: the first is renewal of the Governing Committees. Both *Sûreté Générale* and *Salut Public*, thinned by the Guillotine, need filling up: we naturally fill them up with Talliens, Frérons, victorious Thermidorian men. Still more to the purpose, we appoint that they shall, as Law directs, not in name only but in deed, be renewed and changed from period to period; a fourth part of them going out monthly. The Convention will no more lie under bondage of Committees, under terror of death; but be a free Convention; free to follow its own judgment, and the Force of Public Opinion. Not less natural is it to enact that Prisoners and Persons under Accusation shall have right to demand some "Writ of Accusation," and see clearly what they are accused of. Very natural acts: the harbingers of hundreds not less so.

For now Fouquier's trade, shackled by Writ of Accusation, and legal proof, is as good as gone; effectual only against Robespierre's Tail. The Prisons give up their Suspects; emit them faster and faster. The Committees see themselves besieged with Prisoners' friends; complain that they are hindered in their work: it is as with men rushing out of a crowded place; and obstructing one another. Turned are the tables: Prisoners pouring out in floods; Jailors, *Moutons* and the Tail of Robespierre going now whither they were wont to send!—The Hundred and thirty-two Nantese Republicans, whom we saw marching in irons, have arrived; shrunk to Ninety-four, the fifth man of them choked by the road. They arrive: and suddenly find themselves not pleaders for life, but denouncers to death. Their Trial is for acquittal, and more. As the voice of a trumpet, their testimony sounds far and wide, mere atrocities of a Reign of Terror. For a space of nineteen days; with all solemnity and publicity. Representative Carrier, Company of Marat; Noyadings, Loire Marriages, things done in darkness, come forth into light: clear is the voice of these poor resuscitated Nantese; and Journals and Speech and universal Committee of Mercy reverberate it loud enough, into all ears and hearts. Deputation arrives from Arras; denouncing the atrocities of Representative Lebon. A tamed Convention loves its own life: yet what help? Representative Lebon, Representative Carrier must wend towards the Revolutionary Tribunal; struggle and delay as we will, the cry of a Nation pursues them louder and louder. Them also Tinville must abolish;—if indeed Tinville himself be not abolished.

We must note moreover the decrepit condition into which a once omnipotent Mother Society has fallen. Legendre flung her keys on the Convention table, that Thermidor night; her President was guillotined with Robespierre. The once mighty Mother came, some time after, with a subdued countenance, begging back her keys: the keys were restored her; but the strength could not be restored her; the strength had departed forever. Alas, one's day is done. Vain that the Tribune in mid air sounds as of old: to the general ear it has become a horror, and even a weariness. By and by, Affiliation is prohibited: the mighty Mother sees herself suddenly childless; mourns, as so hoarse a Rachel may.

The Revolutionary Committees, without Suspects to prey upon, perish fast; as it were of famine. In Paris the whole Forty-eight of them are reduced to Twelve, their Forty *sous* are abolished: yet a little while, and Revolutionary Committees are no more. *Maximum* will be abolished; let Sansculottism find food where it can.[757] Neither is there now any Municipality; any centre at the Townhall. Mayor Fleuriot and Company perished; whom we shall not be in haste to replace. The Townhall remains in a broken submissive state; knows not well what it is growing to; knows only that it is grown weak, and must obey. What if we should split Paris into, say, a Dozen separate Municipalities; incapable of concert! The Sections were thus rendered safe to act with:—or indeed might not the Sections themselves be abolished? You had then merely your Twelve manageable pacific Townships, without centre or subdivision;[758] and sacred right of Insurrection fell into abeyance!

So much is getting abolished; fleeting swiftly into the Inane. For the Press speaks, and the human tongue; Journals, heavy and light, in Philippic and Burlesque: a renegade Fréron, a renegade Prudhomme, loud they as ever, only the contrary way. And Ci-*devants* show themselves, almost parade themselves; resuscitated as from death-sleep; publish what death-pains they have had. The very Frogs of the Marsh croak with emphasis.

Your protesting Seventy-three shall, with a struggle, be emitted out of Prison, back to their seats; your Louvets, Isnards, Lanjuinais, and wrecks of Girondism, recalled from their haylofts, and caves in Switzerland, will resume their place in the Convention:[759] natural foes of Terror!

Thermidorian Talliens, and mere foes of Terror, rule in this Convention, and out of it. The compressed Mountain shrinks silent more and more. Moderatism rises louder and louder: not as a tempest, with threatenings; say rather, as the rushing of a mighty organ-blast, and melodious deafening Force of Public Opinion, from the Twenty-five million windpipes of a Nation all in Committee of Mercy: which how shall any detached body of individuals withstand?

Chapter 3.7.II.
La Cabarus

How, above all, shall a poor National Convention, withstand it? In this poor National Convention, broken, bewildered by long terror, perturbations, and guillotinement, there is no Pilot, there is not now even a Danton, who could undertake to steer you anywhither, in such press of weather. The utmost a bewildered Convention can do, is to veer, and trim, and try to keep itself steady: and rush, undrowned, before the wind. Needless to struggle; to fling helm a-lee, and make *'bout ship!* A bewildered Convention sails not in the teeth of the wind; but is rapidly blown round again. So strong is the wind, we say; and so changed; blowing fresher and fresher, as from the sweet South-West; your devastating North-Easters, and wild tornado-gusts of Terror, blown utterly out! All Sansculottic things are passing away; all things are becoming Culottic.

Do but look at the cut of clothes; that light visible Result, significant of a thousand things which are not so visible. In winter 1793, men went in red nightcaps; Municipals themselves in *sabots;* the very Citoyennes had to petition against such headgear. But now in this winter 1794, where is the red nightcap? With the thing beyond the Flood. Your monied Citoyen ponders in what elegantest style he shall dress himself: whether he shall not even dress himself as the Free Peoples of Antiquity. The more adventurous Citoyenne has already done it. Behold her, that beautiful adventurous Citoyenne: in costume of the Ancient Greeks, such Greek as Painter David could teach; her sweeping tresses snooded by glittering antique fillet; bright-eyed tunic of the Greek women; her little feet naked, as in Antique Statues, with mere sandals, and winding-strings of riband, —defying the frost!

There is such an effervescence of Luxury. For your Emigrant *Ci-devants* carried not their mansions and furnitures out of the country with them; but left them standing here: and in the swift changes of property, what with money coined on the Place de la Révolution, what with Army-furnishings, sales of Emigrant Domain and Church Lands and King's Lands, and then with the Aladdin's-lamp of Agio in a time of Paper-money, such mansions have found new occupants. Old wine, drawn from *Ci-devant* bottles, descends new throats. Paris has swept herself, relighted herself; Salons, Soupers not Fraternal, beam once more with suitable effulgence, very singular in colour. The fair Cabarus is come out of Prison; wedded to her red-gloomy Dis, whom they say she treats too loftily: fair Cabarus gives the most brilliant soirées. Round her is gathered a new Republican Army, of Citoyennes in sandals; *Ci-devants* or other: what remnants soever of the old grace survive, are rallied there. At her right-hand, in this cause, labours fair Josephine the Widow Beauharnais, though in straitened circumstances: intent, both of them, to blandish down the grimness of Republican austerity, and recivilise mankind.

Recivilise, as of old they were civilised: by witchery of the Orphic fiddle-bow, and Euterpean rhythm; by the Graces, by the Smiles! Thermidorian Deputies are there in those soirées; Editor Fréron, *Orateur du Peuple;* Barras, who has known other dances than the Carmagnole. Grim Generals of the Republic are there; in enormous horse-collar neckcloth, good against sabre-cuts; the hair gathered all into one knot, "flowing down behind, fixed with a comb." Among which latter do we not recognise, once more, the little bronzed-complexioned Artillery-Officer of Toulon, home from the Italian Wars! Grim enough; of lean, almost cruel aspect: for he has been in trouble, in ill health; also in ill favour, as a man promoted, deservingly or not, by the Terrorists and Robespierre Junior. But does not Barras know him? Will not Barras speak a word for him? Yes,—if at any time it will serve Barras so to do. Somewhat forlorn of fortune, for the present, stands that Artillery-Officer; looks, with those deep earnest eyes of his, into a future as waste as the most. Taciturn; yet with the strangest utterances in him, if you awaken him, which smite home, like light or lightning:—on the whole, rather dangerous? A "dissociable" man? Dissociable enough; a natural terror and horror to all Phantasms, being himself of the genus Reality! He stands here, without work or outlook, in this forsaken manner;—glances nevertheless, it would seem, at the kind glance of Josephine Beauharnais; and, for the rest, with severe countenance, with open eyes and closed lips, waits what will betide.

That the Balls, therefore, have a new figure this winter, we can see. Not Carmagnoles, rude "whirlblasts of rags," as Mercier called them "precursors of storm and destruction:" no, soft Ionic motions; fit for the light sandal, and antique Grecian tunic! Efflorescence of Luxury has come out: for men have wealth; nay new-got wealth; and under the Terror you durst not dance except in rags. Among the innumerable kinds of Balls, let the hasty reader mark only this single one: the kind they call Victim Balls, *Bals à Victime*. The dancers, in choice costume, have all crape round the left arm: to be admitted, it needs that you be a *Victime;* that you have lost a relative under the Terror. Peace to the Dead; let us *dance* to their memory! For in all ways one must dance.

It is very remarkable, according to Mercier, under what varieties of figure this great business of dancing goes on. "The women," says he, "are Nymphs, Sultanas; sometimes Minervas, Junos, even Dianas. In light-unerring gyrations they swim there; with such earnestness of purpose; with perfect silence, so absorbed are they. What is singular," continues he, "the onlookers are as it were mingled with the dancers; form as it were a circumambient element round the different contre-dances, yet without deranging them. It is rare, in fact, that a Sultana in such circumstances experience the smallest collision. Her pretty foot darts down, an inch from mine; she is off again; she is as a flash of light: but soon the measure recalls her to the point she set out from. Like a glittering comet she travels her eclipse, revolving on herself, as by a double effect of gravitation and attraction."[760] Looking forward a little way, into Time, the same Mercier discerns *Merveilleuses* in "flesh-coloured drawers" with gold circlets; mere dancing Houris of an artificial Mahomet's-Paradise: much too Mahometan. Montgaillard, with his splenetic eye, notes a no less strange thing; that every fashionable Citoyenne you meet is in an interesting situation. Good Heavens, *every?* Mere pillows and stuffing! adds the acrid man;—such, in a time of depopulation by war and guillotine, being the fashion.[761] No further seek its merits to disclose.

Behold also instead of the old grim *Tappe-durs* of Robespierre, what new street-groups are these? Young men habited not in black-shag Carmagnole spencer, but in superfine *habit carré* or spencer with rectangular tail appended to it; "square-tailed coat," with elegant antiguillotinish specialty of collar; "the hair plaited at the temples," and knotted back, long-flowing, in military wise: young men of what they call the *Muscadin* or Dandy species! Fréron, in his fondness names them *Jeunesse Dorée,* Golden, or Gilt Youth. They have come out, these Gilt Youths, in a kind of resuscitated state; they wear crape round the left arm, such of them as were *Victims.* More they carry clubs loaded with lead; in an angry manner: any *Tappe-dur* or remnant of Jacobinism they may fall in with, shall fare the worse. They have suffered much: their friends guillotined; their pleasures, frolics, superfine collars ruthlessly repressed: "ware now the base Red Nightcaps who did it! Fair Cabarus and the Army of Greek sandals smile approval. In the Théâtre Feydeau, young Valour in square-tailed coat eyes Beauty in Greek sandals, and kindles by her glances: Down with Jacobinism! No Jacobin hymn or demonstration, only Thermidorian ones, shall be permitted here: we beat down Jacobinism with clubs loaded with lead.

But let any one who has examined the Dandy nature, how petulant it is, especially in the gregarious state, think what an element, in sacred right of insurrection, this Gilt Youth was! Broils and battery; war without truce or measure! Hateful is Sansculottism, as Death and Night. For indeed is not the Dandy *culottic*, habilatory, by law of existence; "a cloth-animal: one that lives, moves, and has his being in cloth?" —

So goes it, waltzing, bickering; fair Cabarus, by Orphic witchery, struggling to recivilise mankind. Not unsuccessfully, we hear. What utmost Republican grimness can resist Greek sandals, in Ionic motion, the very toes covered with gold rings?[762] By degrees the indisputablest new-politeness rises; grows, with vigour. And yet, whether, even to this day, that inexpressible tone of society known under the old Kings, when Sin had "lost all its deformity" (with or without advantage to us), and airy Nothing had obtained such a local habitation and establishment as she never had,—be recovered? Or even, whether it be not lost beyond recovery?[763] —Either way, the world must contrive to struggle on.

Chapter 3.7.III.
Quiberon

But indeed do not these long-flowing hair-queues of a *Jeunesse Dorée* in semi-military costume betoken, unconsciously, another still more important tendency? The Republic, abhorrent of her Guillotine, loves her Army.

And with cause. For, surely, if good fighting be a kind of honour, as it is, in its season; and be with the vulgar of men, even the chief kind of honour, then here is good fighting, in good season, if there ever was. These Sons of the Republic, they rose, in mad wrath, to deliver her from Slavery and Cimmeria. And have they not done it? Through Maritime Alps, through gorges of Pyrenees, through Low Countries, Northward along the Rhine-valley, far is Cimmeria hurled back from the sacred Motherland. Fierce as fire, they have carried her Tricolor over the faces of all her enemies;—over scarped heights, over cannon-batteries; down, as with the Vengeur, into the dead deep sea. She has "Eleven hundred thousand fighters on foot," this Republic: "At one particular moment she had," or supposed she had, "seventeen hundred thousand."[764] Like a ring of lightning, they, volleying and *ça-ira*-ing, begirdle her from shore to shore. Cimmerian Coalition of Despots recoils; smitten with astonishment, and strange pangs.

Such a fire is in these Gaelic Republican men; high-blazing; which no Coalition can withstand! Not scutcheons, with four degrees of nobility; but *ci-devant* Sergeants, who have had to clutch Generalship out of the cannon's throat, a Pichegru, a Jourdan, a Hoche, lead them on. They have bread, they have iron; "with bread and iron you can get to China."—See Pichegru's soldiers, this hard winter, in their looped and windowed destitution, in their "straw-rope shoes and cloaks of bass-mat," how they overrun Holland, like a demon-host, the ice having bridged all waters; and rush shouting from victory to victory! Ships in the Texel are taken by huzzars on horseback: fled is York; fled is the Stadtholder, glad to escape to England, and leave Holland to fraternise.[765] Such a Gaelic fire, we say, blazes in this People, like the conflagration of grass and dry-jungle; which no mortal can withstand—for the moment.

And even so it will blaze and run, scorching all things; and, from Cadiz to Archangel, mad Sansculottism, drilled now into Soldiership, led on by some "armed Soldier of Democracy" (say, that Monosyllabic Artillery-Officer), will set its foot cruelly on the necks of its enemies; and its shouting and their shrieking shall fill the world!—Rash Coalised Kings, such a fire have ye kindled; yourselves fireless, *your* fighters animated only by drill-serjeants, messroom moralities, and the drummer's cat! However, it is begun, and will not end: not for a matter of twenty years. So long, this Gaelic fire, through its successive changes of colour and character, will blaze over the face of Europe, and afflict the scorch all men:—till it provoke all men; till it kindle another kind of fire, the Teutonic kind, namely; and be swallowed up, so to speak, in a day! For there is a fire comparable to the burning of dry-jungle and grass; most sudden, high-blazing: and another fire which we liken to the burning of coal, or even of anthracite coal; difficult to kindle, but then which nothing will put out. The ready Gaelic fire, we can remark further, and remark not in Pichegrus only, but in innumerable Voltaires, Racines, Laplaces, no less; for a man, whether he fight, or sing, or think, will remain the same unity of a man,—is admirable for roasting eggs, in every conceivable sense. The Teutonic anthracite again, as we see in Luthers, Leibnitzes, Shakespeares, is preferable for smelting metals. How happy is our Europe that has both kinds!—

But be this as it may, the Republic is clearly triumphing. In the spring of the year Mentz Town again sees itself besieged; will again change master: did not Merlin the Thionviller, "with wild beard and look," say it was not for the last time they saw him there? The Elector of Mentz circulates among his brother Potentates this pertinent query, Were it not advisable to treat of Peace? Yes! answers many an Elector from the bottom of his heart. But, on the other hand, Austria hesitates; finally refuses, being subsidied by Pitt. As to Pitt, whoever hesitate, he, suspending his Habeas-corpus, suspending his Cash-payments, stands inflexible,—spite of foreign reverses; spite of domestic obstacles, of Scotch National Conventions and English Friends of the People, whom he is obliged to arraign, to hang, or even to see acquitted with jubilee: a lean inflexible man. The Majesty of Spain, as we predicted, makes Peace; also the Majesty of Prussia: and there is a Treaty of Bâle.[766] Treaty with black Anarchists and Regicides! Alas, what help? You cannot hang this Anarchy; it is like to hang you: you must needs treat with it.

Likewise, General Hoche has even succeeded in pacificating La Vendée. Rogue Rossignol and his "Infernal Columns" have vanished: by firmness and justice, by sagacity and industry, General Hoche has done it. Taking "Movable Columns," not infernal; girdling-in the Country; pardoning the submissive, cutting down the resistive, limb after limb of the Revolt is brought under. La Rochejacquelin, last of our Nobles, fell in battle; Stofflet himself makes terms; Georges-Cadoudal is back to Brittany, among his Chouans: the frightful gangrene of La Vendée seems veritably extirpated. It has cost, as they reckon in round numbers, the lives of a Hundred Thousand fellow-mortals; with noyadings, conflagratings by infernal column, which defy arithmetic. This is the La Vendée War.[767]

Nay in few months, it does burst up once more, but once only:—blown upon by Pitt, by our Ci-devant Puisaye of Calvados, and others. In the month of July 1795, English Ships will ride in Quiberon roads. There will be debarkation of chivalrous Ci-devants, of volunteer Prisoners-of-war—eager to desert; of fire-arms, Proclamations, clothes-chests, Royalists and specie. Whereupon also, on the Republican side, there will be rapid stand-to-arms; with ambuscade marchings by Quiberon beach, at midnight; storming of Fort Penthievre; war-thunder mingling with the roar of the nightly main; and such a morning light as has seldom dawned; debarkation hurled back into its boats, or into the devouring billows, with wreck and wail;—in one word, a Ci-devant Puisaye as totally ineffectual here as he was in Calvados, when he rode from Vernon Castle without boots.[768]

Again, therefore, it has cost the lives of many a brave man. Among whom the whole world laments the brave Son of Sombreuil. Ill-fated family! The father and younger son went to the guillotine; the heroic daughter languishes, reduced to want, hides her woes from History: the elder son perishes here; shot by military tribunal as an Emigrant; Hoche himself cannot save him. If all wars, civil and other, are misunderstandings, what a thing must right-understanding be!

Chapter 3.7.IV.
Lion not Dead

The Convention, borne on the tide of Fortune towards foreign Victory, and driven by the strong wind of Public Opinion towards Clemency and Luxury, is rushing fast; all skill of pilotage is needed, and more than all, in such a velocity.

Curious to see, how we veer and whirl, yet must ever whirl round again, and scud before the wind. If, on the one hand, we re-admit the Protesting Seventy-Three, we, on the other hand, agree to consummate the Apotheosis of Marat; lift his body from the Cordeliers Church, and transport it to the Pantheon of Great Men,—flinging out Mirabeau to make room for him. To no purpose: so strong blows Public Opinion! A Gilt Youthhood, in plaited hair-tresses, tears down his Busts from the Theatre Feydeau; tramples them under foot; scatters them, with vociferation into the Cesspool of Montmartre. [769] Swept is his Chapel from the Place du Carrousel; the Cesspool of Montmartre will receive his very dust. Shorter godhood had no divine man. Some four months in this Pantheon, Temple of All the Immortals; then to the Cesspool, grand *Cloaca* of Paris and the World! "His Busts at one time amounted to four thousand." Between Temple of All the Immortals and Cloaca of the World, how are poor human creatures whirled!

Furthermore the question arises, When will the Constitution of *Ninety-three*, of 1793, come into action? Considerate heads surmise, in all privacy, that the Constitution of Ninety-three will never come into action. Let them busy themselves to get ready a better.

Or, again, where now are the Jacobins? Childless, most decrepit, as we saw, sat the mighty Mother; gnashing not teeth, but empty gums, against a traitorous Thermidorian Convention and the current of things. Twice were Billaud, Collot and Company accused in Convention, by a Lecointre, by a Legendre; and the second time, it was not voted calumnious. Billaud from the Jacobin tribune says, 'The lion is not dead, he is only sleeping.' They ask him in Convention, What he means by the awakening of the lion? And bickerings, of an extensive sort, arose in the Palais-Egalité between *Tappe-*

durs and the Gilt Youthhood; cries of 'Down with the Jacobins, the *Jacoquins*,' *coquin* meaning scoundrel! The Tribune in mid-air gave battle-sound; answered only by silence and uncertain gasps. Talk was, in Government Committees, of "suspending" the Jacobin Sessions. Hark, there!—it is in Allhallow-time, or on the Hallow-eve itself, month *ci-devant* November, year once named of Grace 1794, sad eve for Jacobinism,—volley of stones dashing through our windows, with jingle and execration! The female Jacobins, famed *Tricoteuses* with knitting-needles, take flight; are met at the doors by a Gilt Youthhood and "mob of four thousand persons;" are hooted, flouted, hustled; fustigated, in a scandalous manner, *cotillons retroussés*;—and vanish in mere hysterics. Sally out ye male Jacobins! The male Jacobins sally out; but only to battle, disaster and confusion. So that armed Authority has to intervene: and again on the morrow to intervene; and suspend the Jacobin Sessions forever and a day.[770] Gone are the Jacobins; into invisibility; in a storm of laughter and howls. Their place is made a Normal School, the first of the kind seen; it then vanishes into a "Market of Thermidor Ninth;" into a Market of Saint-Honoré, where is now peaceable chaffering for poultry and greens. The solemn temples, the great globe itself; the baseless fabric! Are not we such stuff, we and this world of ours, as Dreams are made of?

Maximum being abrogated, Trade was to take its own free course. Alas, Trade, shackled, topsyturvied in the way we saw, and now suddenly let go again, can for the present take no course at all; but only reel and stagger. There is, so to speak, no Trade whatever for the time being. Assignats, long sinking, emitted in such quantities, sink now with an alacrity beyond parallel. '*Combien?*' said one, to a Hackney-coachman, 'What fare?' 'Six thousand livres,' answered he: some three hundred pounds sterling, in Paper-money. [771] Pressure of Maximum withdrawn, the things it compressed likewise withdraw. "Two ounces of bread per day" in the modicum allotted: wide-waving, doleful are the Bakers' Queues; Farmers' houses are become pawnbrokers' shops.

One can imagine, in these circumstances, with what humour Sansculottism growled in its throat, '*La Cabarus*;' beheld Ci-devants return dancing, the Thermidor effulgence of recivilisation, and Balls in flesh-coloured drawers. Greek tunics and sandals; hosts of *Muscadins* parading, with their clubs loaded with lead;—and we here, cast out, abhorred, "picking offals from the street;"[772] agitating in Baker's Queue for our two ounces of bread! Will the Jacobin lion, which they say is meeting secretly "at the Archevêché, in *bonnet rouge* with loaded pistols," not awaken? Seemingly not. Our Collot, our Billaud, Barrère, Vadier, in these last days of March 1795, are found worthy of *Déportation*, of Banishment beyond seas; and shall, for the present, be trundled off to the Castle of Ham. The lion is dead;—or writhing in death-throes!

Behold, accordingly, on the day they call Twelfth of Germinal (which is also called First of April, not a lucky day), how lively are these streets of Paris once more! Floods of hungry women, of squalid hungry men; ejaculating: 'Bread, Bread and the Constitution of Ninety-three!' Paris has risen, once again, like the Ocean-tide; is flowing towards the Tuileries, for Bread and a Constitution. Tuileries Sentries do their best; but it serves not: the Ocean-tide sweeps them away; inundates the Convention Hall itself; howling, 'Bread, and the Constitution!'

Unhappy Senators, unhappy People, there is yet, after all toils and broils, no Bread, no Constitution. *'Du pain, pas tant de longs discours*, Bread, not bursts of Parliamentary eloquence!' so wailed the Menads of Maillard, five years ago and more; so wail ye to this hour. The Convention, with unalterable countenance, with what thought one knows not, keeps its seat in this waste howling chaos; rings its stormbell from the Pavilion of Unity. Section Lepelletier, old *Filles Saint-Thomas*, who are of the money-changing species; these and Gilt Youthhood fly to the rescue; sweep chaos forth again, with levelled bayonets. Paris is declared "in a state of siege." Pichegru, Conqueror of Holland, who happens to be here, is named Commandant, till the disturbance end. He, in one day, so to speak, ends it. He accomplishes the transfer of Billaud, Collot and Company; dissipating all opposition "by two cannon-shots," blank cannon-shots, and the terror of his name; and thereupon announcing, with a Laconicism which should be imitated, 'Representatives, your decrees are executed,'[773] lays down his Commandantship.

This Revolt of Germinal, therefore, has passed, like a vain cry. The Prisoners rest safe in Ham, waiting for ships; some nine hundred "chief Terrorists of Paris" are disarmed. Sansculottism, swept forth with bayonets, has vanished, with its misery, to the bottom of Saint-Antoine and Saint-Marceau.—Time was when Usher Maillard with Menads could alter the course of Legislation; but that time is not. Legislation seems to have got bayonets; Section Lepelletier takes its firelock, not for us! We retire to our dark dens; our cry of hunger is called a Plot of Pitt; the Saloons glitter, the flesh-coloured Drawers gyrate as before. It was for *'The Cabarus'* then, and her *Muscadins* and Money-changers, that we fought? It was for Balls in flesh-coloured drawers that we took Feudalism by the beard, and did, and dared, shedding our blood like water? Expressive Silence, muse thou their praise!—

Chapter 3.7.V.
Lion Sprawling its Last

Representative Carrier went to the Guillotine, in December last; protesting that he acted by orders. The Revolutionary Tribunal, after all it has devoured, has now only, as Anarchic things do, to devour itself. In the early days of May, men see a remarkable thing: Fouquier-Tinville pleading at the Bar once his own. He and his chief Jurymen, Leroi *August-Tenth*, Juryman Vilate, a Batch of Sixteen; pleading hard, protesting that they acted by orders: but pleading in vain. Thus men break the axe with which they have done hateful things; the axe itself having grown hateful. For the rest, Fouquier died hard enough: 'Where are thy Batches?' howled the People.— 'Hungry *canaille*,' asked Fouquier, 'is thy Bread cheaper, wanting them?'

Remarkable Fouquier; once but as other Attorneys and Law-beagles, which hunt ravenous on this Earth, a well-known phasis of human nature; and now thou art and remainest the most remarkable Attorney that ever lived and hunted in the Upper Air! For, in this terrestrial Course of Time, there was to be an *Avatar* of Attorneyism; the Heavens had said, Let there be an Incarnation, not divine, of the venatory Attorney-spirit which keeps its eye on the bond only;—and lo, this was it; and they have attorneyed it in its turn. Vanish, then, thou rat-eyed Incarnation of Attorneyism; who at bottom wert but as other Attorneys, and too hungry Sons of Adam! Juryman Vilate had striven hard for life, and published, from his Prison, an ingenious Book, not unknown to us; but it would not stead: he also had to vanish; and this his Book of the *Secret Causes of Thermidor*, full of lies, with particles of truth in it undiscoverable otherwise, is all that remains of him.

Revolutionary Tribunal has done; but vengeance has not done. Representative Lebon, after long struggling, is handed over to the ordinary Law Courts, and by them guillotined. Nay, at Lyons and elsewhere, resuscitated Moderatism, in its vengeance, will not wait the slow process of Law; but bursts into the Prisons, sets fire to the prisons; burns some three score imprisoned Jacobins to dire death, or chokes them "with the smoke of straw." There go vengeful truculent "Companies of Jesus," "Companies of the Sun;" slaying Jacobinism wherever they meet with it; flinging it into the Rhone-stream; which, once more, bears seaward a horrid cargo.[774] Whereupon, at Toulon, Jacobinism rises in revolt; and is like to hang the National Representatives.—With such action and reaction, is not a poor National Convention hard bested? It is like the settlement of winds and waters, of seas long tornado-beaten; and goes on with jumble and with jangle. Now flung aloft, now sunk in trough of the sea, your Vessel of the Republic has need of all pilotage and more.

What Parliament that ever sat under the Moon had such a series of destinies, as this National Convention of France? It came together to make the Constitution; and instead of that, it has had to make nothing but destruction and confusion: to burn up Catholicisms, Aristocratisms, to worship Reason and dig Saltpetre, to fight Titanically with itself and with the whole world. A Convention decimated by the Guillotine; above the tenth man has bowed his neck to the axe. Which has seen Carmagnoles danced before it, and patriotic strophes sung amid Church-spoils; the wounded of the Tenth of August defile in handbarrows; and, in the Pandemonial Midnight, Egalité's dames in tricolor drink lemonade, and spectrum of Sieyes mount, saying, *Death sans phrase*. A Convention which has effervesced, and which has congealed; which has been red with rage, and also pale with rage: sitting with pistols in its pocket, drawing sword (in a moment of effervescence): now storming to the four winds, through a Danton-voice, Awake, O France, and smite the tyrants; now frozen mute under its Robespierre, and answering his dirge-voice by a dubious gasp. Assassinated, decimated; stabbed at, shot at, in baths, on streets and staircases; which has been the nucleus of Chaos. Has it not heard the chimes at midnight? It has deliberated, beset by a Hundred thousand armed men with artillery-furnaces and provision-carts. It has been betocsined, bestormed; over-flooded by black deluges of Sansculottism; and has heard the shrill cry, *Bread and Soap*. For, as we say, its the nucleus of Chaos; it sat as the centre of Sansculottism; and had spread its pavilion on the waste Deep, where is neither path nor landmark, neither bottom nor shore. In intrinsic valour, ingenuity, fidelity, and general force and manhood, it has perhaps not far surpassed the average of Parliaments: but in frankness of purpose, in singularity of position, it seeks its fellow. One other Sansculottic submersion, or at most two, and this wearied vessel of a Convention reaches land.

Revolt of Germinal Twelfth ended as a vain cry; moribund Sansculottism was swept back into invisibility. There it has lain moaning, these six weeks: moaning, and also scheming. Jacobins disarmed, flung forth from their Tribune in mid air, must needs try to help themselves, in secret conclave under ground. Lo, therefore, on the First day of the month *Prairial*, 20th of May 1795, sound of the *générale* once more; beating sharp, ran-tan, To arms, To arms!

Sansculottism has risen, yet again, from its death-lair; waste wild-flowing, as the unfruitful Sea. Saint-Antoine is a-foot: 'Bread and the Constitution of Ninety-three,' so sounds it; so stands it written with chalk on the hats of men. They have their pikes, their firelocks; Paper of Grievances; standards; printed Proclamation, drawn up in quite official manner, —considering this, and also considering that, they, a much-enduring Sovereign People, are in Insurrection; will have Bread and the Constitution of Ninety-three. And so the Barriers are seized, and the *générale* beats, and tocsins discourse discord. Black deluges overflow the Tuileries; spite of sentries, the Sanctuary itself is invaded: enter, to our Order of the Day, a torrent of dishevelled women, wailing, 'Bread! Bread!' President may well cover himself; and have his own tocsin rung in "the Pavilion of Unity;" the ship of the State again labours and leaks; overwashed, near to swamping, with unfruitful brine.

What a day, once more! Women are driven out: men storm irresistibly in; choke all corridors, thunder at all gates. Deputies, putting forth head, obtest, conjure; Saint-Antoine rages, 'Bread and Constitution.' Report has risen that the "Convention is assassinating the women:" crushing and rushing, clangor and furor! The oak doors have become as oak tambourines, sounding under the axe of Saint-Antoine; plaster-work crackles, woodwork booms and jingles; door starts up;—bursts-in Saint-Antoine with frenzy and vociferation, Rag-standards, printed Proclamation, drum-music: astonishment to eye and ear. Gendarmes, loyal Sectioners charge through the other door; they are recharged; musketry exploding: Saint-Antoine cannot be expelled. Obtesting Deputies obtest vainly; Respect the President; approach not the President! Deputy Féraud, stretching out his hands, baring his bosom scarred in the Spanish wars, obtests vainly: threatens and resists vainly. Rebellious Deputy of the Sovereign, if thou have fought, have not we too? We have no bread, no Constitution! They wrench poor Féraud; they tumble him, trample him, wrath waxing to see itself work: they drag him into the corridor, dead or near it; sever his head, and fix it on a pike. Ah, did an unexampled Convention want this variety of destiny too, then? Féraud's bloody head goes on a pike. Such a game has begun; Paris and the Earth may wait how it will end.

And so it billows free though all Corridors; within, and without, far as the eye reaches, nothing but Bedlam, and the great Deep broken loose! President Boissy d'Anglas sits like a rock: the rest of the Convention is floated "to the upper benches;" Sectioners and Gendarmes still ranking there to form a kind of wall for them. And Insurrection rages; rolls its drums; will read its Paper of Grievances, will have this decreed, will have that. Covered sits President Boissy, unyielding; like a rock in the beating of seas. They menace him, level muskets at him, he yields not; they hold up Féraud's bloody head to him, with grave stern air he bows to it, and yields not.

And the Paper of Grievances cannot get itself read for uproar; and the drums roll, and the throats bawl; and Insurrection, like sphere-music, is inaudible for very noise: Decree us this, Decree us that. One man we discern bawling "for the space of an hour at all intervals," '*Je demande l'arrestation des coquins et des lâches.*' Really one of the most comprehensive Petitions ever put up: which indeed, to this hour, includes all that you can reasonably ask Constitution of the Year One, Rotten-Borough, Ballot-Box, or other miraculous Political Ark of the Covenant to do for you to the end of the world! I also *demand arrestment of the Knaves and Dastards,* and nothing more whatever. National Representation, deluged with black Sansculottism glides out; for help elsewhere, for safety elsewhere: here is no help.

About four in the afternoon, there remain hardly more than some Sixty Members: mere friends, or even secret-leaders; a remnant of the Mountain-crest, held in silence by Thermidorian thraldom. Now is the time for them; now or never let them descend, and speak! They descend, these Sixty, invited by Sansculottism: Romme of the New Calendar, Ruhl of the Sacred Phial, Goujon, Duquesnoy, Soubrany, and the rest. Glad Sansculottism forms a ring for them; Romme takes the President's chair; they begin resolving and decreeing. Fast enough now comes Decree after Decree, in alternate brief strains, or strophe and antistrophe,—what will cheapen bread, what will awaken the dormant lion. And at every new Decree, Sansculottism shouts, Decreed, Decreed; and rolls its drums.

Fast enough; the work of months in hours,—when see, a Figure enters, whom in the lamp-light we recognise to be Legendre; and utters words: fit to be hissed out! And then see, Section Lepelletier or other Muscadin Section enters, and Gilt Youth, with levelled bayonets, countenances screwed to the sticking-place! Tramp, tramp, with bayonets gleaming in the lamp-light: what can one do, worn down with long riot, grown heartless, dark, hungry, but roll back, but rush back, and escape who can? The very windows need to be thrown up, that Sansculottism may escape fast enough. Money-changer Sections and Gilt Youth sweep them forth, with steel besom, far into the depths of Saint-Antoine. Triumph once more! The Decrees of that Sixty are not so much as rescinded; they are declared null and non-extant. Romme, Ruhl, Goujon and the ringleaders, some thirteen in all, are decreed Accused. Permanent-session ends at three in the morning.[775] Sansculottism, once more flung resupine, lies sprawling; sprawling its *last.*

Such was the First of Prairial, 20th May, 1795. Second and Third of Prairial, during which Sansculottism still sprawled, and unexpectedly rang its tocsin, and assembled in arms, availed Sansculottism nothing. What though with our Rommes and Ruhls, accused but not yet arrested, we make a new "True National Convention" of our own, over in the East; and put the others Out of Law? What though we rank in arms and march? Armed Force and Muscadin Sections, some thirty thousand men, environ that old False Convention: we can but bully one another: bandying nicknames, 'Muscadins,' against 'Blooddrinkers, Buveurs de Sang.' Féraud's Assassin, taken with the red hand, and sentenced, and now near to Guillotine and Place de Grève, is retaken; is carried back into Saint-Antoine: to no purpose. Convention Sectionaries and Gilt Youth come, according to Decree, to seek him; nay to disarm Saint-Antoine! And they do disarm it: by rolling of cannon, by springing upon enemy's cannon; by military audacity, and terror of the Law. Saint-Antoine surrenders its arms; Santerre even advising it, anxious for life and brewhouse. Féraud's Assassin flings himself from a high roof: and all is lost.[776]

Discerning which things, old Ruhl shot a pistol through his old white head; dashed his life in pieces, as he had done the Sacred Phial of Rheims. Romme, Goujon and the others stand ranked before a swiftly-appointed, swift Military Tribunal. Hearing the sentence, Goujon drew a knife, struck it into his breast, passed it to his neighbour Romme; and fell dead. Romme did the like; and another all but did it; Roman-death rushing on there, as in electric-chain, before your Bailiffs could intervene! The Guillotine had the rest.

They were the *Ultimi Romanorum*. Billaud, Collot and Company are now ordered to be tried for life; but are found to be already off, shipped for Sinamarri, and the hot mud of Surinam. There let Billaud surround himself with flocks of tame parrots; Collot take the yellow fever, and drinking a whole bottle of brandy, burn up his entrails.[777] Sansculottism spraws no more. The dormant lion has become a dead one; and now, as we see, any hoof may smite him.

Chapter 3.7.VI.
Grilled Herrings

So dies Sansculottism, the *body* of Sansculottism, or is changed. Its ragged Pythian Carmagnole-dance has transformed itself into a Pyrrhic, into a dance of Cabarus Balls. Sansculottism is dead; extinguished by new *isms* of that kind, which were its own natural progeny; and is buried, we may say, with such deafening jubilation and disharmony of funeral-knell on their part, that only after some half century or so does one begin to learn clearly why it ever was alive.

And yet a meaning lay in it: Sansculottism verily was alive, a New-Birth of TIME; nay it still lives, and is not dead, but changed. The *soul* of it still lives; still works far and wide, through one bodily shape into another less amorphous, as is the way of cunning Time with his New-Births:—till, in some perfected shape, it embrace the whole circuit of the world! For the wise man may now everywhere discern that he must found on his manhood, not on the garnitures of his manhood. He who, in these Epochs of our Europe, founds on garnitures, formulas, culottisms of what sort soever, is founding on old cloth and sheep-skin, and cannot endure. But as for the body of Sansculottism, that is dead and buried,—and, one hopes, need not reappear, in primary amorphous shape, for another thousand years!

It was the frightfullest thing ever borne of Time? One of the frightfullest. This Convention, now grown Anti-Jacobin, did, with an eye to justify and fortify itself, publish Lists of what the Reign of Terror had perpetrated: Lists of Persons Guillotined. The Lists, cries splenetic Abbé Montgaillard, were not complete. They contain the names of, How many persons thinks the reader?—Two Thousand all but a few. There were above Four Thousand, cries Montgaillard: so many were guillotined, fusilladed, noyaded, done to dire death; of whom Nine Hundred were women.[778] It is a horrible sum of human lives, M. l'Abbé:—some ten times as many shot rightly on a field of battle, and one might have had his Glorious-Victory with *Te-Deum*. It is not far from the two-hundredth part of what perished in the entire Seven Years War. By which Seven Years War, did not the great Fritz wrench Silesia from the great Theresa; and a Pompadour, stung by epigrams, satisfy herself that she could not be an Agnes Sorel? The head of man is a strange vacant sounding-shell, M. l'Abbé; and studies Cocker to small purpose.

But what if History, somewhere on this Planet, were to hear of a Nation, the third soul of whom had not for thirty weeks each year as many third-rate potatoes as would sustain him?[779] History, in that case, feels bound to consider that starvation is starvation; that starvation from age to age presupposes much: History ventures to assert that the French Sansculotte of Ninety-three, who, roused from long death-sleep, could rush at once to the frontiers, and die fighting for an immortal Hope and Faith of Deliverance for him and his, was but the *second*-miserablest of men! The Irish Sans-potato, had he not senses then, nay a soul? In his frozen darkness, it was bitter for him to die famishing; bitter to see his children famish. It was bitter for him to be a beggar, a liar and a knave. Nay, if that dreary Greenland-wind of benighted Want, perennial from sire to son, had frozen him into a kind of torpor and numb callosity, so that he saw not, felt not, was this, for a creature with a soul in it, some assuagement; or the cruellest wretchedness of all?

Such things were, such things are; and they go on in silence peaceably: and Sansculottisms follow them. History, looking back over this France through long times, back to Turgot's time for instance, when dumb Drudgery staggered up to its King's Palace, and in wide expanse of sallow faces, squalor and winged raggedness, presented hieroglyphically its Petition of Grievances; and for answer got hanged on a "new gallows forty feet high,"—confesses mournfully that there is no period to be met with, in which the general Twenty-five Millions of France suffered *less* than in this period which they name Reign of Terror! But it was not the Dumb Millions that suffered here; it was the Speaking Thousands, and Hundreds, and Units; who shrieked and published, and made the world ring with their wail, as they could and should: that is the grand peculiarity. The frightfullest Births of Time are never the loud-speaking ones, for these soon die; they are the silent ones, which can live from century to century! Anarchy, hateful as Death, is abhorrent to the whole nature of man; and must itself soon die.

Wherefore let all men know what of depth and of height is still revealed in man; and, with fear and wonder, with just sympathy and just antipathy, with clear eye and open heart, contemplate it and appropriate it; and draw innumerable inferences from it. This inference, for example, among the first: "That if the gods of this lower world will sit on their glittering thrones, indolent as Epicurus' gods, with the living Chaos of Ignorance and Hunger weltering uncared for at their feet, and smooth Parasites preaching, Peace, peace, when there is no peace," then the dark Chaos, it would seem, will rise; has risen, and O Heavens! has it not tanned their skins into breeches for itself? That there be no second Sansculottism in our Earth for a thousand years, let us understand well what the first was; and let Rich and Poor of us go and do *otherwise*.—But to our tale.

The Muscadin Sections greatly rejoice; Cabarus Balls gyrate: the well-nigh insoluble problem *Republic without Anarchy*, have we not solved it?—Law of Fraternity or Death is gone: chimerical *Obtain-who-need* has become practical *Hold-who-have*. To anarchic Republic of the Poverties there has succeeded orderly Republic of the Luxuries; which will continue as long as it can.

On the Pont au Change, on the Place de Grève, in long sheds, Mercier, in these summer evenings, saw working men at their repast. One's allotment of daily bread has sunk to an ounce and a half. "Plates containing each three grilled herrings, sprinkled with shorn onions, wetted with a little vinegar; to this add some morsel of boiled prunes, and lentils swimming in a clear sauce: at these frugal tables, the cook's gridiron hissing near by, and the pot simmering on a fire between two stones, I have seen them ranged by the hundred; consuming, without bread, their scant messes, far too moderate for the keenness of their appetite, and the extent of their stomach."[780] Seine water, rushing plenteous by, will supply the deficiency.

O man of Toil, thy struggling and thy daring, these six long years of insurrection and tribulation, thou hast profited nothing by it, then? Thou consumest thy herring and water, in the blessed gold-red evening. O why was the Earth so beautiful, becrimsoned with dawn and twilight, if man's dealings with man were to make it a vale of scarcity, of tears, not even soft tears? Destroying of Bastilles, discomfiting of Brunswicks, fronting of Principalities and Powers, of Earth and Tophet, all that thou hast dared and endured,—it was for a Republic of the Cabarus Saloons? Patience; thou must have patience: the end is not yet.

Chapter 3.7.VII.
The Whiff of Grapeshot

In fact, what can be more natural, one may say inevitable, as a Post-Sansculottic transitionary state, than even this? Confused wreck of a Republic of the Poverties, which ended in Reign of Terror, is arranging itself into such composure as it can. Evangel of Jean-Jacques, and most other Evangels, becoming incredible, what is there for it but return to the old Evangel of Mammon? *Contrat-Social* is true or untrue, Brotherhood is Brotherhood or Death; but money always will buy money's worth: in the wreck of human dubitations, this remains indubitable, that Pleasure is pleasant. Aristocracy of Feudal Parchment has passed away with a mighty rushing; and now, by a natural course, we arrive at Aristocracy of the Moneybag. It is the course through which all European Societies are at this hour travelling. Apparently a still baser sort of Aristocracy? An infinitely baser; the basest yet known!

In which however there is this advantage, that, like Anarchy itself, it cannot continue. Hast thou considered how Thought is stronger than Artillery-parks, and (were it fifty years after death and martyrdom, or were it two thousand years) writes and unwrites Acts of Parliament, removes mountains; models the World like soft clay? Also how the beginning of all Thought, worth the name, is Love; and the wise head never yet was, without first the generous heart? The Heavens cease not their bounty: they send us generous hearts into every generation. And now what generous heart can pretend to itself, or be hoodwinked into believing, that Loyalty to the Moneybag is a noble Loyalty? Mammon, cries the generous heart out of all ages and countries, is the basest of known Gods, even of known Devils. In him what glory is there, that ye should worship him? No glory discernable; not even terror: at best, detestability, ill-matched with despicability!— Generous hearts, discerning, on this hand, widespread Wretchedness, dark without and within, moistening its ounce-and-half of bread with tears; and on that hand, mere Balls in fleshcoloured drawers, and inane or foul glitter of such sort,—cannot but ejaculate, cannot but announce: Too much, O divine Mammon; somewhat too much!—The voice of these, once announcing itself, carries *fiat* and *pereat* in it, for all things here below.

Meanwhile, we will hate Anarchy as Death, which it is; and the things worse than Anarchy shall be hated *more*. Surely Peace alone is fruitful. Anarchy is destruction: a burning up, say, of Shams and Insupportabilities; but which leaves Vacancy behind. Know this also, that out of a world of Unwise nothing but an Unwisdom can be made. Arrange it, Constitution-build it, sift it through Ballot-Boxes as thou wilt, it is and remains an Unwisdom,—the new prey of new quacks and unclean things, the latter end of it slightly better than the beginning. Who can bring a wise thing out of men unwise? Not one. And so Vacancy and general Abolition having come for this France, what can Anarchy do more? Let there be Order, were it under the Soldier's Sword; let there be Peace, that the bounty of the Heavens be not spilt; that what of Wisdom they do send us bring fruit in its season!— It remains to be seen how the quellers of Sansculottism were themselves quelled, and sacred right of Insurrection was blown away by gunpowder: wherewith this singular eventful History called *French Revolution* ends.

The Convention, driven such a course by wild wind, wild tide, and steerage and non-steerage, these three years, has become weary of its own existence, sees all men weary of it; and wishes heartily to finish. To the last, it has to strive with contradictions: it is now getting fast ready with a Constitution, yet knows no peace. Sieyes, we say, is making the Constitution once more; has as good as made it. Warned by experience, the great Architect alters much, admits much. Distinction of Active and Passive Citizen, that is, Money-qualification for Electors: nay Two Chambers, "Council of Ancients," as well as "Council of Five Hundred;" to that conclusion have we come! In a like spirit, eschewing that fatal self-denying ordinance of your Old Constituents, we enact not only that actual Convention Members are re-eligible, but that Two-thirds of them must be re-elected. The Active Citizen Electors shall for this time have free choice of only One-third of their National Assembly. Such enactment, of Two-thirds to be re-elected, we append to our Constitution; we submit our Constitution to the Townships of France, and say, Accept *both*, or reject both. Unsavoury as this appendix may be, the Townships, by overwhelming majority, accept and ratify. With Directory of Five; with Two good Chambers, double-majority of them nominated by ourselves, one hopes this Constitution may prove final. *March* it will; for the legs of it, the re-elected Two-thirds, are already there, able to march. Sieyes looks at his Paper Fabric with just pride.

But now see how the contumacious Sections, Lepelletier foremost, kick against the pricks! Is it not manifest infraction of one's Elective Franchise, Rights of Man, and Sovereignty of the People, this appendix of re-electing *your* Two-thirds? Greedy tyrants who would perpetuate yourselves!—For the truth is, victory over Saint-Antoine, and long right of Insurrection, has spoiled these men. Nay spoiled all men. Consider too how each man was free to hope what he liked; and now there is to be no hope, there is to be fruition, fruition of *this*.

In men spoiled by long right of Insurrection, what confused ferments will rise, tongues once begun wagging! Journalists declaim, your Lacretelles, Laharpes; Orators spout. There is Royalism traceable in it, and Jacobinism. On the West Frontier, in deep secrecy, Pichegru, durst he trust his Army, is treating with Condé: in these Sections, there spout wolves in sheep's clothing, masked Emigrants and Royalists![781] All men, as we say, had hoped, each that the Election would do something for his own side: and now there is no Election, or only the third of one. Black is united with white against this clause of the Two-thirds; all the Unruly of France, who see their trade thereby near ending.

Section Lepelletier, after Addresses enough, finds that such clause is a manifest infraction; that it, Lepelletier, for one, will simply not conform thereto; and invites all other free Sections to join it, "in central Committee," in resistance to oppression.[782] The Sections join it, nearly all; strong with their Forty Thousand fighting men. The Convention therefore may look to itself! Lepelletier, on this 12th day of Vendémiaire, 4th of October 1795, is sitting in open contravention, in its Convent of Filles Saint-Thomas, Rue Vivienne, with guns primed. The Convention has some Five Thousand regular troops at hand; Generals in abundance; and a Fifteen Hundred of miscellaneous persecuted Ultra-Jacobins, whom in this crisis it has hastily got together and armed, under the title *Patriots of Eighty-nine*. Strong in Law, it sends its General Menou to disarm Lepelletier.

General Menou marches accordingly, with due summons and demonstration; with no result. General Menou, about eight in the evening, finds that he is standing ranked in the Rue Vivienne, emitting vain summonses; with primed guns pointed out of every window at him; and that he cannot disarm Lepelletier. He has to return, with whole skin, but without success; and be thrown into arrest as "a traitor." Whereupon the whole Forty Thousand join this Lepelletier which cannot be vanquished: to what hand shall a quaking Convention now turn? Our poor Convention, after such voyaging, just entering harbour, so to speak, has *struck on the bar;*—and labours there frightfully, with breakers roaring round it, Forty thousand of them, like to wash it, and its Sieyes Cargo and the whole future of France, into the deep! Yet one last time, it struggles, ready to perish.

Some call for Barras to be made Commandant; he conquered in Thermidor. Some, what is more to the purpose, bethink them of the Citizen Buonaparte, unemployed Artillery Officer, who took Toulon. A man of head, a man of action: Barras is named Commandant's-Cloak; this young Artillery Officer is named Commandant. He was in the Gallery at the moment, and heard it; he withdrew, some half hour, to consider with himself: after a half hour of grim compressed considering, to be or not to be, he answers *Yea*.

And now, a man of head being at the centre of it, the whole matter gets vital. Swift, to Camp of Sablons; to secure the Artillery, there are not twenty men guarding it! A swift Adjutant, Murat is the name of him, gallops; gets thither some minutes within time, for Lepelletier was also on march that way: the Cannon are ours. And now beset this post, and beset that; rapid and firm: at Wicket of the Louvre, in Cul de Sac Dauphin, in Rue Saint-Honoré, from Pont Neuf all along the north Quays, southward to Pont *ci-devant* Royal,—rank round the Sanctuary of the Tuileries, a ring of steel discipline; let every gunner have his match burning, and all men stand to their arms!

Thus there is Permanent-session through night; and thus at sunrise of the morrow, there is seen sacred Insurrection once again: vessel of State labouring on the bar; and tumultuous sea all round her, beating *générale*, arming and sounding,—not ringing tocsin, for we have left no tocsin but our own in the Pavilion of Unity. It is an imminence of shipwreck, for the whole world to gaze at. Frightfully she labours, that poor ship, within cable-length of port; huge peril for her. However, she has a man at the helm. Insurgent messages, received, and not received; messenger admitted blindfolded; counsel and counter-counsel: the poor ship labours!—Vendémiaire 13th, year 4: curious enough, of all days, it is the Fifth day of October, anniversary of that Menad-march, six years ago; by sacred right of Insurrection we are got thus far.

Lepelletier has seized the Church of Saint-Roch; has seized the Pont Neuf, our piquet there retreating without fire. Stray shots fall from Lepelletier; rattle down on the very Tuileries staircase. On the other hand, women advance dishevelled, shrieking, Peace; Lepelletier behind them waving its hat in sign that we shall fraternise. Steady! The Artillery Officer is steady as bronze; can be quick as lightning. He sends eight hundred muskets with ball-cartridges to the Convention itself; honourable Members shall act with these in case of extremity: whereat they look grave enough. Four of the afternoon is struck.[783]   Lepelletier, making nothing by messengers, by fraternity or hat-waving, bursts out, along the Southern Quai Voltaire, along streets, and passages, treble-quick, in huge veritable onslaught! Whereupon, thou bronze Artillery Officer—? 'Fire!' say the bronze lips. Roar and again roar, continual, volcano-like, goes his great gun, in the Cul de Sac Dauphin against the Church of Saint-Roch; go his great guns on the Pont Royal; go all his great guns;—blow to air some two hundred men, mainly about the Church of Saint-Roch! Lepelletier cannot stand such horse-play; no Sectioner can stand it; the Forty-thousand yield on all sides, scour towards covert. "Some hundred or so of them gathered both Theatre de la République; but," says he, "a few shells dislodged them. It was all finished at six."

The Ship is *over* the bar, then; free she bounds shoreward,—amid shouting and vivats! Citoyen Buonaparte is "named General of the Interior, by acclamation;" quelled Sections have to disarm in such humour as they may; sacred right of Insurrection is gone for ever! The Sieyes Constitution can disembark itself, and begin marching. The miraculous Convention Ship has got to land;—and is there, shall we figuratively say, changed, as Epic Ships are wont, into a kind of *Sea Nymph*, never to sail more; to roam the waste Azure, a Miracle in History!

"It is false," says Napoleon, "that we fired first with blank charge; it had been a waste of life to do that." Most false: the firing was with sharp and sharpest shot: to all men it was plain that here was no sport; the rabbets and plinths of Saint-Roch Church show splintered by it, to this hour.—Singular: in old Broglie's time, six years ago, this Whiff of Grapeshot was promised; but it could not be given then, could not have profited then. Now, however, the time is come for it, and the man; and behold, you have it; and the thing we specifically call *French Revolution* is blown into space by it, and become a thing that was!—

Chapter 3.7.VIII.
Finis

Homer's Epos, it is remarked, is like a Bas-relief sculpture: it does not conclude, but merely ceases. Such, indeed, is the Epos of Universal History itself. Directorates, Consulates, Emperorships, Restorations, Citizen-Kingships succeed this Business in due series, in due genesis one out of the other. Nevertheless the First-parent of all these may be said to have gone to air in the way we see. A Baboeuf Insurrection, next year, will die in the birth; stifled by the Soldiery. A Senate, if tinged with Royalism, can be purged by the Soldiery; and an Eighteenth of Fructidor transacted by the mere shew of bayonets.[784] Nay Soldiers' bayonets can be used *à posteriori* on a Senate, and make it leap out of window, — still bloodless; and produce an Eighteenth of Brumaire.[785] Such changes must happen: but they are managed by intriguings, caballings, and then by orderly word of command; almost like mere changes of Ministry. Not in general by sacred right of Insurrection, but by milder methods growing ever milder, shall the Events of French history be henceforth brought to pass.

It is admitted that this Directorate, which owned, at its starting, these three things, an "old table, a sheet of paper, and an ink-bottle," and no visible money or arrangement whatever,[786] did wonders: that France, since the Reign of Terror hushed itself, has been a new France, awakened like a giant out of torpor; and has gone on, in the Internal Life of it, with continual progress. As for the External form and forms of Life, — what can we say except that out of the Eater there comes Strength; out of the Unwise there comes *not* Wisdom! Shams are burnt up; nay, what as yet is the peculiarity of France, the very Cant of them is burnt up. The new Realities are not yet come: ah no, only Phantasms, Paper models, tentative Prefigurements of such! In France there are now Four Million Landed Properties; that black portent of an Agrarian Law is as it were *realised*. What is still stranger, we understand all Frenchmen have "the right of duel;" the Hackney-coachman with the Peer, if insult be given: such is the law of Public Opinion. Equality at least in death! The Form of Government is by Citizen King, frequently shot at, not yet shot.

On the whole, therefore, has it not been fulfilled what was prophesied, *ex-postfacto* indeed, by the Archquack Cagliostro, or another? He, as he looked in rapt vision and amazement into these things, thus spake:[787] "Ha! What is *this?* Angels, Uriel, Anachiel, and the other Five; Pentagon of Rejuvenescence; Power that destroyed Original Sin; Earth, Heaven, and thou Outer Limbo, which men name Hell! Does the EMPIRE Of IMPOSTURE waver? Burst there, in starry sheen updarting, Light-rays from out *its* dark foundations; as it rocks and heaves, not in travail-throes, but in death-throes? Yea, Light-rays, piercing, clear, that salute the Heavens,—lo, they *kindle* it; their starry clearness becomes as red Hellfire!

"IMPOSTURE is in flames, Imposture is burnt up: one red sea of Fire, wild-billowing enwraps the World; with its fire-tongue, licks at the very Stars. Thrones are hurled into it, and Dubois mitres, and Prebendal Stalls that drop fatness, and—ha! what see I?—all the *Gigs* of Creation; all, all! Wo is me! Never since Pharaoh's Chariots, in the Red-sea of water, was there wreck of Wheel-vehicles like this in the Sea of Fire. Desolate, as ashes, as gases, shall they wander in the wind.

Higher, higher yet flames the Fire-Sea; crackling with new dislocated timber; hissing with leather and prunella. The metal Images are molten; the marble Images become mortar-lime; the stone Mountains sulkily explode. RESPECTABILITY, with all her collected Gigs inflamed for funeral pyre, wailing, leaves the earth: not to return save under new Avatar. Imposture, how it burns, through generations: how it is burnt up; for a time. The World is black ashes; which, ah, when will they grow green? The Images all run into amorphous Corinthian brass; all Dwellings of men destroyed; the very mountains peeled and riven, the valleys black and dead: it is an empty World! Wo to them that shall be born then!—A King, a Queen (ah me!) were hurled in; did rustle once; flew aloft, crackling, like paper-scroll. Iscariot Egalité was hurled in; thou grim De Launay, with thy grim Bastille; whole kindreds and peoples; five millions of mutually destroying Men. For it is the End of the Dominion of IMPOSTURE (which is Darkness and opaque Firedamp); and the burning up, with unquenchable fire, of all the Gigs that are in the Earth." This Prophecy, we say, has it not been fulfilled, is it not fulfilling?

And so here, O Reader, has the time come for us two to part. Toilsome was our journeying together; not without offence; but it is done. To me thou wert as a beloved shade, the disembodied or not yet embodied spirit of a

Brother. To thee I was but as a Voice. Yet was our relation a kind of sacred one; doubt not that! Whatsoever once sacred things become hollow jargons, yet while the Voice of Man speaks with Man, hast thou not there the living fountain out of which all sacrednesses sprang, and will yet spring? Man, by the nature of him, is definable as "an incarnated Word." Ill stands it with me if I have spoken falsely: thine also it was to hear truly. Farewell.

INDEX

ARRAS, guillotine at.

ARRESTS in August 1792.

ARSENAL, attempted destruction of.

ARTOIS, M. d', ways of, unpopularity of, memorial by, flies, at Coblentz, refusal to return.

ASSEMBLIES, Primary and Secondary.

ASSEMBLY, National, Third Estate becomes, to be extruded, stands grouped in the rain, occupies Tennis-Court, scene there, joined by clergy, doings on King's speech, ratified by King, cannon pointed at, regrets Necker, after Bastille.

ASSEMBLY, Constituent, National, becomes, pedantic, Irregular Verbs, what it can do, Night of Pentecost, Left and Right side, raises money, on the Veto, Fifth October, women, in Paris Riding-Hall, on deficit, assignats, on clergy, and riot, prepares for Louis's visit, on Federation, Anacharsis Clootz, eldest of men, on Franklin's death, on state of army, thanks Bouillé, on Nanci affair, on Emigrants, on death of Mirabeau, on escape of King, after capture of King, completes Constitution, dissolves itself, what it has done.

ASSEMBLY, Legislative, First French Parliament, book of law, dispute with King, Baiser de Lamourette, High Court, decrees vetoed, scenes in, reprimands King's ministers, declares war, declares France in danger, reinstates Pétion, nonplused, Lafayette, King and Swiss, August Tenth, becoming defunct, September massacres, dissolved.

ASSIGNATS, origin of, false Royalist, forgers of, coach-fare in.

AUBRIOT, Sieur, after King's capture.

AUBRY, Colonel, at Jalès.

AUCH, M. Martin d', in Versailles Court.

AUSTRIA quarrels with France.

AUSTRIAN Committee, at Tuileries.

AUSTRIAN Army, invades France, defeated at Jemappes, Dumouriez escapes to, repulsed, Watigny.

AVIGNON, Union of, described, state of, riot in church at, occupied by Jourdan, massacre at.

BACHAUMONT, his thirty volumes.

BAILLE, involuntary epigram of.

BAILLY, Astronomer, account of, President of National Assembly, Mayor of Paris, receives Louis in Paris, and Paris Parlement, on Petition for Deposition, decline of, in prison, at Queen's trial, guillotined cruelly.

BAKERS', French in tail at.

BARBAROUX and Marat, Marseilles Deputy, and the Rolands, on Map of France, demand of, to Marseilles, meets Marseillese, in National Convention, against Robespierre, cannot be heard, the Girondins declining, arrested, and Charlotte Corday, retreats to Bourdeaux, farewell of, shoots himself.

BARDY, Abbé, massacred.

BARENTIN, Keeper of Seals.

BARNAVE, at Grenoble, member of Assembly, one of a trio, Jacobin, duel with Cazalès, escorts the King from Varennes, conciliates Queen, becomes Constitutional, retires to Grenoble, treason, in prison, guillotined.

BARRAS, Paul-François, in National Convention, commands in Thermidor, appoints Napoleon in Vendémiaire.

BARRERE, Editor, at King's trial, peace-maker, levy in mass, plot, banished.

BARTHOLOMEW massacre.

BASTILLE, Linguet's Book on, meaning of, shots fired at, summoned by insurgents, besieged, capitulates, treatment of captured, Queret-Demery, demolished, key sent to Washington, Heroes.

BAZIRE, of Mountain, imprisoned.

BEARN, riot at.

BEAUHARNAIS in Champ-de-Mars, Josephine, imprisoned, and Napoleon, at La Cabarus's.

BEAUMARCHAIS, Caron, his lawsuit, his "Mariage de Figaro," commissions arms from Holland, his distress.

BEAUMONT, Archbishop, notice of.

BEAUREPAIRE, Governor of Verdun, shoots himself.

BENTHAM, Jeremy, naturalised.

BERLINE, towards Varennes.

BERTHIER, Intendant, fled, arrested and massacred.

BERTHIER, Commandant, at Versailles.

BESENVAL, Baron, Commandant of Paris, on French Finance, in riot of Rue St. Antoine, on corruption of Guards, at Champ-de-Mars, apparition to, decamps, and Louis XVI.

BETHUNE, riot at.

BEURNONVILLE, with Dumouriez, imprisoned.

BILLAUD-VARENNES, Jacobin, cruel, at massacres, September 1792, in Salut Committee, and Robespierre's Être Suprême, accuses Robespierre, accused, banished.

BLANC, Le, landlord at Varennes, escape of family.

BLOOD, baths of.

BONCHAMPS, in La Vendée War.

BONNEMERE, Aubin, at Siege of Bastille.

BOUILLE, at Metz, account of, character of, troops mutinous, and Salm regiment, intrepidity of, marches on Nanci, quells Nanci mutineers, at Mirabeau's funeral, expects fugitive King, would liberate King, emigrates.

BOUILLE, Junior, asleep at Varennes, flies to father.

BOURDEAUX, priests hanged at, for Girondism.

BOYER, duellist.

BREST, sailors revolt, state of, in 1791, Fédérés in Paris, in 1793.

BRETEUIL, Home-Secretary.

BRETON Club, germ of Jacobins.

BRETONS, deputations of, Girondins.

BREZE, Marquis de, his mode of ushering, and National Assembly, extraordinary etiquette.

BRIENNE, Loménie, anti-protestant, in Notables, incapacity of, failure of, arrests Paris Parlement, secret scheme, scheme discovered, arrests two Parlementeers, bewildered, desperate shifts by, wishes for Necker, dismissed, and provided for, his effigy burnt.

BRISSAC, Duke de, commands Constitutional Guard, disbanded.

BRISSOT, edits "Moniteur," friend of Blacks, in First Parliament, plans in 1792, active in Assembly, in Jacobins, at Roland's, pelted in Assembly, arrested, trial of, guillotined.

BRITTANY, disturbances in.

BROGLIE, Marshal, against Plenary Court, in command, in office, dismissed.

BRUNSWICK, Duke, marches on France, advances, Proclamation, at Verdun, at Argonne, retreats.

BUFFON, Mme. de, and Duke d'Orléans, at d'Orléans execution.

BUTTAFUOCO, Napoleon's letter to.

BUZOT, in National Convention, arrested, retreats to Bourdeaux, end of.

CABANIS, Physician to Mirabeau.

CABARUS, Mlle., and Tallien, imprisoned.

CAEN, Girondins at.

CALENDAR, Romme's new, comparative ground-scheme of.

CALONNE, M. de, Financier, character of, suavity and genius of, his difficulties, dismissed, marriage and after-course.

CALVADOS, for Girondism.

CAMUS, Archivist, in National Convention, with Dumouriez, imprisoned.

CANNON, Siamese, wooden, fever, Goethe on.

CARMAGNOLE, costume, what, dances in Convention.

CARNOT, Hippolyte, notice of, plan for Toulon, discovery in Robespierre's pocket.

CARPENTRAS, against Avignon.

CARRA, on plots for King's flight, in National Convention.

CARRIER, a Revolutionist, in National Assembly, Nantes noyades, guillotined.

CARTAUX, General, fights Girondins, at Toulon.

CASTRIES, Duke de, duel with Lameth.

CATHELINEAU, of La Vendée.

CAVAIGNAC, Convention Representative.

CAZALES, Royalist, in Constituent Assembly.

CAZOTTE, author of "Diable Amoureux," seized, saved for a time by his daughter.

CERCLE, Social, of Fauchet.

CLAVIERE, edits "Moniteur," account of, Finance Minister, arrested, suicide of.

CLERGY, French, in States-General, conciliators of orders, joins Third Estate, lands, national, power of, &c.

CLERMONT, flight of King through, Prussians near.

CLERY, on Louis's last scene.

CLOOTZ, Anacharsis, Baron de, account of, disparagement of, in National Convention, universal republic of, on nullity of religion, purged from the Jacobins, guillotined.

CLOVIS, in the Champ-de-Mars.

CLUB, Electoral, at Paris, becomes Provisional Municipality, permanent.

CLUGNY, M., as Finance Minister.

COBLENTZ, Emigrants at.

COBOURG and Dumouriez.

COCKADES, green, tricolor, black, national, trampled, white.

COFFINHAL, Judge, delivers Henriot.

COIGNY, Duke de, a sinecurist.

COMMISSIONERS, Convention, like Kings.

COMMITTEE of Defence, Central, of Watchfulness, of Public Salvation, Circular of, of the Constitution, Revolutionary.

COMMUNE, Council-General of the, Sovereign of France, enlisting.

CONDE, Prince de, attends Louis XV., departure of.

CONDE, Town, surrender of.

CONDORCET, Marquis, edits "Moniteur," Girondist, prepares Address, on Robespierre, death of.

CONSTITUTION, French, completed, will not march, burst in pieces, new, of 1793.

CONVENTION, National, in what case to be summoned, demanded by some, determined on, Deputies elected, constituted, motions in, work to be done, hated, politeness, effervescence of, on September Massacres, guard for, try the King, debate on trial, invite to revolt, condemn Louis, armed Girondins in, power of, removes to Tuileries, besieged, June 2nd, 1793, extinction of Girondins, Jacobins and, on forfeited property, Carmagnole, Goddess of Reason, Representatives, at Feast of Être Suprême, end of Robespierre, retrospect of, Féraud, Germinal, Prairial, termination, its successor.

CORDAY, Charlotte, account of, in Paris, assissinates Marat, examined, executed.

CORDELIERS, Club, Hébert in.

COURT, Chevalier de.

COUTHON, of Mountain, in Legislative, in National Convention, at Lyons, in Salut Committee, his question in Jacobins, decree of, arrest and execution.

COVENANT, Scotch, French.

CRUSSOL, Marquise de, executed.

CUISSA, massacre of, at La Force.

CUSSY, Girondin, retreats to Bourdeaux.

CUSTINE, General, takes Mentz, retreats, censured, guillotined, his son guillotined.

CUSTOMS and morals.

DAMAS, Colonel Comte de, at Clermont, at Varennes.

DAMPIERRE, General, killed.

DAMPMARTIN, Captain, at riot in Rue St. Antoine, on condition of army, on state of France, at Avignon, on Marseillese.

DANDOINS, Captain, Flight to Varennes.

DANTON, notice of, President of Cordeliers, and Marat, served with writs, in Cordeliers Club, elected Councillor, Mirabeau of Sansculottes, in Jacobins, for Deposition, of Committee, August Tenth, Minister of Justice, after September massacre, after Jemappes, and Robespierre, in Netherlands, at King's trial, on war, rebukes Marat, peace-maker, and Dumouriez, in Salut Committee, breaks with Girondins, his law of Forty sous, and Revolutionary Government, and Paris Municipality, retires to Arcis, and Robespierre, arrested, tried, and guillotined.

DAVID, Painter, in National Convention, works by, hemlock with Robespierre.

DEMOCRACY, on Bunker Hill, spread of, in France.

DEPARTMENTS, France divided into.

DESEZE, Pleader for Louis.

DESHUTTES massacred, Fifth October.

DESILLES, Captain, in Nanci.

DESLONS, Captain, at Varennes, would liberate the King.

DESMOULINS, Camille, notice of, in arms at Café de Foy, on Insurrection of Women, in Cordeliers Club, and Brissot, in National Convention, on Sansculottism, on plots, suspect, for a committee of mercy, ridicules law of the suspect, his Journal, trial of, guillotined, widow guillotined.

DIDEROT, prisoner in Vincennes.

DINNERS, defined.

DOPPET, General, at Lyons.

DROUET, Jean B., notice of, discovers Royalty in flight, raises Varennes, blocks the bridge, defends his prize, rewarded, to be in Convention, captured by Austrians.

DUBARRY, Dame, and Louis XV., flight of, imprisoned.

DUBOIS Crancé bombards and captures Lyons.

DUCHATEL votes, wrapped in blankets, at Caen.

DUCOS, Girondin.

DUGOMMIER, General, at Toulon.

DUHAMEL, killed by Marseillese.

DUMONT, on Mirabeau.

DUMOURIEZ, notice by, account of him, in Brittany, at Nantes, in La Vendée, sent for to Paris, Foreign Minister, dismissed, to Army, disobeys Lückner, Commander-in-Chief, his army, Council of War, seizes Argonne Forest, Grand Pre, and mutineers, and Marat in Paris, to Netherlands, at Jemappes, in Paris, discontented, retreats, beaten, will join the enemy, arrests his arresters, escapes to Austrians.

DUPONT, Deputy, Atheist.

DUPORT, Adrien, in Paris Parlement, in Constituent Assembly, one of a trio, law-reformer.

DUPORTAIL, in office.

DUROSOY, Royalist, guillotined.

DUSAULX, M., on taking of Bastille, notice of.

DUTERTRE, in office.

EDGEWORTH, Abbé, attends Louis, at execution of Louis.

EGLANTINE, Fabre d', in National Convention, assists in New Calendar, imprisoned.

ELIE, Capt., at Siege of Bastille, after victory.

ELIZABETH, Princess, flight to Varennes, August 10th, in Temple Prison, guillotined.

ENGLAND declares war on France, captures Toulon.

ENRAGED Club, the.

EQUALITY, reign of.

ESCUYER, Patriot l', at Avignon.

ESPREMENIL, Duval d', notice of, patriot, speaker in Paris Parlement, with crucifix, discovers Brienne's plot, arrest and speech of, turncoat, in Constituent Assembly, beaten by populace, guillotined, widow guillotined.

ESTAING, Count d', notice of, National Colonel, Royalist, at Queen's Trial.

ESTATE, Fourth, of Editors.

ETOILE, beginning of Federation at.

FAMINE, in France, in 1788-1792, Louis and Assembly try to relieve, in 1792, and remedy, remedy by maximum, &c.

FAUCHET, Abbé, at siege of Bastille, his Te-Deums, his harangue on Franklin, his Cercle Social, in First Parliament, motion by, doffs his insignia, King's death, lamentation, will demit, trial of.

FAUSSIGNY, sword in hand.

FAVRAS, Chevalier, execution of.

FEDERATION, spread of, of Champ-de-Mars, deputies to, human species at, ceremonies of, a new, 1792.

FERAUD, in National Convention, massacred there.

FERSEN, Count, gets Berline built, acts coachman in King's flight.

FEUILLANS, Club, denounce Jacobins, decline, extinguished, Battalion, Justices and Patriotism.

FINANCES, serious state of, how to be improved.

FLANDERS, how Louis XV. conquers.

FLANDRE, regiment de, at Versailles.

FLESSELLES, Paris Provost, shot.

FLEURIOT, Mayor, guillotined.

FLEURY, Joly de, Controller of Finance.

FONTENAI, Mme.

FORSTER (FOSTER), and French soldier, account of.

FOUCHE, at Lyons.

FOULON, bad repute of, sobriquet, funeral of, alive, judged, massacred.

FOURNIER, and Orleans Prisoners.

FOY, Café de, revolutionary.

FRANCE, abject, under Louis XV., Kings of, early history of, decay of Kingship in, on accession of Louis XVI., and Philosophy, famine in, 1775, state of, prior Revolution, aids America, in 1788, inflammable, July 1789, gibbets, general overturn, how to reform, riotousness of, Mirabeau and, after King's flight, petitions against Royalty, warfare of towns in, European league against, terror of, in Spring 1792, decree of war, France in danger, general enlisting, rage of, Autumn 1792, Marat's Circular, September, Sansculottic, declaration of war, Mountain and Girondins divide, communes of, coalition against, levy in mass.

FRANKLIN, Ambassador to France, his death lamented, bust in Jacobins.

FRENCH Anglomania, character of the, literature, in 1784, Parlements, nature of, Mirabeau, type of the, mob, character of.

FRERON, notice of, renegade, Gilt Youth of.

FRETEAU, at Royal Session, arrested, liberated.

FREYS, the Jew brokers, imprisoned.

GALLOIS, to La Vendée.

GAMAIN, Sieur, informer.

GARAT, Minister of Justice.

GENLIS, Mme., account of, and D'Orléans, to Switzerland.

GENSONNE, Girondist, to La Vendée, arrested, trial of.

GEORGES-CADOUDAL, in La Vendée.

GEORGET, at taking of Bastille.

GERARD, Farmer, Rennes deputy.

GERLE, Dom, at Theot's.

GERMINAL Twelfth, First of April 1795.

GIRONDINS, origin of term, in National Convention, against Robespierre, on King's trial, and Jacobins, formula of, favourers of, schemes of, to be seized? break with Danton, armed against Mountain, accuse Marat, departments, commission of twelve, commission broken, arrested, dispersed, war by, retreat of eleven, trial and death of.

GOBEL, Archbishop to be, renounces religion, arrested, guillotined.

GOETHE, at Argonne, in Prussian retreat, at Mentz.

GOGUELAT, Engineer, assists Louis's flight, intrigues.

GONDRAN, captain of Guard.

GORSAS, Journalist, pleads for Swiss, in National Convention, his house broken into, guillotined.

GOUJON, Member of Convention, in riot of Prairial, suicide of.

GOUPIL, on extreme left.

GOUVION, Major-General, at Paris, flight to Varennes, death of.

GOVERNMENT, Maurepas's, bad state of French, French revolutionary, Danton on.

GRAVE, Chev. de, War Minister, loses head.

GREGOIRE, Curé, notice of, in National Convention, detained in Convention, and destruction of religion.

GUADET, Girondin, cross-questions Ministers, arrested, guillotined.

GUARDS, Swiss, and French, at Réveillon riot, French refuse to fire, come to Palais-Royal, fire on Royal-Allemand, to Bastille, name changed, National origin of, number of, Body at Versailles, October Fifth, fight, fly in Château, Body, and French, at Versailles, National, at Nanci, French, last appearance of, National, how commanded, 1791, Constitutional, dismissed, Filles-St.-Thomas, routed, Swiss, at Tuileries, ordered to cease, destroyed, eulogy of, Departmental, for National Convention.

GUILLAUME, Clerk, pursues King.

GUILLOTIN, Doctor, summoned by Paris Parlement, invents the guillotine, deputed to King.

GUILLOTINE invented, described, in action, to be improved, number of sufferers by.

HASSENFRATZ, in War-office.

HÉBERT, Editor of "Père Duchene," signs petition, arrested, at Queen's trial, quickens Revolutionary Tribunal, arrested, and guillotined, widow guillotined.

HENAULT, President, on Surnames.

HENRIOT, General of National Guard, and the Convention, to deliver Robespierre, seized, rescued, end of.

HERBOIS, Collot d', notice of, in National Convention, at Lyons massacre, in Salut Committee, attempt to assassinate, bullied at Jacobins, President, night of Thermidor, accused, banished.

HERITIER, Jerome l', shot at Versailles.

HOCHE, Sergeant Lazare, General against Prussia, pacifies La Vendée,

HONDSCHOOTEN, Battle of.

HOTEL des Invalides, plundered.

HOTEL de Ville, after Bastille taken, harangues at.

HOUCHARD, General, unsuccessful.

HOWE, Lord, defeats French.

HUGUENIN, Patriot, tocsin in heart, 20th June 1792.

HULIN, half-pay, at siege of Bastille.

INISDAL'S, Count d', plot.

INSURRECTION, most sacred of duties, of Women, of August Tenth, difficult, of Paris, against Girondins, sacred right of, last Sansculottic, of Baboeuf.

ISNARD, Max, notice of, in First Parliament, on Ministers, to demolish Paris.

JACOB, Jean Claude, father of men.

JACOBINS, Society, beginning of, Hall, described, and members, Journal &c., of, daughters of, at Nanci, suppressed, Club increases, and Mirabeau, prospers, "Lords of the Articles," extinguishes Feuillans, Hall enlarged, described, and Marseillese, and Lavergne, message to Dumouriez, missionaries in Army, on King's trial, on accusation of Robespierre, against Girondins, National Convention and, Popular Tribunals of, purges members, to become dominant, locked out by Legendre, begs back its keys, decline of, mobbed, suspended, hunted down.

JALES, Camp of, Royalists at, destroyed.

JAUCOURT, Chevalier, and Liberty.

JAY, Dame le.

JONES, Paul, equipped for America, at Paris, account of, burial of.

JOUNNEAU, Deputy, in danger in September.

JOURDAN, General, repels Austria.

JOURDAN, Coupe-tete, at Versailles, leader of Brigands, supreme in Avignon, massacre by, flight of, guillotined.

JULIEN, Sieur Jean, guillotined.

KAUNITZ, Prince, denounces Jacobins.

KELLERMANN, at Valmy.

KLOPSTOCK, naturalised.

KNOX, John, and the Virgin.

KORFF, Baroness de, in flight to Varennes.

LAFARGE, President of Jacobins, Madame Lavergne and.

LAFAYETTE, bust of, erected, against Calonne, demands by, in Notables, Cromwell-Grandison, Bastille time, Vice-President of National Assembly, General of National Guard, resigns and reaccepts, Scipio-Americanus, thanked, rewarded, French Guards and, to Versailles, Fifth October, at Versailles, swears the Guards, Feuillant, on abolition of Titles, at Champ-de-Mars Federation, at De Castries' riot, character of, in Day of Poniards, difficult position of, at King's going to St. Cloud, resigns and reaccepts, at flight from Tuileries, after escape of King, moves for amnesty, resigns, decline of, doubtful against Jacobins, journey to Paris, to be accused, flies to Holland.

LAFLOTTE, poison-plot, informer.

LAIS, Sieur, Jacobin, with Louis Philippe.

LALLY, death of.

LAMARCHE, guillotined.

LAMARCK'S, illness of Mirabeau at.

LAMBALLE, Princess de, to England, intrigues for Royalists, at La Force, massacred.

LAMETH, in Constituent Assembly, one of a trio, brothers, notice of, Jacobins, Charles, Duke de Castries, brothers become constitutional, Theodore, in First Parliament.

LAMOIGNON, Keeper of Seals, dismissed, effigy burned, and death of.

LAMOTTE, Countess de, and Diamond Necklace, in the Salpêtrière, "Memoirs" burned, in London, M. de, in prison.

LAMOURETTE, Abbé, kiss of, guillotined.

LANJUINAIS, Girondin, clothes torn, arrested, recalled.

LAPORTE, Intendant, guillotined.

LARIVIERE, Justice, imprisoned.

LA ROCHEJACQUELIN, in La Vendée, death of.

LASOURCE, accuses Danton, president, and Marat, arrested, condemned.

LATOUR-MAUBOURG, notice of.

LAUNAY, Marquis de, Governor of Bastille, besieged, unassisted, to blow up Bastille, massacred.

LAVERGNE, surrenders Longwi.

LAVOISIER, Chemist, guillotined.

LAW, Martial, in Paris, Book of the.

LAWYERS, their influence on the Revolution, number of, in Tiers Etat, in Parliament First.

LAZARE, Maison de St., plundered.

LEBAS at Strasburg, arrested,

LEBON, Priest, in National Convention, at Arras, guillotined.

LECHAPELIER, Deputy, and Insurrection of Women.

LECOINTRE, National Major, will not fight, active, in First Parliament.

LEFEVRE, Abbé, distributes powder.

LEGENDRE, in danger, at Tuileries riot, in National Convention, against Girondins, for Danton, locks out Jacobins, in First of Prairial.

LENFANT, Abbé, on Protestant claims, massacred.

LEPELLETIER, Section for Convention, revolt of, in Vendémiaire.

LETTRES-DE-CACHET, and Parlement of Paris.

LEVASSEUR, in National Convention, Convention Representative.

LIANCOURT, Duke de, Liberal, not a revolt, but a revolution.

LIES, Philosophism on, to be extinguished, how.

LIGNE, Prince de, death of.

LILLE, Colonel Rouget de, Marseillese Hymn.

LILLE, besieged.

LINGUET, his "Bastille Unveiled," returns.

LOISEROLLES, General, guillotined for his son.

LONGWI, surrender of, fugitives at Paris.

LORDS of the Articles, Jacobins as.

LORRAINE Fédérés and the Queen, state of, in 1790.

LOUIS XIV., l'etat c'est moi, booted in Parlement, pursues Louvois.

LOUIS XV., origin of his surname, last illness of, dismisses Dame Dubarry, Choiseul, wounded, has small-pox, his mode of conquest, impoverishes France, his daughters, on death, on ministerial capacity, death and burial of.

LOUIS XVI., at his accession, good measures of, temper and pursuits of, difficulties of, commences governing, and Notables, holds Royal Session, receives States-General Deputies, in States-General procession, speech to States-General, National Assembly, unwise policy of, dismisses Necker, apprised of the Revolution, conciliatory, visits Assembly, Bastille, visits Paris, deserted, will fly, languid, at Dinner of Guards, deposition of, proposed, October Fifth, women deputies, to fly or not? grants the acceptance, Paris propositions to, in the Château tumult, appears to mob, will go to Paris, his wisest course, procession to Paris, review of his position, lodged at Tuileries, Restorer of French Liberty, no hunting, locksmith, schemes, visits Assembly, Federation, Hereditary Representative, will fly, and D'Inisdal's plot, Mirabeau, useless, indecision of, ill of catarrh, prepares for St. Cloud, hindered by populace, effect, should he escape, prepares for flight, his circular, flies, letter to Assembly, manner of flight, loiters by the way, detected by Drouet, captured at Varennes, indecision there, return to Paris, reception there, to be deposed? reinstated, reception of Legislative, position of, proposes war, with tears, vetoes, dissolves Roland Ministry, in riot of, June 20, and Pétion, at Federation, with cuirass, declared forfeited, last levee of, Tenth August, quits Tuileries for Assembly, in Assembly, sent to Temple prison, in Temple, to be tried, and the Locksmith Gamain, at the bar, his will, condemned, parting scene, and execution of, his son.

LOUIS-PHILIPPE, King of the French, Jacobin door-keeper, at Valmy, bravery at Jemappes, and sister, with Dumouriez to Austrians, to Switzerland.

LOUSTALOT, Editor.

LOUVET, his "Chevalier de Faublas," his "Sentinelles," and Robespierre, in National Convention, Girondin accuses Robespierre, arrested, retreats to Bourdeaux, escape of, recalled.

LUCKNER, Supreme General, and Dumouriez, guillotined.

LUNEVILLE, Inspector Malseigne at.

LUX, Adam, guillotined.

LYONS, Federation at, disorders in, Chalier, Jacobin, executed at, capture of magazine, massacres at.

MAILHE, Deputy, on trial of Louis.

MAILLARD, Usher, at siege of Bastille, Insurrection of Women, drum, Champs Elysées, entering Versailles, addresses National Assembly there, signs Déchéance petition, in September Massacres.

MAILLE, Camp-Marshal, at Tuileries, massacred at La Force.

MAILLY, Marshal, one of Four Generals.

MALESHERBES, M. de, in King's Council, defends Louis.

MALSEIGNE, Army Inspector, at Nanci, imprisoned, liberated.

MANDAT, Commander of Guards, August, 1792.

MANUEL, Jacobin, slow-sure, in August Tenth, in Governing Committee, haranguing at La Force, in National Convention, motions in, vote at King's trial, in prison, guillotined.

MARAT, Jean Paul, horseleech to D'Artois, notice of, against violence, at siege of Bastille, summoned by Constituent, not to be gagged, astir, how to regenerate France, police and, on abolition of titles, would gibbet Mirabeau, bust in Jacobins, concealed in cellars, in seat of honour, signs circular, elected to Convention, and Dumouriez, oaths by, in Convention, on sufferings of People, and Girondins, arrested, returns in triumph, fall of Girondins.

MARECHAL, Atheist, Calendar by.

MARECHALE, the Lady, on nobility.

MARSEILLES, Brigands at, on Déchéance, the bar of iron, for Girondism.

MARSEILLESE, March and Hymn of, at Charenton, at Paris, Filles-St.-Thomas and, barracks.

MASSACRE, Avignon, September, number slain in, compared to Bartholomew.

MATON, Advocate, his "Resurrection."

MAUPEOU, under Louis XV., and Dame Dubarry.

MAUREPAS, Prime Minister, character of, government of, death of.

MAURY, Abbé, character of, in Constituent Assembly, seized emigrating, dogmatic, efforts fruitless, made Cardinal.

MEMMAY, M., of Quincey, explosion of rustics.

MENOU, General, arrest of.

MENTZ, occupied by French, siege of, surrender of.

MERCIER, on Paris revolting, Editor, the September Massacre, in National Convention, King's trial.

MERLIN of Thionville in Mountain, irascible, at Mentz.

MERLIN of Douai, Law of Suspect.

METZ, Bouillé at, troops mutinous at.

MEUDON tannery.

MIOMANDRE de Ste. Marie, Bodyguard, October Fifth, left for dead, revives, rewarded.

MIRABEAU, Marquis, on the state of France in 1775, and his son, his death.

MIRABEAU, Count, his pamphlets, the Notables, Lettres-de-Cachet against, expelled by the Provence Noblesse, cloth-shop, is Deputy for Aix, king of Frenchmen, family of, wanderings of, his future course, groaned at, in Assembly, his newspaper suppressed, silences Usher de Brézé, at Bastille ruins, on Robespierre, fame of, on French deficit, populace, on veto, Mounier, October Fifth, insight of, defends veto, courage, revenue of, saleable? and Danton, on Constitution, at Jacobins, his courtship, on state of Army, Marat would gibbet, his power in France, on D'Orléans, on duelling, interview with Queen, speech on emigrants, the "trente voix," in Council, his plans for France, probable career of, last appearance in Assembly, anxiety of populace for, last sayings of, death and funeral of, burial-place of, character of, last of Mirabeaus, bust in Jacobins, bust demolished.

MIRABEAU the younger, nicknamed Tonneau, in Constituent Assembly, breaks his sword.

MIRANDA, General, attempts Holland.

MIROMENIL, Keeper of Seals.

MOLEVILLE, Bertrand de, Historian, minister, his plan, frivolous policy of, and D'Orléans, Jesuitic, concealed.

MOMORO, Bookseller, agrarian, arrested, guillotined, his Wife, "Goddess of Reason."

MONGE, Mathematician, in office, assists in new Calendar.

MONSABERT, G. de, President of Paris Parlement, arrested.

MONTELIMART, covenant sworn at.

MONTESQUIOU, General, takes Savoy.

MONTGAILLARD, on captive Queen, on September Massacres.

MONTMARTRE, trenches at.

MONTMORIN, War-Secretary.

MOORE, Doctor, at attack of Tuileries, at La Force.

MORANDE, De, newspaper by, will return, in prison.

MORELLET, Philosophe.

MOUCHETON, M. de, of King's Bodyguard.

MOUDON, Abbé, confessor to Louis XV.

MOUNIER, at Grenoble, proposes Tennis-Court oath, October Fifth, President of Constituent Assembly, deputed to King, dilemma of.

MOUNTAIN, members of the, re-elected in National Convention, Gironde and, favourers of the, vulnerable points of, prevails, Danton, Duperret, after Gironde dispersed, in labour.

MULLER, General, expedition to Spain.

MURAT, in Vendémiaire revolt.

NANCI, revolt at, description of town, deputation imprisoned, deputation of mutineers, state of mutineers in, Bouillé's fight, Paris thereupon, military executions at, Assembly Commissioners.

NANTES, after King's flight, massacres at.

NAPOLEON Buonaparte (Buonaparte) studying mathematics, pamphlet by, democratic, in Corsica, August Tenth, under General Cartaux, at Toulon, Josephine and, at La Cabarus's, Vendémiaire.

NARBONNE, Louis de, assists flight of King's Aunts, to be War-Minister, demands by, secreted, escapes.

NAVY, Louis XV. on French.

NECKER, and finance, account of, dismissed, refuses Brienne, recalled, difficulty as to States-General, reconvokes Notables, opinion of himself, popular, dismissed, recalled, returns in glory, his plans, becoming unpopular, departs, with difficulty.

NECKLACE, Diamond.

NERWINDEN, battle of.

NIEVRE-CHOL, Mayor of Lyons.

NOBLES, state of the, under Louis XV., new, join Third Estate.

NOTABLES, Calonne's convocation of, assembled 22nd February 1787, members of, effects of dismissal of, reconvoked, 6th November 1788, dismissed again.

NOYADES, Nantes.

OCTOBER Fifth, 1789

OGE, condemned.

ORLEANS, High Court at, prisoners massacred at Versailles.

ORLEANS, a Duke d', in Louis XV."s sick-room.

ORLEANS, Philippe (Egalité), Duc d', Duke de Chartres (till 1785), waits on Dauphin, Father, with Louis XV., not Admiral, wealth, debauchery, Palais-Royal buildings, in Notables (Duke d'Orléans now), looks of, Bed-of-Justice, 1787, arrested, liberated, in States-General Procession, joins Third Estate, his party, in Constituent Assembly, Fifth October and, shunned in England, Mirabeau, cash deficiency, use of, in Revolution, accused by Royalists, at Court, insulted, in National Convention, decline of, in Convention, vote on King's trial, at King's execution, arrested, imprisoned, condemned, and executed.

ORMESSON, d', Controller of Finance.

PACHE, Swiss, account of, Minister of War, Mayor, dismissed, reinstated, imprisoned.

PAN, Mallet du, solicits for Louis.

PANIS, Advocate, in Governing Committee, and Beaumarchais, confidant of Danton.

PANTHEON, first occupant of.

PARENS, Curate, renounces religion.

PARIS, origin of city, police in 1750, ship Ville-de-Paris, riot at Palais-de-Justice, beautified, in 1788, election, 1789, troops called to, military preparations in, July Fourteenth, cry for arms, search for arms, Bailly, mayor of, trade-strikes in, Lafayette patrols, October Fifth, propositions to Louis, Louis in, Journals, bill-stickers, undermined, after Champ-de-Mars Federation, on Nanci affair, on death of Mirabeau, on flight to Varennes, on King's return, Directory suspends Pétion, enlisting, 1792, on forfeiture of King, Sections, rising of, August Tenth, prepares for insurrection, Municipality supplanted, statues destroyed, King and Queen to prison, September, 1792, names printed on house-door, in insurrection, Girondins, May 1793, Municipality in red caps, brotherly supper, Sections to be abolished.

PARIS, Guardsman, assassinates Lepelletier.

PARIS, friend of Danton.

PARLEMENT, patriotic, against Taxation, remonstrates, at Versailles, arrested, origin of, nature of, corrupt, at Troyes, yields, Royal Session in, how to be tamed, oath and declaration of, firmness of, scene in, and dismissal of, reinstated, unpopular, summons Dr. Guillotin, abolished.

PARLEMENTS, Provincial, adhere to Paris, rebellious, exiled, grand deputations of, reinstated, abolished.

PELTIER, Royalist Pamphleteer, "Père Duchene," Editor of.

PEREYRA (Peyreyra), Walloon, account of, imprisoned.

PETION, account of, Dutch-built, and D'Espréménil, to be mayor, Varennes, meets King, and Royalty, at close of Assembly, in London, Mayor of Paris, in Twentieth June, suspended, reinstated, welcomes Marseillese, August Tenth, in Tuileries, rebukes Septemberers, in National Convention, declines mayorship, against Mountain, retreat to Bourdeaux, end of.

PÉTION, National-Pique, christening of.

PETITION of famishing French, at Fatherland's altar, of the Eight Thousand.

PETITIONS, on capture of King, for deposition, &c.

PHELIPPEAUX, purged out of the Jacobins.

PHILOSOPHISM, influence of, on Revolution, what it has done with Church, with Religion.

PICHEGRU, General, account of, in Germinal.

PILNITZ, Convention at.

PIN, Latour du, War-Minister, dismissed.

PITT, against France, and Girondins, inflexible.

PLOTS, of King's flight, various, of Aristocrats, October Fifth, Royalist, of Favras and others, cartels, Twelve bullies from Switzerland, D'Inisdal, will-o'-wisp, Mirabeau and Queen, poniards, Mallet du Pan, Narbonne's, traces of, in Armoire-de-Fer, against Girondins, Desmoulins on, prison.

POLIGNAC, Duke de, a sinecurist, dismissed, at Bale, younger, in Ham.

POMPIGNAN, President of National Assembly.

POPE PIUS VI., excommunicates Talleyrand, his effigy burned.

PRAIRIAL First to Third, May 20-22, 1795.

PRECY, siege of, Lyons.

PRIESTHOOD, disrobing of, costumes in Carmagnole.

PRIESTLEY, Dr., riot against, naturalised, elected to National Convention.

PRIESTS, dissident, marry in France, Anti-national, hanged, many killed near the Abbaye, number slain in September Massacre, to rescue Louis, drowned at Nantes.

PRISONS, Paris, in Bastille time, full, August 1792, number of, in France, state of, in Terror, thinned after Terror.

PRISON, Abbaye, refractory Members sent to, Temple, Louis sent to, Abbaye, Priests killed near, massacres at La Force, Chatelet, and Conciergerie.

PROCESSION, of States-General Deputies, of Necker and D'Orléans busts, of Louis to Paris, again, after Varennes, of Louis to trial, at Constitution of 1793.

PROVENCE Noblesse, expel Mirabeau.

PRUDHOMME, Editor, on assassins, on Cavaignac.

PRUSSIA, Fritz of, against France, army of, ravages France, King of, and French Princes.

PUISAYE, Girondin General, at Quiberon.

QUERET-DEMERY, in Bastille.

QUIBERON, debarkation at.

RABAUT, St. Etienne, French Reformer, in National Convention, in Commission of Twelve, arrested, between two walls, guillotined.

RAYNAL, Abbé, Philosophe, his letter to Constituent Assembly.

REBECQUI, of Marseilles, in National Convention, against Robespierre, retires, drowns himself.

REDING, Swiss, massacred.

RELIGION, Christian, and French Revolution, abolished, Clootz on, a new.

REMY, Cornet, at Clermont.

RENAULT, Cecile, to assassinate Robespierre, guillotined.

RENE, King, bequeathed Avignon to Pope.

RENNES, riot in.

RENWICK, last of Cameronians.

REPAIRE, Tardivet du, Bodyguard, Fifth October, rewarded.

REPRESENTATIVES, Paris, Town.

REPUBLIC, French, first mention of, first year of, established, universal, Clootz's, Girondin, one and indivisible, its triumphs.

RESSON, Sieur, reports Lafayette to Jacobins.

REVEILLON, house destroyed.

REVOLT, Paris, in, of Gardes Françaises, becomes Revolution, military, what, of Lepelletier section.

REVOLUTION, French, causes of the, Lord Chesterfield on the, not a revolt, meaning of the term, whence it grew, general commencement of, prosperous characters in, Philosophes and, state of army in, progress of, duelling in, Republic decided on, European powers and, Royalist opinion of, cardinal movements in, Danton and the, changes produced by the, effect of King's death on, Girondin idea of, suspicion in, Terror and, and Christian religion, Revolutionary Committees, Government doings in, Robespierre essential to, end of.

RHEIMS, in September massacre.

RICHELIEU, at death of Louis XV., death of.

RIOT, Paris, in May 1750, Cornlaw (in 1775), at Palais de Justice (1787), triumph, of Rue St. Antoine, of July Fourteenth (1789), and Bastille, at Strasburg, Paris, on the veto, Versailles Château, October Fifth (1789), uses of, to National Assembly, Paris, on Nanci affair, at De Castries' Hotel, on flight of King's Aunts, at Vincennes, on King's proposed journey to St. Cloud, in Champ-de-Mars, with sharp shot, Paris, Twentieth June, 1792, August Tenth, 1792, Grain, Paris, at Theatre de la Nation, selling sugar, of Thermidor, 1794, of Germinal, 1795, of Prairial, final, of Vendémiaire.

RIOUFFE, Girondin, to Bourdeaux, in prison, on death of Girondins, on Mme. Roland.

ROBESPIERRE, Maximilien, account of, derided in Constituent Assembly, Jacobin, incorruptible, on tip of left, elected public accuser, after King's flight, at close of Assembly, at Arras, position of, plans in 1792, chief priest of Jacobins, invisible on August Tenth, reappears, on September Massacre, in National Convention, accused by Girondins, accused by Louvet, acquitted, King's trial, Condorcet on, at Queen's trial, in Salut Committee, and Paris Municipality, embraces Danton, Desmoulins and, and Danton, Danton on, at trial, his three scoundrels, supreme, to be assassinated, at Feast of Être Suprême, apocalyptic, Theot, on Couthon's plot-decree, reserved, his schemes, fails in Convention, applauded at Jacobins, accused, rescued, at Townhall, declared out of law, half-killed, guillotined, essential to Revolution.

ROBESPIERRE, Augustin, decreed accused, guillotined.

ROCHAMBEAU, one of Four Generals, retires.

ROCHE-AYMON, Grand Almoner of Louis XV.

ROCHEFOUCAULT, Duke de la, Liberal, President of Directory, killed.

ROEDERER, Syndic, Feuillant, "Chronicle of Fifty Days," on Fédérés Ammunition, dilemma at Tuileries, August 10th.

ROHAN, Cardinal, Diamond Necklace.

ROLAND, Madame, notice of, at Lyons, narrative by, in Paris, after King's flight, and Barbaroux, public dinners and business, character of, misgivings of, accused, Girondin declining, arrested, condemned and guillotined.

ROLAND, M., notice of, in Paris, Minister, letter, and dismissal of, recalled, decline of, on September Massacres, and Pache, doings of, resigns, flies, suicide of.

ROMME, in National Convention, in Caen prison, his new Calendar, in riot of Prairial, 1795, suicide.

ROMOEUF, pursues King.

RONSIN, General of Revolutionary Army, arrested and guillotined.

ROSIERE, Thuriot de la, summons Bastille, in First Parliament, in National Convention, President at Robespierre's fall.

ROSSIGNOL, in September Massacre, in La Vendée.

ROUSSEAU, Jean-Jacques, Contrat Social of, Gospel according to, burial-place of, statue decreed to.

ROUX, M., "Histoire Parlementaire."

ROYALTY, signs of demolished, abolition of.

RUAMPS, Deputy, against Couthon.

RUHL, notice of, in riot of Prairial, suicide.

SABATIER de Cabre, at Royal Session, arrested, liberated.

ST. ANTOINE to Versailles, Warhorse supper, Nanci affair, at Vincennes, at Jacobins, and Marseillese, August Tenth.

ST. CLOUD, Louis prohibited from.

ST. DENIS, Mayor of, hanged.

ST. FARGEAU, Lepelletier, in National Convention, at King's trial, assassinated, burial of.

ST. HURUGE, Marquis, bull-voice, imprisoned, at Versailles, and Pope's effigy, at Jacobins, on King's trial.

ST. JUST in National Convention, on King's trial, in Salut Committee, at Strasburg, repels Prussians, on Revolution, in Committee-room, Thermidor, his report, arrested.

ST. LOUIS Church, States-General procession from.

ST. MEARD, Jourgniac de, in prison, his "Agony" at La Force.

ST. MERY, Moreau de, prostrated.

SALLES, Deputy, guillotined.

SANSCULOTTISM, apparition of, effects of, growth of, at work, origin of term, and Royalty, above theft, a fact, French Nation and, Revolutionary Tribunal and, how it lives, consummated, fall of, last rising of, death of.

SANTERRE, Brewer, notice of, at siege of Bastille, at Tuileries, June Twentieth, meets Marseillese, Commander of Guards, how to relieve famine, at King's trial, at King's execution, fails in La Vendée, St. Antoine disarmed.

SAPPER, Fraternal.

SAUSSE, M., Procureur of Varennes, scene at his house, flies from Prussians.

SAVONNIERES, M., de, Bodyguard, October Fifth, loses temper.

SAVOY, occupied by French.

SECHELLES, Herault de, in National Convention, leads Convention out, arrested and guillotined.

SECTIONS, of Paris, denounce Girondins, Committee of.

SEIGNEURS, French, compelled to fly.

SERGENT, Agate, Engraver, in Committee, nicknamed "Agate," signs circular.

SERVAN, War-Minister, proposals of.

SEVRES, Potteries, Lamotte's "Mémoires" burnt at.

SICARD, Abbé, imprisoned, in danger near the Abbaye, account of massacre there.

SIDE, Right and Left, of Constituent Assembly, Right and Left, tip of Left, popular, Right after King's flight, Right quits Assembly, Right and Left in First Parliament.

SIEYES, Abbé, account of, Constitution-builder, in Champ-de-Mars, in National Convention, of Constitution Committee, 1790, vote at King's trial, making fresh Constitution.

SILLERY, Marquis.

SIMON, Cordwainer, Dauphin committed to, guillotined.

SIMONEAU, Mayor of Etampes, death of, festival for.

SOMBREUIL, Governor of Hôtel des Invalides, examined, seized, saved by his daughter, guillotined, his son shot.

SPAIN, at war with France, invaded by France.

STAAL, Dame de, on liberty.

STAEL, Mme. de, at States-General procession, intrigue for Narbonne, secretes Narbonne.

STANHOPE and Price, their club and Paris.

STATES-GENERAL, first suggested, meeting announced, how constituted, orders in, Representatives to, Parlements against, Deputies to, in Paris, number of Deputies, place of Assembly, procession of, installed, union of orders.

STRASBURG, riot at, in 1789.

SUFFREN, Admiral, notice of.

SULLEAU, Royalist, editor, massacred.

SUSPECT, Law of the, Chaumette jeered on.

SWEDEN, King of, to assist Marie Antoinette, shot by Ankarstrom.

SWISS Guards at Brest, prisoners at La Force.

TALLEYRAND-PERIGORD, Bishop, notice of, at fatherland's altar, his blessing, excommunicated, in London, to America.

TALLIEN, notice of, editor of "Ami des Citoyens," in Committee of Townhall, August 1792, in National Convention, at Bourdeaux, and Madame Cabarus, recalled, suspect, accuses Robespierre, Thermidorian.

TALMA, actor, his soirée.

TANNERY of human skins, improvements in.

TARGET, Advocate, declines King's defence.

TASSIN, M., and black cockade.

TENNIS-COURT, National Assembly in, Club of, and procession to, master of, rewarded.

TERROR, consummation of, reign of, designated, number guillotined in.

THEATINS Church, granted to Dissidents.

THEOT, Prophetess, on Robespierre.

THERMIDOR, Ninth and Tenth, July 27 and 28, 1794.

THEROIGNE, Mlle., notice of, in Insurrection of Women, at Versailles (October Fifth), in Austrian prison, in Jacobin tribune, armed for insurrection (August Tenth), keeps her carriage, fustigated, insane.

THIONVILLE besieged, siege raised.

THOURET, Law-reformer, dissolves Assembly, guillotined.

THOUVENOT and Dumouriez.

TINVILLE, Fouquier, revolutionist, Jacobin, Attorney-General in Tribunal Revolutionnaire, at Queen's trial, at trial of Girondins, at trial of Mme. Roland, at trial of Danton, and Salut Public, his prison-plots, his batches, the prisons under, mock doom of, at trial of Robespierre, accused, guillotined.

TOLLENDAL, Lally, pleads for father, in States-General, popular, crowned.

TORNE, Bishop.

TOULON, Girondin, occupied by English, besieged, surrenders.

TOULONGEON, Marquis, notice of, on Barnave triumvirate, describes Jacobins Hall.

TOURNAY, Louis, at siege of Bastille.

TOURZELLE, Dame de, escape of.

TRONCHET, Advocate, defends King.

TUILERIES, Louis XVI. lodged at, a tile-field, Twentieth June at, tickets of entry, "Coblentz," Marseillese chase Filles-Saint-Thomas to, August Tenth, King quits, attacked, captured, occupied by National Convention.

TURGOT, Controller of France, on Corn-law, dismissed, death of.

TYRANTS, French people rise against.

UNITED STATES, declaration of Liberty, embassy to Louis XVI., aided by France, of Congress in.

USHANT, battle off.

VALADI, Marquis, Gardes Françaises and, guillotined.

VALAZE, Girondin, on trial of Louis, plots at his house, trial of, kills himself.

VALENCIENNES, besieged, surrendered.

VARENNE, Maton de la, his experiences in September.

VARIGNY, Bodyguard, massacred.

VARLET, "Apostle of Liberty," arrested.

VENDEE, La, Commissioners to, state of, in 1792, insurrection in, war, after King's death, on fire, pacificated.

VENDÉMIAIRE, Thirteenth, October 4, 1795.

VERDUN, to be besieged, surrendered.

VERGENNES, M. de, Prime Minister, death of.

VERGNIAUD, notice of, August Tenth, orations of, President at King's condemnation, in fall of Girondins, trial of, at last supper of Girondins.

VERMOND, Abbé de.

VERSAILLES, death of Louis XV. at, in Bastille time, National Assembly at, troops to, march of women on, of French Guards on, insurrection scene at, the Château forced, prisoners massacred at.

VIARD, Spy.

VILATE, Juryman, guillotined, book by.

VILLARET-JOYEUSE, Admiral, defeated by Howe.

VILLEQUIER, Duke de, emigrates.

VINCENNES, riot at, saved by Lafayette.

VINCENT, of War-Office, arrested, guillotined.

VOLTAIRE, at Paris, described, burial-place of.

WAR, civil, becomes general.

WASHINGTON, key of Bastille sent to, formula for Lafayette.

WATIGNY, Battle of.

WEBER, in Insurrection of Women, Queen leaving Vienna.

WESTERMANN, August Tenth, purged out of the Jacobins, tried and guillotined.

WIMPFEN, Girondin General.

YORK, Duke of, besieges Valenciennes and Dunkirk.

YOUNG, Arthur, at French Revolution.

FOOTNOTES

512 Moore's *Journal*, i. 85.

513 *Hist. Parl.* xvii. 467.

514 Ibid. xvii. 437.

515 *Mémoires de Buzot* (Paris, 1823), p. 88.

516 Moore's *Journal*, i. 159-168.

517 See Toulongeon, *Hist. de France.* ii. c. 5.

518 *Hist. Parl.* xvii. 148.

519 *Hist. Parl.* xix. 300.

520 De Staël, *Considérations sur la Révolution*, ii. 67-81.

521 Beaumarchais' Narrative, *Mémoires sur les Prisons* (Paris, 1823), i. 179-90.

522 Dumouriez, *Mémoires*, ii. 383.

523 Helen Maria Williams, *Letters from France* (London, 1791-93), iii. 96.

524 Dumouriez, ii. 391.

525 Moore, i. 178.

526 *Hist. Parl.* xvii. 409.

527 *Biographie des Ministres* (Bruxelles, 1826), p. 96.

528 *Moniteur* (in *Hist. Parl.* xvii. 347).

529 Félémhesi (anagram for Méhée Fils), *La Verité tout entière, sur les vrais auteurs de la journée du 2 Septembre* 1792 (reprinted in *Hist. Parl.* xviii. 156-181), p. 167.

530 Félémhesi, *La Verité tout entière* (ut supra), p. 173.

531 Moore's *Journal*, i. 185-195.

532 Dulaure: *Esquisses Historiques des principaux événemens de la Révolution*, ii. 206 (cited in Montgaillard, iii. 205.

533 Bertrand-Moleville, *Mém. Particuliers*, ii.213, &c. &c.

534 Jourgniac Saint-Méard, *Mon Agonie de Trente-huit heures* (reprinted in *Hist. Parl.* xviii. 103-135).

535 Maton de la Varenne, *Ma Résurrection* (in *Hist. Parl.* xviii. 135-156).

536 Abbé Sicard, *Relation adressée à un de ses amis* (in *Hist. Parl.* xviii. 98-103).

537 *Mon Agonie* (ut supra, *Hist. Parl.* xviii. 128).

538 *Moniteur*, Debate of 2nd September, 1792.

539 Méhée Fils (ut supra, in *Hist. Parl.* xviii. p. 189).

540 Montgaillard, iii. 191.

541 Helen Maria Williams, iii. 27.

542 See *Hist. Parl.* xvii. 421, 422.

543 *Moniteur* of 6th November, Debate of 5th November, 1793.

544 *Etat des sommes payées par la Commune de Paris* (*Hist. Parl.* xviii. 231).

545 Mercier, *Nouveau Paris*, vi. 21.

546 9th to 13th September, 1572 (Dulaure, *Hist. de Paris*, iv. 289).

547 Dulaure, iii. 494.

548 *Hist. Parl.* xvii. 433.

549 Ibid. xvii. 434.

550 *Pièces officielles relatives au massacre des Prisonniers à Versailles* (in *Hist. Parl.* xviii. 236-249).

551 *Biographie des Ministres*, p. 97.

552 Ibid. p. 103.

553 *Dictionnaire des Hommes Marquans*, § Barras.

554 Bertrand-Moleville, *Mémoires*, ii. 225.

555 See Helen Maria Williams. *Letters*, iii. 79-81.

556 Dumouriez, *Mémoires*, iii. 29.

557 Dumouriez, *Mémoires*, iii. 55.

558 Helen Maria Williams, iii. 32.

559 Goethe, *Campagne in Frankreich* (*Werke*, xxx. 73.

560 *Hist. Parl.* xix. 177.

561 Goethe, xxx. 49.

562 *Hist. Parl.* xix. 19.

563 Williams, iii. 71.

564 1st October, 1792; Dumouriez, iii. 73.

565 *Bombardement de Lille* (in *Hist. Parl.* xx. 63-71).

566 *Campagne in Frankreich*, p. 103.

567 See *Hermann und Dorothea* (also by Goethe), Buch *Kalliope*.

568 *Campagne in Frankreich*, Goethe's *Werke* (Stuttgart, 1829), xxx. 133-137.

569 *Campagne in Frankreich*, Goethe's *Werke*, xxx. 152.

570 Ibid. 210-12.

571 Dumouriez, iii. 115.—Marat's account, In the *Débats des Jacobins* and *Journal de la République* (*Hist. Parl.* xix. 317-21), agrees to the turning on the heel, but strives to interpret it differently.

572 Johann Georg Forster's *Briefwechsel* (Leipzig, 1829), i. 88.

573 *Hist. Parl.* xx. 184.

574 *Moniteur* Newspaper, Nos. 271, 280, 294, Annee premiere; Moore's *Journal*, ii. 21, 157, &c. (which, however, may perhaps, as in similar cases, be only a copy of the Newspaper).

575 *Moniteur*, ut supra; Séance du 25 Septembre.

576 Madame Roland, *Mémoires*, ii. 237, &c.

577 *Dictionnaire des Hommes Marquans*, § Chambon.

578 *Moniteur* (in *Hist. Parl.* xx. 412).

579 *Hist. Parl.* xx. 431-440.

580 Ibid. 409.

581 Mercier, *Nouveau Paris*.

582 Moore, i. 123; ii. 224, &c.

583 *Moniteur*, Séance du 21 Septembre, An 1er (1792).

584 Moore's *Journal*, ii. 165.

585 Dumouriez, *Mémoires*, iii. 174.

586 Moore, ii. 148.

587 Louvet, *Mémoires* (Paris, 1823) p. 52; *Moniteur* (Séances du 29 Octobre, 5 Novembre, 1792); Moore (ii. 178), &c.

588 See *Hist. Parl.* xvii. 401; Newspapers by Gorsas and others (cited *ibid.* 428).

589 *Journal des Débats des Jacobins* in *Hist. Parl.* xxii. 296.

590 Prudhomme's Newspaper in *Hist. Parl.* xxi. 314.

591 See Extracts from their Newspapers, in *Hist. Parl.* xxi. 1-38, &c.

592 *Moniteur*, Séance du 14 Décembre 1792.

593 Mrs. Hannah More, *Letter to Jacob Dupont* (London, 1793); &c. &c.

594 *Hist. Parl.* xxii. 131; Moore, &c.

595 *Hist. Parl.* xxiii. 31, 48, &c.

596 *Moniteur*, Séance du 7 Decembre 1792.

597 Dumouriez, *Mémoires*, iii. c. 4.

598 Mercier, *Nouveau Paris*, vi. 156-59; Montgaillard, iii. 348-87; Moore, &c.

599 *Moniteur* in *Hist. Parl.* xxiii. 210. See Boissy d'Anglas, *Vie de Malesherbes*, ii. 139.

600 *Biographie des Ministres*, p. 157.

601 See Prudhomme's Newspaper, *Révolutions de Paris* in *Hist. Parl.* xxiii. 318.

602 *Hist. Parl.* xxiii. 275, 318; Félix Lepelletier, *Vie de Michel Lepelletier son Frère*, p. 61. &c. Félix, with due love of the miraculous, will have it that the Suicide in the inn was not Paris, but some *double-ganger* of his.

603 Cléry's *Narrative* (London, 1798), cited in Weber, iii. 312.

604 Newspapers, Municipal Records, &c. &c. in *Hist. Parl.* xxiii. 298-349; *Deux Amis*, ix. 369-373; Mercier, *Nouveau Paris*, iii. 3-8.

605 His Letter in the Newspapers (*Hist. Parl.* ubi supra).

606 Forster's *Briefwechsel*, i. 473.

607 *Hist. Parl.* ubi supra.

608 *Annual Register* of 1793, pp. 114-128.

609 23d March, *Annual Register*, p. 161.

610 1st February; 7th March, Moniteur of these dates.

611 *Moniteur* &c. *Hist. Parl.* xxiv. 332-348.

612 *Hist. Parl.* xxiv. 353-356.

613 Dumouriez, *Mémoires*, iii. 314.

614 *Moniteur*, 1793, No. 140, &c.

615 *Hist. Parl.* xxv. 25, &c.

616 *Hist. Parl.* xxiv. 385-93; xxvi. 229, &c.

617 *Moniteur*, Séance du 20 Mai 1793.

618 Genlis, *Mémoires* (London, 1825), iv. 118.

619 *Mémoires de Meillan, Représentant du Peuple* (Paris, 1823), p. 51.

620 Dumouriez, iv. 16-73.

621 Forster's *Briefwechsel*, ii. 514, 460, 631.

622 See Dampmartin, *Evénemens*, ii. 213-30.

623 *Moniteur* in *Hist. Parl.* xxv. 6.

624 *Choix des Rapports*, xi. 277.

625 *Hist. Parl.* xxv. 72.

626 Louvet, *Mémoires*, p. 72.

627 Meillan, pp. 23, 24; Louvet, pp. 71-80.

628 *Moniteur* (Séance du 12 Mars), 15 Mars.

629 Meillan, *Mémoires*, pp. 85, 24.

630 *Moniteur*, No. 70, (du 11 Mars), No. 76, &c.

631 *Moniteur*, No. 83 (du 24 Mars 1793), Nos. 86, 98, 99, 100.

632 *Moniteur*, du 20 Avril, &c. to 20 Mai, 1793.

633 Dumouriez, *Mémoires*, iv. c. 7-10.

634 Genlis, iv. 139.

635 Dumouriez, iv. 159, &c.

636 Their Narrative, written by Camus in Toulongeon, iii. app. 60-87.

637 *Mémoires*, iv. 162-180.

638 See Montgaillard, iv. 144.

639 *Mémoires de Réné Levasseur* (Bruxelles, 1830), i. 164.

640 Séance du 1er Avril, 1793 in *Hist. Parl.* xxv. 24-35.

641 *Hist. Parl.* xv. 397.

642 *Moniteur*, du 16 Avril 1793, et seqq.

643 Séance du 26 Avril, An 1er (in *Moniteur*, No. 116).

644 Levasseur, *Mémoires*, i. c. 6.

645 Buzot, *Mémoires*, pp. 69, 84; Meillan, *Mémoires*, pp. 192, 195, 196. See *Commission des Douze* in *Choix des Rapports*, xii. 69-131.

646 *Deux Amis*, vii. 77-80; Forster, i. 514; Moore, i. 70. She did not die till 1817; in the Salpêtrière, in the most abject state of insanity; see Esquirol, *Des Maladies Mentales* (Paris, 1838), i. 445-50.

647 Mercier, *Nouveau Paris*, vi. 63.

648 See *Histoire des Brissotins*, par Camille Desmoulins, a Pamphlet of Camille's, Paris, 1793.

649 *Moniteur*, Séance du 25 Mai, 1793.

650 Meillan, *Mémoires*, p. 195; Buzot, pp. 69, 84.

651 *Debats de la Convention* (Paris, 1828), iv. 187-223; *Moniteur*, Nos. 152, 3, 4, An 1er.

652 Louvet, *Mémoires*, p. 89.

653 Buzot, *Mémoires*, p. 310. See *Pièces Justificatives*, of Narratives, Commentaries, &c. in Buzot, Louvet, Meillan: *Documens Complémentaires*, in *Hist. Parl.* xxviii. 1-78.

654 Meillan, p. 72, 73; Louvet, p. 129.

655 *Belagerung von Mainz*, Goethe's *Werke*, xxx. 278-334.

656 Meillan, p.75; Louvet, p. 114.

657 *Moniteur*, Nos. 197, 198, 199; *Hist. Parl.* xxviii. 301-5; *Deux Amis*, x. 368-374.

658 See *Eloge funèbre de Jean-Paul Marat*, prononcé à Strasbourg in Barbaroux, p. 125-131; Mercier, &c.

659 Séance du 16 Septembre 1793.

660 *Procès de Charlotte Corday*, &c. *Hist. Parl.* xxviii. 311-338.

661 *Deux Amis*, x. 374-384.

662 *Briefwechsel*, i. 508.

663 See Hazlitt, ii. 529-41.

664 Barbaroux, p. 29.

665 *Deux Amis*, x. 345.

666 *Mémoires de Puisaye* (London, 1803), ii. 142-67.

667 Louvet, pp. 101-37; Meillan, pp. 81, 241-70.

668 Meillan, pp. 119-137.

669 Louvet, pp. 138-164.

670 *Belagerung von Maintz*, Goethe's *Werke*, xxx. 315.

671 *Deux Amis*, xi. 73.

672 *Choix des Rapports*, xii. 432-42.

673 September 22nd of 1792 is Vendémiaire 1st of Year One, and the new months are all of 30 days each; therefore:

To the number of the day in	Add	We have the number of the day in	Days
Vendémiaire	21	September	30
Brumaire	21	October	31
Frimaire	20	November	30
Nivose	20	December	31
Pluviose	19	January	31
Ventose	18	February	28
Germinal	20	March	31
Floréal	19	April	30
Prairial	19	May	31
Messidor	18	June	30
Thermidor	18	July	31
Fructidor	17	August	31

There are 5 Sansculottides, and in leap-year a sixth, to be added at the end of Fructidor. Romme's first Leap-year is '*An* 4'(1795, not 1796), which is another troublesome circumstance, every fourth year, from "September 23d" round to "February 29" again.

The New Calendar ceased on the 1st of January 1806. See *Choix des Rapports*, xiii. 83-99; xix. 199.

674 *Deux Amis*, xi. 147; xiii. 160-92, &c.

675 *Deux Amis*, xi. 80-143.

676 Louvet, p. 180-199.

677 *Moniteur*, Séance du 5 Septembre, 1793.

678 *Débats*, Séance du 23 Août 1793.

679 *Moniteur*, Séance du 17 Septembre 1793.

680 *Moniteur*, Séances du 5, 9, 11 Septembre.

681 *Deux Amis*, xi. 148-188.

682 See *Mémoires particuliers de la Captivité à la Tour du Temple*, by the Duchesse d'Angoulême, Paris, 21 Janvier 1817.

683 *Procès de la Reine* (*Deux Amis*, xi. 251-381).

684 Vilate, *Causes secrètes de la Révolution de Thermidor* (Paris, 1825), p. 179.

685 Weber, i. 6.

686 *Deux Amis*, xi. 301.

687 Δημοσθένους εἰπόντος, Ἀποκτενοῦδί σε Ἀθηναῖοι, φωκίων· Ἀν μανῶσιν, εἴτε σὲ δ', ἐὰν σαφρονῶσι.—Plut. *Opp.* t. iv. p. 310. ed. Reiske, 1776.

688 *Mémoires de Riouffe* in *Mémoires sur les Prisons*, Paris, 1823, p. 48-55.

689 Louvet, p. 213.

690 *Recherches Historiques sur les Girondins* in *Mémoires de Buzot*, p. 107.

691 *Hist. Parl.* Introd., i. 1 et seqq.

692 *Deux Amis*, xii. 78.

693 Mercier. ii. 124.

694 *Moniteur* of these months, passim.

695 Foster, ii. 628; Montgaillard, iv. 141-57.

696 *Mémoires (Sur les Prisons*, i.), pp. 55-7.

697 *Mémoires de Madame Roland* (Introd.), i. 68.

698 Vie de Bailly in *Mémoires*, i., p. 29.

699 *Mémoires de Madame Roland* (Introd.), i. 88.

700 Foster, ii. 629.

701 *Moniteur*, 11 Decembre, 30 Decembre, 1793; Louvet, p. 287.

702 See Louvet, p. 301.

703 *Deux Amis*, xii. 249-51.

704 *Deux Amis*, xi. 145.

705 *Moniteur* (du 17 Novembre 1793), &c.

706 *Deux Amis*, xii. 251-62.

707 *Moniteur*, 1793, Nos. 101 (31 Decembre), 95, 96, 98, &c.

708 *Deux Amis*, xii. 266-72; *Moniteur*, du 2 Janvier 1794.

709 *Procès de Carrier*, 4 tomes, Paris, 1795.

710 *Les Horreures des Prisons d'Arras*, Paris, 1823.

711 Montgaillard, iv. 200.

712 *Moniteur*, Séance du 17 Brumaire (7th November), 1793.

713 *Analyse du Moniteur* (Paris, 1801), ii. 280.

714 Mercier, iv. 134. See *Moniteur*, Séance du 10 Novembre.

715 See also *Moniteur*, Séance du 26 Novembre.

716 Mercier, iv. 127-146.

717 *Deux Amis*, xii. 62-5.

718 *Débats*, du 10 Novembre, 1723.

719 *Dictionnaire des Hommes Marquans*, i. 115.

720 *Moniteur*, du 27 Novembre 1793.

721 *Choix des Rapports*, xiii. 189.

722 Ibid. xv. 360.

723 There is, in *Prudhomme*, an atrocity *à la* Captain-Kirk reported of this Cavaignac; which has been copied into Dictionaries of *Hommes Marquans*, of *Biographie Universelle*, &c.; which not only has no truth in it, but, much more singular, is still capable of being proved to have none.

724 *Deux Amis*, xiii. 205-30; Toulongeon, &c.

725 Levasseur, *Mémoires*, ii. c. 2-7.

726 His narrative in *Deux Amis*, xiv. 177-86.

727 Compare Barrère (*Chois des Rapports*, xiv. 416-21); Lord Howe (*Annual Register* of 1794, p. 86), &c.

728 Carlyle's *Miscellanies*, § Sinking of the Vengeur.

729 *Chois des Rapports*, xv. 378, 384.

730 26th June, 1794, (see *Rapport de Guyton-Morveau sur les Aérostats*, in *Moniteur* du 6 Vendémiaire, An 2).

731 Mercier, v. 25; *Deux Amis*, xii. 142-199.

732 See *Deux Amis*, xv. 189-192; *Mémoires de Genlis; Founders of the French Republic*, &c. &c.

733 Mercier, ii. 134.

734 Montgaillard, iv. 290.

735 *Moniteur*, du 17 Ventose (7th March) 1794.

736 *Biographie de Ministres*, § Danton.

737 *Aperçus sur Camille Desmoulins* in *Vieux Cordelier*, Paris, 1825, pp. 1-29.

738 Montgaillard, iv. 200.

739 Duchesse d'Angoulême, *Captivité à la Tour du Temple*, pp. 37-71.

740 *Tribunal Révolutionnaire*, du 8 Mai 1794, *Moniteur*, No. 231.

741 *Tableaux de la Révolution*, § Soupers Fraternels; Mercier, ii. 150.

742 Riouffe, p. 73; *Deux Amis*, xii. 298-302.

743 Vilate, *Causes Secrètes de la Révolution de 9 Thermidor*.

744 See Vilate, *Causes Secrètes*. (Vilate's Narrative is very curious; but is not to be taken as true, without sifting; being, at bottom, in spite of its title, not a Narrative but a Pleading).

745 Montgaillard, iv. 237.

746 *Maison d'Arrêt de Port-Libre*, par Coittant, &c. *Mémoires sur les Prisons*, ii.

747 Montgaillard, iv. 218; Riouffe, p. 273.

748 *Voyage de Cent Trente-deux Nantais*, (*Prisons*, ii. 288-335).

749 *Relation de ce qu'ont souffert pour la Religion les Prêtres déportés en 1794, dans la rade de l'île d'Aix*, (*Prisons*, ii. 387-485).

750 *Deux Amis*, xii. 347-73.

751 *Deux Amis*, xii. 350-8.

752 See Vilate.

753 *Moniteur*, Nos. 311, 312; *Débats*, iv. 421-42; *Deux Amis*, xii. 390-411.

754 *Précis des Evénemens du Neuf Thermidor*, par C.A. Méda, ancien Gendarme, Paris, 1825.

755 Mémoires sur les Prisons, ii. 277.

756 Méda. p. 384. (Méda asserts that it was he who, with infinite courage, though in a lefthanded manner, shot Robespierre. Méda got promoted for his services of this night; and died General and Baron. Few credited Méda (in what was otherwise incredible).

757 24th December 1794, *Moniteur*, No. 97.

758 October 1795, Dulaure, viii. 454-6.

759 *Deux Amis*, xiii. 3-39.

760 Mercier, *Nouveau Paris*, iii. 138, 153.

761 Montgaillard, iv. 436-42.

762 Montgaillard, Mercier, (ubi supra).

763 De Staël, *Considérations* iii. c. 10, &c.

764 Toulongeon, iii. c. 7; v. c. 10, p. 194.

765 19th January, 1795, Montgaillard, iv. 287-311.

766 5th April, 1795, Montgaillard, iv. 319.

767 *Histoire de la Guerre de la Vendée*, par M. le Comte de Vauban, *Mémoires de Madame de la Rochejacquelin*, &c.

768 *Deux Amis*, xiv. 94-106; Puisaye, *Mémoires*, iii-vii.

769 *Moniteur*, du 25 Septembre 1794, du 4 Février 1795.

770 *Moniteur*, Séances du 10-12 Novembre 1794: *Deux Amis*, xiii. 43-49.

771 Mercier, ii. 94. ("1st February, 1796: at the Bourse of Paris, the gold louis," of 20 francs in silver, "costs 5,300 francs in assignats." Montgaillard, iv. 419).

772 Fantin Desodoards, *Histoire de la Révolution*, vii. c. 4.

773 *Moniteur*, Séance du 13 Germinal (2d April) 1795.

774 *Moniteur*, du 27 Juin, du 31 Août, 1795; *Deux Amis*, xiii. 121-9.

775 *Deux Amis*, xiii. 129-46.

776 Toulongeon, v. 297; *Moniteur*, Nos. 244, 5, 6.

777 *Dictionnaire des Hommes Marquans*, §§ Billaud, Collot.

778 Montgaillard, iv. 241.

779 *Report of the Irish Poor-Law Commission*, 1836.

780 *Nouveau Paris*, iv. 118.

781 Napoleon, Las Cases, *Choix des Rapports*, xvii. 398-411.

782 *Deux Amis*, xiii. 375-406.

783 *Moniteur*, Séance du 5 Octobre 1795.

784 *Moniteur*, du 4 Septembre 1797.

785 9th November 1799, *Choix des Rapports*, xvii. 1-96.

786 Bailleul, *Examen critique des Considérations de Madame de Staël*, ii. 275.

787 *Diamond Necklace*, (Carlyle's *Miscellanies*).